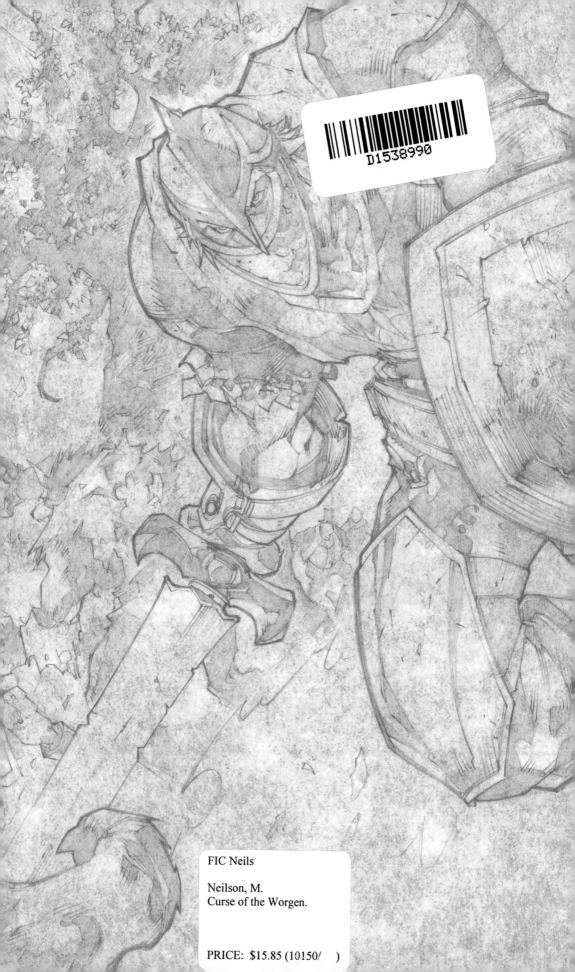

World of Warcraft®

Curse of the Worgen

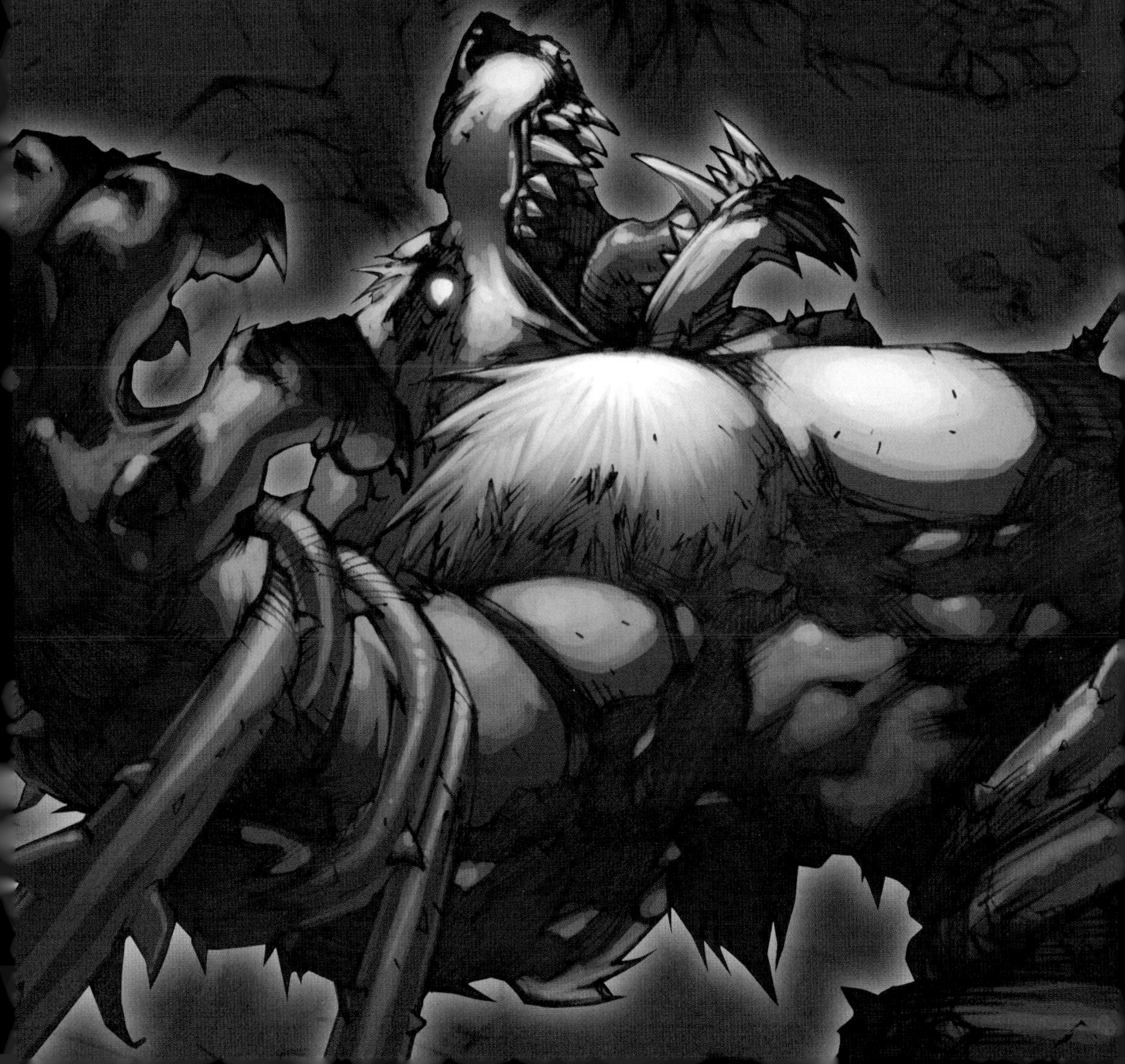

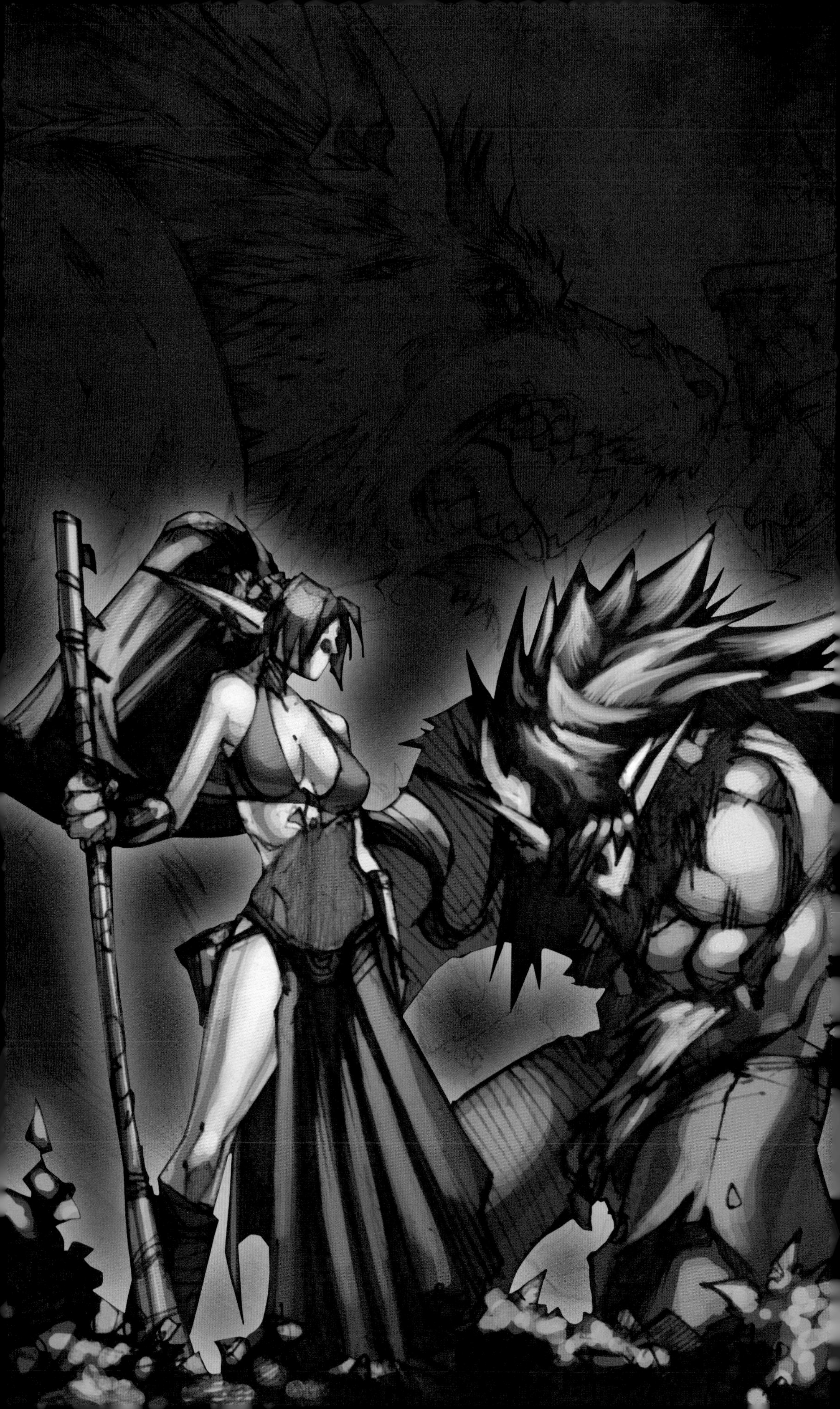

WORLD OF WARCRAFT®

Curse of the Worgen

Writers:
Micky Neilson & James Waugh

Artists:
Ludo Lullabi & Tony Washington

Letterer: Wes Abbott

Story Consultants
Chris Metzen, Alex Afrasiabi & Luis Barriga

Collection Cover
by John Polidora

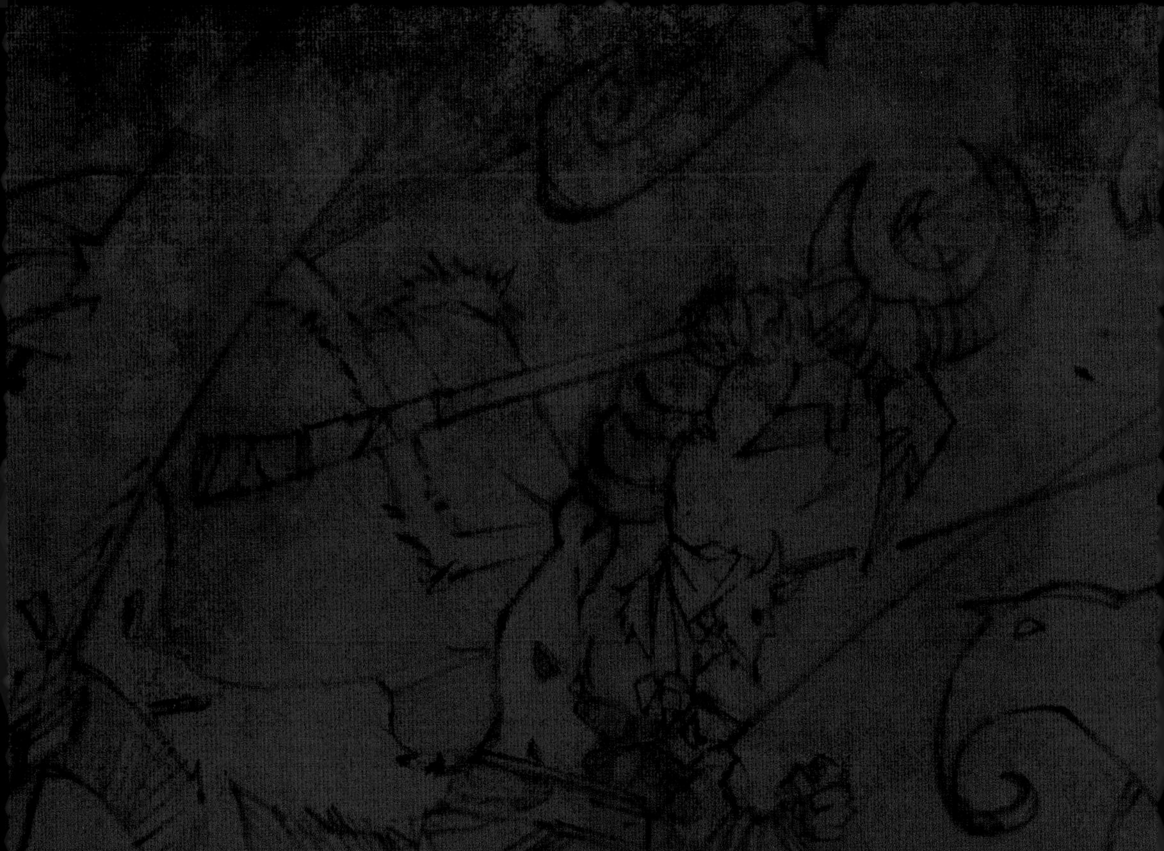

Hank Kanalz Sarah Gaydos	Editors – Original Series
Ian Sattler	Director Editorial, Special Projects and Archival Editions
Robbin Brosterman	Design Director – Books
Eddie Berganza	Executive Editor
Bob Harras	VP – Editor in Chief
Diane Nelson	President
Dan DiDio and Jim Lee	Co-Publishers
Geoff Johns	Chief Creative Officer
John Rood	Executive VP – Sales, Marketing and Business Development
Amy Genkins	Senior VP – Business and Legal Affairs
Nairi Gardiner	Senior VP – Finance
Jeff Boison	VP – Publishing Operations
Mark Chiarello	VP – Art Direction and Design
John Cunningham	VP – Marketing
Terri Cunningham	VP – Talent Relations and Services
Alison Gill	Senior VP – Manufacturing and Operations
David Hyde	VP – Publicity
Hank Kanalz	Senior VP – Digital
Jay Kogan	VP – Business and Legal Affairs, Publishing
Jack Mahan	VP – Business Affairs, Talent
Nick Napolitano	VP – Manufacturing Administration
Ron Perazza	VP – Online
Sue Pohja	VP – Book Sales
Courtney Simmons	Senior VP – Publicity
Bob Wayne	Senior VP – Sales

WORLD OF WARCRAFT: CURSE OF THE WORGEN

DC Comics, 1700 Broadway, New York, NY 10019. A Warner Bros. Entertainment Company
Printed by RR Donnelley, Salem, VA, USA. 9/14/11. First Printing. HC ISBN: 978-1-4012-3267-2 SC ISBN: 978-1-4012-3445-4

SUSTAINABLE FORESTRY INITIATIVE
Certified Chain of Custody
Promoting Sustainable Forest Management
www.sfiprogram.org

Fiber used in this product line meets the sourcing requirements of the SFI program.
www.sfiprogram.org SGS-SFI/COC-US10/81072

LICENSED BLIZZARD ENTERTAINMENT PRODUCT

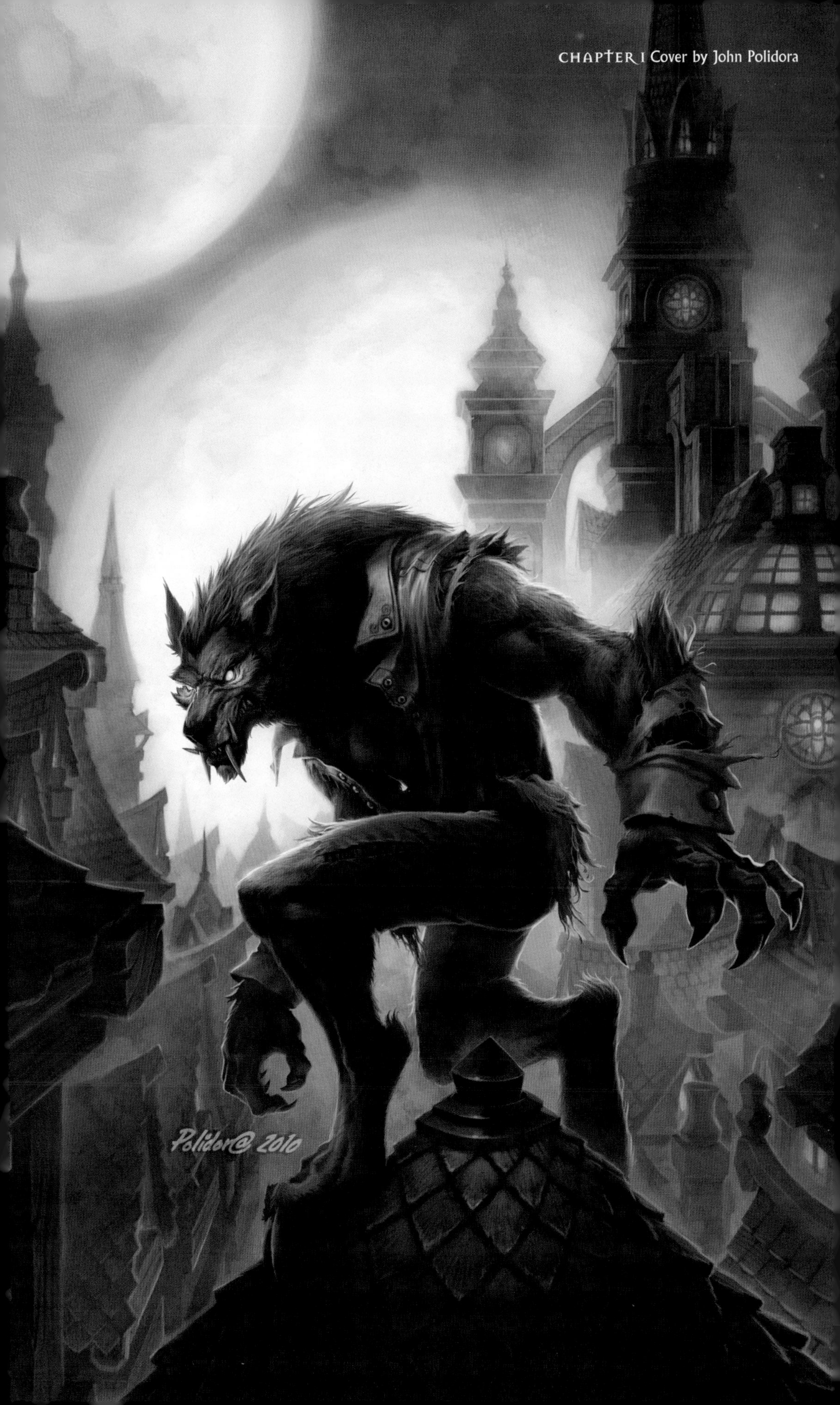
Polidora 2010
CHAPTER 1 Cover by John Polidora

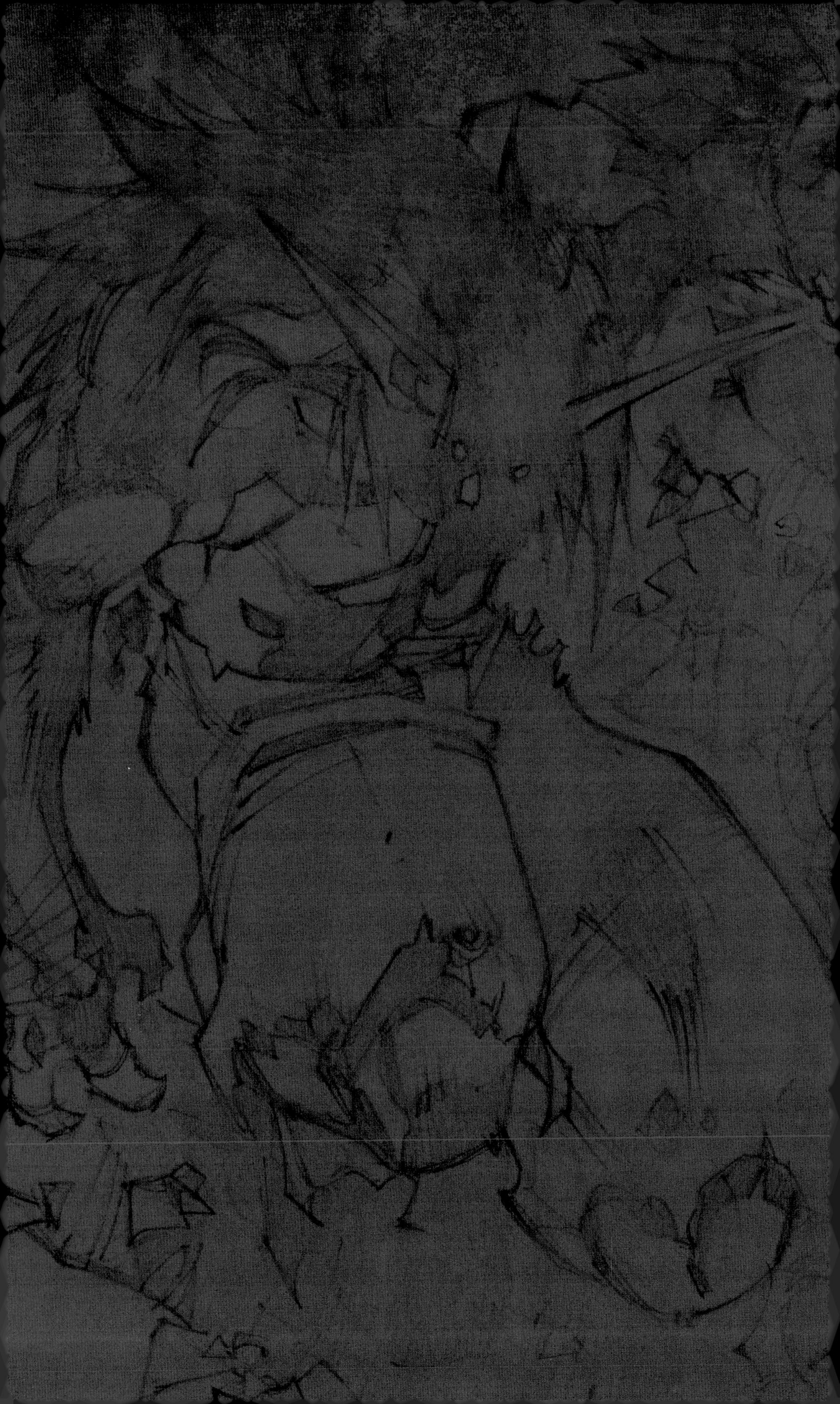

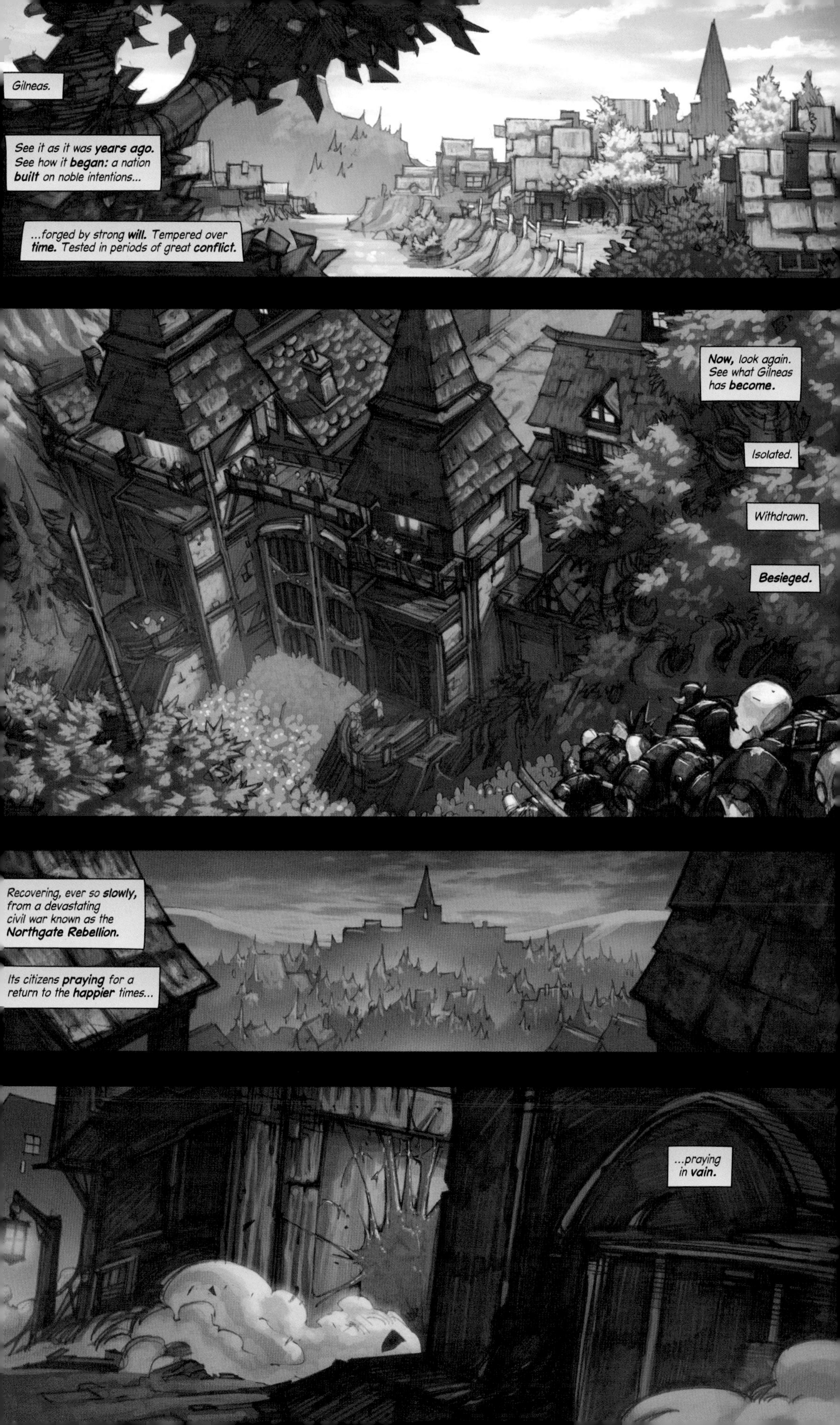
Gilneas.
See it as it was years ago. See how it began: a nation built on noble intentions...
...forged by strong will. Tempered over time. Tested in periods of great conflict.
Now, look again. See what Gilneas has become.
Isolated.
Withdrawn.
Besieged.
Recovering, ever so slowly, from a devastating civil war known as the Northgate Rebellion.
Its citizens praying for a return to the happier times...
...praying in vain.

I **know** now that when the **attack** came, amid the **screaming** and the **bleeding** and the **dying**...

...some **wondered**, with their final **thoughts**...

...if perhaps this **new** enemy held ties to the marauding **undead** clamoring outside the **Greymane Wall**.

A wall built to **protect**. Built to prevent the **rest** of the world's **troubles** from becoming our **own**.

Interesting thing about walls: while they quite often **excel** at shutting things out...

...they're equally as **effective** at trapping things **within**.

Before the attack, this **enemy** had existed only in the timid **whispers** of the **old**.

Or the fanciful **embellishments** of the **young**.

Not a single victim **truly** knew where the nightmarish **beasts** came **from** or how they came to **be**.

Among the **doomed**, desperate citizens of **Gilneas**, no one knew.

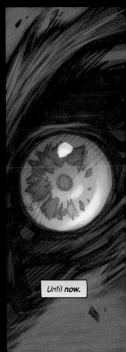

Until **now**.

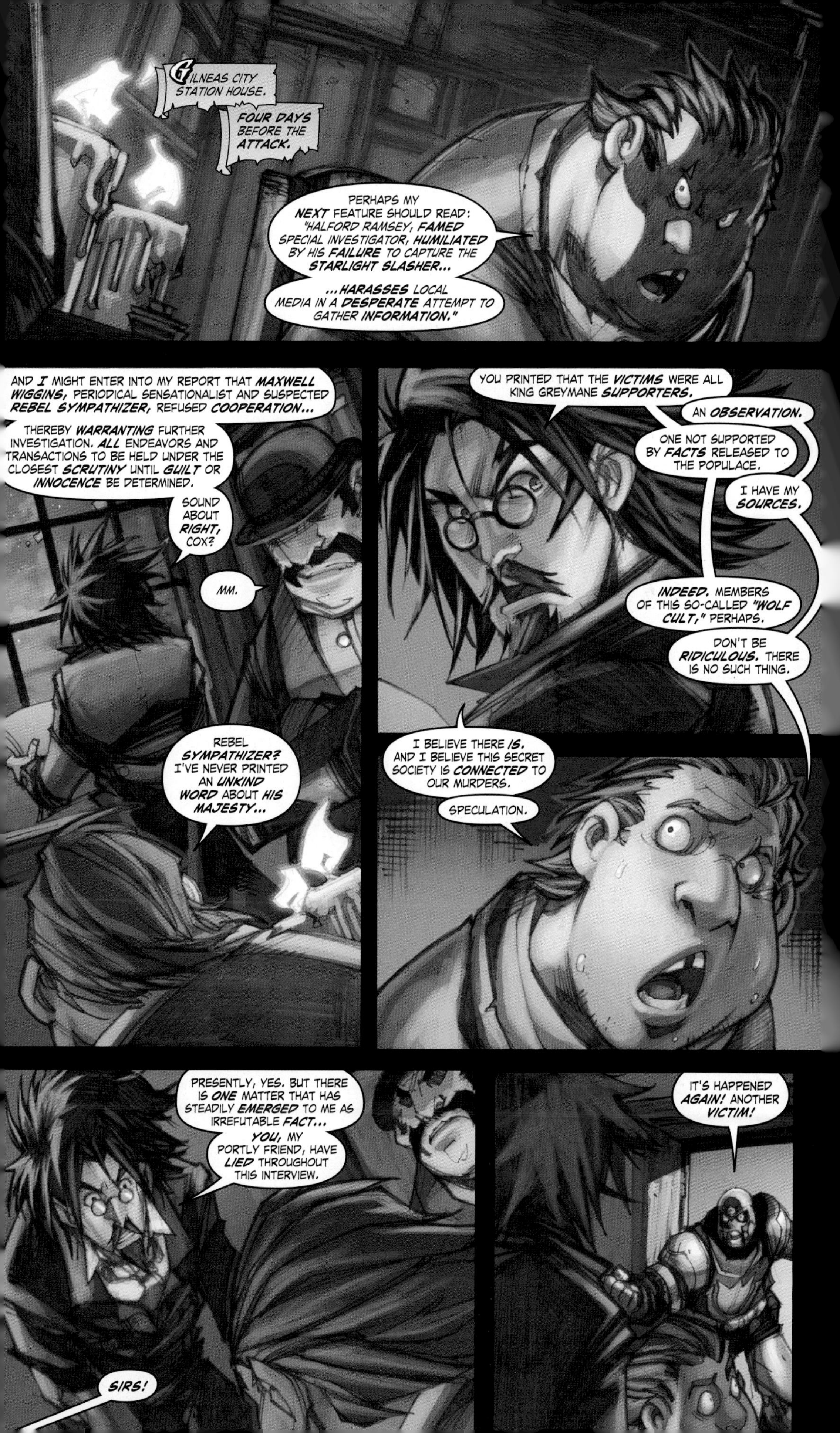
GILNEAS CITY STATION HOUSE.
FOUR DAYS BEFORE THE ATTACK.
PERHAPS MY NEXT FEATURE SHOULD READ: "HALFORD RAMSEY, FAMED SPECIAL INVESTIGATOR, HUMILIATED BY HIS FAILURE TO CAPTURE THE STARLIGHT SLASHER...
...HARASSES LOCAL MEDIA IN A DESPERATE ATTEMPT TO GATHER INFORMATION."
AND I MIGHT ENTER INTO MY REPORT THAT MAXWELL WIGGINS, PERIODICAL SENSATIONALIST AND SUSPECTED REBEL SYMPATHIZER, REFUSED COOPERATION...
THEREBY WARRANTING FURTHER INVESTIGATION. ALL ENDEAVORS AND TRANSACTIONS TO BE HELD UNDER THE CLOSEST SCRUTINY UNTIL GUILT OR INNOCENCE BE DETERMINED.
SOUND ABOUT RIGHT, COX?
MM.
REBEL SYMPATHIZER? I'VE NEVER PRINTED AN UNKIND WORD ABOUT HIS MAJESTY...
YOU PRINTED THAT THE VICTIMS WERE ALL KING GREYMANE SUPPORTERS.
AN OBSERVATION.
ONE NOT SUPPORTED BY FACTS RELEASED TO THE POPULACE.
I HAVE MY SOURCES.
INDEED. MEMBERS OF THIS SO-CALLED "WOLF CULT," PERHAPS.
DON'T BE RIDICULOUS. THERE IS NO SUCH THING.
I BELIEVE THERE IS. AND I BELIEVE THIS SECRET SOCIETY IS CONNECTED TO OUR MURDERS.
SPECULATION.
PRESENTLY, YES. BUT THERE IS ONE MATTER THAT HAS STEADILY EMERGED TO ME AS IRREFUTABLE FACT...
YOU, MY PORTLY FRIEND, HAVE LIED THROUGHOUT THIS INTERVIEW.
SIRS!
IT'S HAPPENED AGAIN! ANOTHER VICTIM!

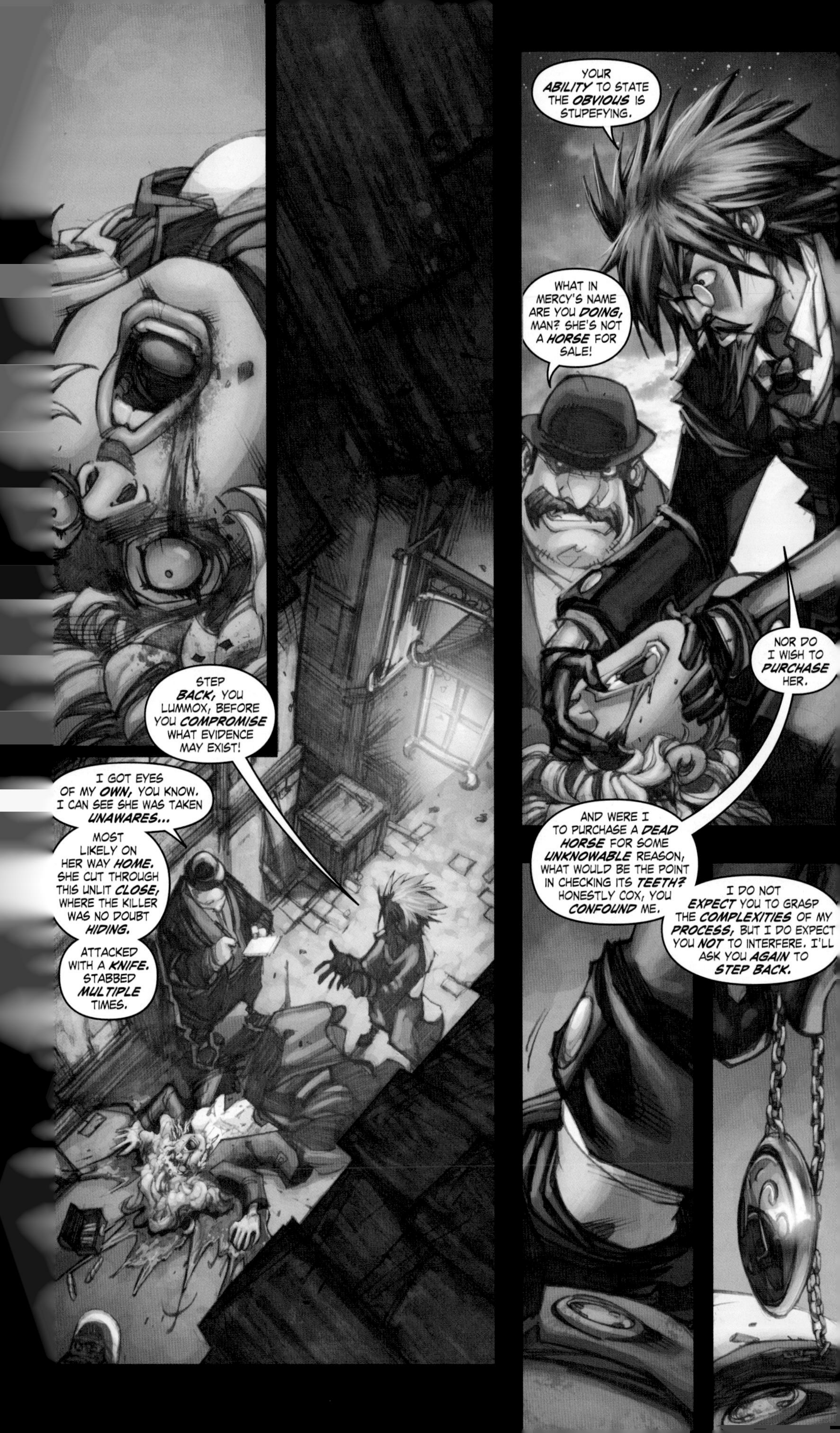
STEP BACK, YOU LUMMOX, BEFORE YOU COMPROMISE WHAT EVIDENCE MAY EXIST!
I GOT EYES OF MY OWN, YOU KNOW. I CAN SEE SHE WAS TAKEN UNAWARES...
MOST LIKELY ON HER WAY HOME. SHE CUT THROUGH THIS UNLIT CLOSE, WHERE THE KILLER WAS NO DOUBT HIDING.
ATTACKED WITH A KNIFE. STABBED MULTIPLE TIMES.
YOUR ABILITY TO STATE THE OBVIOUS IS STUPEFYING.
WHAT IN MERCY'S NAME ARE YOU DOING, MAN? SHE'S NOT A HORSE FOR SALE!
NOR DO I WISH TO PURCHASE HER.
AND WERE I TO PURCHASE A DEAD HORSE FOR SOME UNKNOWABLE REASON, WHAT WOULD BE THE POINT IN CHECKING ITS TEETH? HONESTLY COX, YOU CONFOUND ME.
I DO NOT EXPECT YOU TO GRASP THE COMPLEXITIES OF MY PROCESS, BUT I DO EXPECT YOU NOT TO INTERFERE. I'LL ASK YOU AGAIN TO STEP BACK.

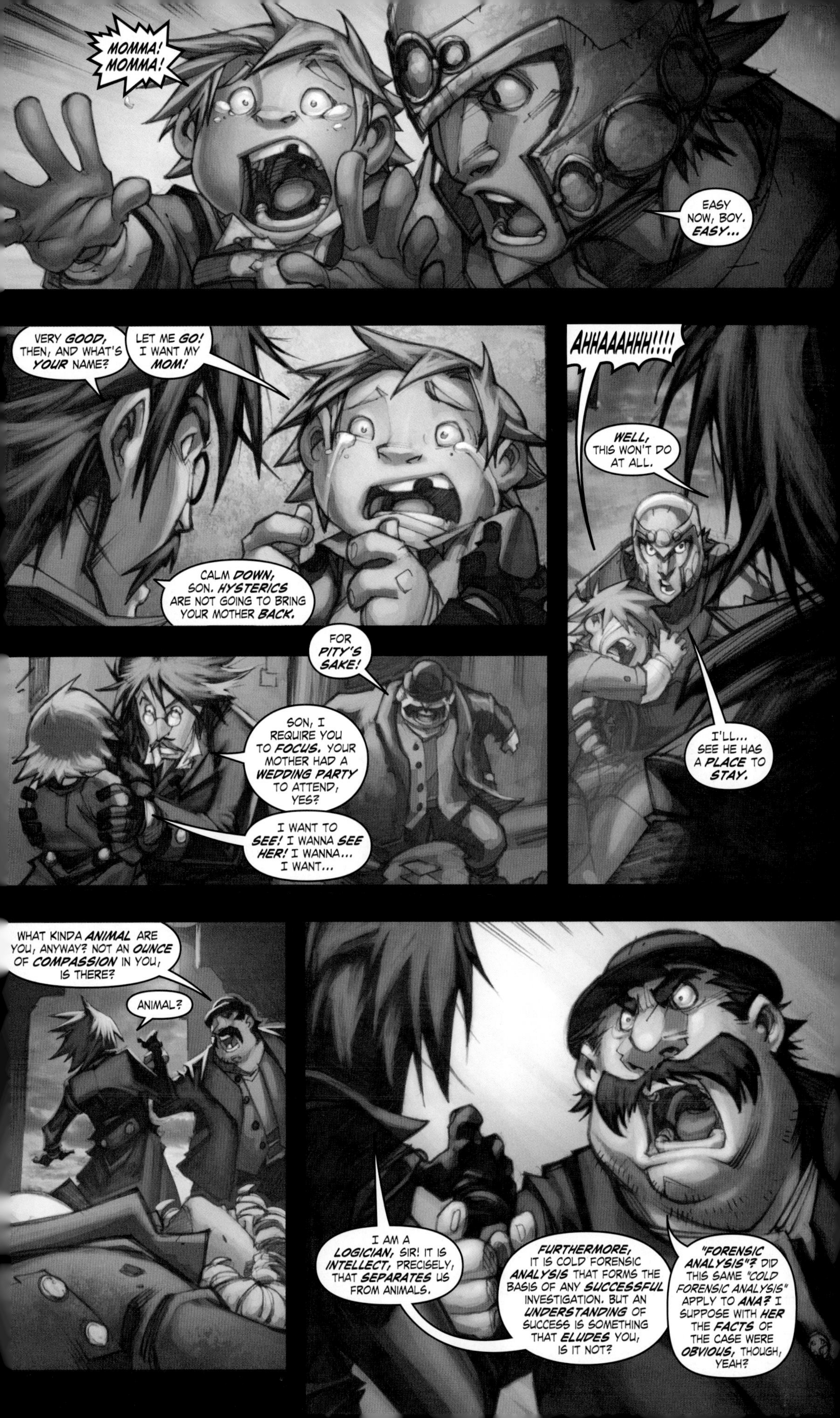
MOMMA! MOMMA!
EASY NOW, BOY. EASY...
VERY GOOD, THEN, AND WHAT'S YOUR NAME?
LET ME GO! I WANT MY MOM!
CALM DOWN, SON. HYSTERICS ARE NOT GOING TO BRING YOUR MOTHER BACK.
FOR PITY'S SAKE!
SON, I REQUIRE YOU TO FOCUS. YOUR MOTHER HAD A WEDDING PARTY TO ATTEND, YES?
I WANT TO SEE! I WANNA SEE HER! I WANNA... I WANT...
AHHHAAAHHH!!!!
WELL, THIS WON'T DO AT ALL.
I'LL... SEE HE HAS A PLACE TO STAY.
WHAT KINDA ANIMAL ARE YOU, ANYWAY? NOT AN OUNCE OF COMPASSION IN YOU, IS THERE?
ANIMAL?
I AM A LOGICIAN, SIR! IT IS INTELLECT, PRECISELY, THAT SEPARATES US FROM ANIMALS.
FURTHERMORE, IT IS COLD FORENSIC ANALYSIS THAT FORMS THE BASIS OF ANY SUCCESSFUL INVESTIGATION. BUT AN UNDERSTANDING OF SUCCESS IS SOMETHING THAT ELUDES YOU, IS IT NOT?
"FORENSIC ANALYSIS"? DID THIS SAME "COLD FORENSIC ANALYSIS" APPLY TO ANA? I SUPPOSE WITH HER THE FACTS OF THE CASE WERE OBVIOUS, THOUGH, YEAH?

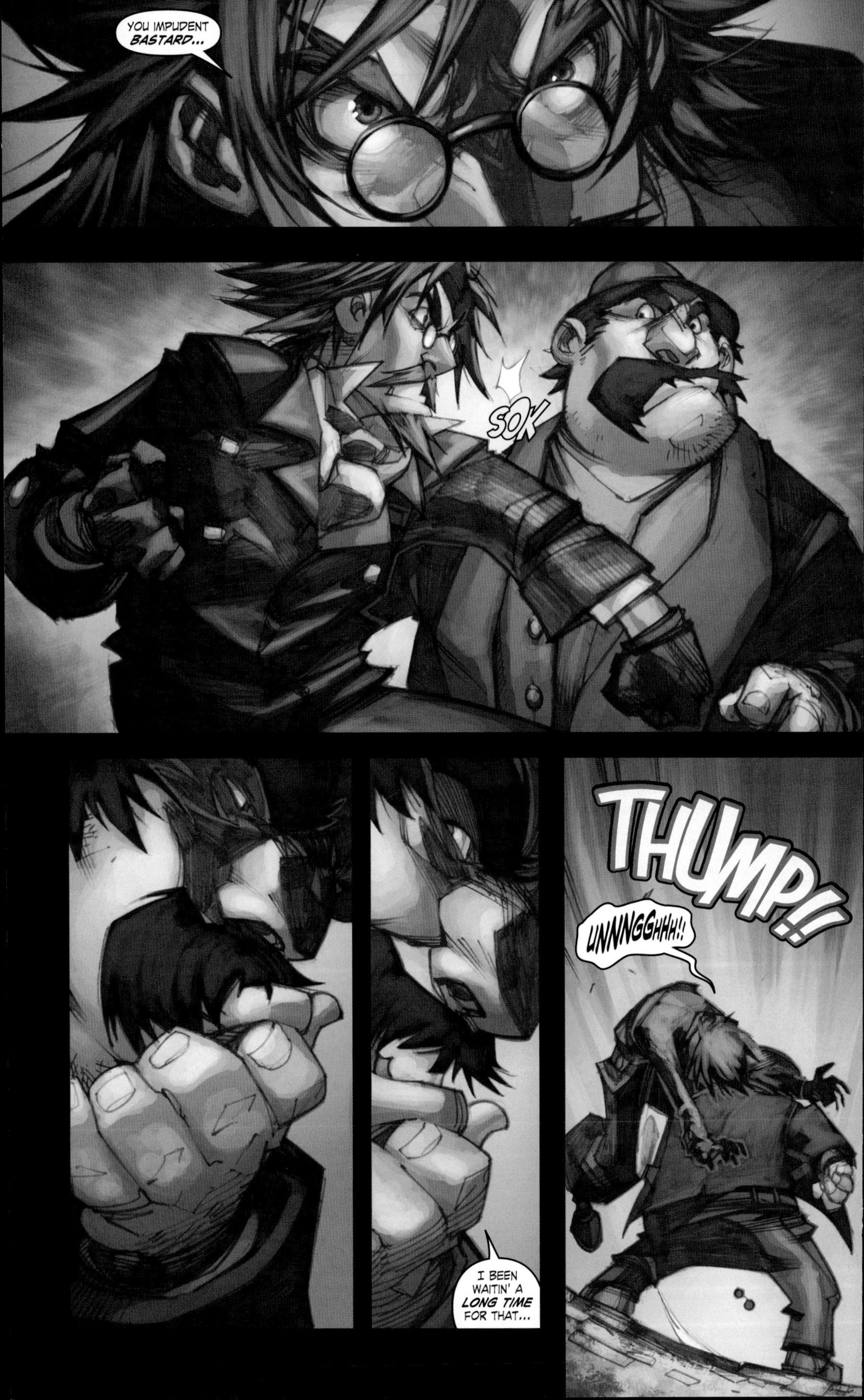
YOU IMPUDENT BASTARD...
SOK
I BEEN WAITIN' A LONG TIME FOR THAT...
THUMP!!
UNNNGGHHH!!

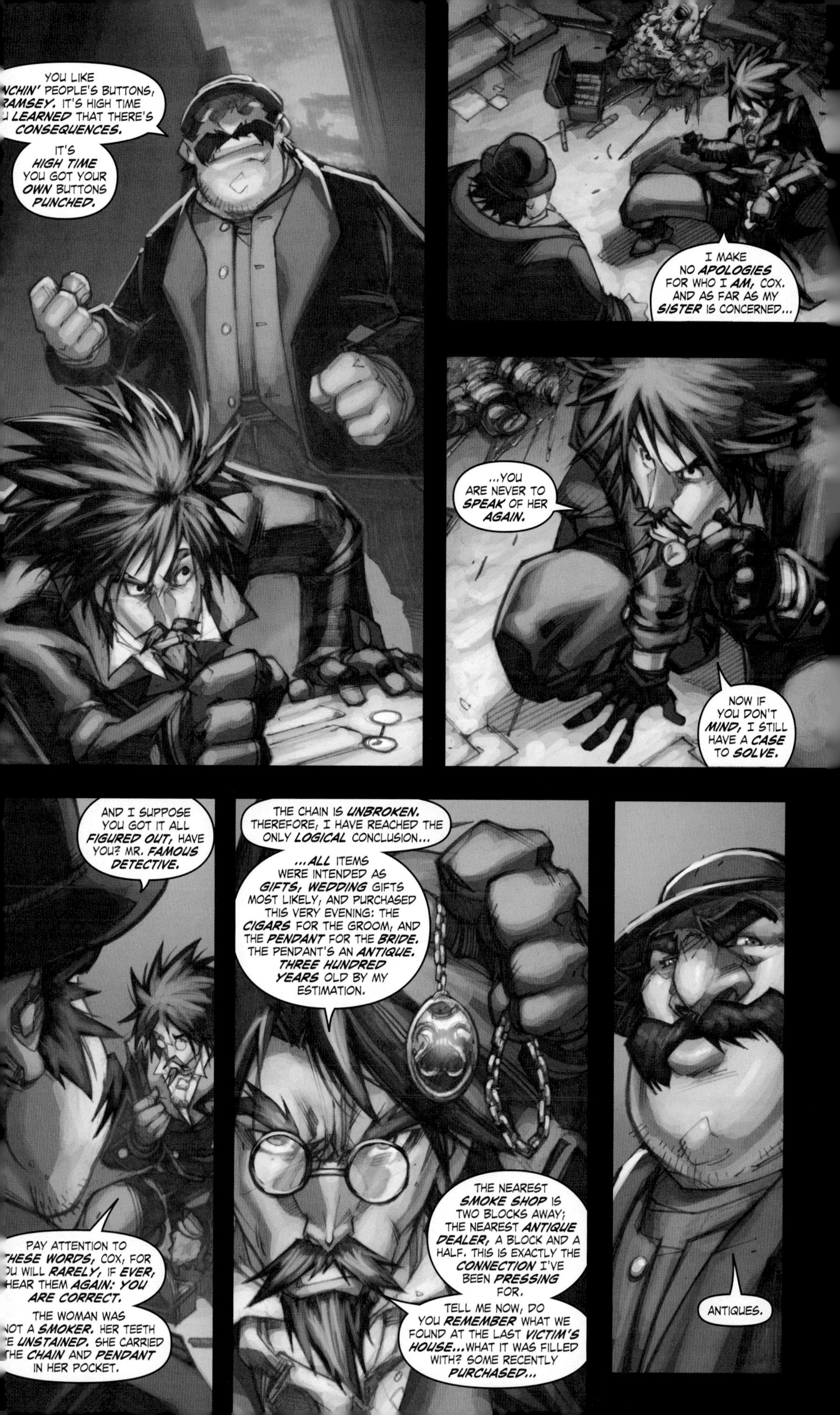

YOU LIKE NCHIN' PEOPLE'S BUTTONS, RAMSEY. IT'S HIGH TIME U LEARNED THAT THERE'S CONSEQUENCES.
IT'S HIGH TIME YOU GOT YOUR OWN BUTTONS PUNCHED.
I MAKE NO APOLOGIES FOR WHO I AM, COX. AND AS FAR AS MY SISTER IS CONCERNED...
...YOU ARE NEVER TO SPEAK OF HER AGAIN.
NOW IF YOU DON'T MIND, I STILL HAVE A CASE TO SOLVE.
AND I SUPPOSE YOU GOT IT ALL FIGURED OUT, HAVE YOU? MR. FAMOUS DETECTIVE.
PAY ATTENTION TO HESE WORDS, COX, FOR U WILL RARELY, IF EVER, HEAR THEM AGAIN: YOU ARE CORRECT.
THE WOMAN WAS NOT A SMOKER. HER TEETH E UNSTAINED. SHE CARRIED THE CHAIN AND PENDANT IN HER POCKET.
THE CHAIN IS UNBROKEN. THEREFORE, I HAVE REACHED THE ONLY LOGICAL CONCLUSION...
...ALL ITEMS WERE INTENDED AS GIFTS, WEDDING GIFTS MOST LIKELY, AND PURCHASED THIS VERY EVENING: THE CIGARS FOR THE GROOM, AND THE PENDANT FOR THE BRIDE. THE PENDANT'S AN ANTIQUE. THREE HUNDRED YEARS OLD BY MY ESTIMATION.
THE NEAREST SMOKE SHOP IS TWO BLOCKS AWAY; THE NEAREST ANTIQUE DEALER, A BLOCK AND A HALF. THIS IS EXACTLY THE CONNECTION I'VE BEEN PRESSING FOR.
TELL ME NOW, DO YOU REMEMBER WHAT WE FOUND AT THE LAST VICTIM'S HOUSE...WHAT IT WAS FILLED WITH? SOME RECENTLY PURCHASED...
ANTIQUES.

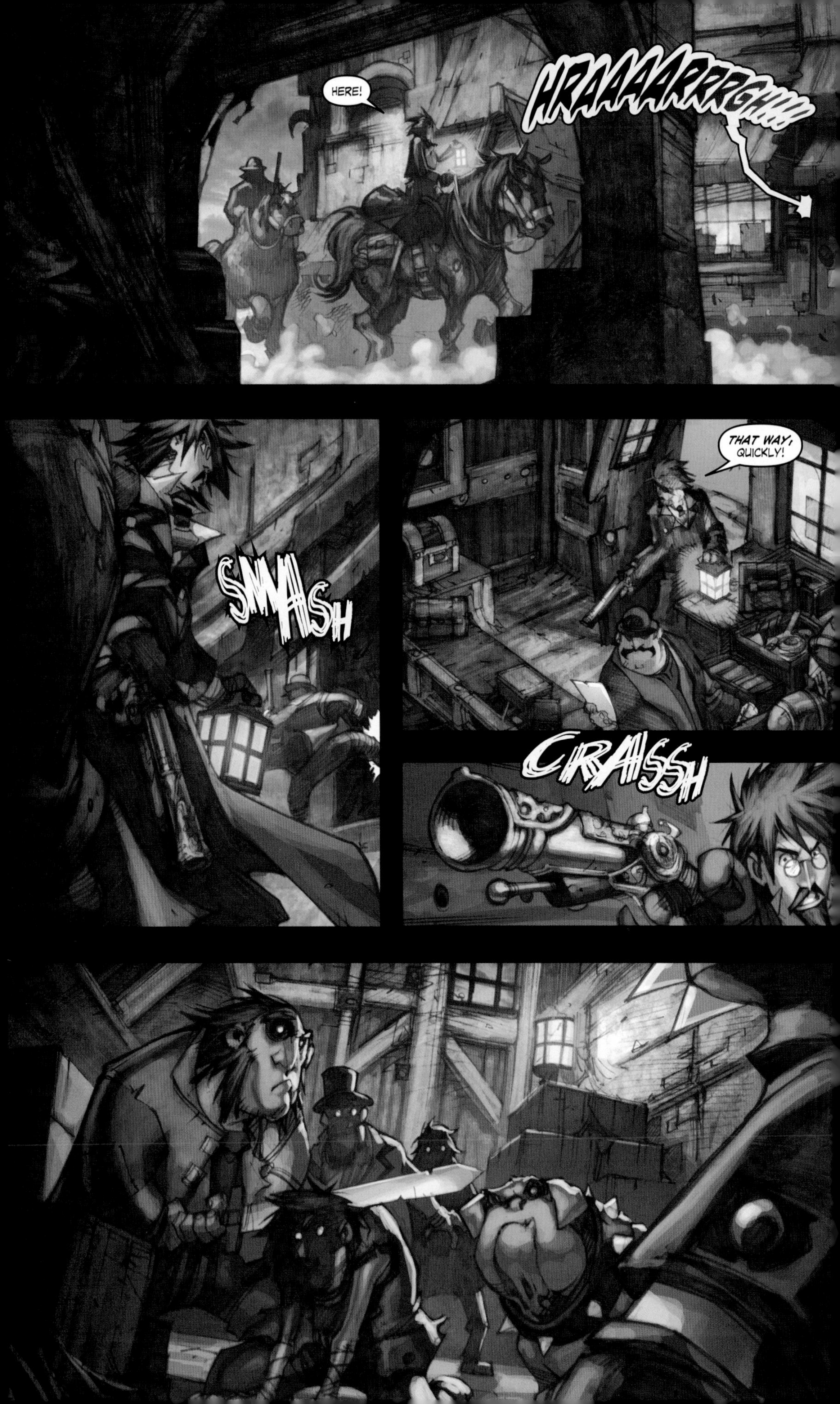
HERE!
HRAAAARRRGH!!!
SMASH
THAT WAY, QUICKLY!
CRASSH

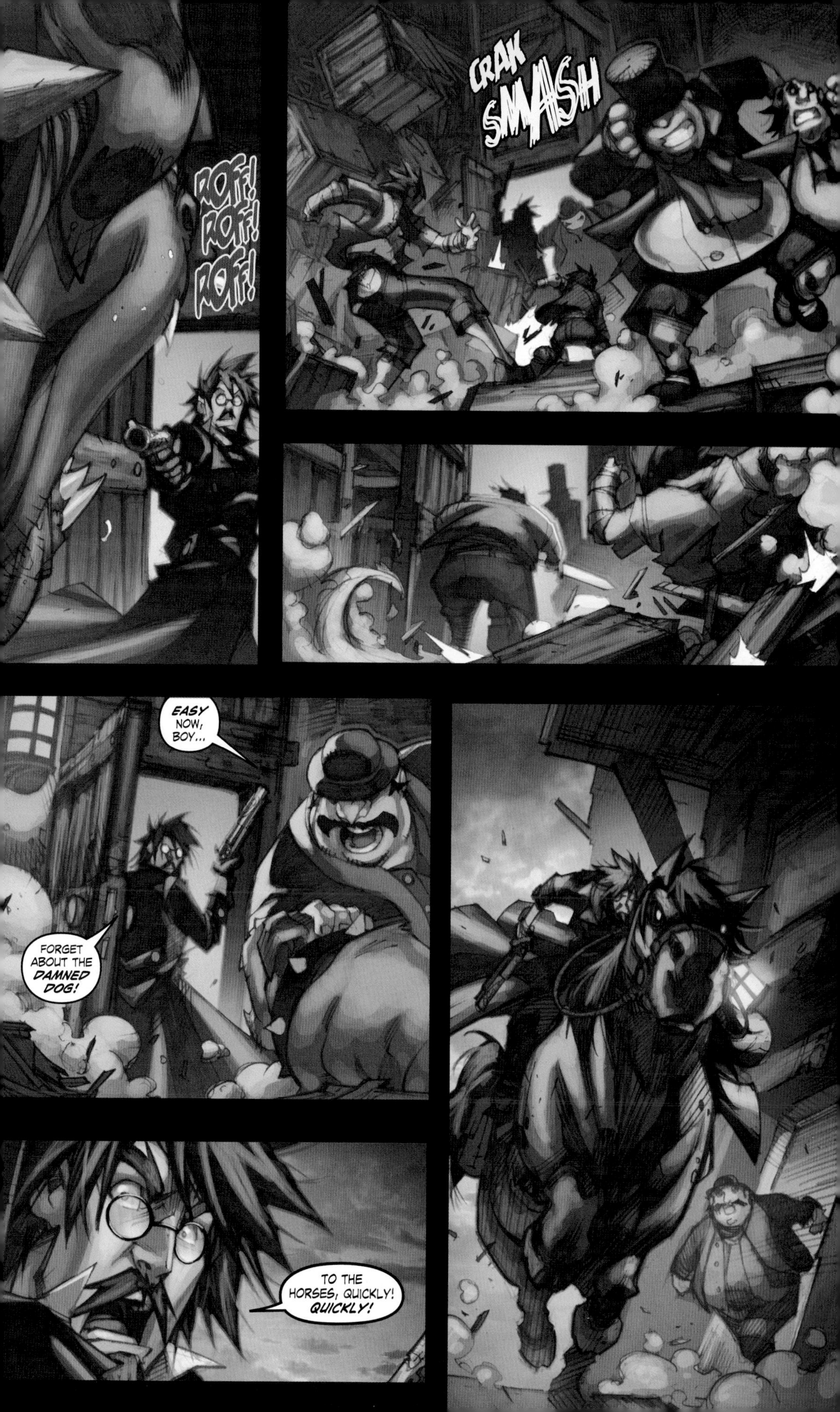
ROFF! ROFF! ROFF!
CRAK
SMASH
EASY NOW, BOY...
FORGET ABOUT THE DAMNED DOG!
TO THE HORSES, QUICKLY! QUICKLY!

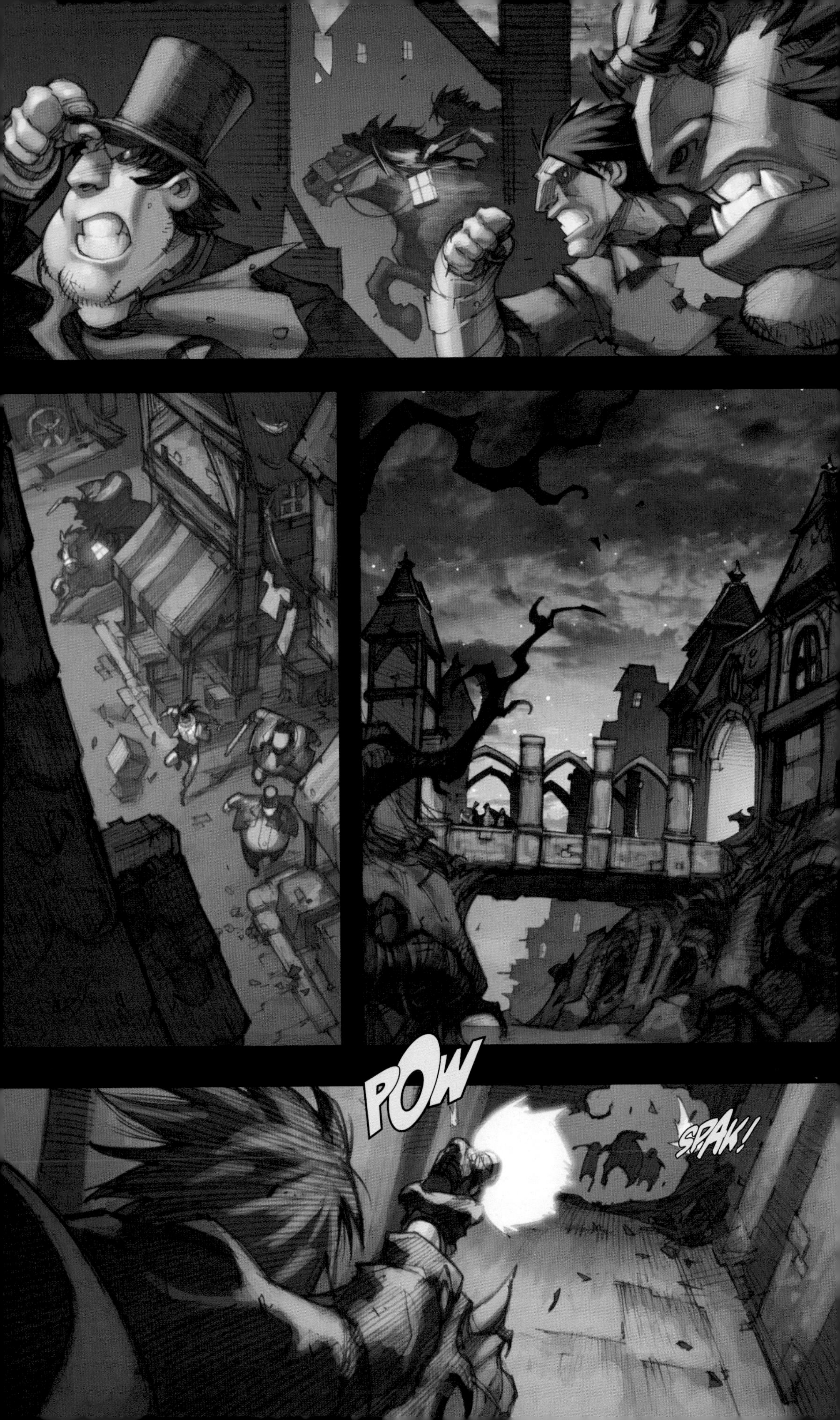
POW
SPAK!

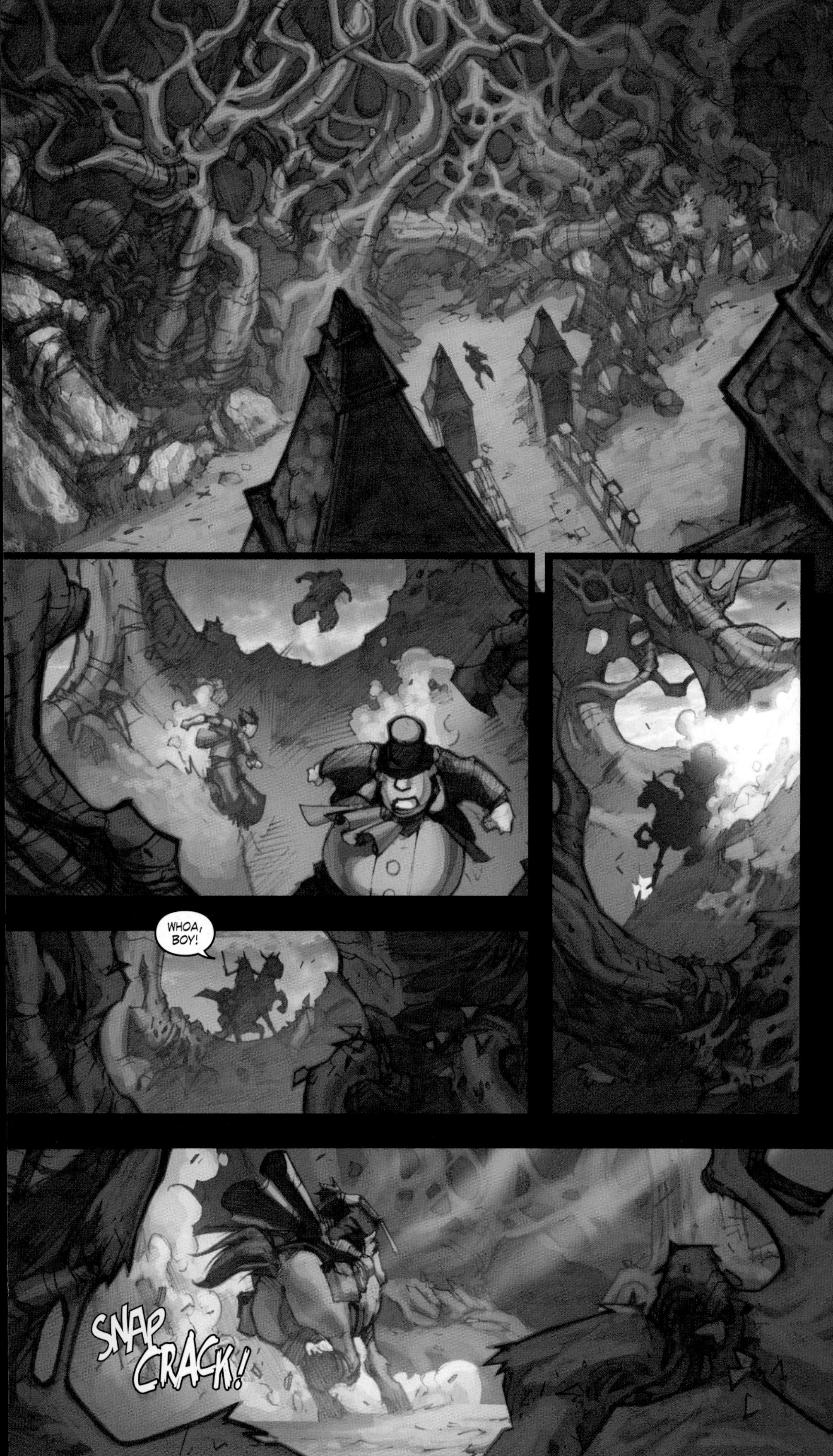
WHOA, BOY!
SNAP CRACK!

GRRRRRRWLLL

RRROWWLLL...

DAMN!

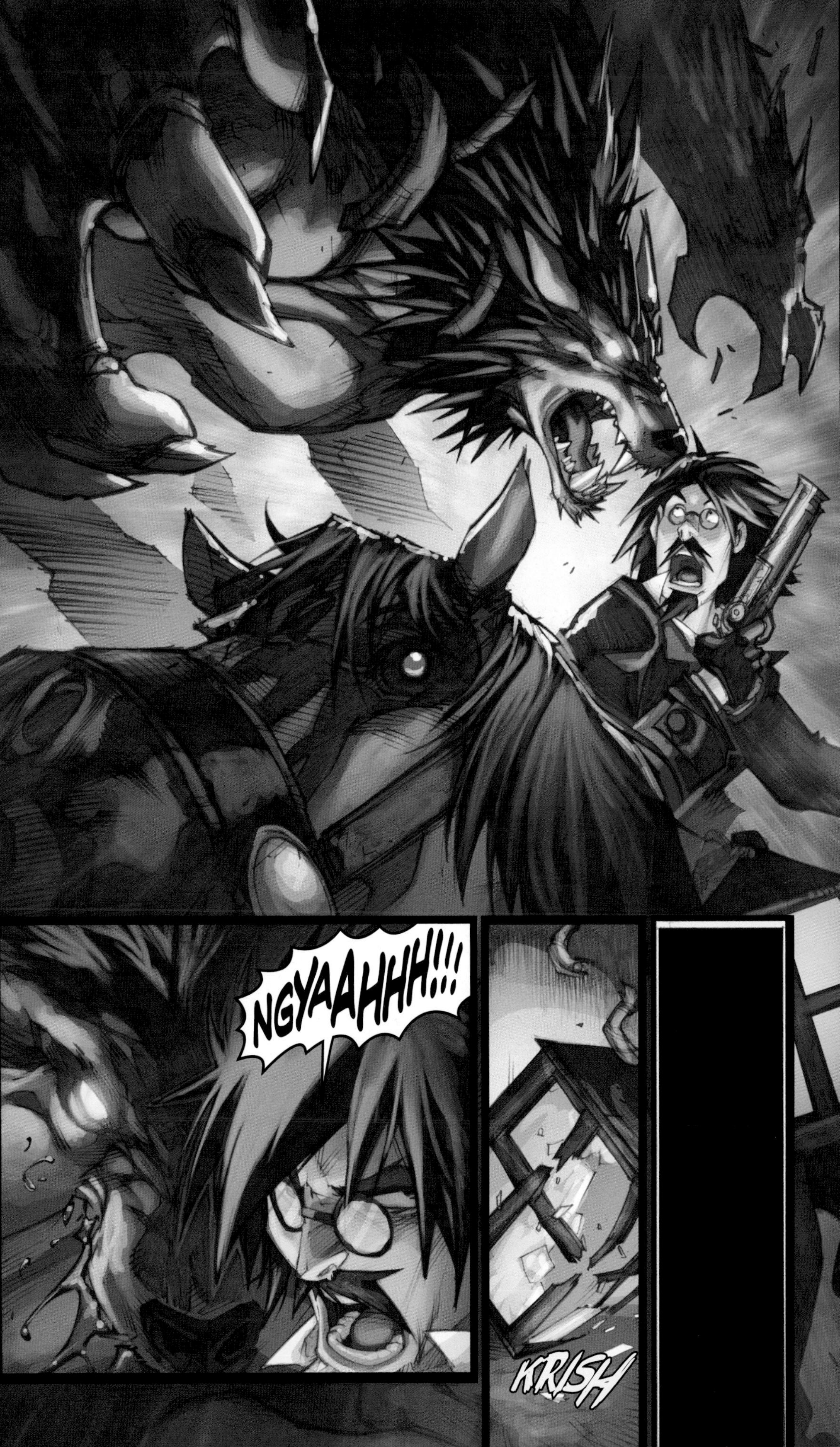
NGYAAHHH!!!
KRISH

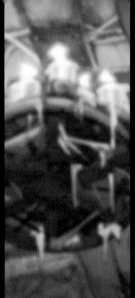

The **pain** in my **shoulder** informed me that I was **alive**.

In a manor house... **abandoned** after the war. It was then that I caught the **scent**...

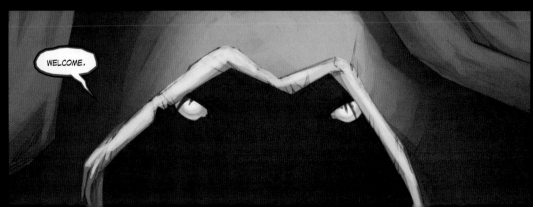

WELCOME.

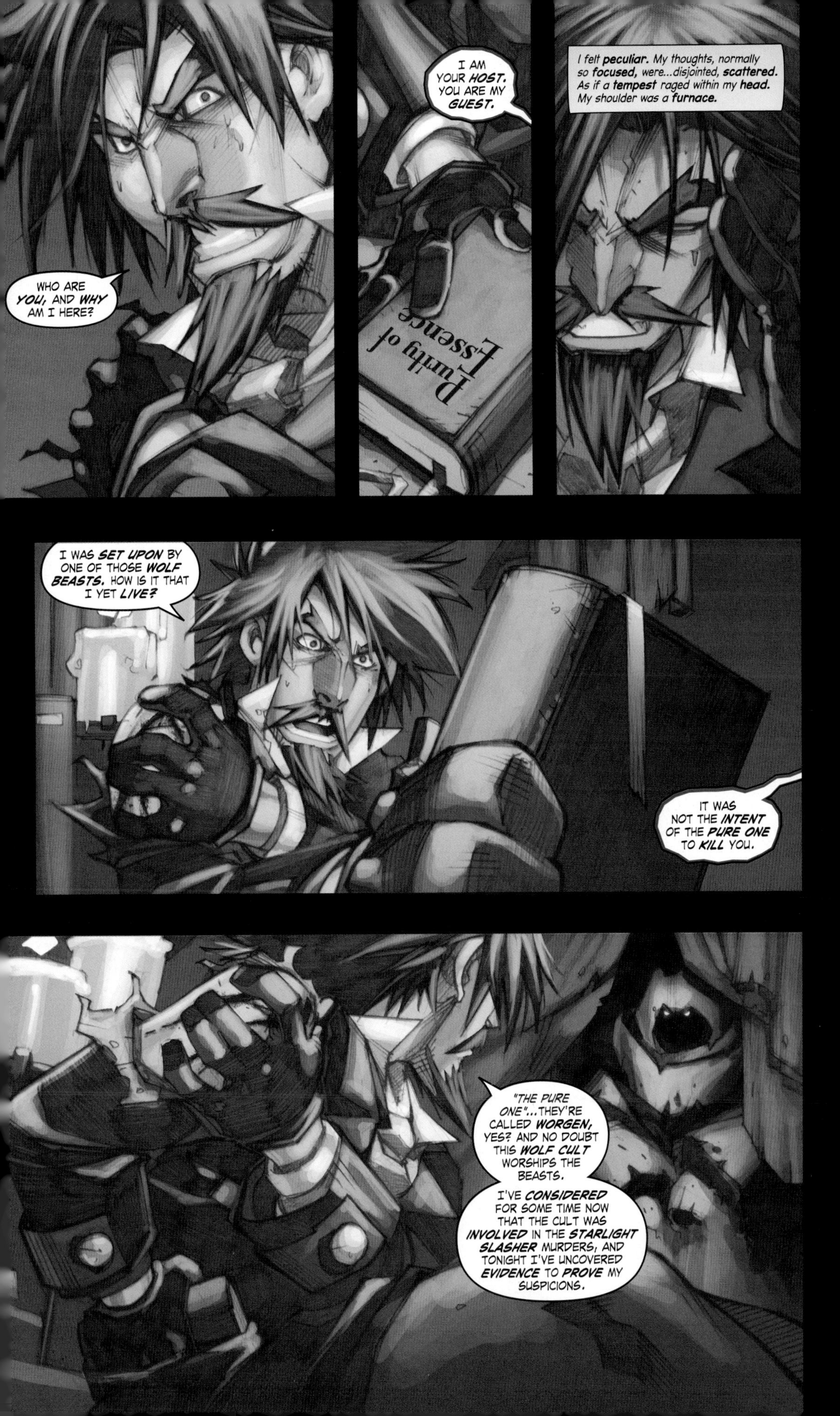
WHO ARE YOU, AND WHY AM I HERE?
I AM YOUR HOST. YOU ARE MY GUEST.
Purity of Essence
I felt peculiar. My thoughts, normally so focused, were...disjointed, scattered. As if a tempest raged within my head. My shoulder was a furnace.
I WAS SET UPON BY ONE OF THOSE WOLF BEASTS. HOW IS IT THAT I YET LIVE?
IT WAS NOT THE INTENT OF THE PURE ONE TO KILL YOU.
"THE PURE ONE"...THEY'RE CALLED WORGEN, YES? AND NO DOUBT THIS WOLF CULT WORSHIPS THE BEASTS.
I'VE CONSIDERED FOR SOME TIME NOW THAT THE CULT WAS INVOLVED IN THE STARLIGHT SLASHER MURDERS, AND TONIGHT I'VE UNCOVERED EVIDENCE TO PROVE MY SUSPICIONS.

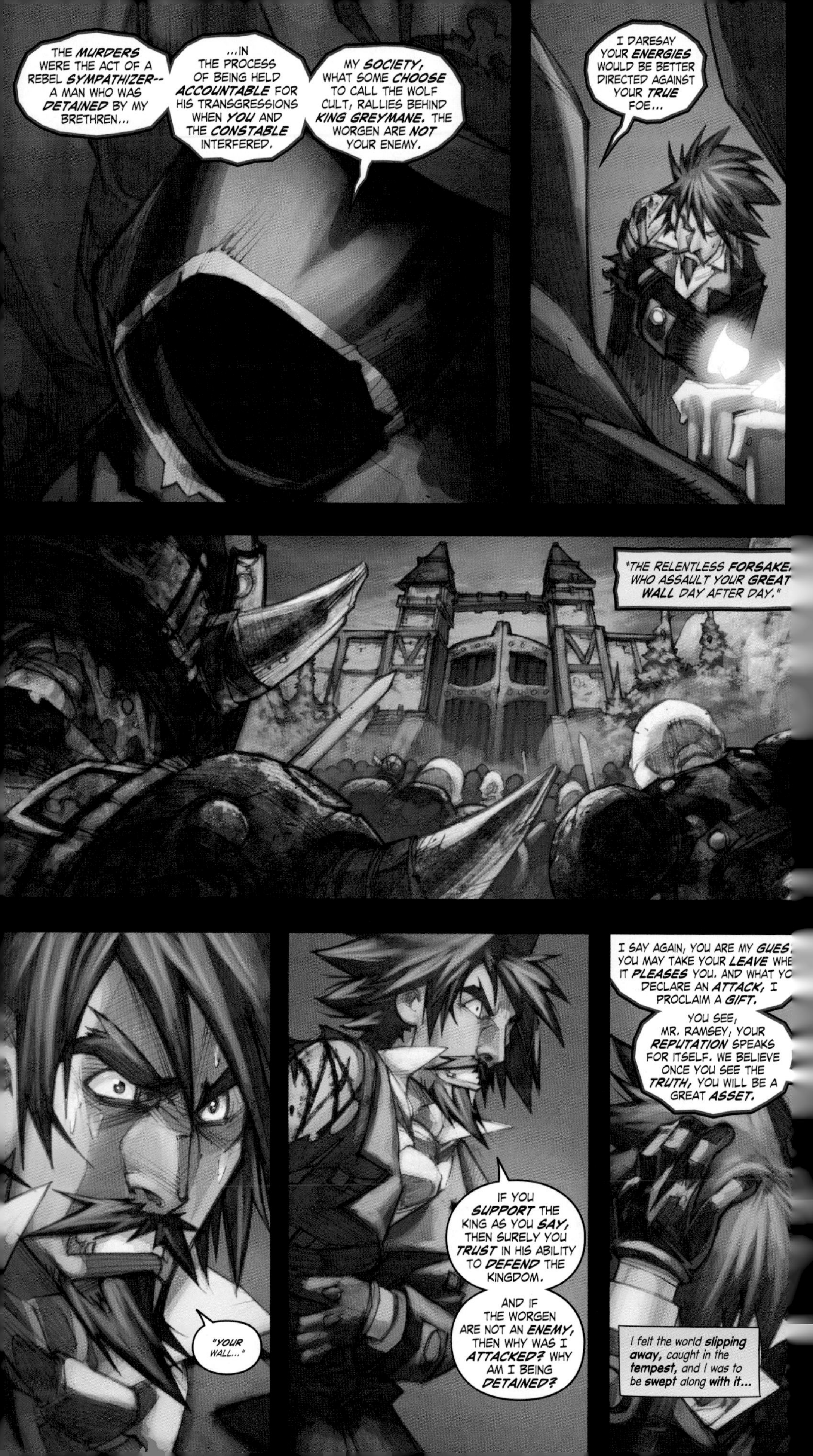

THE MURDERS WERE THE ACT OF A REBEL SYMPATHIZER-- A MAN WHO WAS DETAINED BY MY BRETHREN...
...IN THE PROCESS OF BEING HELD ACCOUNTABLE FOR HIS TRANSGRESSIONS WHEN YOU AND THE CONSTABLE INTERFERED.
MY SOCIETY, WHAT SOME CHOOSE TO CALL THE WOLF CULT, RALLIES BEHIND KING GREYMANE. THE WORGEN ARE NOT YOUR ENEMY.
I DARESAY YOUR ENERGIES WOULD BE BETTER DIRECTED AGAINST YOUR TRUE FOE...
"THE RELENTLESS FORSAKE WHO ASSAULT YOUR GREAT WALL DAY AFTER DAY."
"YOUR WALL..."
IF YOU SUPPORT THE KING AS YOU SAY, THEN SURELY YOU TRUST IN HIS ABILITY TO DEFEND THE KINGDOM.
AND IF THE WORGEN ARE NOT AN ENEMY, THEN WHY WAS I ATTACKED? WHY AM I BEING DETAINED?
I SAY AGAIN, YOU ARE MY GUES YOU MAY TAKE YOUR LEAVE WHE IT PLEASES YOU. AND WHAT YO DECLARE AN ATTACK, I PROCLAIM A GIFT.
YOU SEE, MR. RAMSEY, YOUR REPUTATION SPEAKS FOR ITSELF. WE BELIEVE ONCE YOU SEE THE TRUTH, YOU WILL BE A GREAT ASSET.
I felt the world slipping away, caught in the tempest, and I was to be swept along with it...

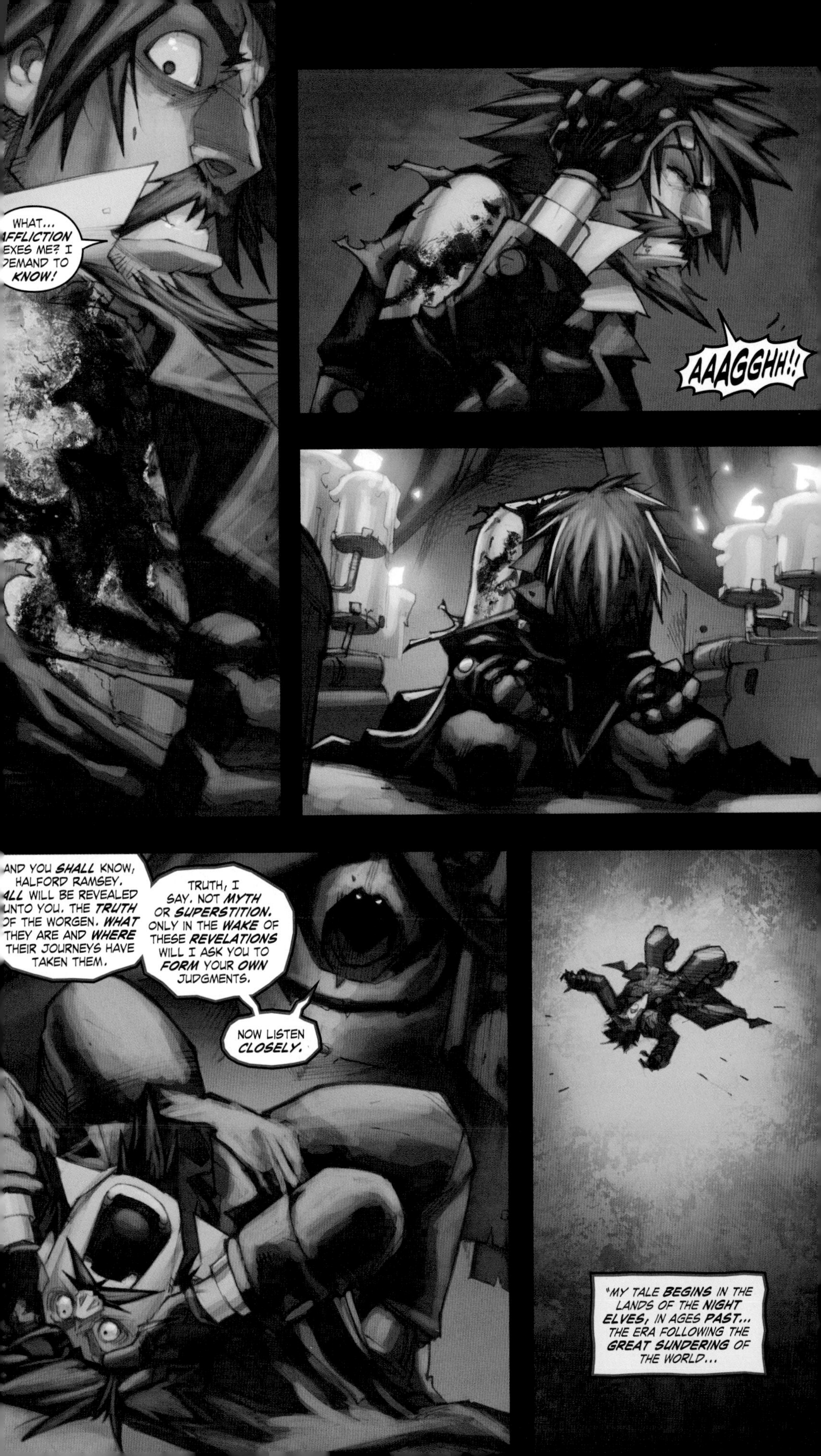

WHAT... AFFLICTION VEXES ME? I DEMAND TO KNOW!
AAAGGHH!!
AND YOU SHALL KNOW, HALFORD RAMSEY. ALL WILL BE REVEALED UNTO YOU. THE TRUTH OF THE WORGEN. WHAT THEY ARE AND WHERE THEIR JOURNEYS HAVE TAKEN THEM.
TRUTH, I SAY. NOT MYTH OR SUPERSTITION. ONLY IN THE WAKE OF THESE REVELATIONS WILL I ASK YOU TO FORM YOUR OWN JUDGMENTS.
NOW LISTEN CLOSELY.
"MY TALE BEGINS IN THE LANDS OF THE NIGHT ELVES, IN AGES PAST... THE ERA FOLLOWING THE GREAT SUNDERING OF THE WORLD...

"DURING WHAT WAS KNOWN AS THE WAR OF THE SATYR...
SENTINELS, SISTERS OF ELUNE, STRIKE FIERCELY!!! DO NOT FAIL!
FORWARD, SOLDIERS OF THE EMERALD FLAME!
"THE NIGHT ELVES OF KALIMDOR FACED, ONCE AGAIN, THE CRUEL REALITY OF CONFLICT--BLOODSHED, DEATH, AND DEEP, TERRIBLE LOSS.
"ARMIES OF SATYRS BURNED WITH UNQUENCHABLE VENGEANCE FOR THEIR FALLEN FATHER, THE SATYR LORD, XAVIUS."

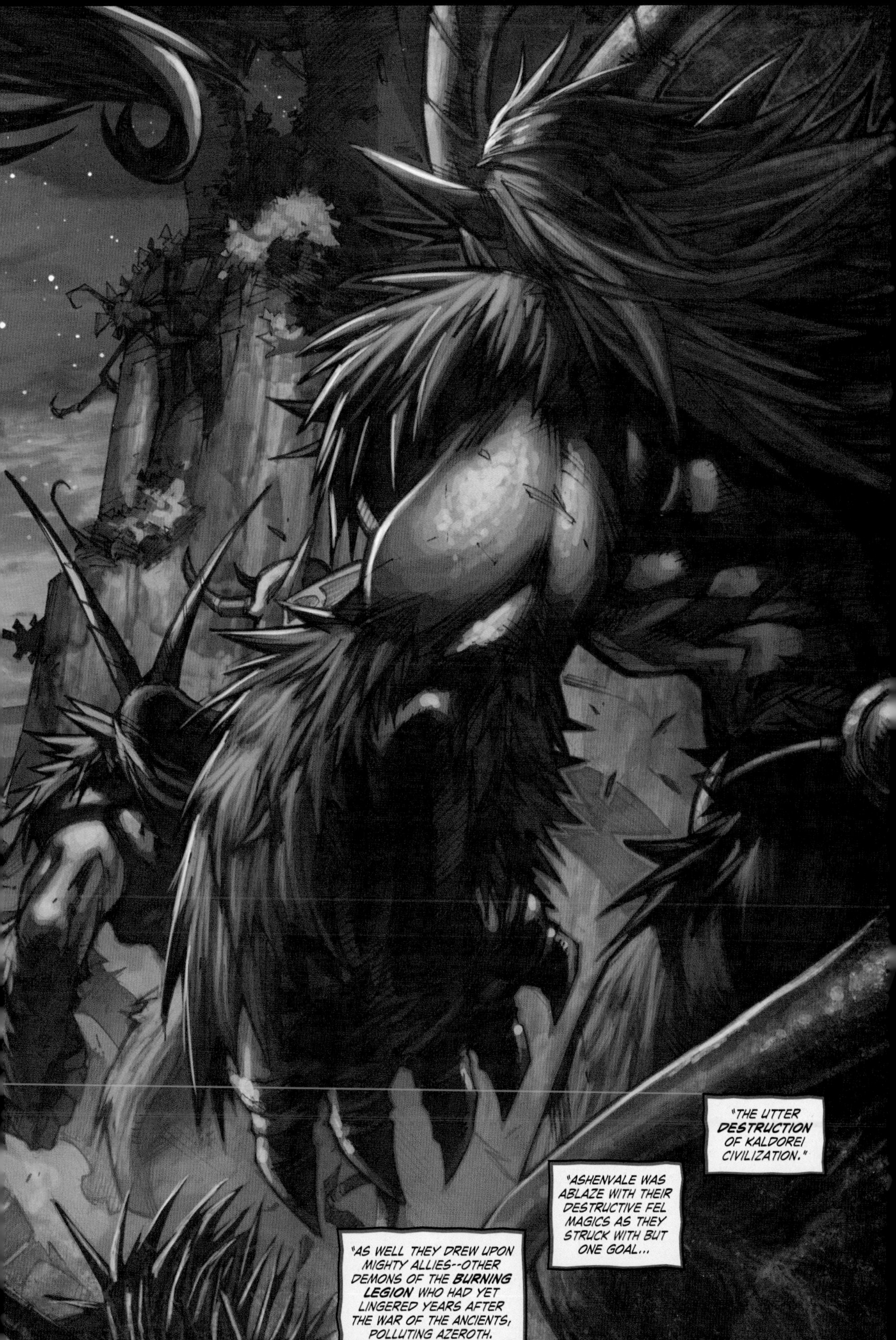
"AS WELL THEY DREW UPON MIGHTY ALLIES--OTHER DEMONS OF THE **BURNING LEGION** WHO HAD YET LINGERED YEARS AFTER THE WAR OF THE ANCIENTS, POLLUTING AZEROTH.
"ASHENVALE WAS ABLAZE WITH THEIR DESTRUCTIVE FEL MAGICS AS THEY STRUCK WITH BUT ONE GOAL...
"THE UTTER **DESTRUCTION** OF KALDOREI CIVILIZATION."

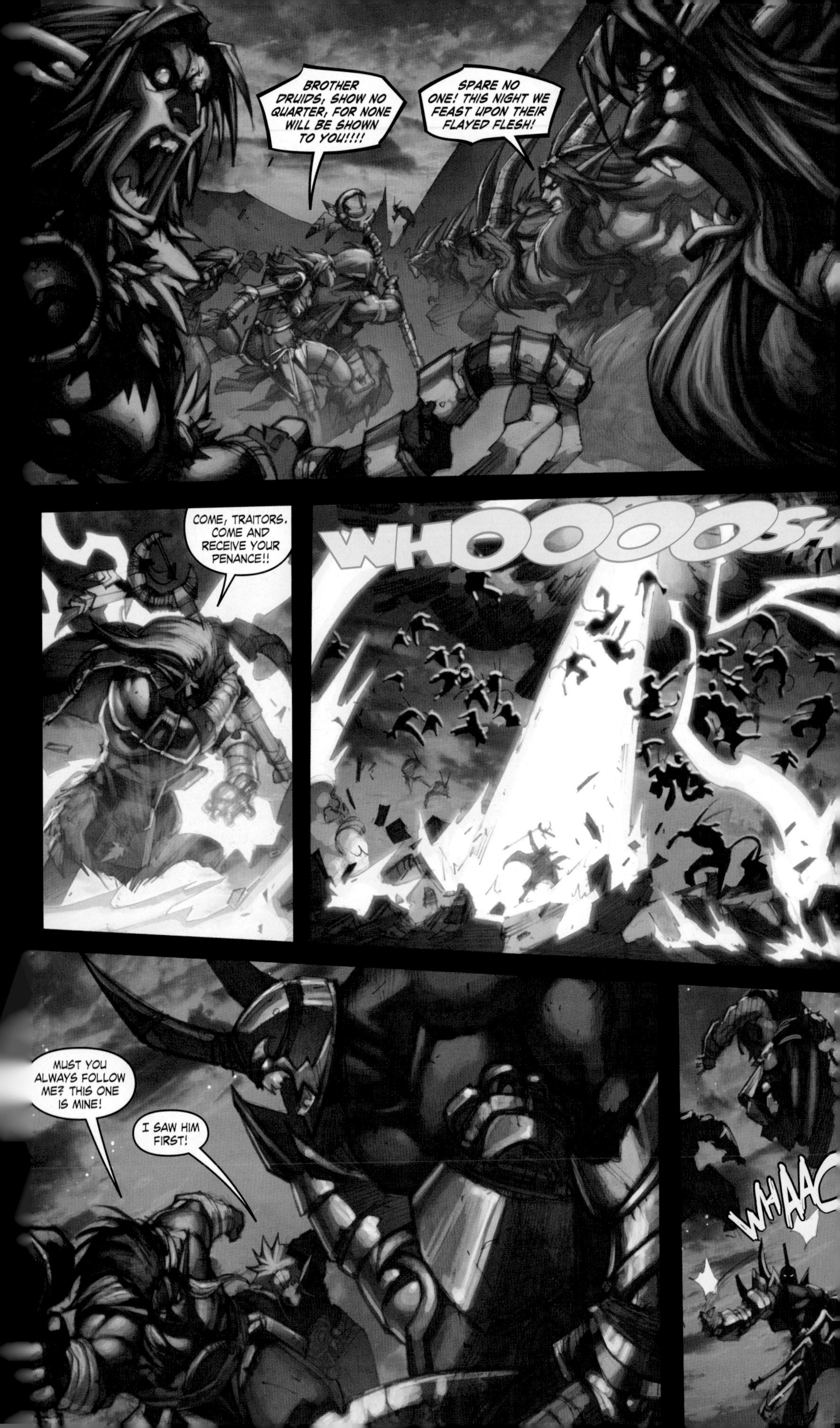
BROTHER DRUIDS; SHOW NO QUARTER, FOR NONE WILL BE SHOWN TO YOU!!!!
SPARE NO ONE! THIS NIGHT WE FEAST UPON THEIR FLAYED FLESH!
COME, TRAITORS, COME AND RECEIVE YOUR PENANCE!!
WHOOOOOOSH
MUST YOU ALWAYS FOLLOW ME? THIS ONE IS MINE!
I SAW HIM FIRST!
WHAAC

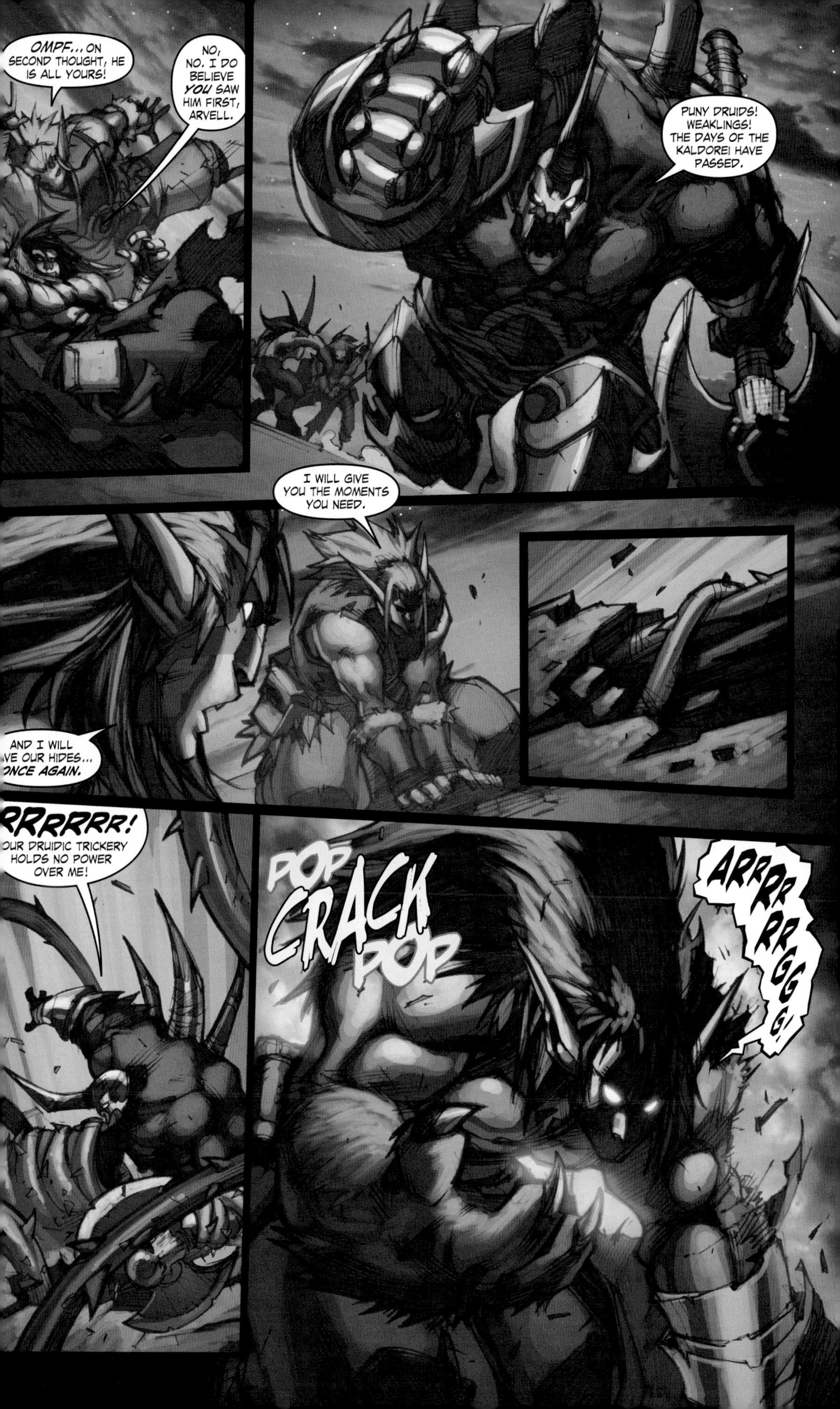
OMPF... ON SECOND THOUGHT, HE IS ALL YOURS!
NO, NO. I DO BELIEVE YOU SAW HIM FIRST, ARVELL.
PUNY DRUIDS! WEAKLINGS! THE DAYS OF THE KALDOREI HAVE PASSED.
I WILL GIVE YOU THE MOMENTS YOU NEED.
AND I WILL
VE OUR HIDES... ONCE AGAIN.
RRRRRR!
OUR DRUIDIC TRICKERY HOLDS NO POWER OVER ME!
POP
CRACK
POP
ARRRRRRGGG!

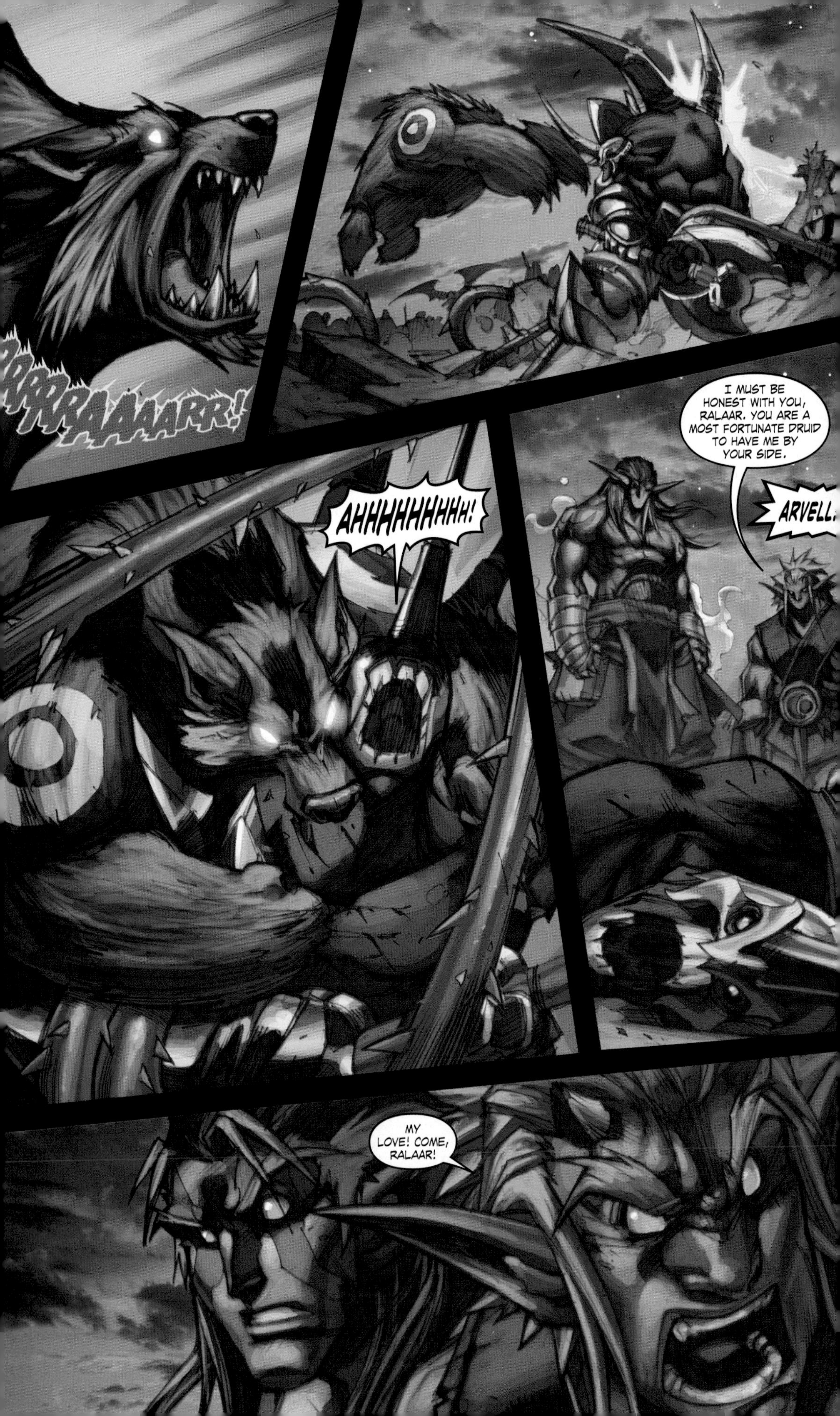
RRRRAAAAARR!
AHHHHHHHHH!
I MUST BE HONEST WITH YOU, RALAAR. YOU ARE A MOST FORTUNATE DRUID TO HAVE ME BY YOUR SIDE.
ARVELL.
MY LOVE! COME, RALAAR!

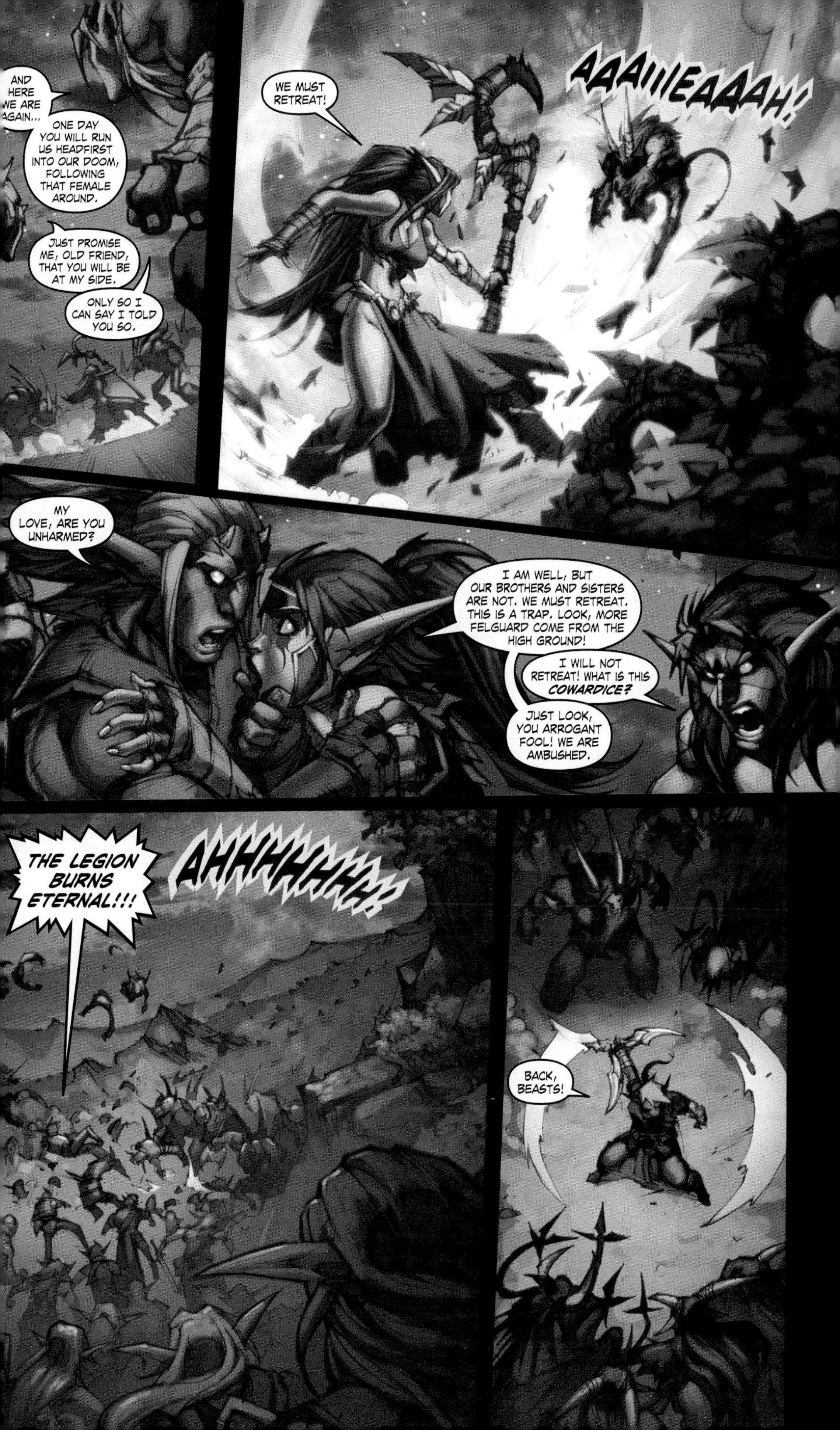
AND HERE WE ARE AGAIN...
ONE DAY YOU WILL RUN US HEADFIRST INTO OUR DOOM, FOLLOWING THAT FEMALE AROUND.
JUST PROMISE ME, OLD FRIEND, THAT YOU WILL BE AT MY SIDE.
ONLY SO I CAN SAY I TOLD YOU SO.
WE MUST RETREAT!
AAAIIIEAAAH!
MY LOVE, ARE YOU UNHARMED?
I AM WELL, BUT OUR BROTHERS AND SISTERS ARE NOT. WE MUST RETREAT. THIS IS A TRAP. LOOK, MORE FELGUARD COME FROM THE HIGH GROUND!
I WILL NOT RETREAT! WHAT IS THIS *COWARDICE?*
JUST LOOK, YOU ARROGANT FOOL! WE ARE AMBUSHED.
THE LEGION BURNS ETERNAL!!!
AHHHHHHH!
BACK, BEASTS!

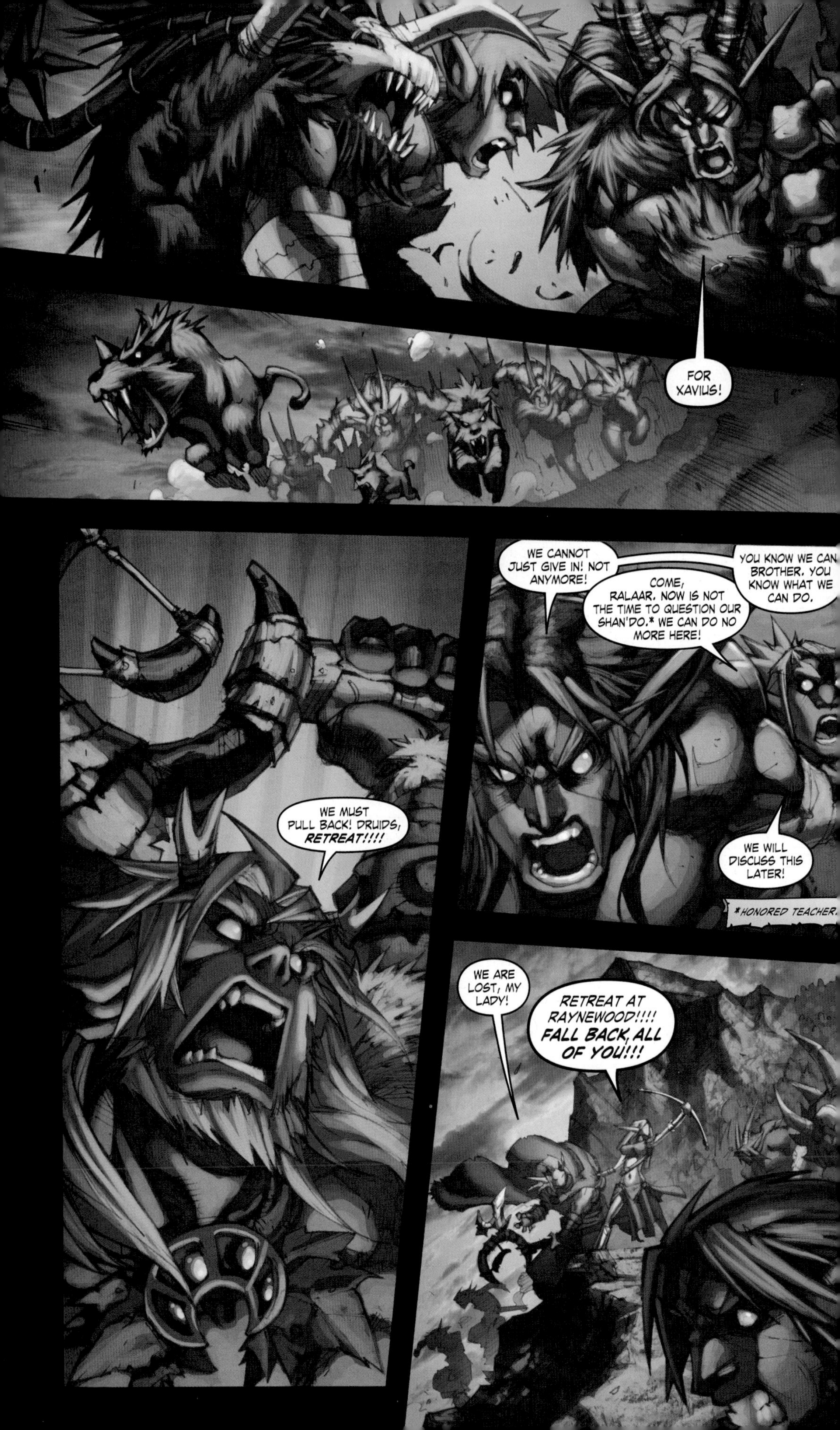
FOR XAVIUS!
WE CANNOT JUST GIVE IN! NOT ANYMORE!
COME, RALAAR. NOW IS NOT THE TIME TO QUESTION OUR SHAN'DO.* WE CAN DO NO MORE HERE!
YOU KNOW WE CAN BROTHER. YOU KNOW WHAT WE CAN DO.
WE MUST PULL BACK! DRUIDS, RETREAT!!!!
WE WILL DISCUSS THIS LATER!
*HONORED TEACHER.
WE ARE LOST, MY LADY!
RETREAT AT RAYNEWOOD!!!! FALL BACK, ALL OF YOU!!!

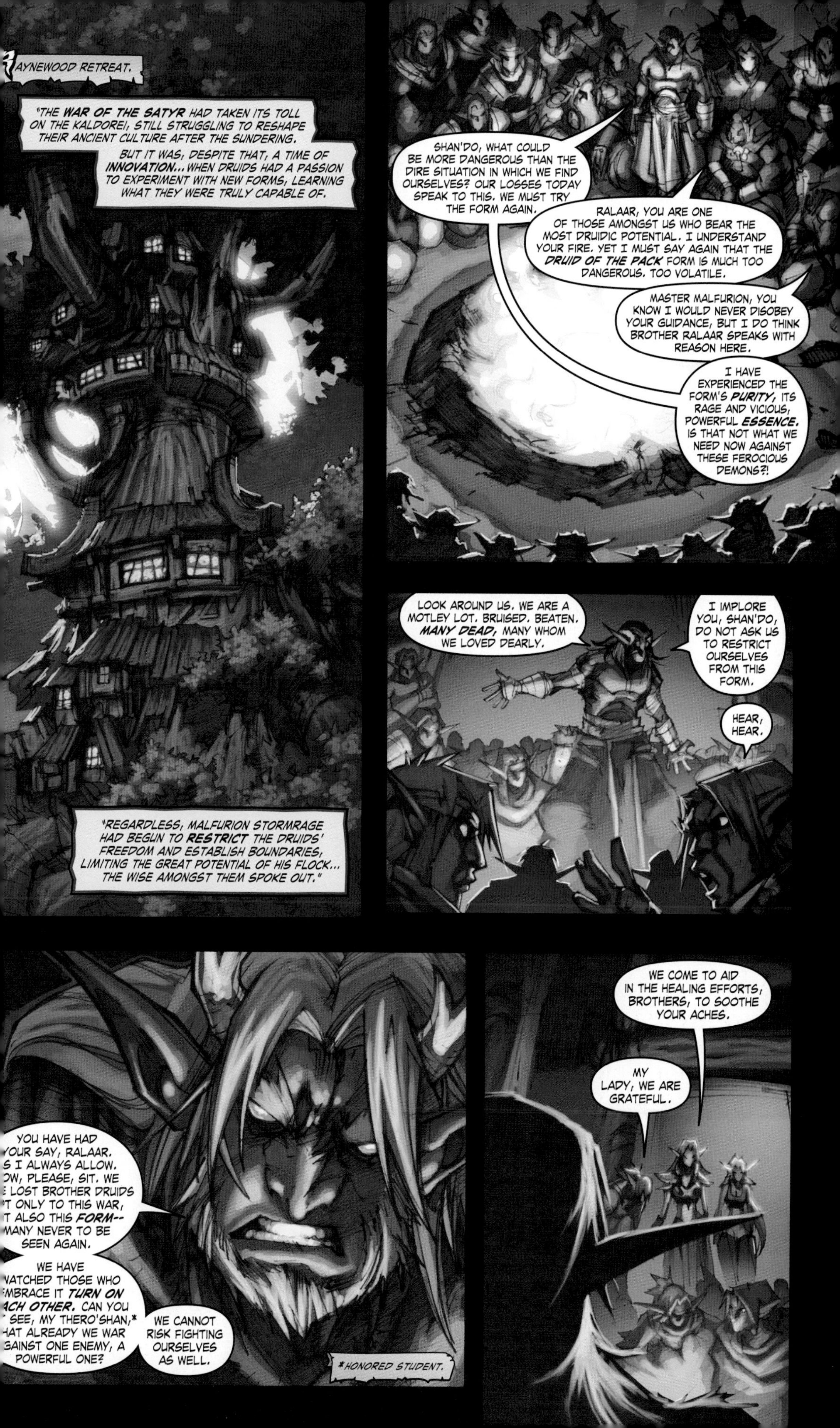
AYNEWOOD RETREAT.
"THE WAR OF THE SATYR HAD TAKEN ITS TOLL ON THE KALDOREI, STILL STRUGGLING TO RESHAPE THEIR ANCIENT CULTURE AFTER THE SUNDERING.
BUT IT WAS, DESPITE THAT, A TIME OF INNOVATION... WHEN DRUIDS HAD A PASSION TO EXPERIMENT WITH NEW FORMS, LEARNING WHAT THEY WERE TRULY CAPABLE OF.
"REGARDLESS, MALFURION STORMRAGE HAD BEGUN TO RESTRICT THE DRUIDS' FREEDOM AND ESTABLISH BOUNDARIES, LIMITING THE GREAT POTENTIAL OF HIS FLOCK... THE WISE AMONGST THEM SPOKE OUT."
SHAN'DO, WHAT COULD BE MORE DANGEROUS THAN THE DIRE SITUATION IN WHICH WE FIND OURSELVES? OUR LOSSES TODAY SPEAK TO THIS. WE MUST TRY THE FORM AGAIN.
RALAAR, YOU ARE ONE OF THOSE AMONGST US WHO BEAR THE MOST DRUIDIC POTENTIAL. I UNDERSTAND YOUR FIRE. YET I MUST SAY AGAIN THAT THE DRUID OF THE PACK FORM IS MUCH TOO DANGEROUS. TOO VOLATILE.
MASTER MALFURION, YOU KNOW I WOULD NEVER DISOBEY YOUR GUIDANCE, BUT I DO THINK BROTHER RALAAR SPEAKS WITH REASON HERE.
I HAVE EXPERIENCED THE FORM'S PURITY, ITS RAGE AND VICIOUS, POWERFUL ESSENCE. IS THAT NOT WHAT WE NEED NOW AGAINST THESE FEROCIOUS DEMONS?!
LOOK AROUND US. WE ARE A MOTLEY LOT. BRUISED. BEATEN. MANY DEAD, MANY WHOM WE LOVED DEARLY.
I IMPLORE YOU, SHAN'DO, DO NOT ASK US TO RESTRICT OURSELVES FROM THIS FORM.
HEAR, HEAR.
YOU HAVE HAD
OUR SAY, RALAAR.
S I ALWAYS ALLOW.
OW, PLEASE, SIT. WE
E LOST BROTHER DRUIDS
T ONLY TO THIS WAR,
T ALSO THIS FORM--
MANY NEVER TO BE
SEEN AGAIN.
WE HAVE
VATCHED THOSE WHO
MBRACE IT TURN ON
ACH OTHER. CAN YOU
SEE, MY THERO'SHAN,*
HAT ALREADY WE WAR
GAINST ONE ENEMY, A
POWERFUL ONE?
WE CANNOT RISK FIGHTING OURSELVES AS WELL.
*HONORED STUDENT.
WE COME TO AID IN THE HEALING EFFORTS, BROTHERS, TO SOOTHE YOUR ACHES.
MY LADY, WE ARE GRATEFUL.

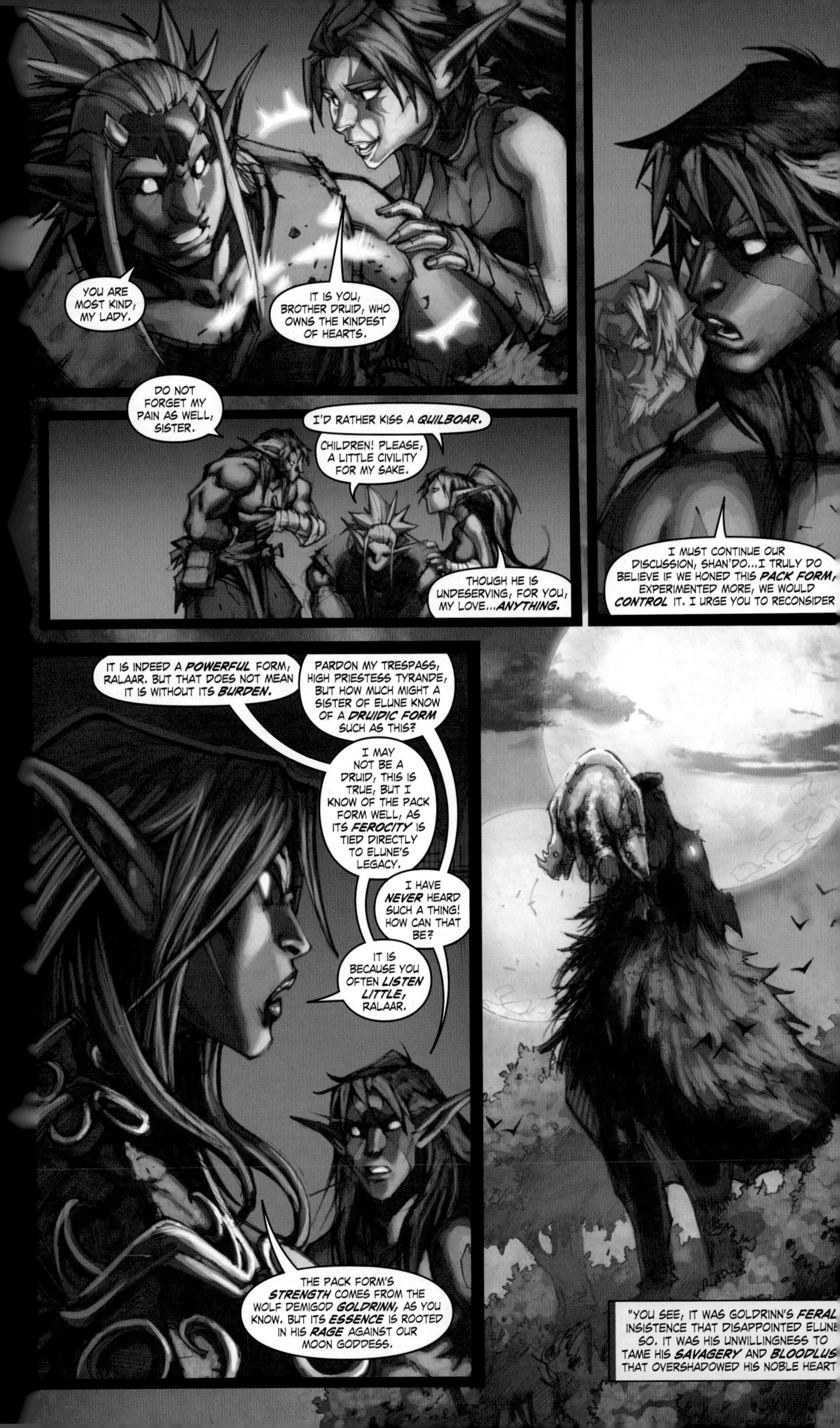
YOU ARE MOST KIND, MY LADY.
IT IS YOU, BROTHER DRUID, WHO OWNS THE KINDEST OF HEARTS.
DO NOT FORGET MY PAIN AS WELL, SISTER.
I'D RATHER KISS A QUILBOAR.
CHILDREN! PLEASE, A LITTLE CIVILITY FOR MY SAKE.
THOUGH HE IS UNDESERVING, FOR YOU, MY LOVE...ANYTHING.
I MUST CONTINUE OUR DISCUSSION, SHAN'DO...I TRULY DO BELIEVE IF WE HONED THIS PACK FORM, EXPERIMENTED MORE, WE WOULD CONTROL IT. I URGE YOU TO RECONSIDER
IT IS INDEED A POWERFUL FORM, RALAAR. BUT THAT DOES NOT MEAN IT IS WITHOUT ITS BURDEN.
PARDON MY TRESPASS, HIGH PRIESTESS TYRANDE, BUT HOW MUCH MIGHT A SISTER OF ELUNE KNOW OF A DRUIDIC FORM SUCH AS THIS?
I MAY NOT BE A DRUID, THIS IS TRUE, BUT I KNOW OF THE PACK FORM WELL, AS ITS FEROCITY IS TIED DIRECTLY TO ELUNE'S LEGACY.
I HAVE NEVER HEARD SUCH A THING! HOW CAN THAT BE?
IT IS BECAUSE YOU OFTEN LISTEN LITTLE, RALAAR.
THE PACK FORM'S STRENGTH COMES FROM THE WOLF DEMIGOD GOLDRINN, AS YOU KNOW. BUT ITS ESSENCE IS ROOTED IN HIS RAGE AGAINST OUR MOON GODDESS.
"YOU SEE, IT WAS GOLDRINN'S FERAL INSISTENCE THAT DISAPPOINTED ELUNE SO. IT WAS HIS UNWILLINGNESS TO TAME HIS SAVAGERY AND BLOODLUST THAT OVERSHADOWED HIS NOBLE HEART

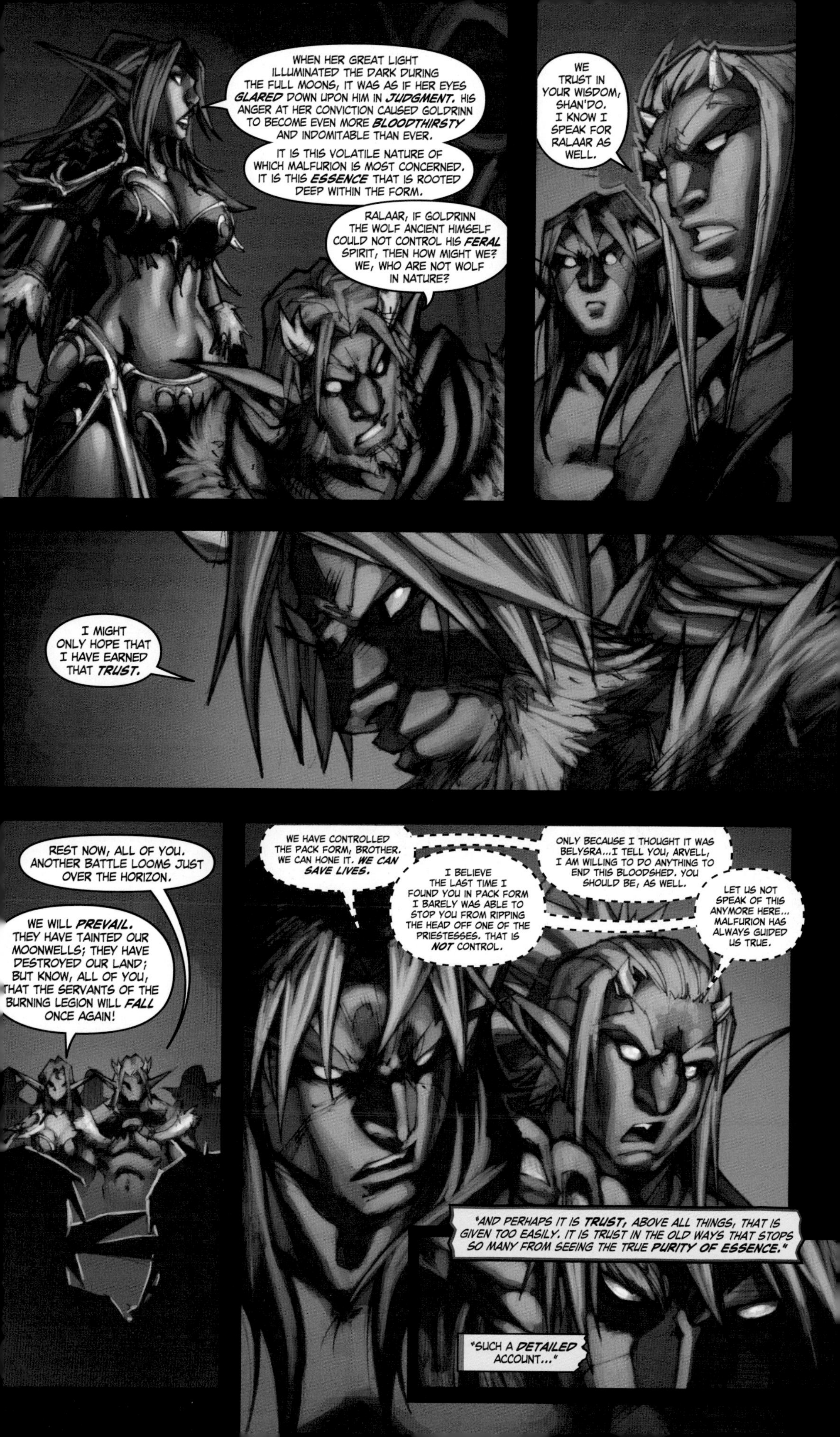

WHEN HER GREAT LIGHT ILLUMINATED THE DARK DURING THE FULL MOONS, IT WAS AS IF HER EYES GLARED DOWN UPON HIM IN JUDGMENT. HIS ANGER AT HER CONVICTION CAUSED GOLDRINN TO BECOME EVEN MORE BLOODTHIRSTY AND INDOMITABLE THAN EVER.
IT IS THIS VOLATILE NATURE OF WHICH MALFURION IS MOST CONCERNED. IT IS THIS ESSENCE THAT IS ROOTED DEEP WITHIN THE FORM.
RALAAR, IF GOLDRINN THE WOLF ANCIENT HIMSELF COULD NOT CONTROL HIS FERAL SPIRIT, THEN HOW MIGHT WE? WE, WHO ARE NOT WOLF IN NATURE?
WE TRUST IN YOUR WISDOM, SHAN'DO. I KNOW I SPEAK FOR RALAAR AS WELL.
I MIGHT ONLY HOPE THAT I HAVE EARNED THAT TRUST.
REST NOW, ALL OF YOU. ANOTHER BATTLE LOOMS JUST OVER THE HORIZON.
WE WILL PREVAIL. THEY HAVE TAINTED OUR MOONWELLS; THEY HAVE DESTROYED OUR LAND; BUT KNOW, ALL OF YOU, THAT THE SERVANTS OF THE BURNING LEGION WILL FALL ONCE AGAIN!
WE HAVE CONTROLLED THE PACK FORM, BROTHER. WE CAN HONE IT. WE CAN SAVE LIVES.
I BELIEVE THE LAST TIME I FOUND YOU IN PACK FORM I BARELY WAS ABLE TO STOP YOU FROM RIPPING THE HEAD OFF ONE OF THE PRIESTESSES. THAT IS NOT CONTROL.
ONLY BECAUSE I THOUGHT IT WAS BELYSRA...I TELL YOU, ARVELL, I AM WILLING TO DO ANYTHING TO END THIS BLOODSHED. YOU SHOULD BE, AS WELL.
LET US NOT SPEAK OF THIS ANYMORE HERE... MALFURION HAS ALWAYS GUIDED US TRUE.
"AND PERHAPS IT IS TRUST, ABOVE ALL THINGS, THAT IS GIVEN TOO EASILY. IT IS TRUST IN THE OLD WAYS THAT STOPS SO MANY FROM SEEING THE TRUE PURITY OF ESSENCE."
"SUCH A DETAILED ACCOUNT..."

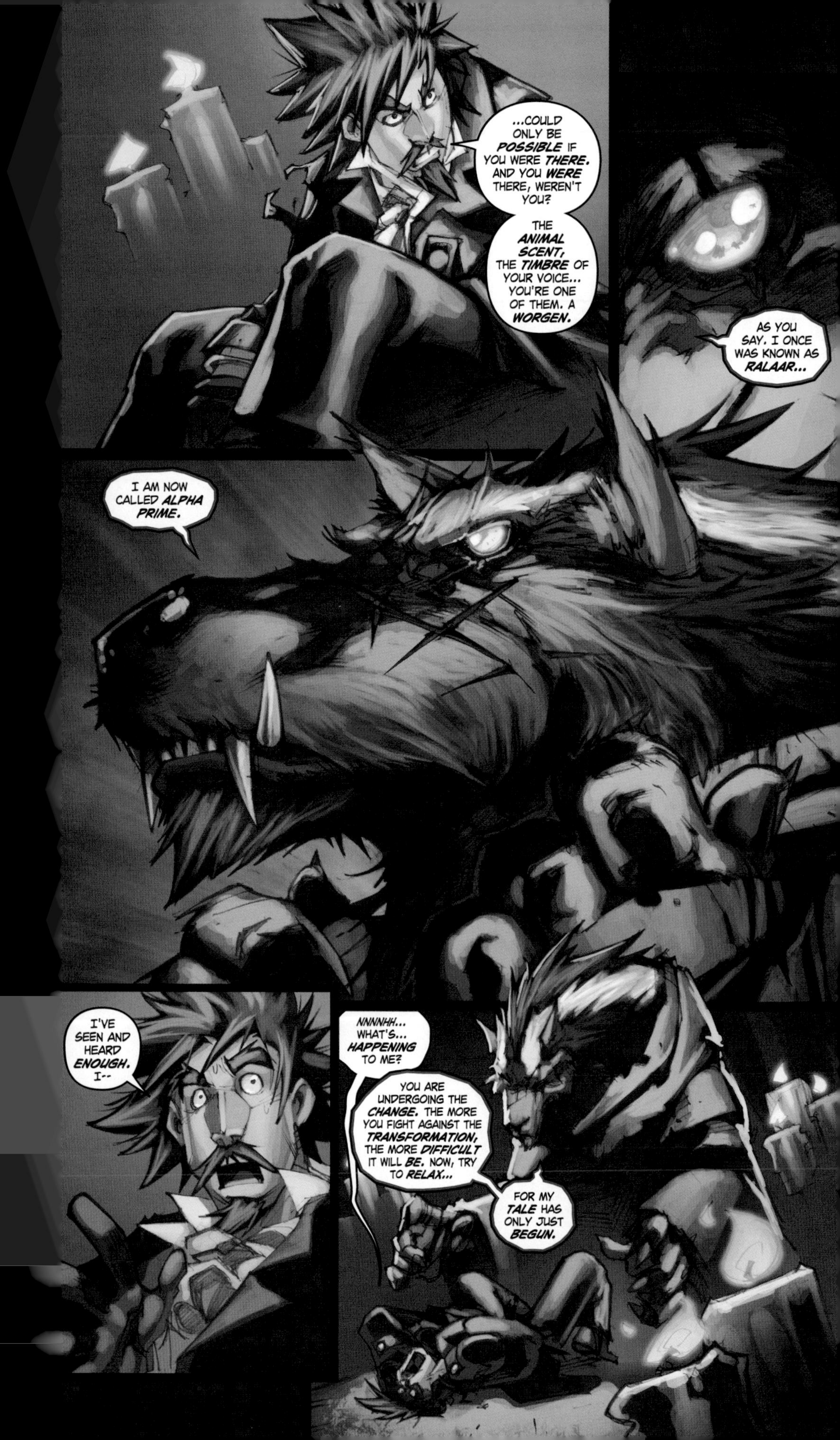
...COULD ONLY BE POSSIBLE IF YOU WERE THERE. AND YOU WERE THERE, WEREN'T YOU?
THE ANIMAL SCENT, THE TIMBRE OF YOUR VOICE... YOU'RE ONE OF THEM. A WORGEN.
AS YOU SAY. I ONCE WAS KNOWN AS RALAAR...
I AM NOW CALLED ALPHA PRIME.
I'VE SEEN AND HEARD ENOUGH. I--
NNNNHH... WHAT'S... HAPPENING TO ME?
YOU ARE UNDERGOING THE CHANGE. THE MORE YOU FIGHT AGAINST THE TRANSFORMATION, THE MORE DIFFICULT IT WILL BE. NOW, TRY TO RELAX...
FOR MY TALE HAS ONLY JUST BEGUN.

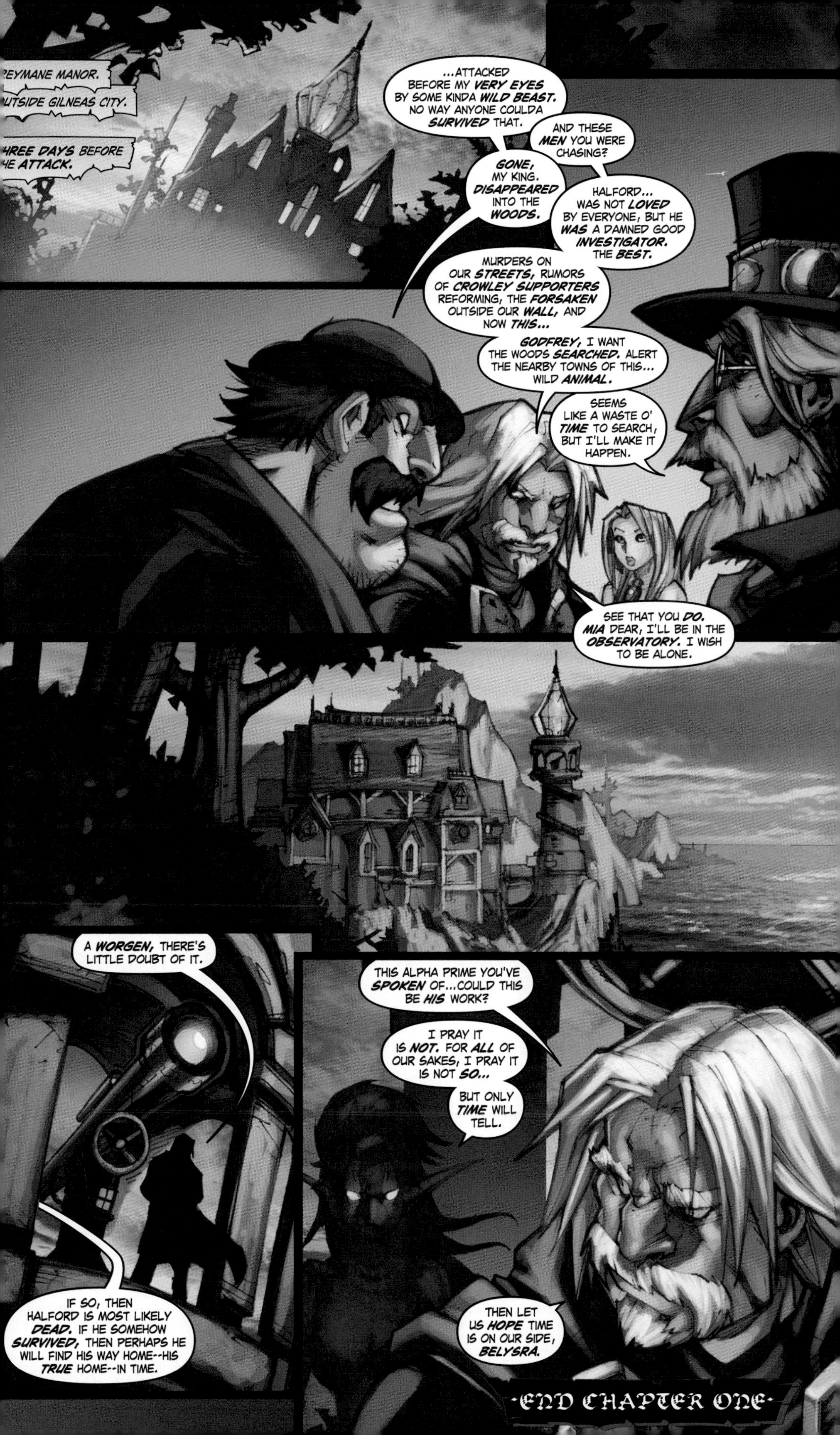

REYMANE MANOR.
OUTSIDE GILNEAS CITY.
THREE DAYS BEFORE THE ATTACK.
...ATTACKED BEFORE MY VERY EYES BY SOME KINDA WILD BEAST. NO WAY ANYONE COULDA SURVIVED THAT.
AND THESE MEN YOU WERE CHASING?
GONE, MY KING. DISAPPEARED INTO THE WOODS.
HALFORD... WAS NOT LOVED BY EVERYONE, BUT HE WAS A DAMNED GOOD INVESTIGATOR. THE BEST.
MURDERS ON OUR STREETS, RUMORS OF CROWLEY SUPPORTERS REFORMING, THE FORSAKEN OUTSIDE OUR WALL, AND NOW THIS...
GODFREY, I WANT THE WOODS SEARCHED. ALERT THE NEARBY TOWNS OF THIS... WILD ANIMAL.
SEEMS LIKE A WASTE O' TIME TO SEARCH, BUT I'LL MAKE IT HAPPEN.
SEE THAT YOU DO. MIA DEAR, I'LL BE IN THE OBSERVATORY. I WISH TO BE ALONE.
A WORGEN, THERE'S LITTLE DOUBT OF IT.
IF SO, THEN HALFORD IS MOST LIKELY DEAD. IF HE SOMEHOW SURVIVED, THEN PERHAPS HE WILL FIND HIS WAY HOME--HIS TRUE HOME--IN TIME.
THIS ALPHA PRIME YOU'VE SPOKEN OF...COULD THIS BE HIS WORK?
I PRAY IT IS NOT. FOR ALL OF OUR SAKES, I PRAY IT IS NOT SO...
BUT ONLY TIME WILL TELL.
THEN LET US HOPE TIME IS ON OUR SIDE, BELYSRA.
-END CHAPTER ONE-

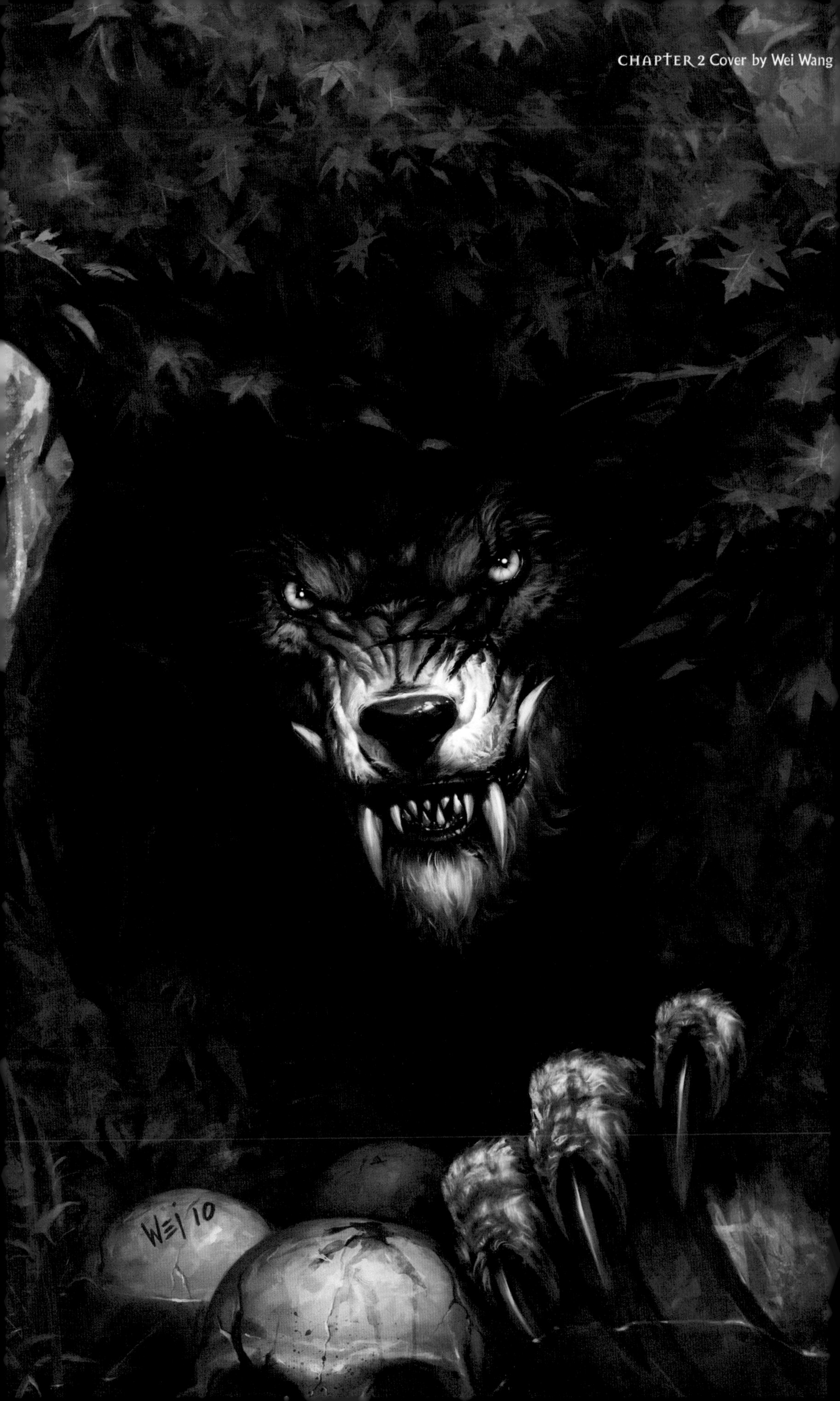

CHAPTER 2 Cover by Wei Wang

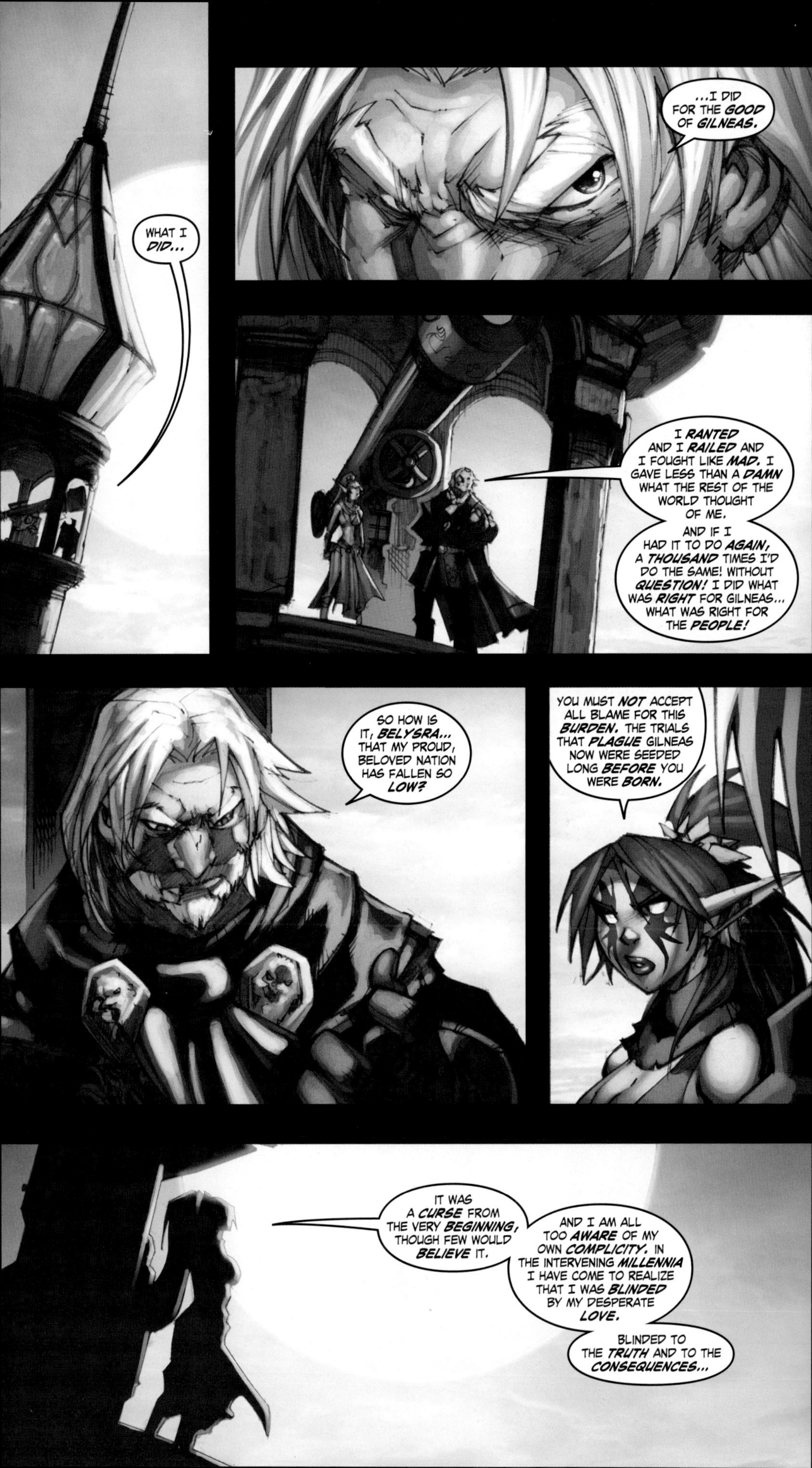
WHAT I DID...
...I DID FOR THE GOOD OF GILNEAS.
I RANTED AND I RAILED AND I FOUGHT LIKE MAD. I GAVE LESS THAN A DAMN WHAT THE REST OF THE WORLD THOUGHT OF ME.
AND IF I HAD IT TO DO AGAIN, A THOUSAND TIMES I'D DO THE SAME! WITHOUT QUESTION! I DID WHAT WAS RIGHT FOR GILNEAS... WHAT WAS RIGHT FOR THE PEOPLE!
SO HOW IS IT, BELYSRA... THAT MY PROUD, BELOVED NATION HAS FALLEN SO LOW?
YOU MUST NOT ACCEPT ALL BLAME FOR THIS BURDEN. THE TRIALS THAT PLAGUE GILNEAS NOW WERE SEEDED LONG BEFORE YOU WERE BORN.
IT WAS A CURSE FROM THE VERY BEGINNING, THOUGH FEW WOULD BELIEVE IT.
AND I AM ALL TOO AWARE OF MY OWN COMPLICITY. IN THE INTERVENING MILLENNIA I HAVE COME TO REALIZE THAT I WAS BLINDED BY MY DESPERATE LOVE.
BLINDED TO THE TRUTH AND TO THE CONSEQUENCES...

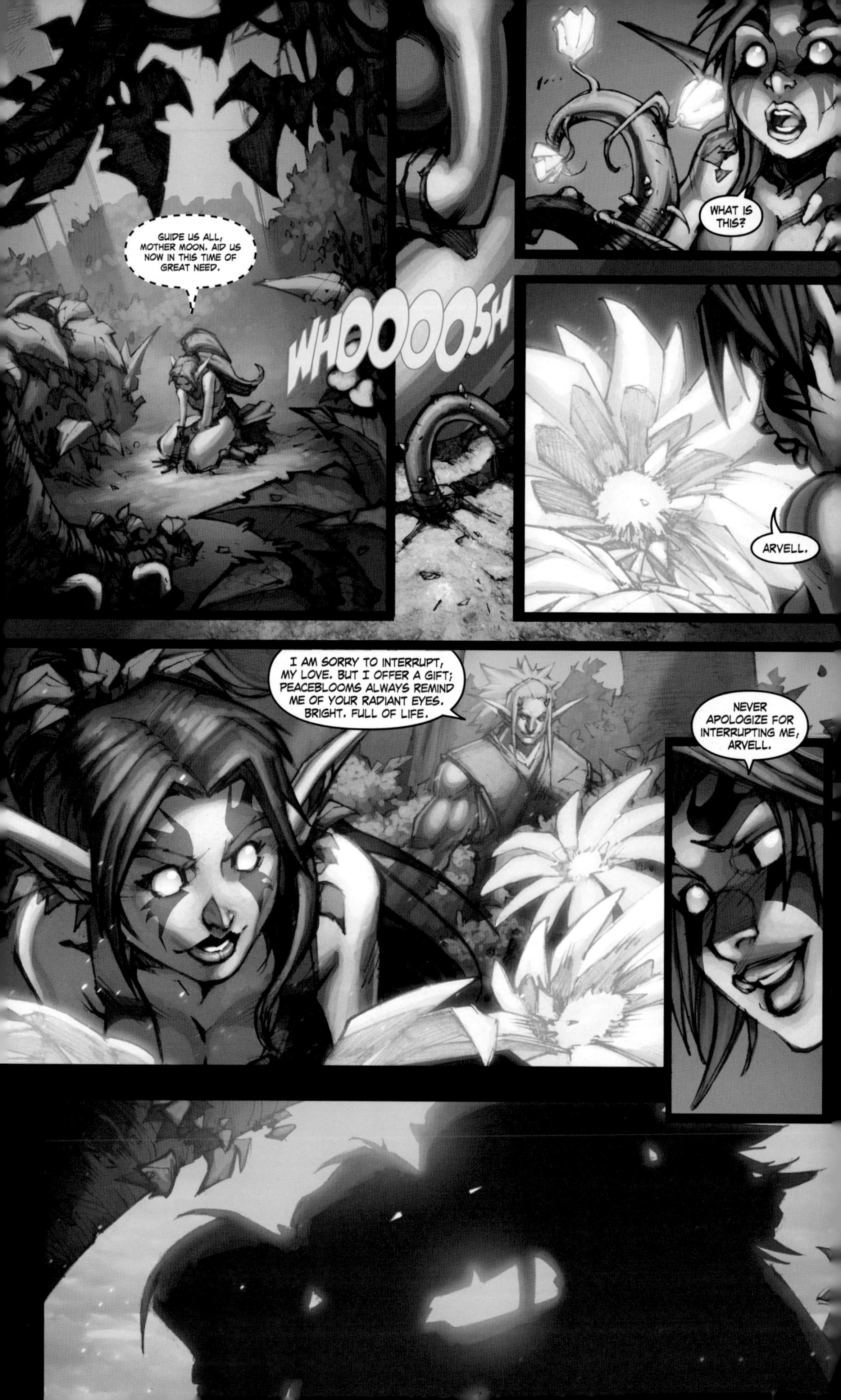
GUIDE US ALL, MOTHER MOON. AID US NOW IN THIS TIME OF GREAT NEED.
WHOOOOOSH
WHAT IS THIS?
ARVELL.
I AM SORRY TO INTERRUPT, MY LOVE. BUT I OFFER A GIFT; PEACEBLOOMS ALWAYS REMIND ME OF YOUR RADIANT EYES. BRIGHT. FULL OF LIFE.
NEVER APOLOGIZE FOR INTERRUPTING ME, ARVELL.

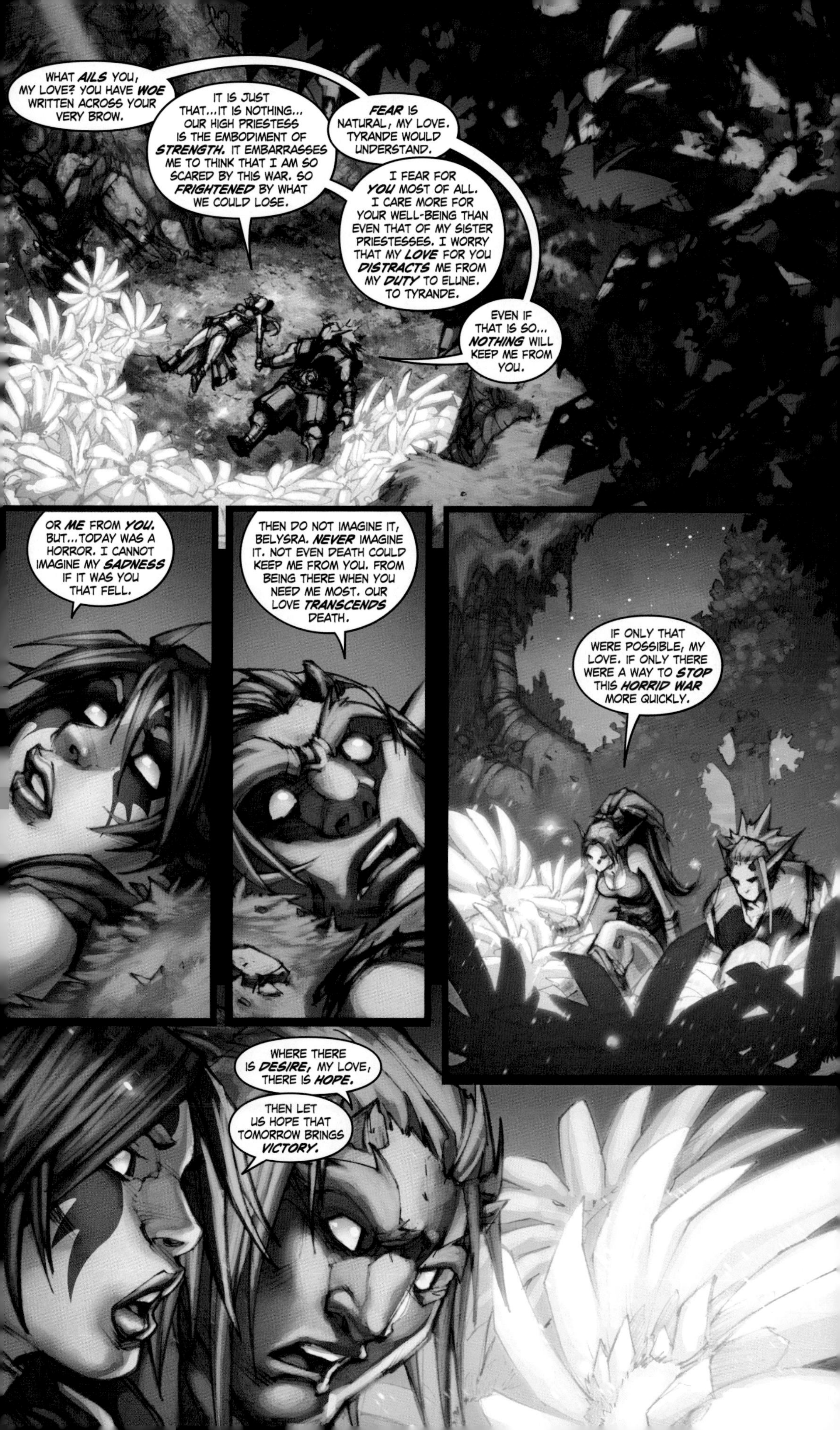
WHAT AILS YOU, MY LOVE? YOU HAVE WOE WRITTEN ACROSS YOUR VERY BROW.
IT IS JUST THAT...IT IS NOTHING... OUR HIGH PRIESTESS IS THE EMBODIMENT OF STRENGTH. IT EMBARRASSES ME TO THINK THAT I AM SO SCARED BY THIS WAR. SO FRIGHTENED BY WHAT WE COULD LOSE.
FEAR IS NATURAL, MY LOVE. TYRANDE WOULD UNDERSTAND.
I FEAR FOR YOU MOST OF ALL. I CARE MORE FOR YOUR WELL-BEING THAN EVEN THAT OF MY SISTER PRIESTESSES. I WORRY THAT MY LOVE FOR YOU DISTRACTS ME FROM MY DUTY TO ELUNE. TO TYRANDE.
EVEN IF THAT IS SO... NOTHING WILL KEEP ME FROM YOU.
OR ME FROM YOU. BUT...TODAY WAS A HORROR. I CANNOT IMAGINE MY SADNESS IF IT WAS YOU THAT FELL.
THEN DO NOT IMAGINE IT, BELYSRA. NEVER IMAGINE IT. NOT EVEN DEATH COULD KEEP ME FROM YOU. FROM BEING THERE WHEN YOU NEED ME MOST. OUR LOVE TRANSCENDS DEATH.
IF ONLY THAT WERE POSSIBLE, MY LOVE. IF ONLY THERE WERE A WAY TO STOP THIS HORRID WAR MORE QUICKLY.
WHERE THERE IS DESIRE, MY LOVE, THERE IS HOPE.
THEN LET US HOPE THAT TOMORROW BRINGS VICTORY.

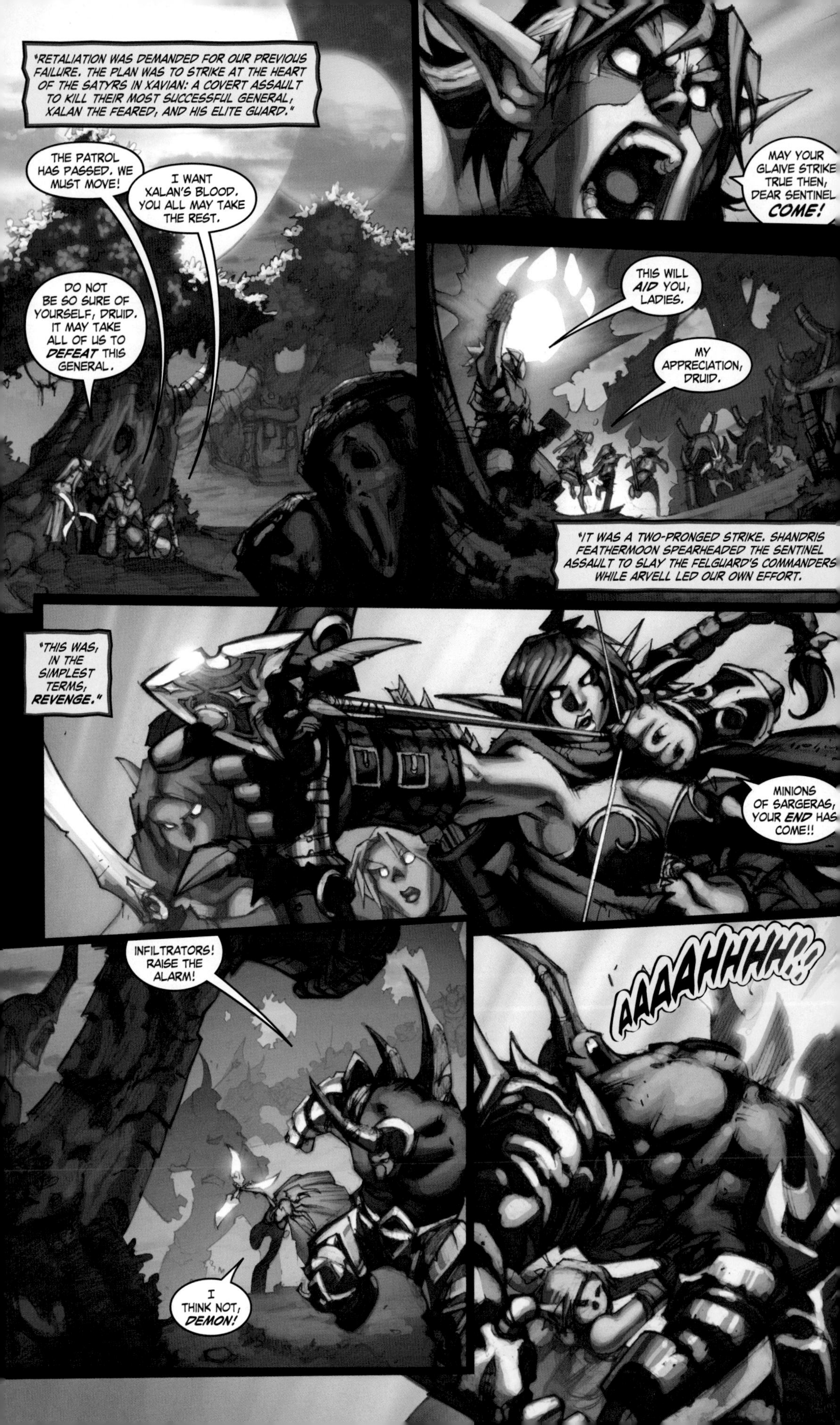
"RETALIATION WAS DEMANDED FOR OUR PREVIOUS FAILURE. THE PLAN WAS TO STRIKE AT THE HEART OF THE SATYRS IN XAVIAN: A COVERT ASSAULT TO KILL THEIR MOST SUCCESSFUL GENERAL, XALAN THE FEARED, AND HIS ELITE GUARD."
THE PATROL HAS PASSED. WE MUST MOVE!
I WANT XALAN'S BLOOD. YOU ALL MAY TAKE THE REST.
DO NOT BE SO SURE OF YOURSELF, DRUID. IT MAY TAKE ALL OF US TO DEFEAT THIS GENERAL.
MAY YOUR GLAIVE STRIKE TRUE THEN, DEAR SENTINEL. COME!
THIS WILL AID YOU, LADIES.
MY APPRECIATION, DRUID.
"IT WAS A TWO-PRONGED STRIKE. SHANDRIS FEATHERMOON SPEARHEADED THE SENTINEL ASSAULT TO SLAY THE FELGUARD'S COMMANDERS WHILE ARVELL LED OUR OWN EFFORT.
"THIS WAS, IN THE SIMPLEST TERMS, REVENGE."
MINIONS OF SARGERAS, YOUR END HAS COME!!
INFILTRATORS! RAISE THE ALARM!
I THINK NOT, DEMON!
AAAAHHHHH!!

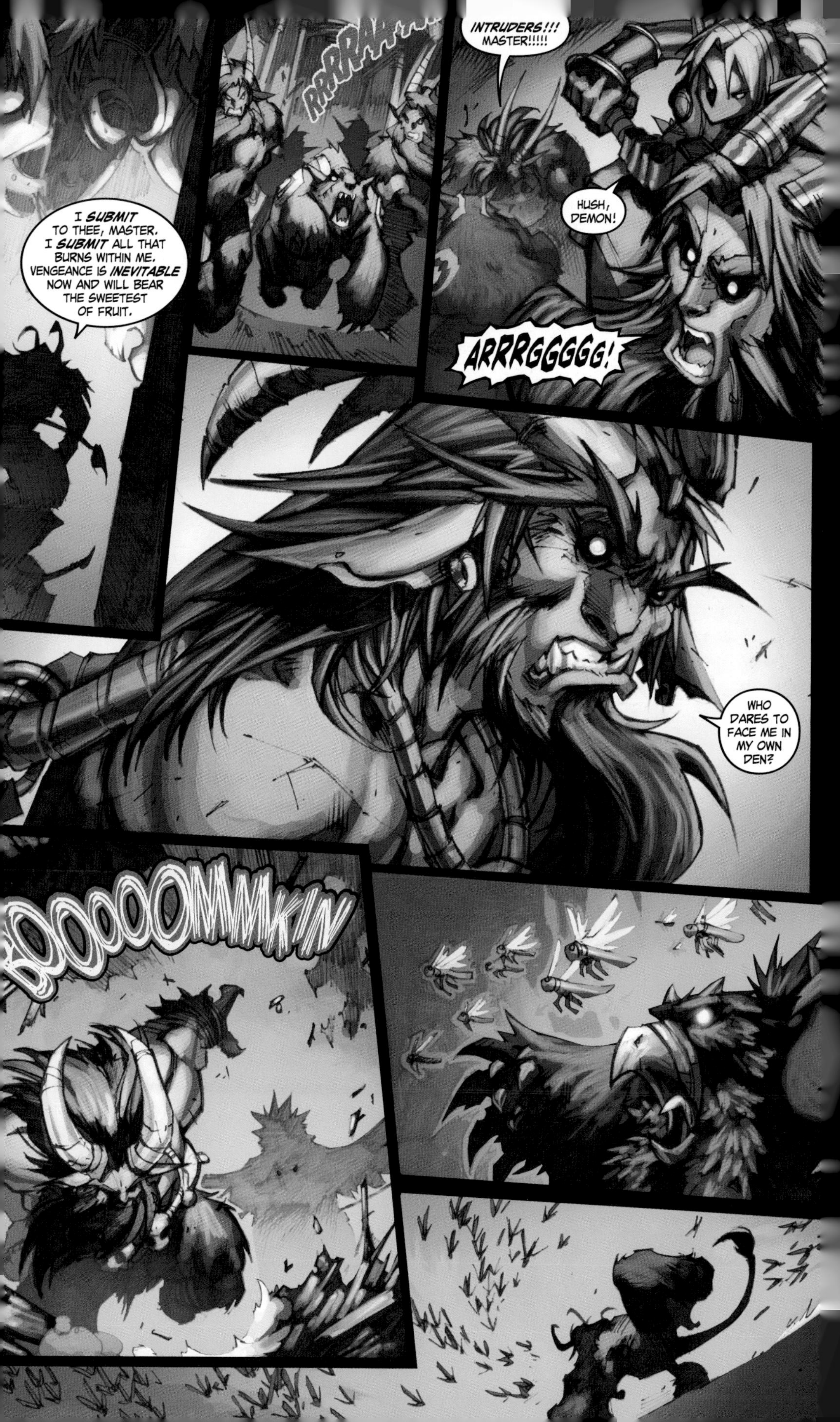

I SUBMIT TO THEE, MASTER. I SUBMIT ALL THAT BURNS WITHIN ME. VENGEANCE IS INEVITABLE NOW AND WILL BEAR THE SWEETEST OF FRUIT.
RRRRAAAA
INTRUDERS!!! MASTER!!!!!
HUSH, DEMON!
ARRRGGGGG!
WHO DARES TO FACE ME IN MY OWN DEN?
BOOOOOMMKIN

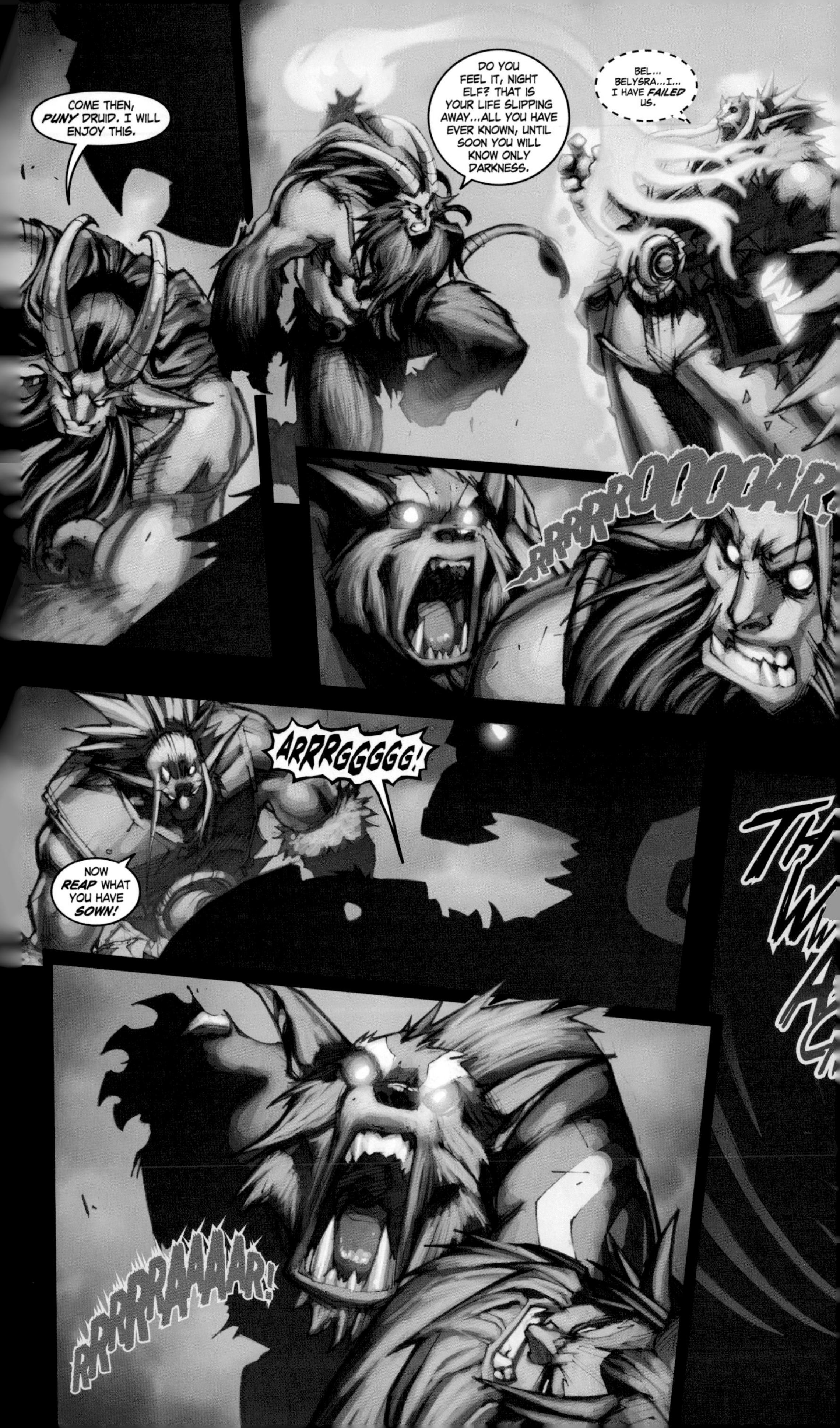
COME THEN, *PUNY* DRUID. I WILL ENJOY THIS.
DO YOU FEEL IT, NIGHT ELF? THAT IS YOUR LIFE SLIPPING AWAY...ALL YOU HAVE EVER KNOWN, UNTIL SOON YOU WILL KNOW ONLY DARKNESS.
BEL... BELYSRA...I... I HAVE *FAILED* US.
RRRRRROOOOOAR!
ARRRGGGGG!
NOW *REAP* WHAT YOU HAVE *SOWN!*
RRRRRAAAAR!

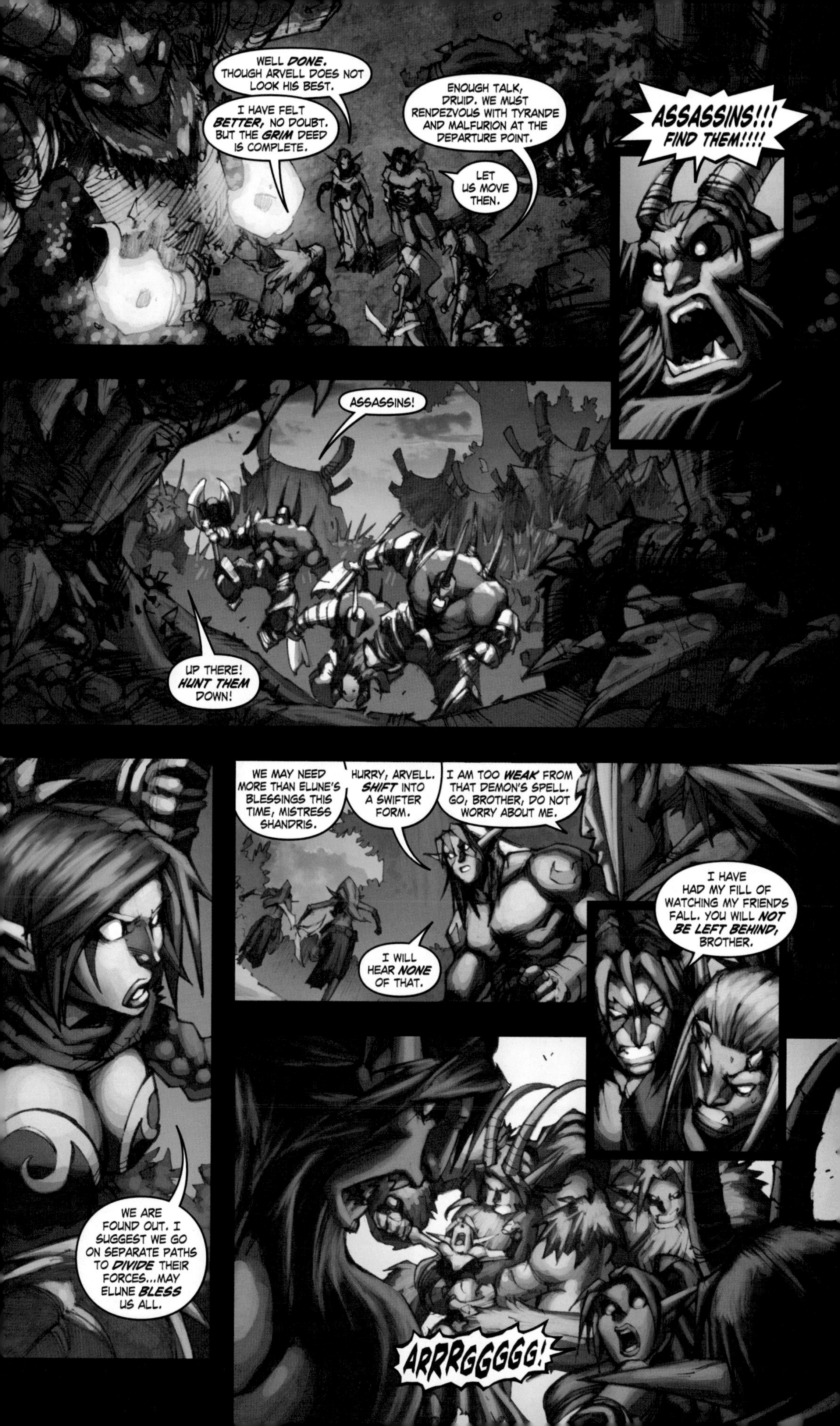
WELL DONE. THOUGH ARVELL DOES NOT LOOK HIS BEST.
I HAVE FELT BETTER, NO DOUBT. BUT THE GRIM DEED IS COMPLETE.
ENOUGH TALK, DRUID. WE MUST RENDEZVOUS WITH TYRANDE AND MALFURION AT THE DEPARTURE POINT.
LET US MOVE THEN.
ASSASSINS!!! FIND THEM!!!!
ASSASSINS!
UP THERE! HUNT THEM DOWN!
WE ARE FOUND OUT. I SUGGEST WE GO ON SEPARATE PATHS TO DIVIDE THEIR FORCES...MAY ELUNE BLESS US ALL.
WE MAY NEED MORE THAN ELUNE'S BLESSINGS THIS TIME, MISTRESS SHANDRIS.
HURRY, ARVELL. SHIFT INTO A SWIFTER FORM.
I AM TOO WEAK FROM THAT DEMON'S SPELL. GO, BROTHER, DO NOT WORRY ABOUT ME.
I WILL HEAR NONE OF THAT.
I HAVE HAD MY FILL OF WATCHING MY FRIENDS FALL. YOU WILL NOT BE LEFT BEHIND, BROTHER.
ARRRGGGGG!

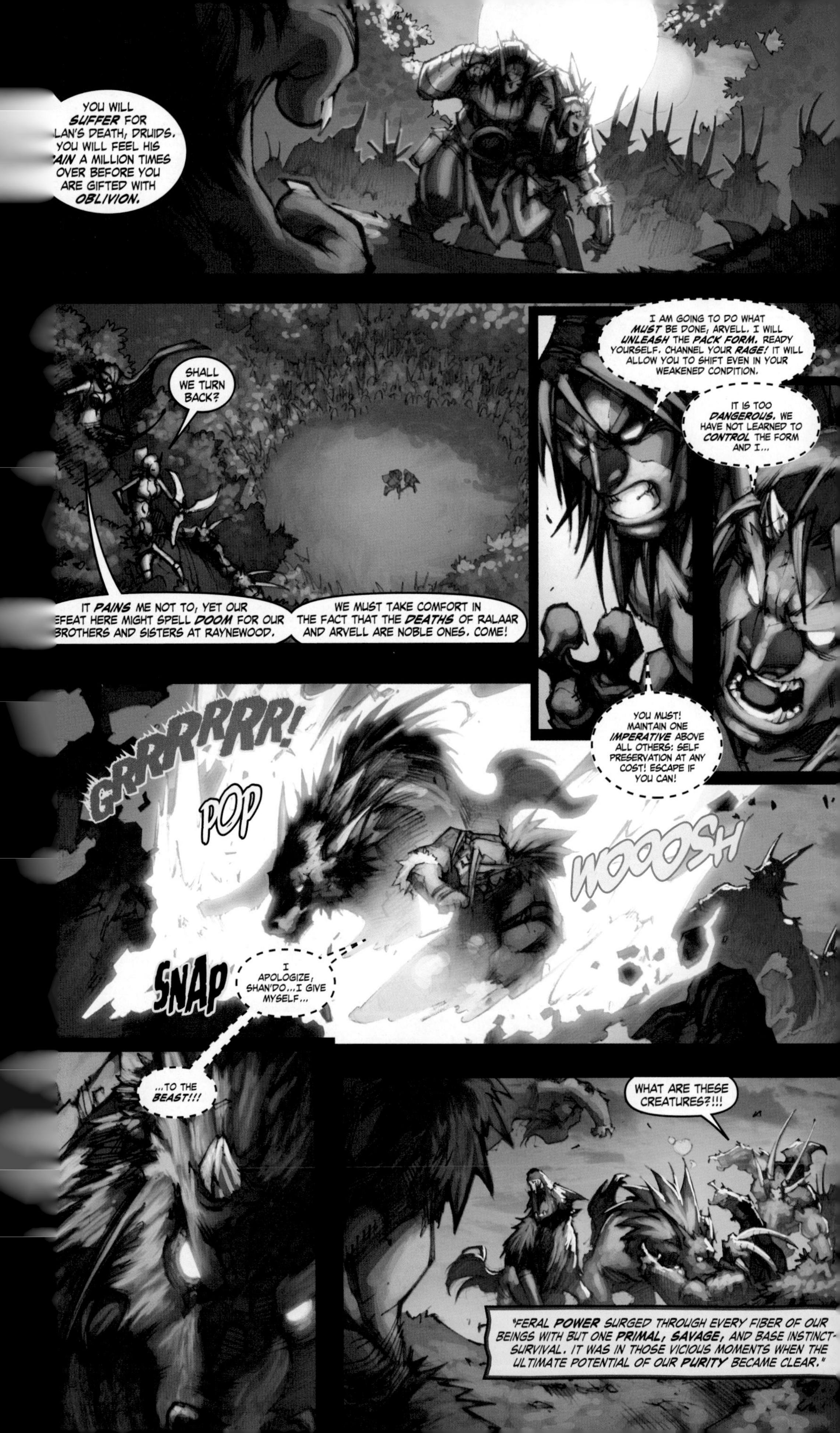

YOU WILL SUFFER FOR LAN'S DEATH, DRUIDS. YOU WILL FEEL HIS AIN A MILLION TIMES OVER BEFORE YOU ARE GIFTED WITH OBLIVION.
SHALL WE TURN BACK?
IT PAINS ME NOT TO, YET OUR EFEAT HERE MIGHT SPELL DOOM FOR OUR BROTHERS AND SISTERS AT RAYNEWOOD.
WE MUST TAKE COMFORT IN THE FACT THAT THE DEATHS OF RALAAR AND ARVELL ARE NOBLE ONES. COME!
I AM GOING TO DO WHAT MUST BE DONE, ARVELL. I WILL UNLEASH THE PACK FORM. READY YOURSELF. CHANNEL YOUR RAGE! IT WILL ALLOW YOU TO SHIFT EVEN IN YOUR WEAKENED CONDITION.
IT IS TOO DANGEROUS. WE HAVE NOT LEARNED TO CONTROL THE FORM AND I...
YOU MUST! MAINTAIN ONE IMPERATIVE ABOVE ALL OTHERS: SELF PRESERVATION AT ANY COST! ESCAPE IF YOU CAN!
GRRRRRR!
POP
WOOOSH
SNAP
I APOLOGIZE, SHAN'DO...I GIVE MYSELF...
...TO THE BEAST!!!
WHAT ARE THESE CREATURES?!!!
"FERAL POWER SURGED THROUGH EVERY FIBER OF OUR BEINGS WITH BUT ONE PRIMAL, SAVAGE, AND BASE INSTINCT-SURVIVAL. IT WAS IN THOSE VICIOUS MOMENTS WHEN THE ULTIMATE POTENTIAL OF OUR PURITY BECAME CLEAR."

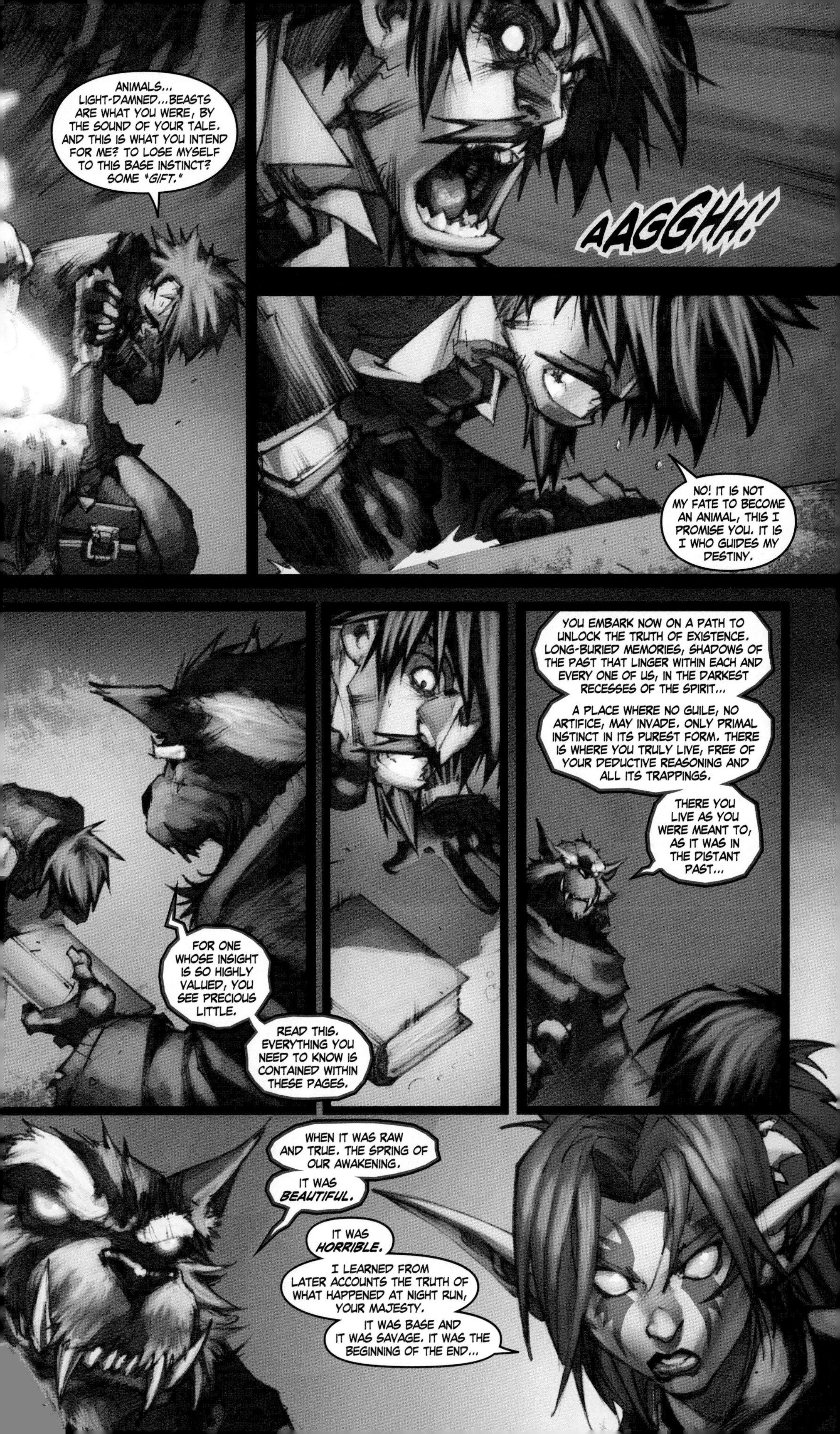

ANIMALS... LIGHT-DAMNED...BEASTS ARE WHAT YOU WERE, BY THE SOUND OF YOUR TALE. AND THIS IS WHAT YOU INTEND FOR ME? TO LOSE MYSELF TO THIS BASE INSTINCT? SOME "GIFT."
AAGGH!!
NO! IT IS NOT MY FATE TO BECOME AN ANIMAL, THIS I PROMISE YOU. IT IS I WHO GUIDES MY DESTINY.
FOR ONE WHOSE INSIGHT IS SO HIGHLY VALUED, YOU SEE PRECIOUS LITTLE.
READ THIS. EVERYTHING YOU NEED TO KNOW IS CONTAINED WITHIN THESE PAGES.
YOU EMBARK NOW ON A PATH TO UNLOCK THE TRUTH OF EXISTENCE. LONG-BURIED MEMORIES, SHADOWS OF THE PAST THAT LINGER WITHIN EACH AND EVERY ONE OF US, IN THE DARKEST RECESSES OF THE SPIRIT...
A PLACE WHERE NO GUILE, NO ARTIFICE, MAY INVADE. ONLY PRIMAL INSTINCT IN ITS PUREST FORM. THERE IS WHERE YOU TRULY LIVE, FREE OF YOUR DEDUCTIVE REASONING AND ALL ITS TRAPPINGS.
THERE YOU LIVE AS YOU WERE MEANT TO, AS IT WAS IN THE DISTANT PAST...
WHEN IT WAS RAW AND TRUE. THE SPRING OF OUR AWAKENING.
IT WAS BEAUTIFUL.
IT WAS HORRIBLE.
I LEARNED FROM LATER ACCOUNTS THE TRUTH OF WHAT HAPPENED AT NIGHT RUN, YOUR MAJESTY.
IT WAS BASE AND IT WAS SAVAGE. IT WAS THE BEGINNING OF THE END...

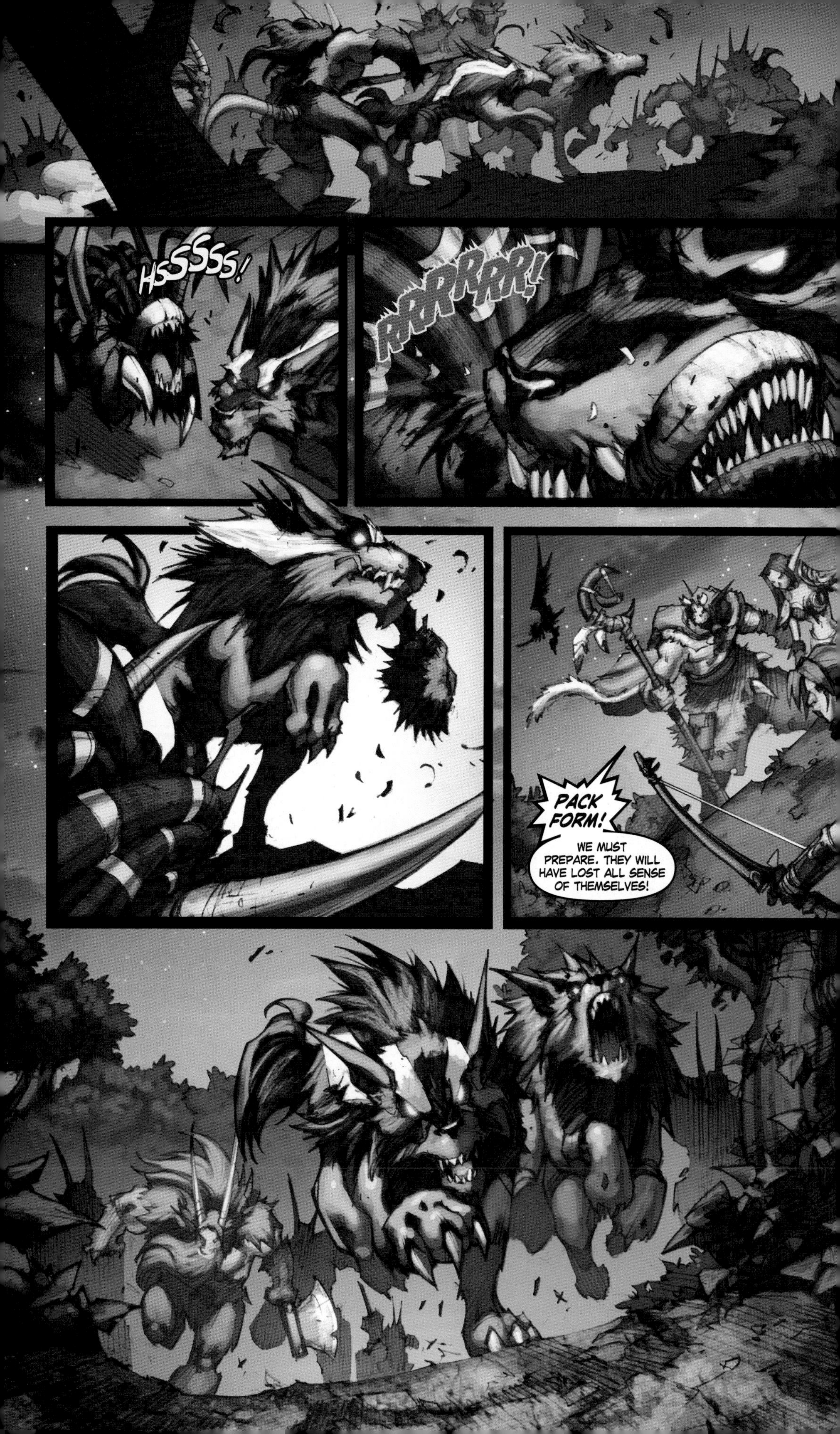
HSSSSS!
RRRRRRR!
PACK FORM!
WE MUST PREPARE. THEY WILL HAVE LOST ALL SENSE OF THEMSELVES!

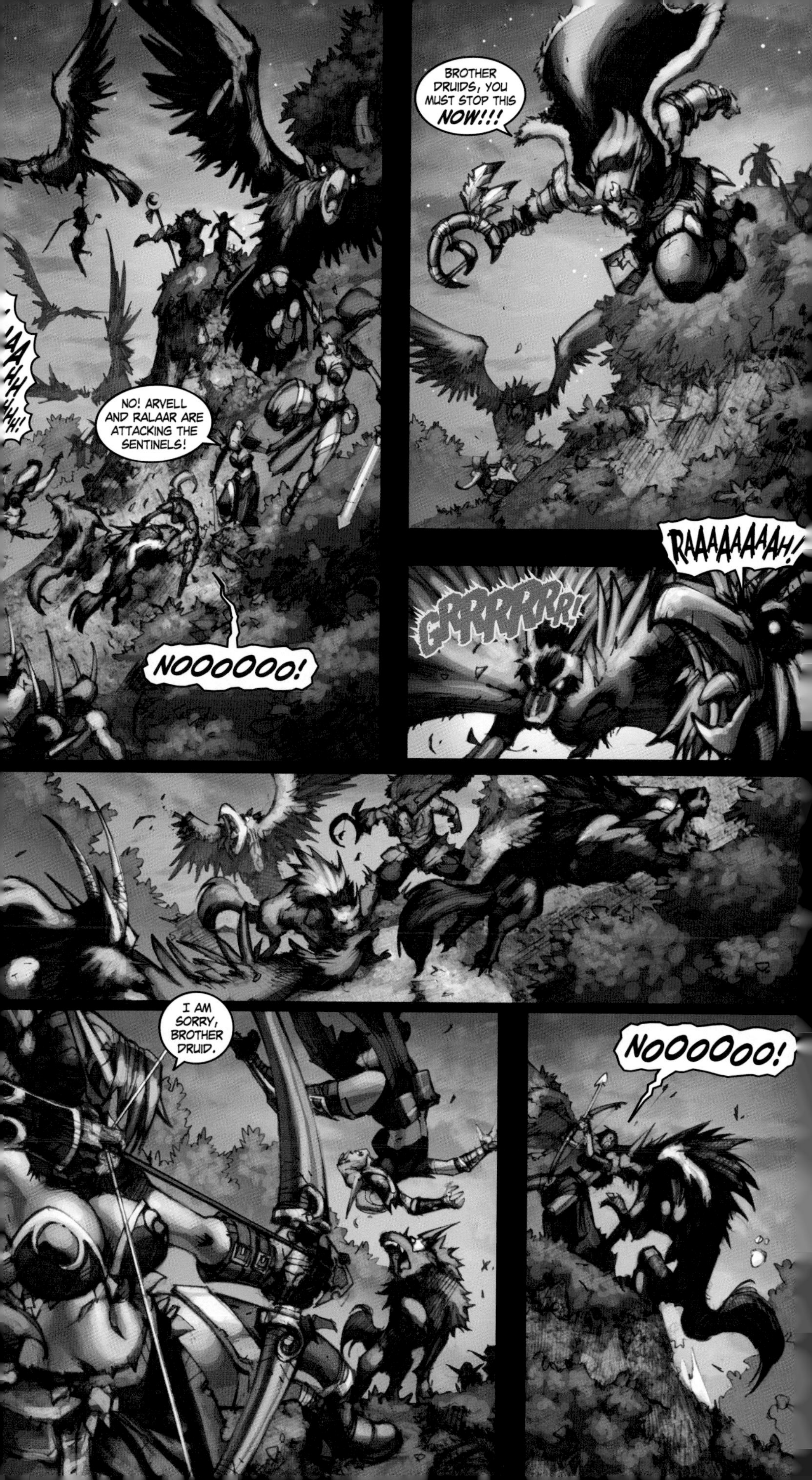
NO! ARVELL AND RALAAR ARE ATTACKING THE SENTINELS!
NOOOOOO!
BROTHER DRUIDS, YOU MUST STOP THIS NOW!!!
RAAAAAAAAH!
GRRRRRRR!
I AM SORRY, BROTHER DRUID.
NOOOOOO!

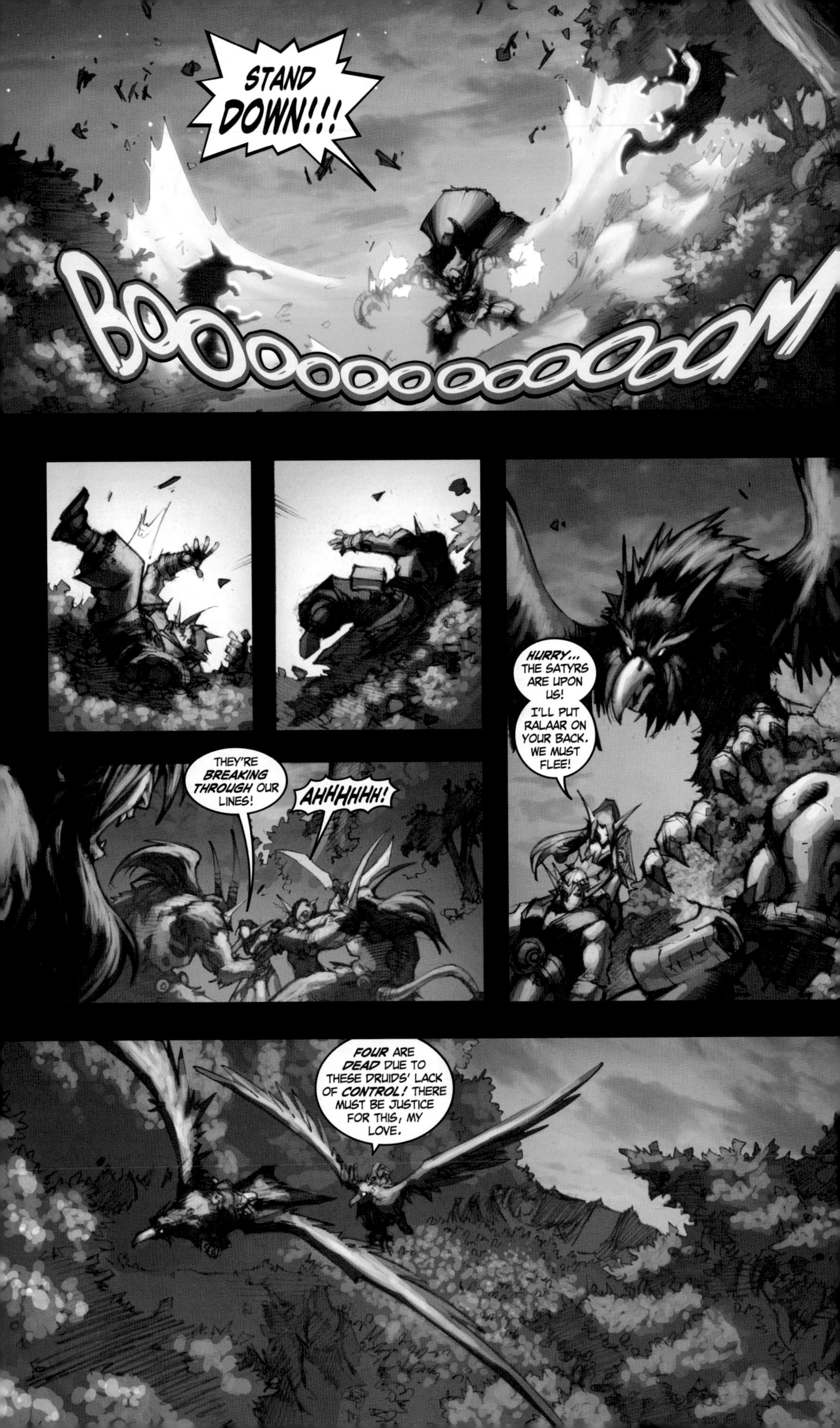
STAND DOWN!!!
BOOOOOOOOOOOOOOOM
HURRY... THE SATYRS ARE UPON US!
I'LL PUT RALAAR ON YOUR BACK. WE MUST FLEE!
THEY'RE BREAKING THROUGH OUR LINES!
AHHHHHH!
FOUR ARE DEAD DUE TO THESE DRUIDS' LACK OF CONTROL! THERE MUST BE JUSTICE FOR THIS, MY LOVE.

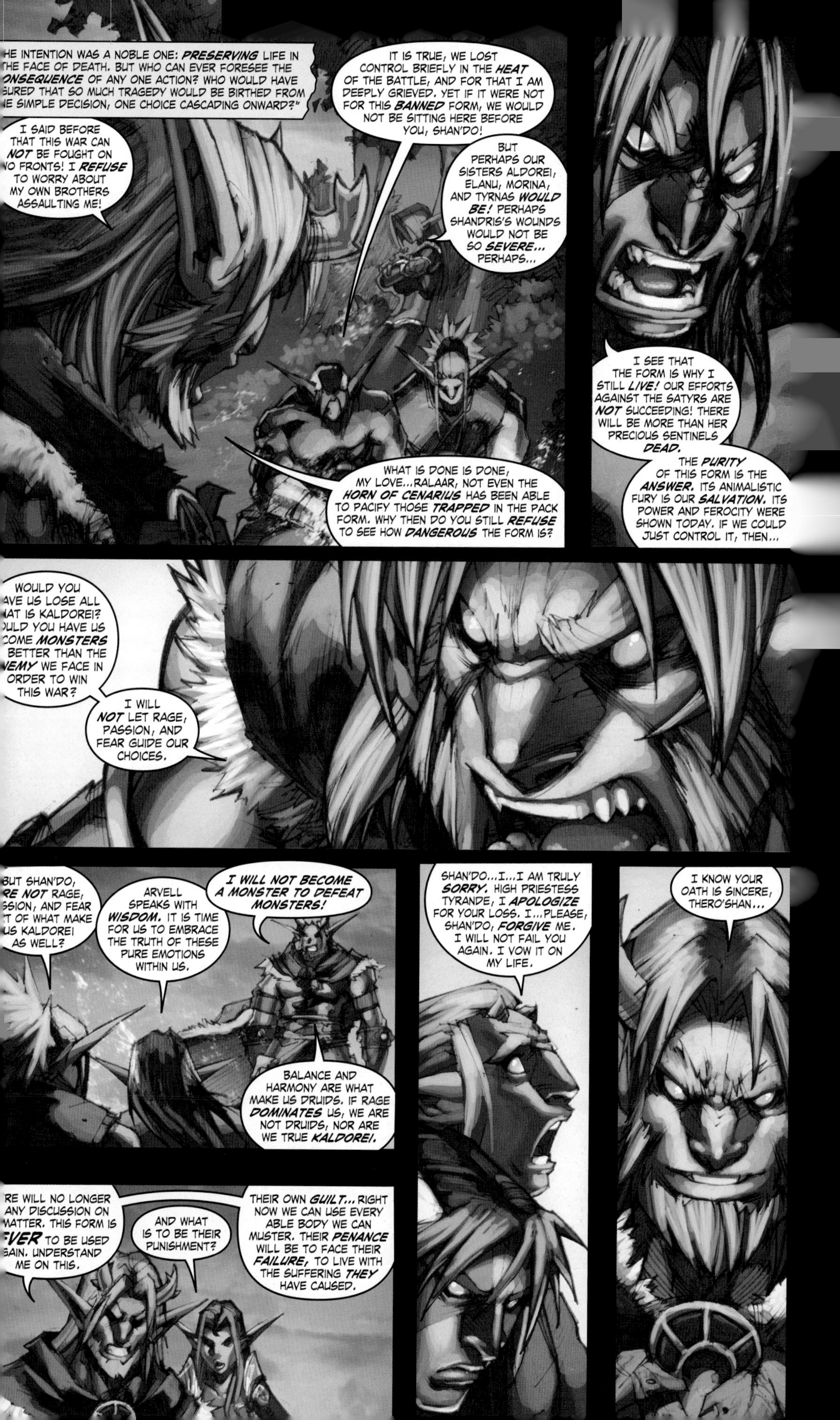
HE INTENTION WAS A NOBLE ONE: PRESERVING LIFE IN THE FACE OF DEATH. BUT WHO CAN EVER FORESEE THE ONSEQUENCE OF ANY ONE ACTION? WHO WOULD HAVE GURED THAT SO MUCH TRAGEDY WOULD BE BIRTHED FROM E SIMPLE DECISION, ONE CHOICE CASCADING ONWARD?"
I SAID BEFORE THAT THIS WAR CAN NOT BE FOUGHT ON O FRONTS! I REFUSE TO WORRY ABOUT MY OWN BROTHERS ASSAULTING ME!
IT IS TRUE, WE LOST CONTROL BRIEFLY IN THE HEAT OF THE BATTLE, AND FOR THAT I AM DEEPLY GRIEVED. YET IF IT WERE NOT FOR THIS BANNED FORM, WE WOULD NOT BE SITTING HERE BEFORE YOU, SHAN'DO!
BUT PERHAPS OUR SISTERS ALDOREI, ELANU, MORINA, AND TYRNAS WOULD BE! PERHAPS SHANDRIS'S WOUNDS WOULD NOT BE SO SEVERE... PERHAPS...
WHAT IS DONE IS DONE, MY LOVE...RALAAR, NOT EVEN THE HORN OF CENARIUS HAS BEEN ABLE TO PACIFY THOSE TRAPPED IN THE PACK FORM. WHY THEN DO YOU STILL REFUSE TO SEE HOW DANGEROUS THE FORM IS?
I SEE THAT THE FORM IS WHY I STILL LIVE! OUR EFFORTS AGAINST THE SATYRS ARE NOT SUCCEEDING! THERE WILL BE MORE THAN HER PRECIOUS SENTINELS DEAD.
THE PURITY OF THIS FORM IS THE ANSWER. ITS ANIMALISTIC FURY IS OUR SALVATION. ITS POWER AND FEROCITY WERE SHOWN TODAY. IF WE COULD JUST CONTROL IT, THEN...
WOULD YOU AVE US LOSE ALL AT IS KALDOREI? OULD YOU HAVE US COME MONSTERS BETTER THAN THE EMY WE FACE IN ORDER TO WIN THIS WAR?
I WILL NOT LET RAGE, PASSION, AND FEAR GUIDE OUR CHOICES.
BUT SHAN'DO, RE NOT RAGE, SSION, AND FEAR T OF WHAT MAKE US KALDOREI AS WELL?
ARVELL SPEAKS WITH WISDOM. IT IS TIME FOR US TO EMBRACE THE TRUTH OF THESE PURE EMOTIONS WITHIN US.
I WILL NOT BECOME A MONSTER TO DEFEAT MONSTERS!
BALANCE AND HARMONY ARE WHAT MAKE US DRUIDS. IF RAGE DOMINATES US, WE ARE NOT DRUIDS, NOR ARE WE TRUE KALDOREI.
SHAN'DO...I...I AM TRULY SORRY. HIGH PRIESTESS TYRANDE, I APOLOGIZE FOR YOUR LOSS. I...PLEASE, SHAN'DO, FORGIVE ME. I WILL NOT FAIL YOU AGAIN. I VOW IT ON MY LIFE.
I KNOW YOUR OATH IS SINCERE, THERO'SHAN...
RE WILL NO LONGER ANY DISCUSSION ON MATTER. THIS FORM IS EVER TO BE USED AIN. UNDERSTAND ME ON THIS.
AND WHAT IS TO BE THEIR PUNISHMENT?
THEIR OWN GUILT... RIGHT NOW WE CAN USE EVERY ABLE BODY WE CAN MUSTER. THEIR PENANCE WILL BE TO FACE THEIR FAILURE, TO LIVE WITH THE SUFFERING THEY HAVE CAUSED.

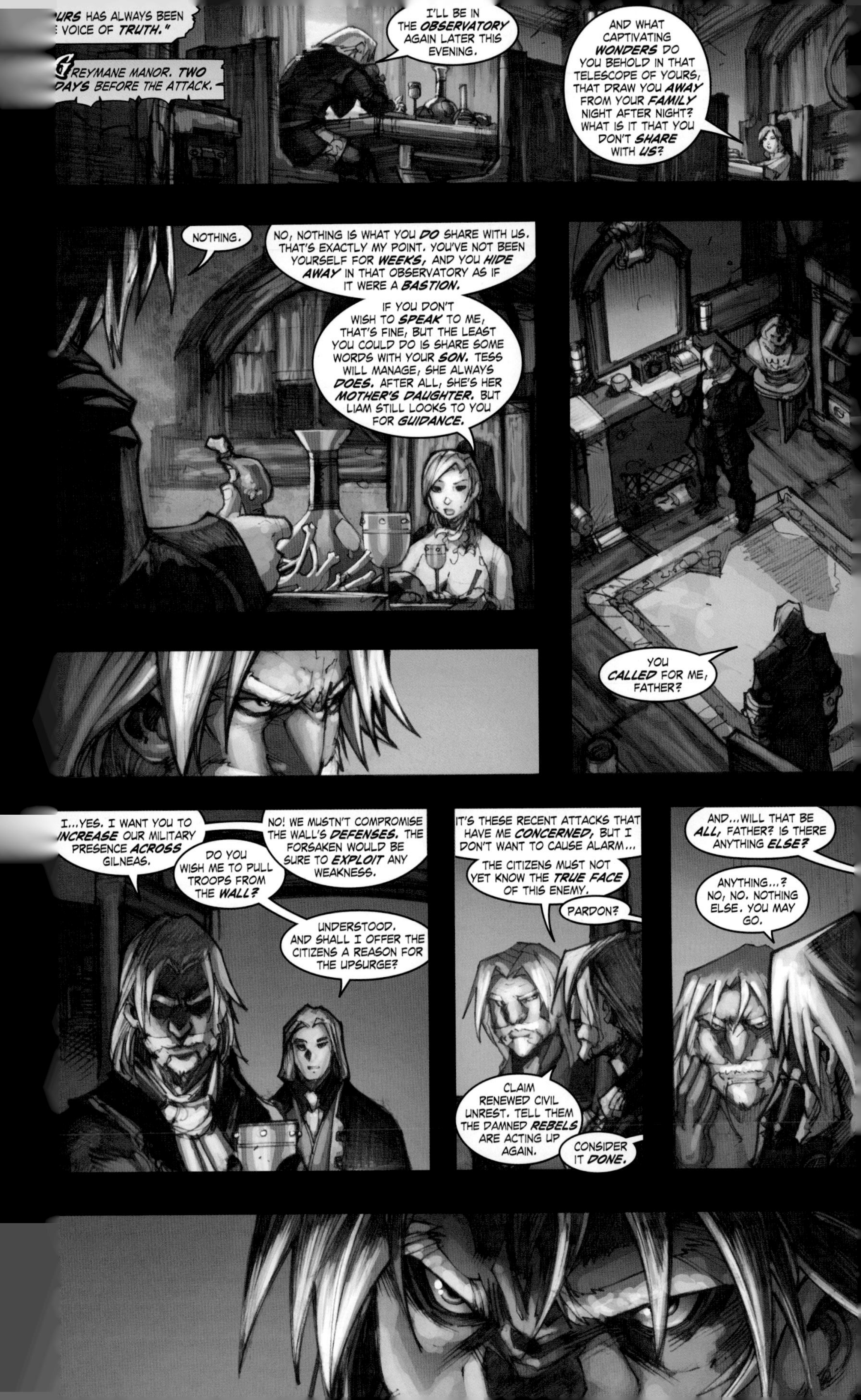
"URS HAS ALWAYS BEEN
E VOICE OF TRUTH."
GREYMANE MANOR. TWO DAYS BEFORE THE ATTACK.
I'LL BE IN THE OBSERVATORY AGAIN LATER THIS EVENING.
AND WHAT CAPTIVATING WONDERS DO YOU BEHOLD IN THAT TELESCOPE OF YOURS, THAT DRAW YOU AWAY FROM YOUR FAMILY NIGHT AFTER NIGHT? WHAT IS IT THAT YOU DON'T SHARE WITH US?
NOTHING.
NO, NOTHING IS WHAT YOU DO SHARE WITH US. THAT'S EXACTLY MY POINT. YOU'VE NOT BEEN YOURSELF FOR WEEKS, AND YOU HIDE AWAY IN THAT OBSERVATORY AS IF IT WERE A BASTION.
IF YOU DON'T WISH TO SPEAK TO ME, THAT'S FINE, BUT THE LEAST YOU COULD DO IS SHARE SOME WORDS WITH YOUR SON. TESS WILL MANAGE, SHE ALWAYS DOES. AFTER ALL, SHE'S HER MOTHER'S DAUGHTER. BUT LIAM STILL LOOKS TO YOU FOR GUIDANCE.
YOU CALLED FOR ME, FATHER?
I...YES. I WANT YOU TO INCREASE OUR MILITARY PRESENCE ACROSS GILNEAS.
DO YOU WISH ME TO PULL TROOPS FROM THE WALL?
NO! WE MUSTN'T COMPROMISE THE WALL'S DEFENSES. THE FORSAKEN WOULD BE SURE TO EXPLOIT ANY WEAKNESS.
UNDERSTOOD. AND SHALL I OFFER THE CITIZENS A REASON FOR THE UPSURGE?
IT'S THESE RECENT ATTACKS THAT HAVE ME CONCERNED, BUT I DON'T WANT TO CAUSE ALARM...
THE CITIZENS MUST NOT YET KNOW THE TRUE FACE OF THIS ENEMY.
PARDON?
CLAIM RENEWED CIVIL UNREST. TELL THEM THE DAMNED REBELS ARE ACTING UP AGAIN.
CONSIDER IT DONE.
AND...WILL THAT BE ALL, FATHER? IS THERE ANYTHING ELSE?
ANYTHING...? NO, NO. NOTHING ELSE. YOU MAY GO.

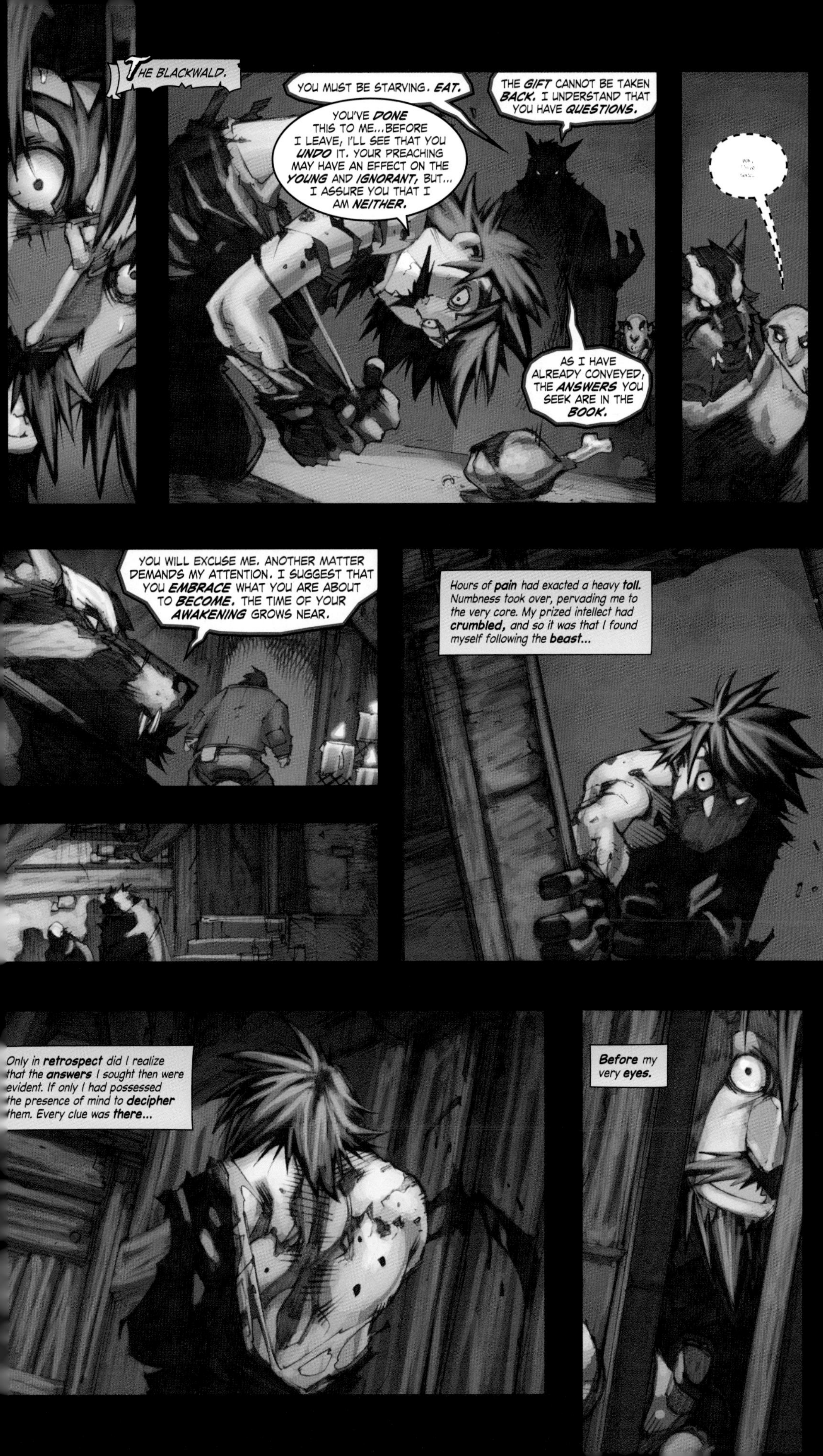
The Blackwald.
You must be starving. Eat.
You've done this to me...before I leave, I'll see that you undo it. Your preaching may have an effect on the young and ignorant, but... I assure you that I am neither.
The gift cannot be taken back. I understand that you have questions.
As I have already conveyed, the answers you seek are in the book.
You will excuse me. Another matter demands my attention. I suggest that you embrace what you are about to become. The time of your awakening grows near.
Hours of pain had exacted a heavy toll. Numbness took over, pervading me to the very core. My prized intellect had crumbled, and so it was that I found myself following the beast...
Only in retrospect did I realize that the answers I sought then were evident. If only I had possessed the presence of mind to decipher them. Every clue was there...
Before my very eyes.

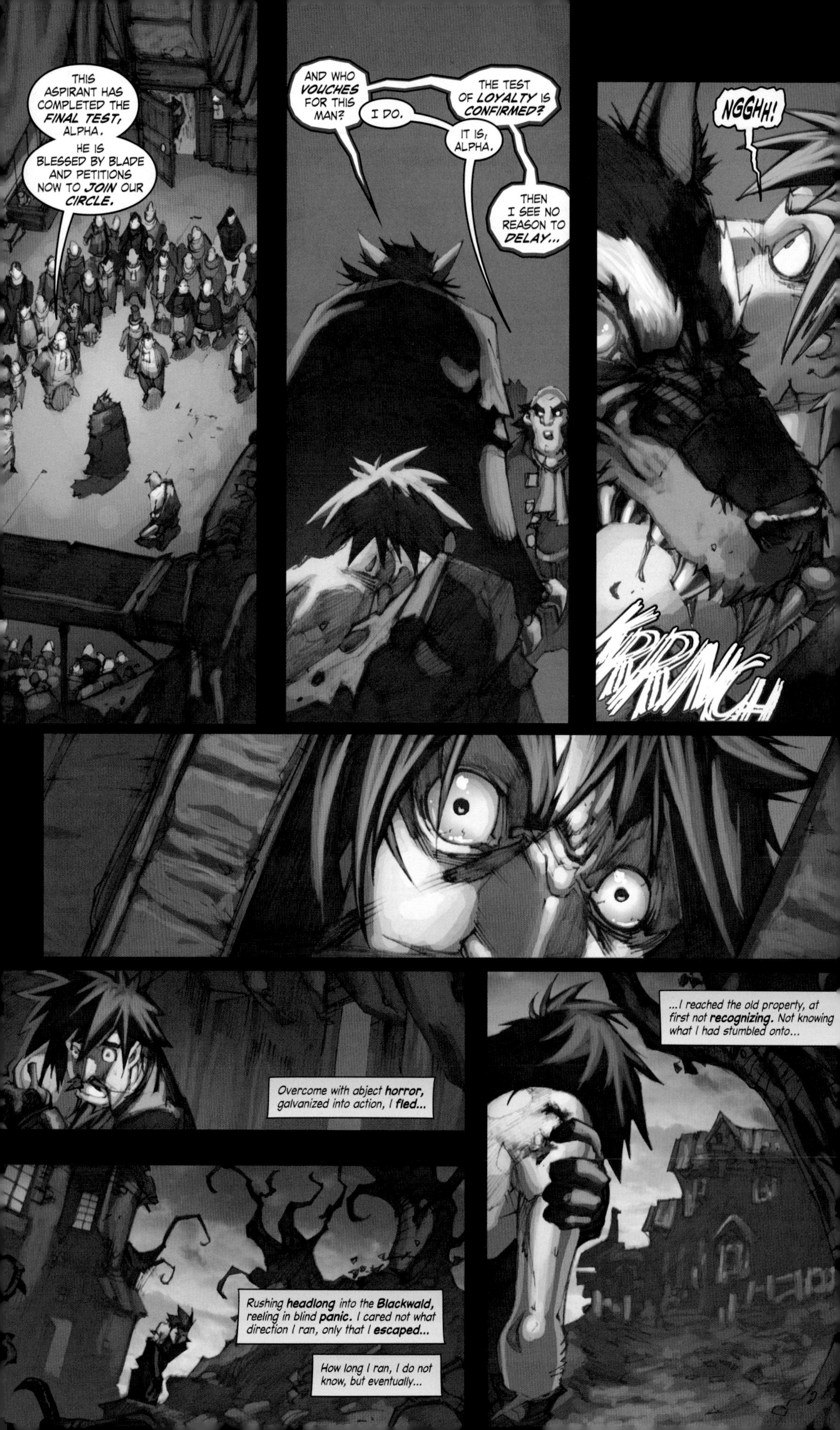

THIS ASPIRANT HAS COMPLETED THE FINAL TEST, ALPHA.
HE IS BLESSED BY BLADE AND PETITIONS NOW TO JOIN OUR CIRCLE.
AND WHO VOUCHES FOR THIS MAN?
I DO.
THE TEST OF LOYALTY IS CONFIRMED?
IT IS, ALPHA.
THEN I SEE NO REASON TO DELAY...
NGGHH!
KRRRUNCH
Overcome with abject horror, galvanized into action, I fled...
Rushing headlong into the Blackwald, reeling in blind panic. I cared not what direction I ran, only that I escaped...
How long I ran, I do not know, but eventually...
...I reached the old property, at first not recognizing. Not knowing what I had stumbled onto...

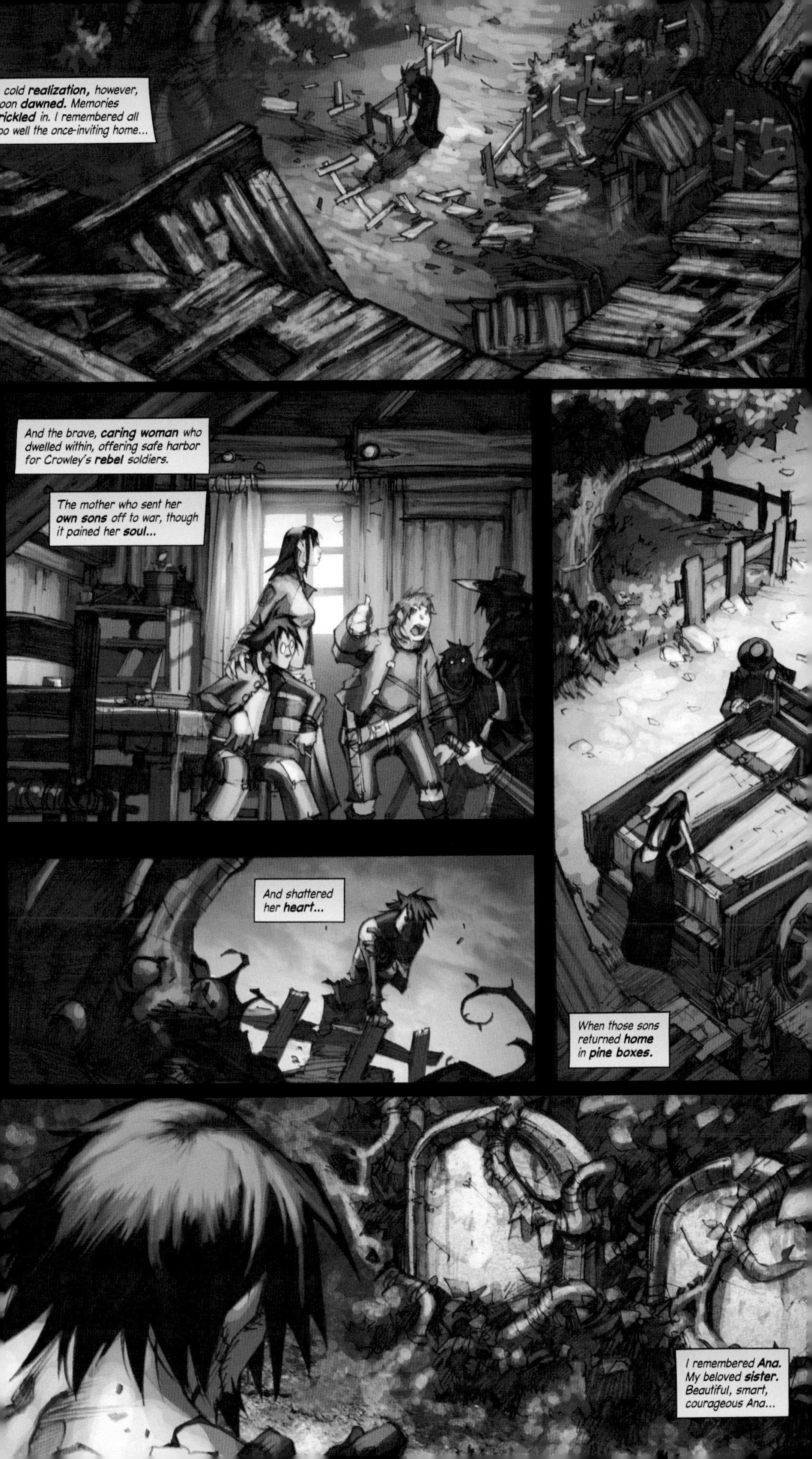

cold **realization,** however, oon **dawned.** Memories rickled in. I remembered all oo well the once-inviting home...
And the brave, **caring woman** who dwelled within, offering safe harbor for Crowley's **rebel** soldiers.
The mother who sent her **own sons** off to war, though it pained her **soul...**
When those sons returned **home** in **pine boxes.**
And shattered her **heart...**
I remembered **Ana.** My beloved **sister.** Beautiful, smart, courageous Ana...

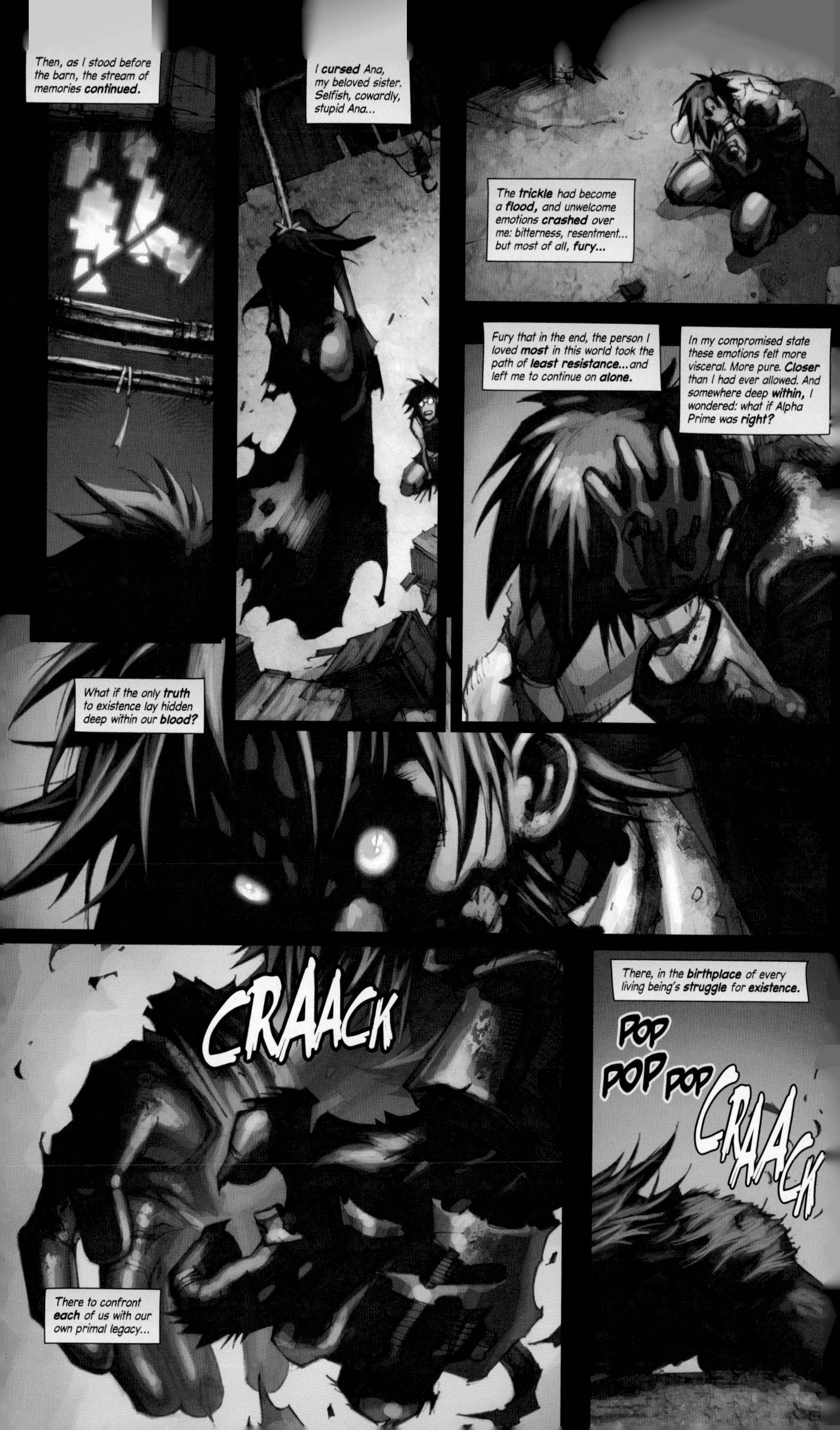

Then, as I stood before the barn, the stream of memories **continued.**
I **cursed** Ana, my beloved sister. Selfish, cowardly, stupid Ana...
The **trickle** had become a **flood,** and unwelcome emotions **crashed** over me: bitterness, resentment... but most of all, **fury...**
Fury that in the end, the person I loved **most** in this world took the path of **least resistance...** and left me to continue on **alone.**
In my compromised state these emotions felt more visceral. More pure. **Closer** than I had ever allowed. And somewhere deep **within,** I wondered: what if Alpha Prime was **right?**
What if the only **truth** to existence lay hidden deep within our **blood?**
CRAACK
There to confront **each** of us with our own primal legacy...
There, in the **birthplace** of every living being's **struggle** for **existence.**
POP
POP POP
CRAACK

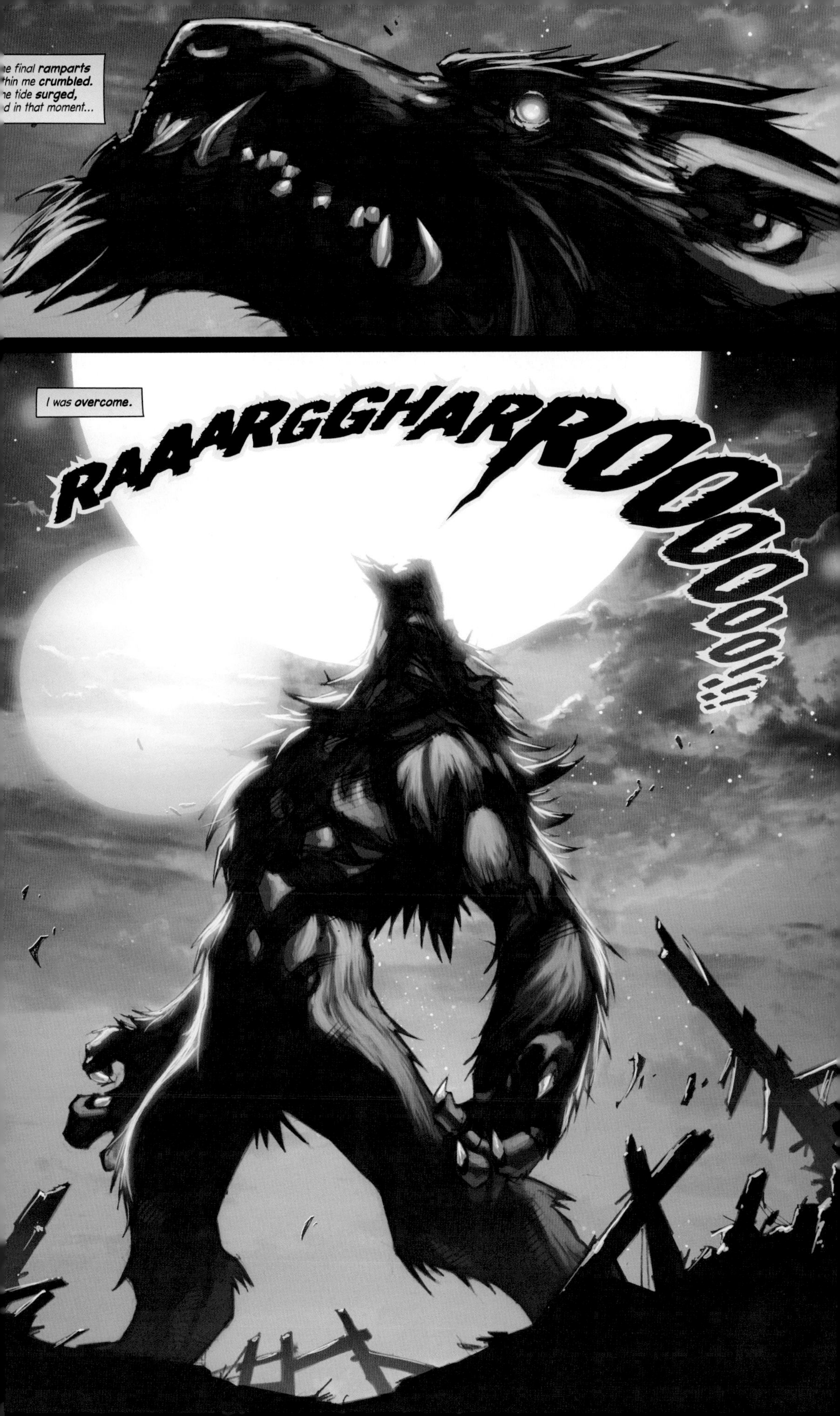
e final ramparts
thin me crumbled.
e tide surged,
d in that moment...
I was overcome.
RAAARGGHARROOOOOOO!!!

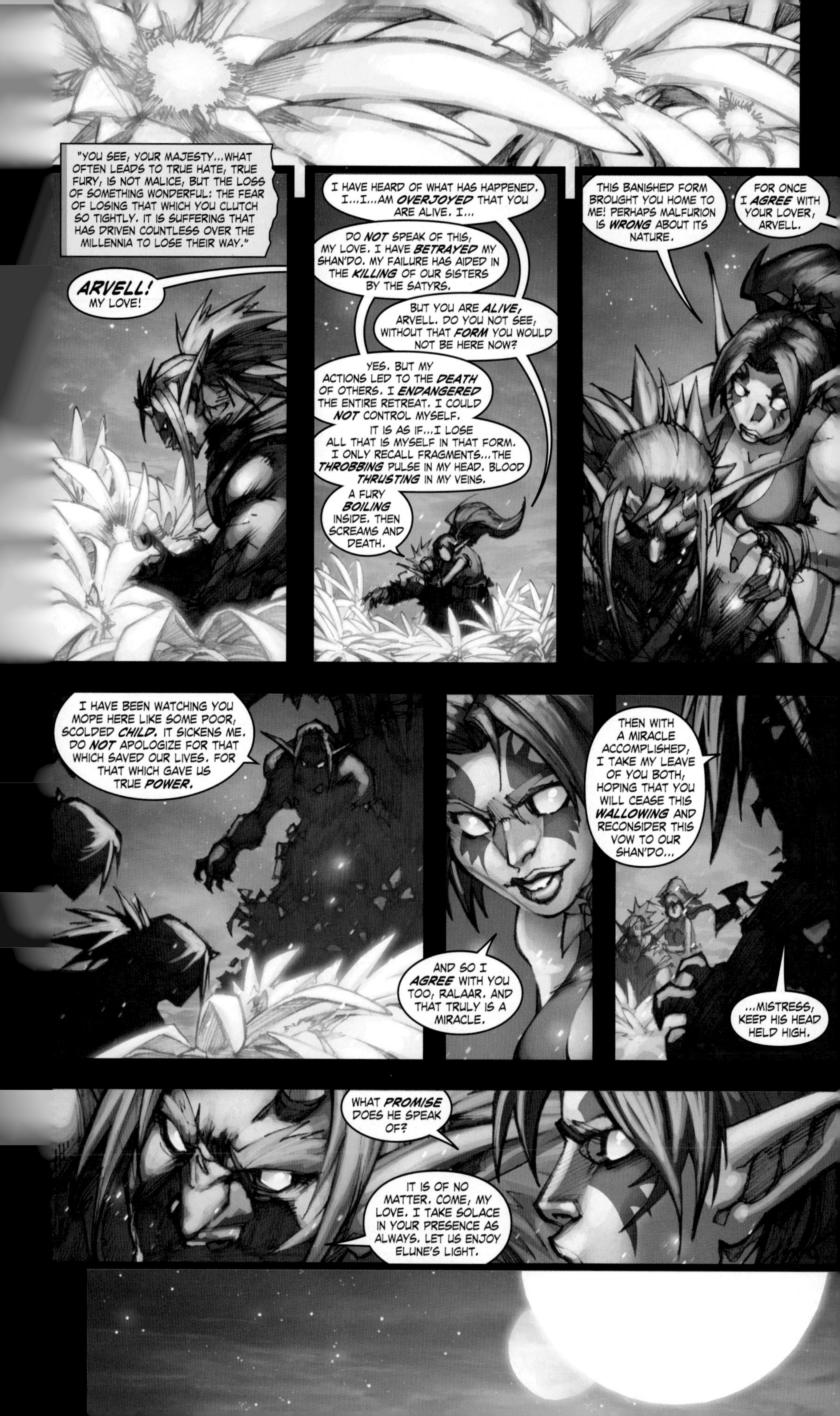
"YOU SEE, YOUR MAJESTY...WHAT OFTEN LEADS TO TRUE HATE, TRUE FURY, IS NOT MALICE, BUT THE LOSS OF SOMETHING WONDERFUL: THE FEAR OF LOSING THAT WHICH YOU CLUTCH SO TIGHTLY. IT IS SUFFERING THAT HAS DRIVEN COUNTLESS OVER THE MILLENNIA TO LOSE THEIR WAY."
ARVELL! MY LOVE!
I HAVE HEARD OF WHAT HAS HAPPENED. I...I...AM OVERJOYED THAT YOU ARE ALIVE. I...
DO NOT SPEAK OF THIS, MY LOVE. I HAVE BETRAYED MY SHAN'DO. MY FAILURE HAS AIDED IN THE KILLING OF OUR SISTERS BY THE SATYRS.
BUT YOU ARE ALIVE, ARVELL. DO YOU NOT SEE, WITHOUT THAT FORM YOU WOULD NOT BE HERE NOW?
YES. BUT MY ACTIONS LED TO THE DEATH OF OTHERS. I ENDANGERED THE ENTIRE RETREAT. I COULD NOT CONTROL MYSELF.
IT IS AS IF...I LOSE ALL THAT IS MYSELF IN THAT FORM. I ONLY RECALL FRAGMENTS...THE THROBBING PULSE IN MY HEAD. BLOOD THRUSTING IN MY VEINS.
A FURY BOILING INSIDE. THEN SCREAMS AND DEATH.
THIS BANISHED FORM BROUGHT YOU HOME TO ME! PERHAPS MALFURION IS WRONG ABOUT ITS NATURE.
FOR ONCE I AGREE WITH YOUR LOVER, ARVELL.
I HAVE BEEN WATCHING YOU MOPE HERE LIKE SOME POOR, SCOLDED CHILD. IT SICKENS ME. DO NOT APOLOGIZE FOR THAT WHICH SAVED OUR LIVES. FOR THAT WHICH GAVE US TRUE POWER.
AND SO I AGREE WITH YOU TOO, RALAAR. AND THAT TRULY IS A MIRACLE.
THEN WITH A MIRACLE ACCOMPLISHED, I TAKE MY LEAVE OF YOU BOTH, HOPING THAT YOU WILL CEASE THIS WALLOWING AND RECONSIDER THIS VOW TO OUR SHAN'DO...
...MISTRESS, KEEP HIS HEAD HELD HIGH.
WHAT PROMISE DOES HE SPEAK OF?
IT IS OF NO MATTER. COME, MY LOVE. I TAKE SOLACE IN YOUR PRESENCE AS ALWAYS. LET US ENJOY ELUNE'S LIGHT.

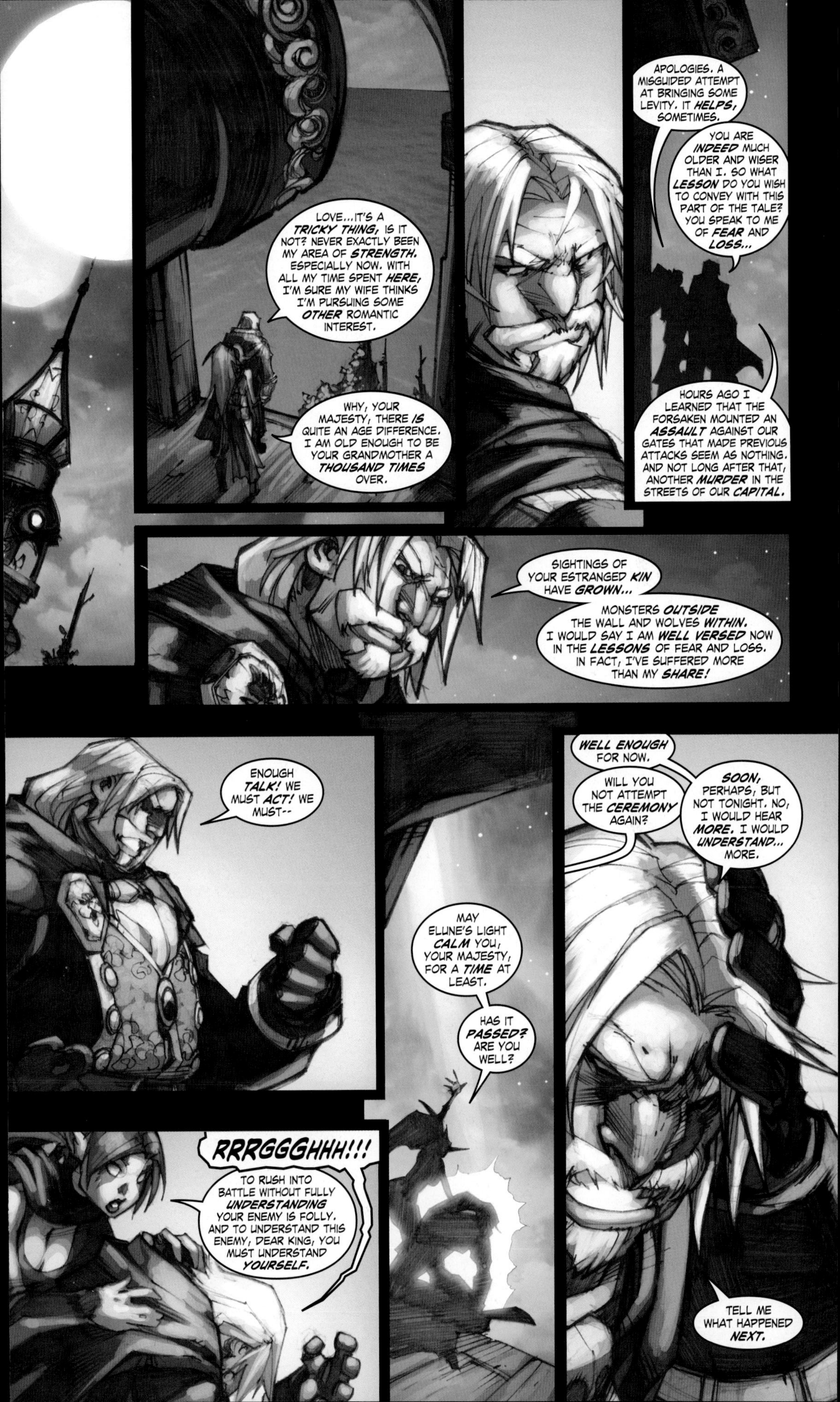
LOVE...IT'S A TRICKY THING, IS IT NOT? NEVER EXACTLY BEEN MY AREA OF STRENGTH. ESPECIALLY NOW. WITH ALL MY TIME SPENT HERE, I'M SURE MY WIFE THINKS I'M PURSUING SOME OTHER ROMANTIC INTEREST.
WHY, YOUR MAJESTY, THERE IS QUITE AN AGE DIFFERENCE. I AM OLD ENOUGH TO BE YOUR GRANDMOTHER A THOUSAND TIMES OVER.
APOLOGIES. A MISGUIDED ATTEMPT AT BRINGING SOME LEVITY. IT HELPS, SOMETIMES.
YOU ARE INDEED MUCH OLDER AND WISER THAN I. SO WHAT LESSON DO YOU WISH TO CONVEY WITH THIS PART OF THE TALE? YOU SPEAK TO ME OF FEAR AND LOSS...
HOURS AGO I LEARNED THAT THE FORSAKEN MOUNTED AN ASSAULT AGAINST OUR GATES THAT MADE PREVIOUS ATTACKS SEEM AS NOTHING. AND NOT LONG AFTER THAT, ANOTHER MURDER IN THE STREETS OF OUR CAPITAL.
SIGHTINGS OF YOUR ESTRANGED KIN HAVE GROWN...
MONSTERS OUTSIDE THE WALL AND WOLVES WITHIN. I WOULD SAY I AM WELL VERSED NOW IN THE LESSONS OF FEAR AND LOSS. IN FACT, I'VE SUFFERED MORE THAN MY SHARE!
ENOUGH TALK! WE MUST ACT! WE MUST--
RRRGGGHHH!!!
TO RUSH INTO BATTLE WITHOUT FULLY UNDERSTANDING YOUR ENEMY IS FOLLY. AND TO UNDERSTAND THIS ENEMY, DEAR KING, YOU MUST UNDERSTAND YOURSELF.
MAY ELUNE'S LIGHT CALM YOU, YOUR MAJESTY, FOR A TIME AT LEAST.
HAS IT PASSED? ARE YOU WELL?
WELL ENOUGH FOR NOW.
WILL YOU NOT ATTEMPT THE CEREMONY AGAIN?
SOON, PERHAPS, BUT NOT TONIGHT. NO, I WOULD HEAR MORE. I WOULD UNDERSTAND... MORE.
TELL ME WHAT HAPPENED NEXT.

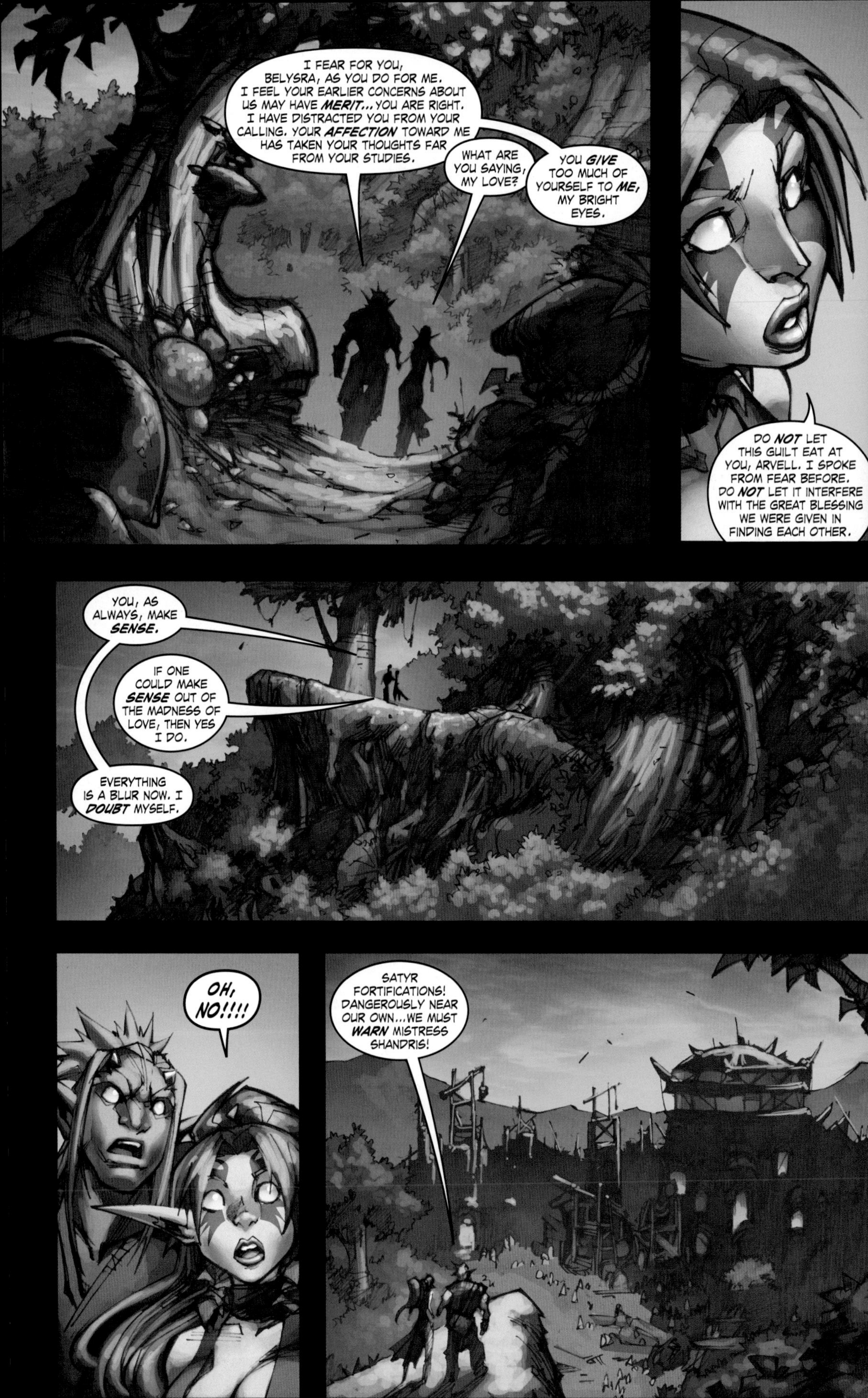
I FEAR FOR YOU, BELYSRA, AS YOU DO FOR ME. I FEEL YOUR EARLIER CONCERNS ABOUT US MAY HAVE MERIT... YOU ARE RIGHT. I HAVE DISTRACTED YOU FROM YOUR CALLING. YOUR AFFECTION TOWARD ME HAS TAKEN YOUR THOUGHTS FAR FROM YOUR STUDIES.
WHAT ARE YOU SAYING, MY LOVE?
YOU GIVE TOO MUCH OF YOURSELF TO ME, MY BRIGHT EYES.
DO NOT LET THIS GUILT EAT AT YOU, ARVELL. I SPOKE FROM FEAR BEFORE. DO NOT LET IT INTERFERE WITH THE GREAT BLESSING WE WERE GIVEN IN FINDING EACH OTHER.
YOU, AS ALWAYS, MAKE SENSE.
IF ONE COULD MAKE SENSE OUT OF THE MADNESS OF LOVE, THEN YES I DO.
EVERYTHING IS A BLUR NOW. I DOUBT MYSELF.
OH, NO!!!!
SATYR FORTIFICATIONS! DANGEROUSLY NEAR OUR OWN... WE MUST WARN MISTRESS SHANDRIS!

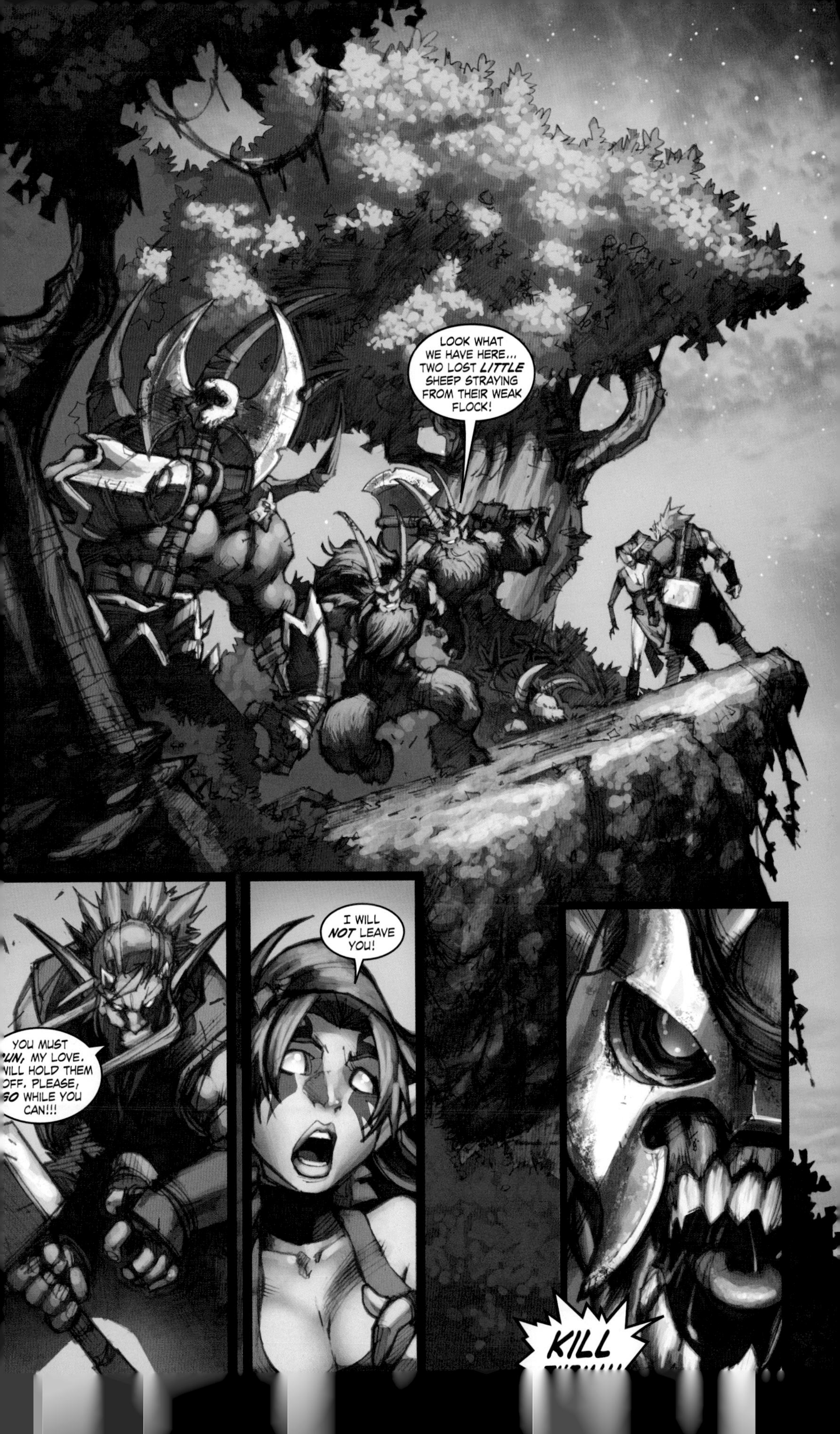
LOOK WHAT WE HAVE HERE... TWO LOST LITTLE SHEEP STRAYING FROM THEIR WEAK FLOCK!
YOU MUST UN, MY LOVE. WILL HOLD THEM OFF. PLEASE, GO WHILE YOU CAN!!!
I WILL NOT LEAVE YOU!
KILL

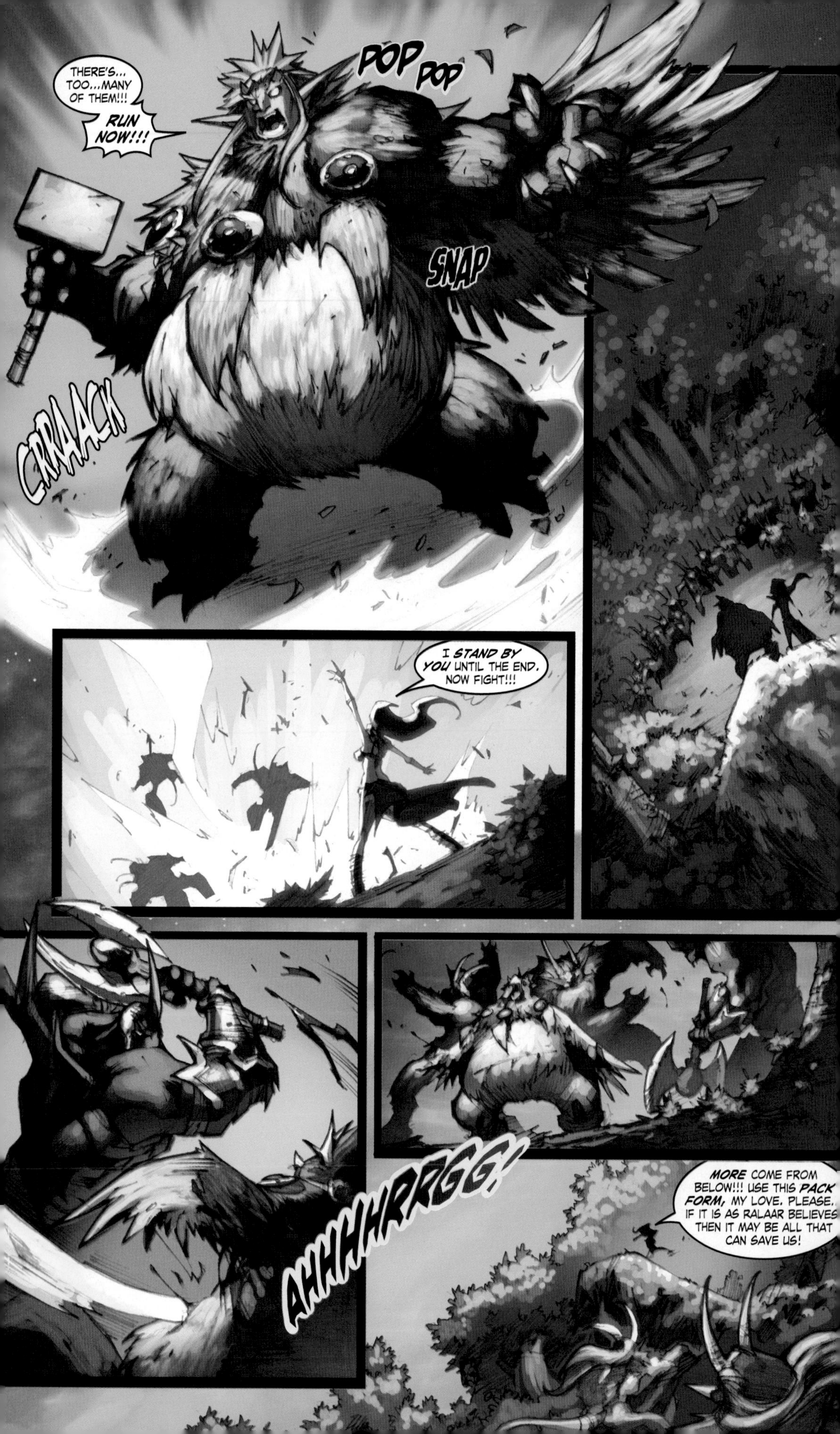
THERE'S... TOO...MANY OF THEM!!!
RUN NOW!!!
POP POP
SNAP
CRRAACK
I STAND BY YOU UNTIL THE END. NOW FIGHT!!!
AHHHHRRGG!
MORE COME FROM BELOW!!! USE THIS PACK FORM, MY LOVE. PLEASE. IF IT IS AS RALAAR BELIEVES THEN IT MAY BE ALL THAT CAN SAVE US!

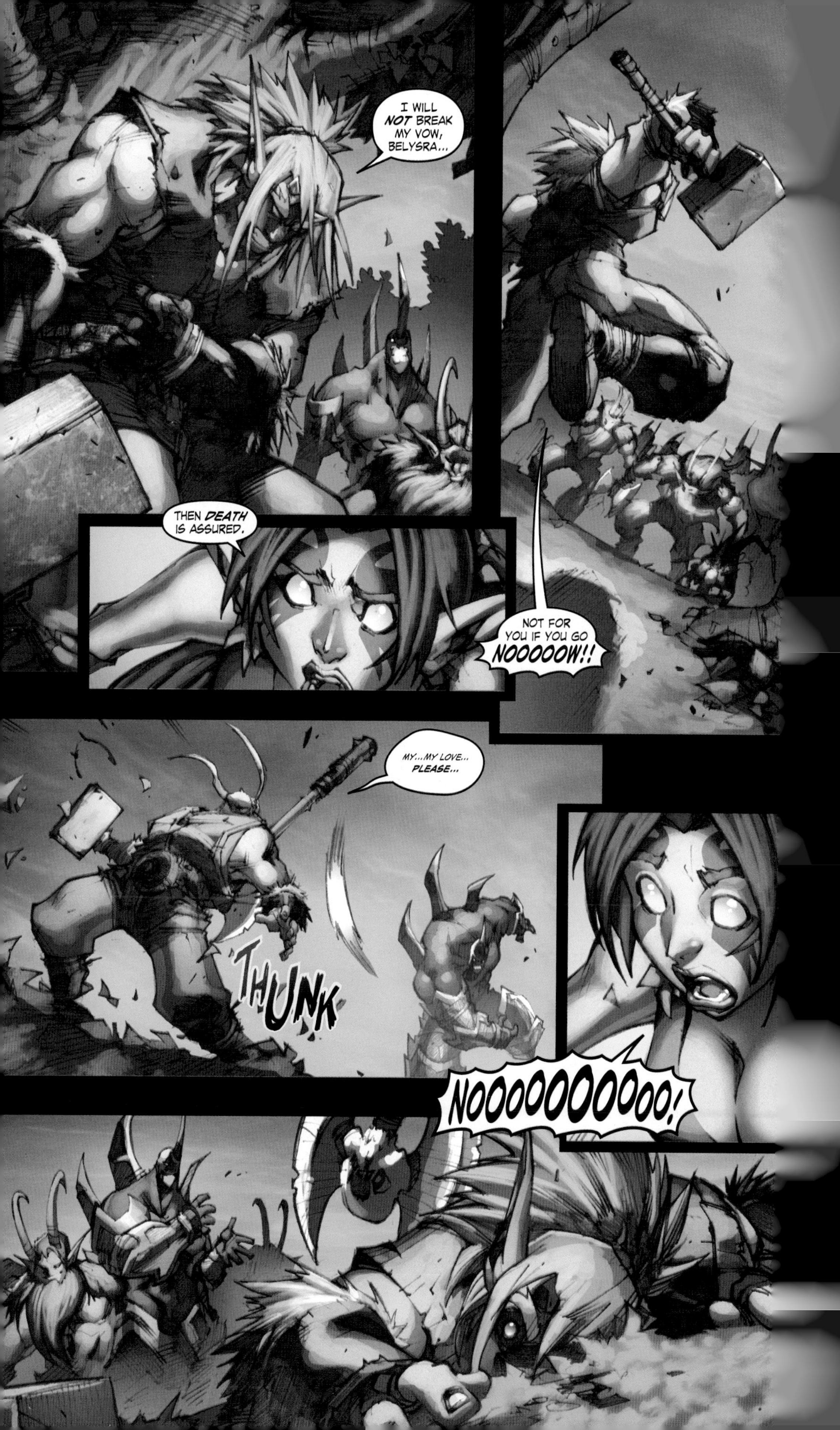
I WILL NOT BREAK MY VOW, BELYSRA...
THEN DEATH IS ASSURED.
NOT FOR YOU IF YOU GO NOOOOOW!!
MY...MY LOVE... PLEASE...
THUNK
NOOOOOOOOOO!

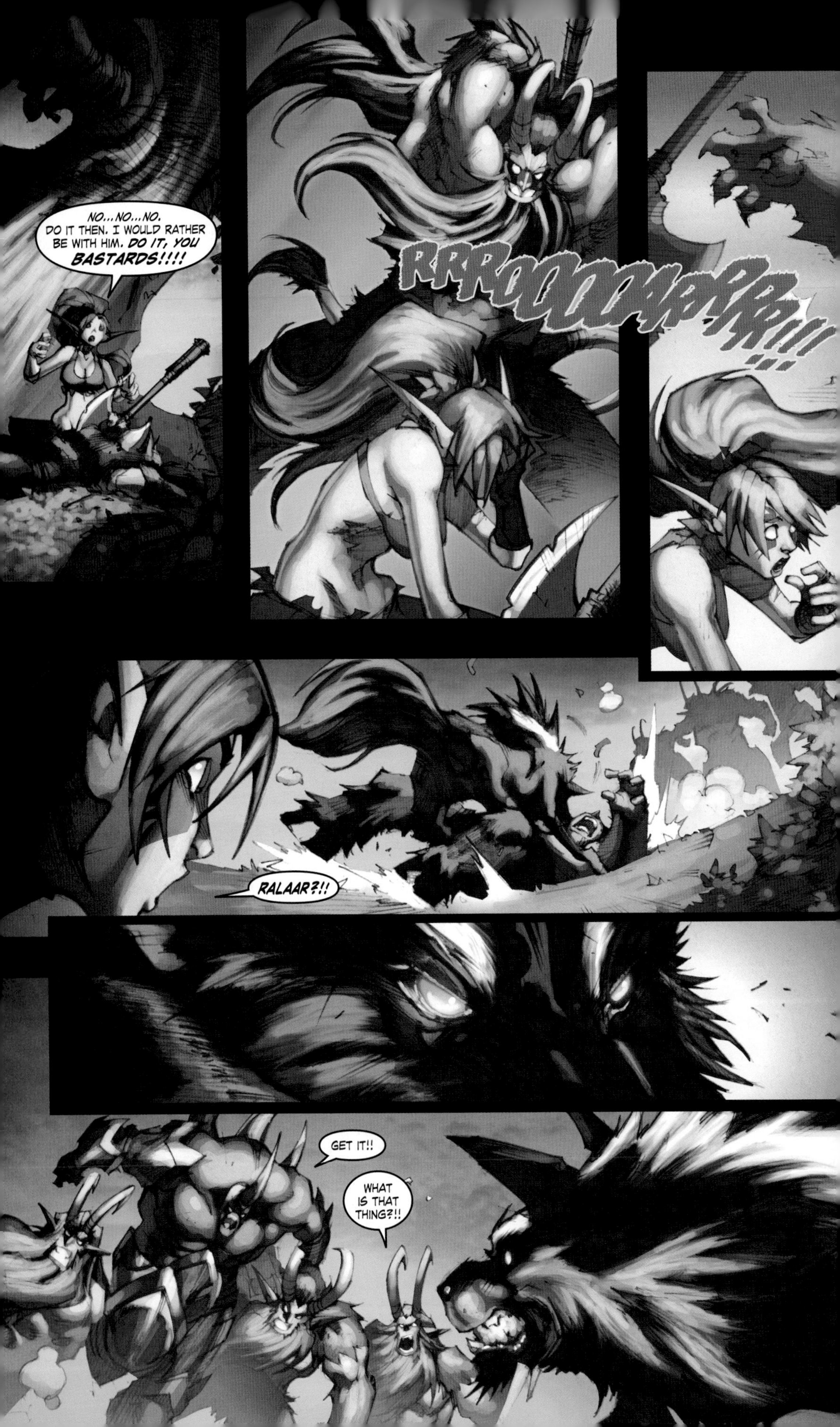
NO...NO...NO. DO IT THEN. I WOULD RATHER BE WITH HIM. DO IT, YOU BASTARDS!!!!
RRROOOOAARRR!!!
RALAAR?!!
GET IT!!
WHAT IS THAT THING?!!

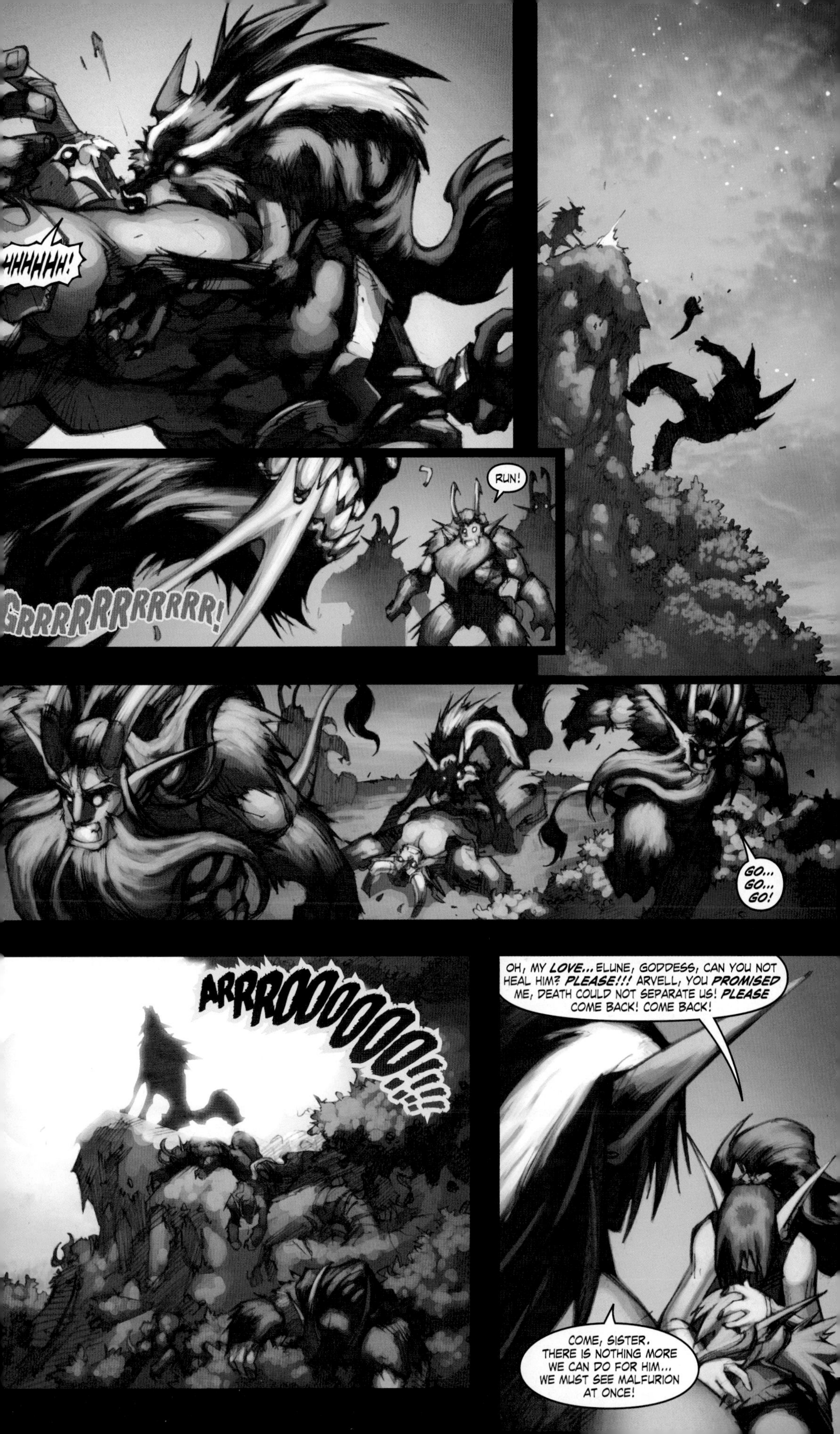
HHHHHH!
RUN!
GRRRRRRRRRR!
GO... GO... GO!
ARRROOOOOOO!!!!
OH, MY LOVE... ELUNE, GODDESS, CAN YOU NOT HEAL HIM? PLEASE!!! ARVELL, YOU PROMISED ME, DEATH COULD NOT SEPARATE US! PLEASE COME BACK! COME BACK!
COME, SISTER. THERE IS NOTHING MORE WE CAN DO FOR HIM... WE MUST SEE MALFURION AT ONCE!

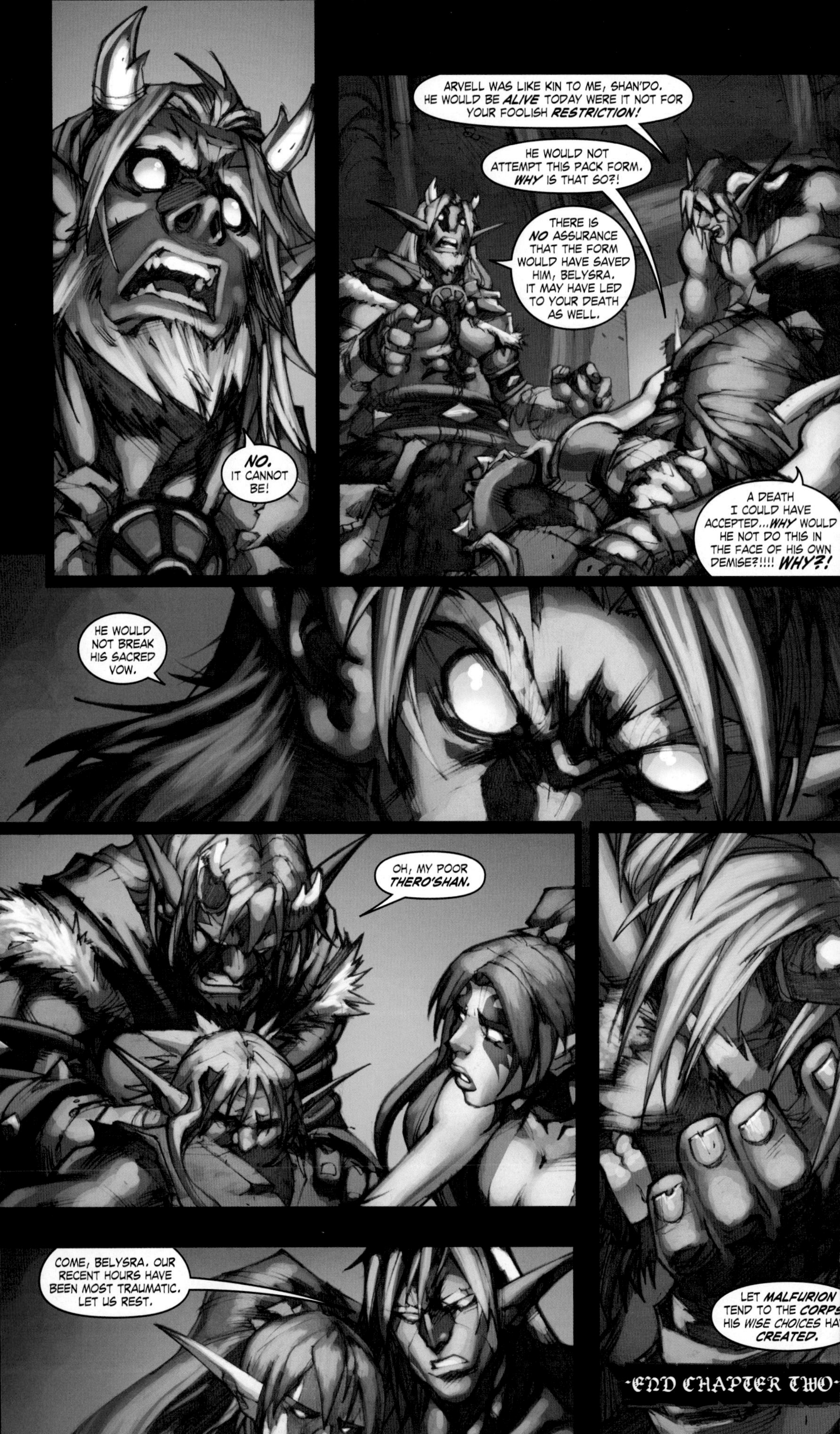
NO. IT CANNOT BE!
ARVELL WAS LIKE KIN TO ME, SHAN'DO. HE WOULD BE ALIVE TODAY WERE IT NOT FOR YOUR FOOLISH RESTRICTION!
HE WOULD NOT ATTEMPT THIS PACK FORM. WHY IS THAT SO?!
THERE IS NO ASSURANCE THAT THE FORM WOULD HAVE SAVED HIM, BELYSRA. IT MAY HAVE LED TO YOUR DEATH AS WELL.
A DEATH I COULD HAVE ACCEPTED...WHY WOULD HE NOT DO THIS IN THE FACE OF HIS OWN DEMISE?!!!! WHY?!
HE WOULD NOT BREAK HIS SACRED VOW.
OH, MY POOR THERO'SHAN.
COME, BELYSRA. OUR RECENT HOURS HAVE BEEN MOST TRAUMATIC. LET US REST.
LET MALFURION TEND TO THE CORPS
HIS WISE CHOICES HA
CREATED.
-END CHAPTER TWO-

Polidor© 2010

CHAPTER 3 Cover by John Polidora

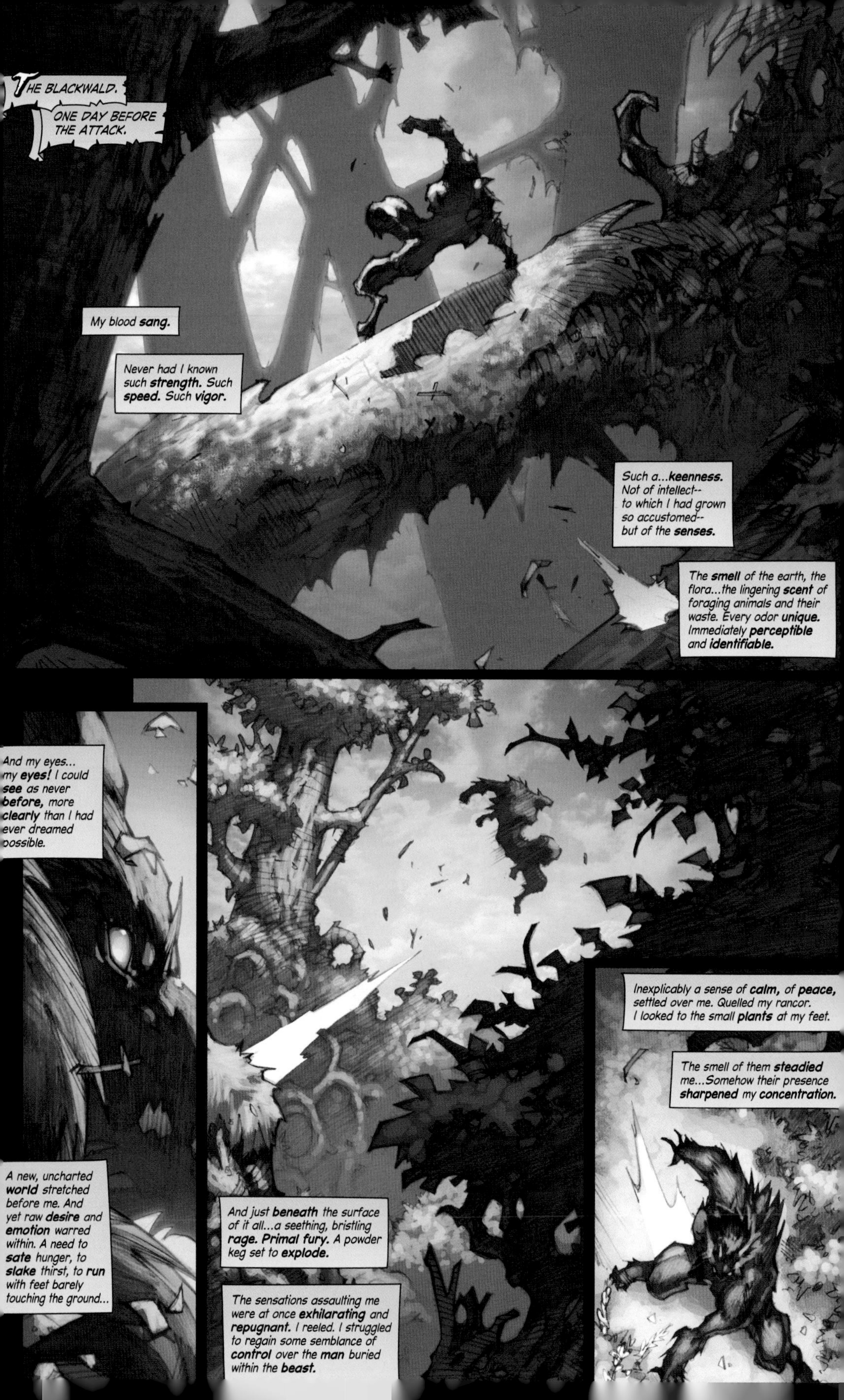
THE BLACKWALD.
ONE DAY BEFORE THE ATTACK.
My blood sang.
Never had I known such strength. Such speed. Such vigor.
Such a...keenness. Not of intellect-- to which I had grown so accustomed-- but of the senses.
The smell of the earth, the flora...the lingering scent of foraging animals and their waste. Every odor unique. Immediately perceptible and identifiable.
And my eyes... my eyes! I could see as never before, more clearly than I had ever dreamed possible.
A new, uncharted world stretched before me. And yet raw desire and emotion warred within. A need to sate hunger, to slake thirst, to run with feet barely touching the ground...
And just beneath the surface of it all...a seething, bristling rage. Primal fury. A powder keg set to explode.
The sensations assaulting me were at once exhilarating and repugnant. I reeled. I struggled to regain some semblance of control over the man buried within the beast.
Inexplicably a sense of calm, of peace, settled over me. Quelled my rancor. I looked to the small plants at my feet.
The smell of them steadied me...Somehow their presence sharpened my concentration.

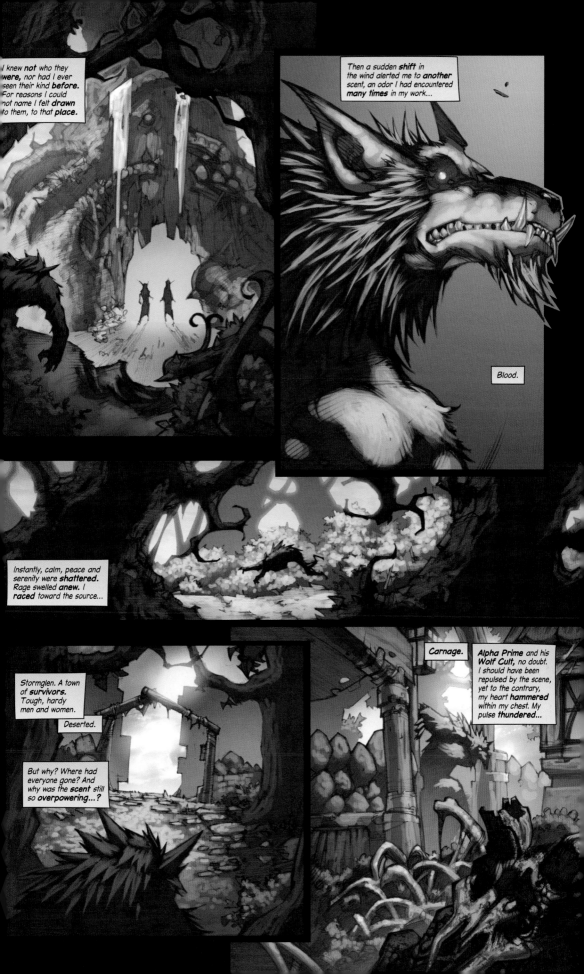

I knew **not** who they **were**, nor had I ever **seen** their kind **before**. For reasons I could **not** name I felt **drawn** to them, to that **place**.

Then a sudden **shift** in the wind alerted me to **another** scent, an odor I had encountered **many times** in my work...

Blood.

Instantly, calm, peace and serenity were **shattered**. Rage swelled **anew**. I **raced** toward the source...

Stormglen. A town of **survivors**. Tough, hardy men and women.

Deserted.

But why? Where had everyone gone? And why was the **scent** still so **overpowering...?**

Carnage.

Alpha Prime and his **Wolf Cult**, no doubt. I should have been repulsed by the scene, yet to the contrary, my heart **hammered** within my chest. My pulse **thundered...**

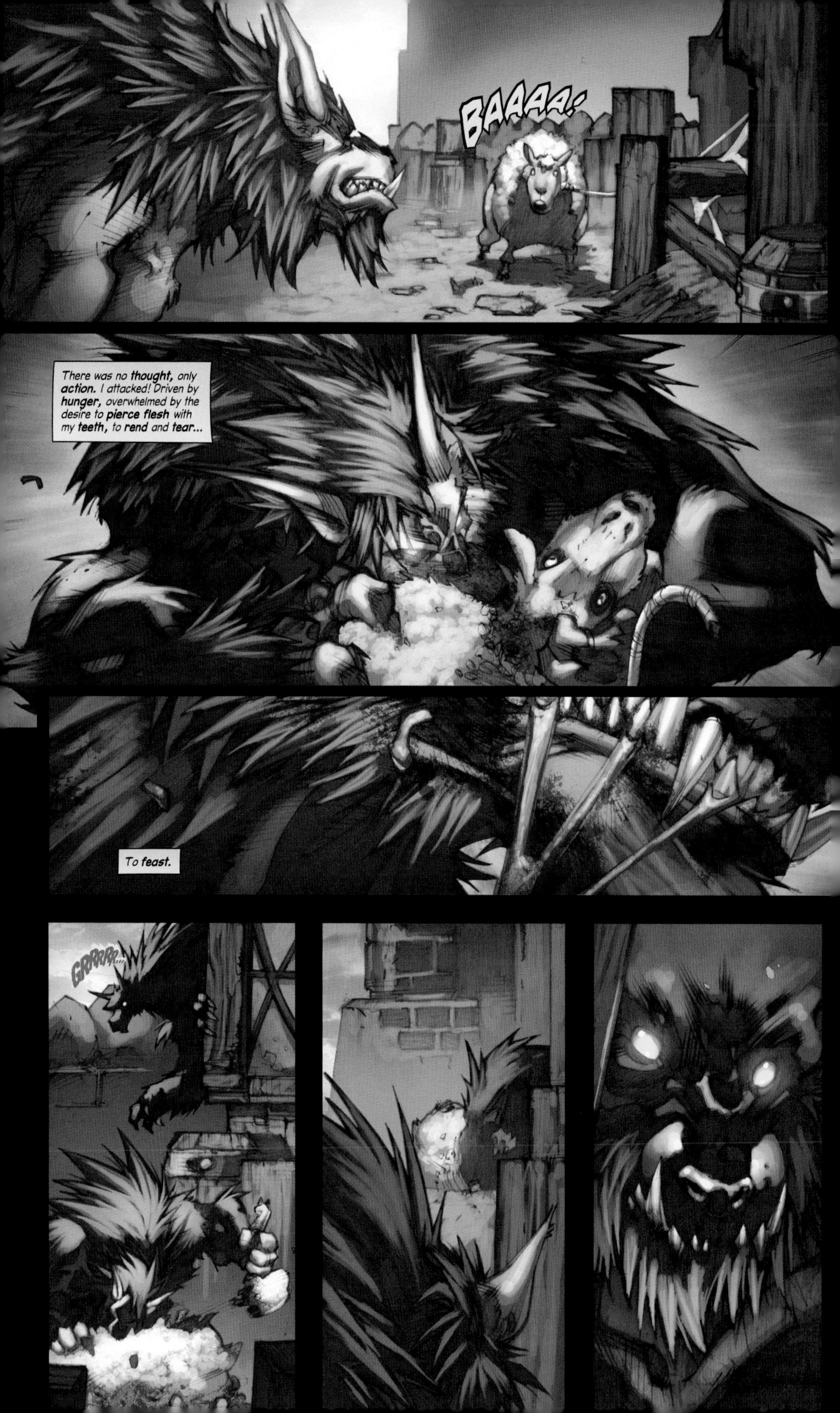

BAAAA!
There was no **thought,** only **action.** I attacked! Driven by **hunger,** overwhelmed by the desire to **pierce flesh** with my **teeth,** to **rend** and **tear...**
To **feast.**
GRRRRR...

GRR-RRRM...

WHUMP

RARGH!!

GRARR!!!

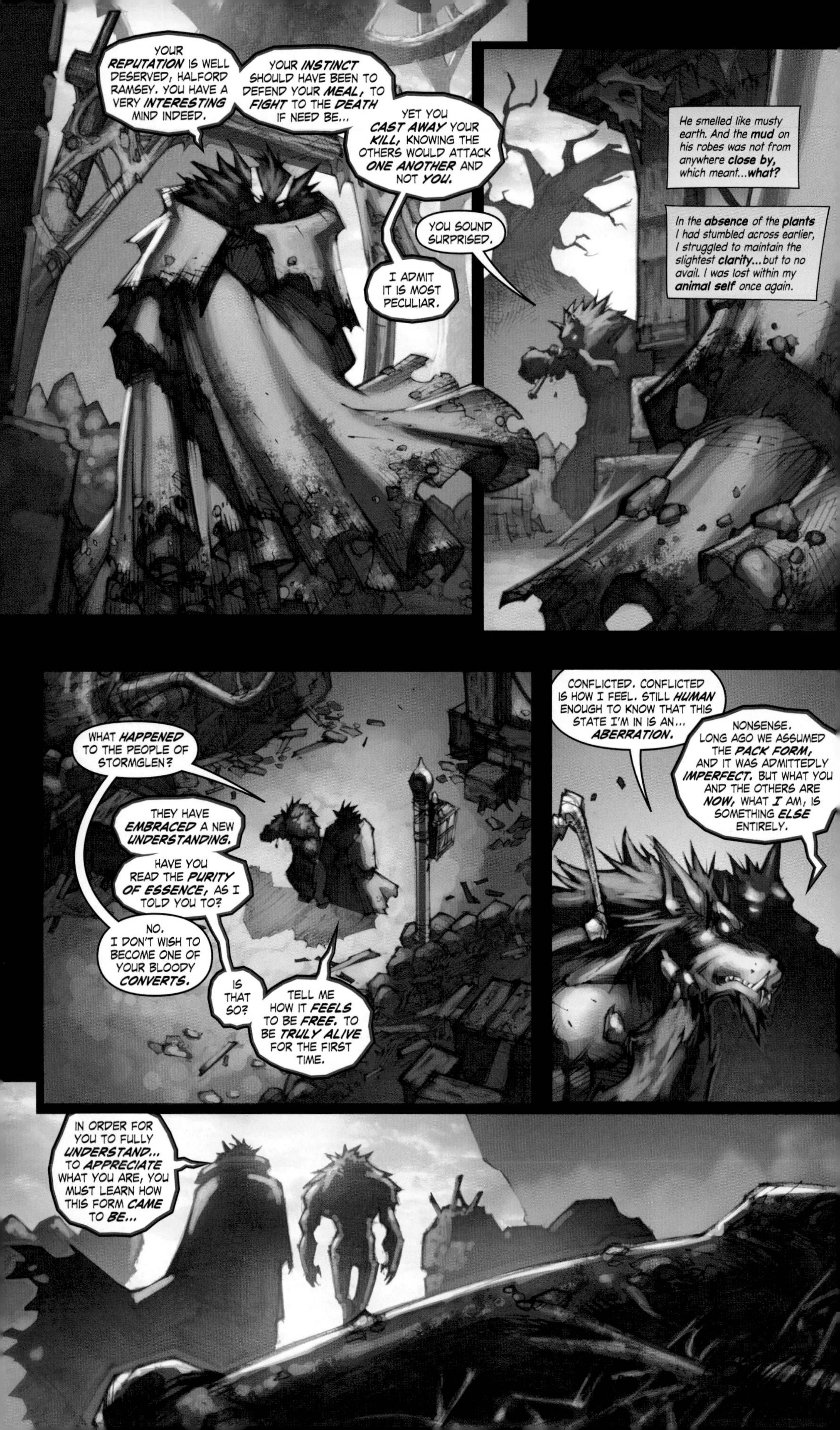
YOUR REPUTATION IS WELL DESERVED, HALFORD RAMSEY. YOU HAVE A VERY INTERESTING MIND INDEED.
YOUR INSTINCT SHOULD HAVE BEEN TO DEFEND YOUR MEAL, TO FIGHT TO THE DEATH IF NEED BE...
YET YOU CAST AWAY YOUR KILL, KNOWING THE OTHERS WOULD ATTACK ONE ANOTHER AND NOT YOU.
YOU SOUND SURPRISED.
I ADMIT IT IS MOST PECULIAR.
He smelled like musty earth. And the mud on his robes was not from anywhere close by, which meant...what?
In the absence of the plants I had stumbled across earlier, I struggled to maintain the slightest clarity...but to no avail. I was lost within my animal self once again.
WHAT HAPPENED TO THE PEOPLE OF STORMGLEN?
THEY HAVE EMBRACED A NEW UNDERSTANDING.
HAVE YOU READ THE PURITY OF ESSENCE, AS I TOLD YOU TO?
NO. I DON'T WISH TO BECOME ONE OF YOUR BLOODY CONVERTS.
IS THAT SO?
TELL ME HOW IT FEELS TO BE FREE. TO BE TRULY ALIVE FOR THE FIRST TIME.
CONFLICTED. CONFLICTED IS HOW I FEEL. STILL HUMAN ENOUGH TO KNOW THAT THIS STATE I'M IN IS AN... ABERRATION.
NONSENSE. LONG AGO WE ASSUMED THE PACK FORM, AND IT WAS ADMITTEDLY IMPERFECT. BUT WHAT YOU AND THE OTHERS ARE NOW, WHAT I AM, IS SOMETHING ELSE ENTIRELY.
IN ORDER FOR YOU TO FULLY UNDERSTAND... TO APPRECIATE WHAT YOU ARE, YOU MUST LEARN HOW THIS FORM CAME TO BE...

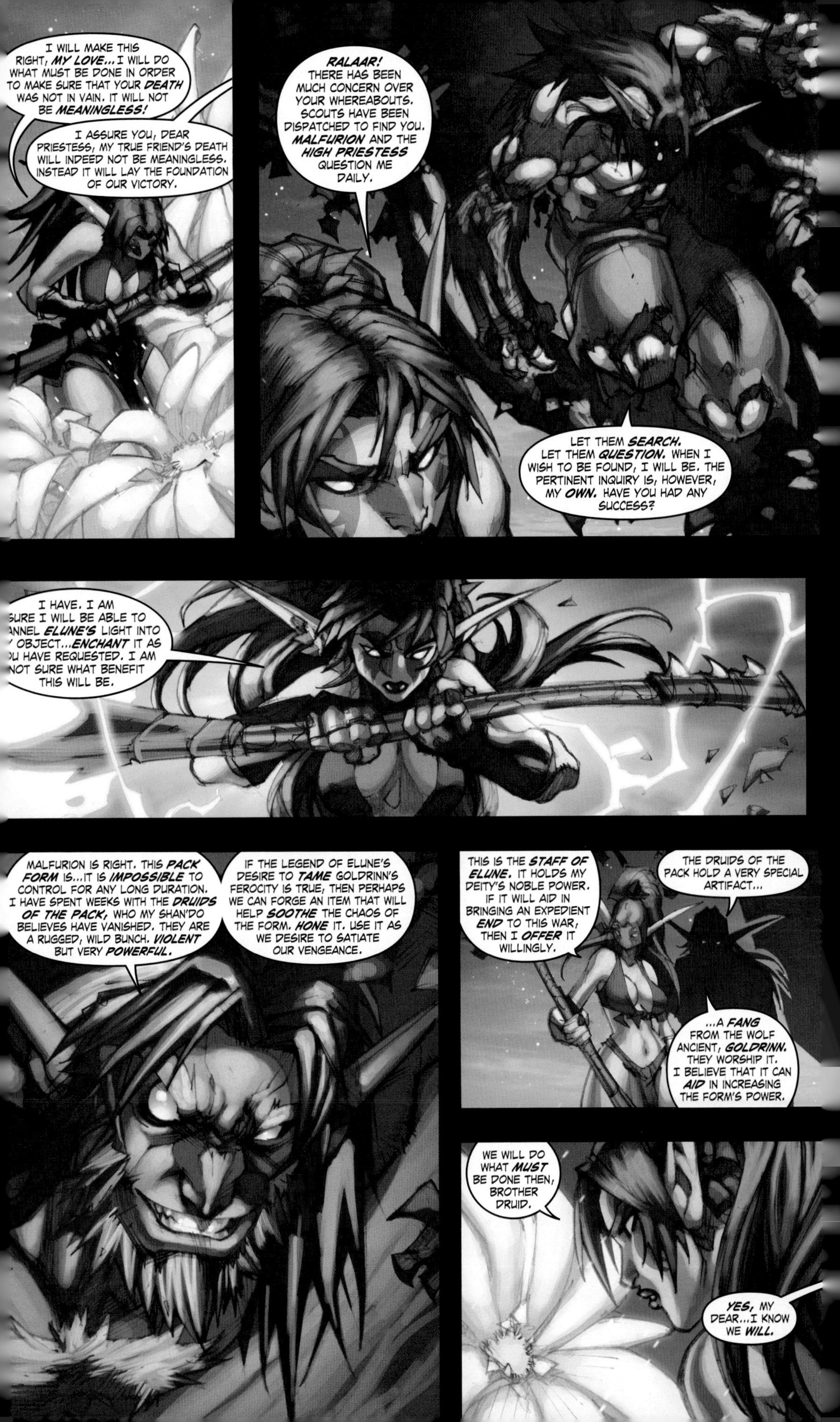
I WILL MAKE THIS RIGHT, MY LOVE... I WILL DO WHAT MUST BE DONE IN ORDER TO MAKE SURE THAT YOUR DEATH WAS NOT IN VAIN. IT WILL NOT BE MEANINGLESS!
I ASSURE YOU, DEAR PRIESTESS, MY TRUE FRIEND'S DEATH WILL INDEED NOT BE MEANINGLESS. INSTEAD IT WILL LAY THE FOUNDATION OF OUR VICTORY.
RALAAR! THERE HAS BEEN MUCH CONCERN OVER YOUR WHEREABOUTS. SCOUTS HAVE BEEN DISPATCHED TO FIND YOU. MALFURION AND THE HIGH PRIESTESS QUESTION ME DAILY.
LET THEM SEARCH. LET THEM QUESTION. WHEN I WISH TO BE FOUND, I WILL BE. THE PERTINENT INQUIRY IS, HOWEVER, MY OWN. HAVE YOU HAD ANY SUCCESS?
I HAVE. I AM SURE I WILL BE ABLE TO ANNEL ELUNE'S LIGHT INTO OBJECT...ENCHANT IT AS OU HAVE REQUESTED. I AM NOT SURE WHAT BENEFIT THIS WILL BE.
MALFURION IS RIGHT. THIS PACK FORM IS...IT IS IMPOSSIBLE TO CONTROL FOR ANY LONG DURATION. I HAVE SPENT WEEKS WITH THE DRUIDS OF THE PACK, WHO MY SHAN'DO BELIEVES HAVE VANISHED. THEY ARE A RUGGED, WILD BUNCH. VIOLENT BUT VERY POWERFUL.
IF THE LEGEND OF ELUNE'S DESIRE TO TAME GOLDRINN'S FEROCITY IS TRUE, THEN PERHAPS WE CAN FORGE AN ITEM THAT WILL HELP SOOTHE THE CHAOS OF THE FORM. HONE IT. USE IT AS WE DESIRE TO SATIATE OUR VENGEANCE.
THIS IS THE STAFF OF ELUNE. IT HOLDS MY DEITY'S NOBLE POWER. IF IT WILL AID IN BRINGING AN EXPEDIENT END TO THIS WAR, THEN I OFFER IT WILLINGLY.
THE DRUIDS OF THE PACK HOLD A VERY SPECIAL ARTIFACT...
...A FANG FROM THE WOLF ANCIENT, GOLDRINN. THEY WORSHIP IT. I BELIEVE THAT IT CAN AID IN INCREASING THE FORM'S POWER.
WE WILL DO WHAT MUST BE DONE THEN, BROTHER DRUID.
YES, MY DEAR...I KNOW WE WILL.

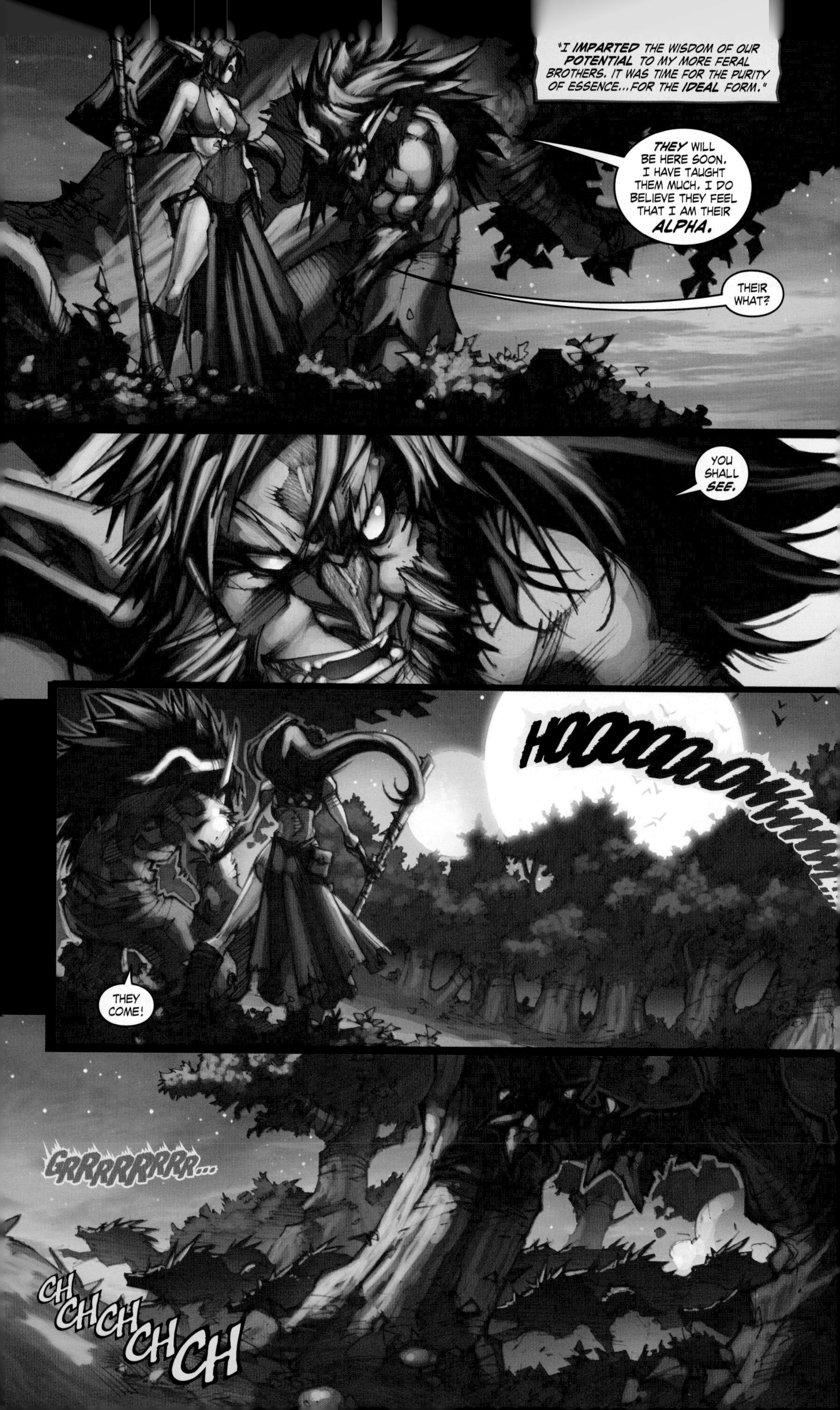
"I IMPARTED THE WISDOM OF OUR POTENTIAL TO MY MORE FERAL BROTHERS. IT WAS TIME FOR THE PURITY OF ESSENCE...FOR THE IDEAL FORM."
THEY WILL BE HERE SOON. I HAVE TAUGHT THEM MUCH. I DO BELIEVE THEY FEEL THAT I AM THEIR ALPHA.
THEIR WHAT?
YOU SHALL SEE.
HOOOOOOOOOWWWWWW...
THEY COME!
GRRRRRRRR...
CH CH CH CH CH CH

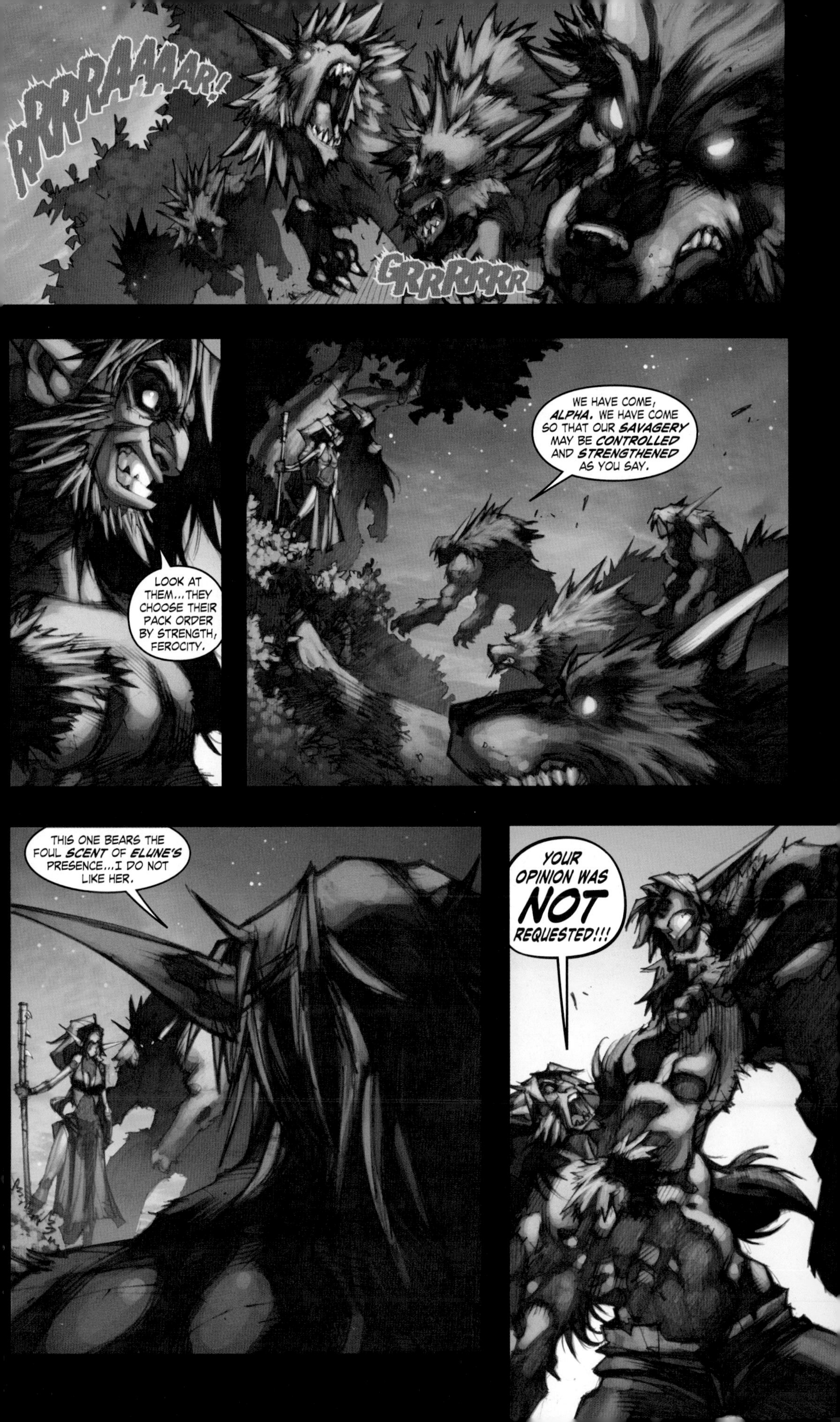
RRRRAAAAR!
GRRRRRRR
LOOK AT THEM...THEY CHOOSE THEIR PACK ORDER BY STRENGTH, FEROCITY.
WE HAVE COME, ALPHA. WE HAVE COME SO THAT OUR SAVAGERY MAY BE CONTROLLED AND STRENGTHENED AS YOU SAY.
THIS ONE BEARS THE FOUL SCENT OF ELUNE'S PRESENCE...I DO NOT LIKE HER.
YOUR OPINION WAS NOT REQUESTED!!!

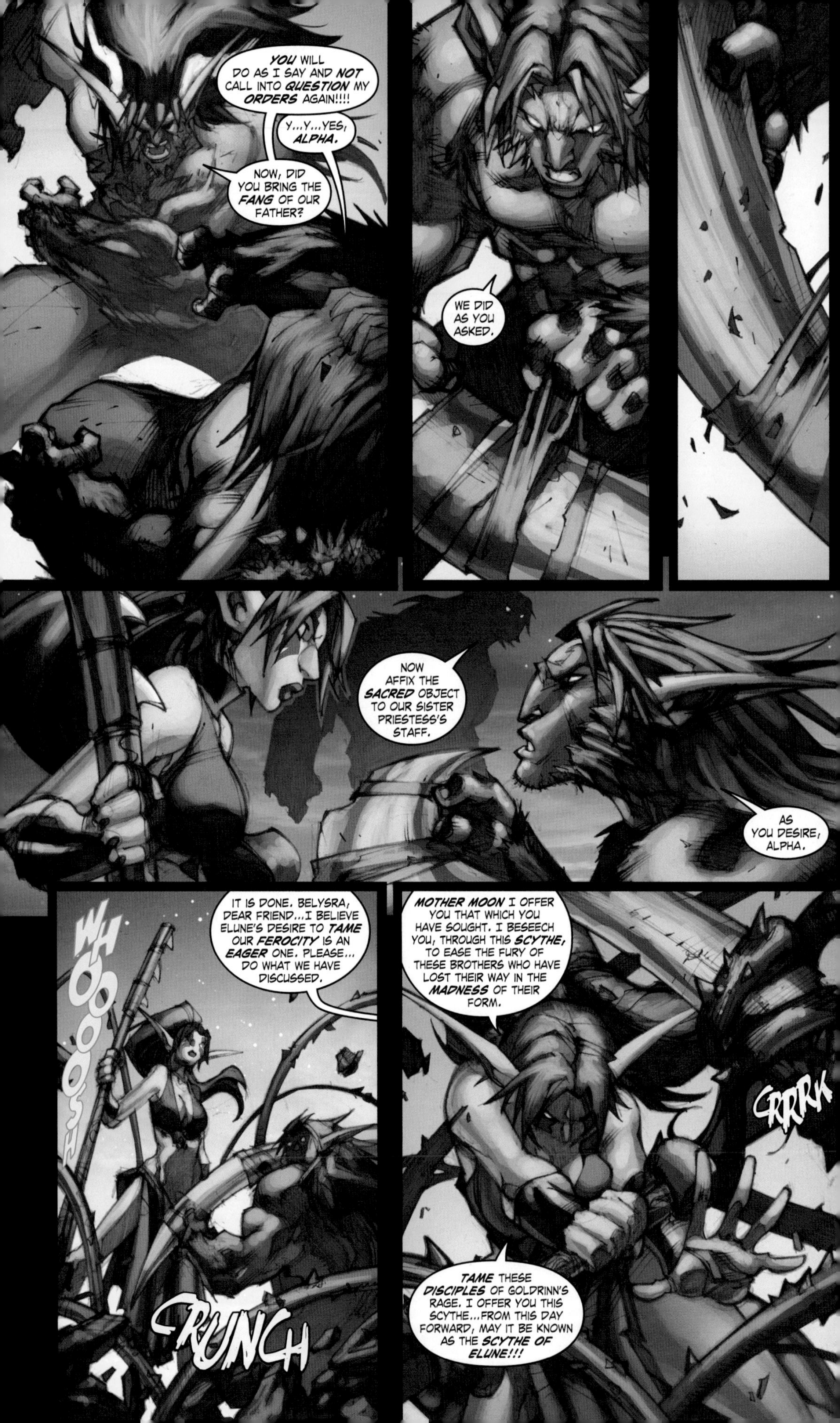

YOU WILL DO AS I SAY AND NOT CALL INTO QUESTION MY ORDERS AGAIN!!!!
Y...Y...YES, ALPHA.
NOW, DID YOU BRING THE FANG OF OUR FATHER?
WE DID AS YOU ASKED.
NOW AFFIX THE SACRED OBJECT TO OUR SISTER PRIESTESS'S STAFF.
AS YOU DESIRE, ALPHA.
IT IS DONE. BELYSRA, DEAR FRIEND...I BELIEVE ELUNE'S DESIRE TO TAME OUR FEROCITY IS AN EAGER ONE. PLEASE... DO WHAT WE HAVE DISCUSSED.
WHOOOOSH
CRUNCH
MOTHER MOON I OFFER YOU THAT WHICH YOU HAVE SOUGHT. I BESEECH YOU, THROUGH THIS SCYTHE, TO EASE THE FURY OF THESE BROTHERS WHO HAVE LOST THEIR WAY IN THE MADNESS OF THEIR FORM.
CRRRK
TAME THESE DISCIPLES OF GOLDRINN'S RAGE. I OFFER YOU THIS SCYTHE...FROM THIS DAY FORWARD, MAY IT BE KNOWN AS THE SCYTHE OF ELUNE!!!

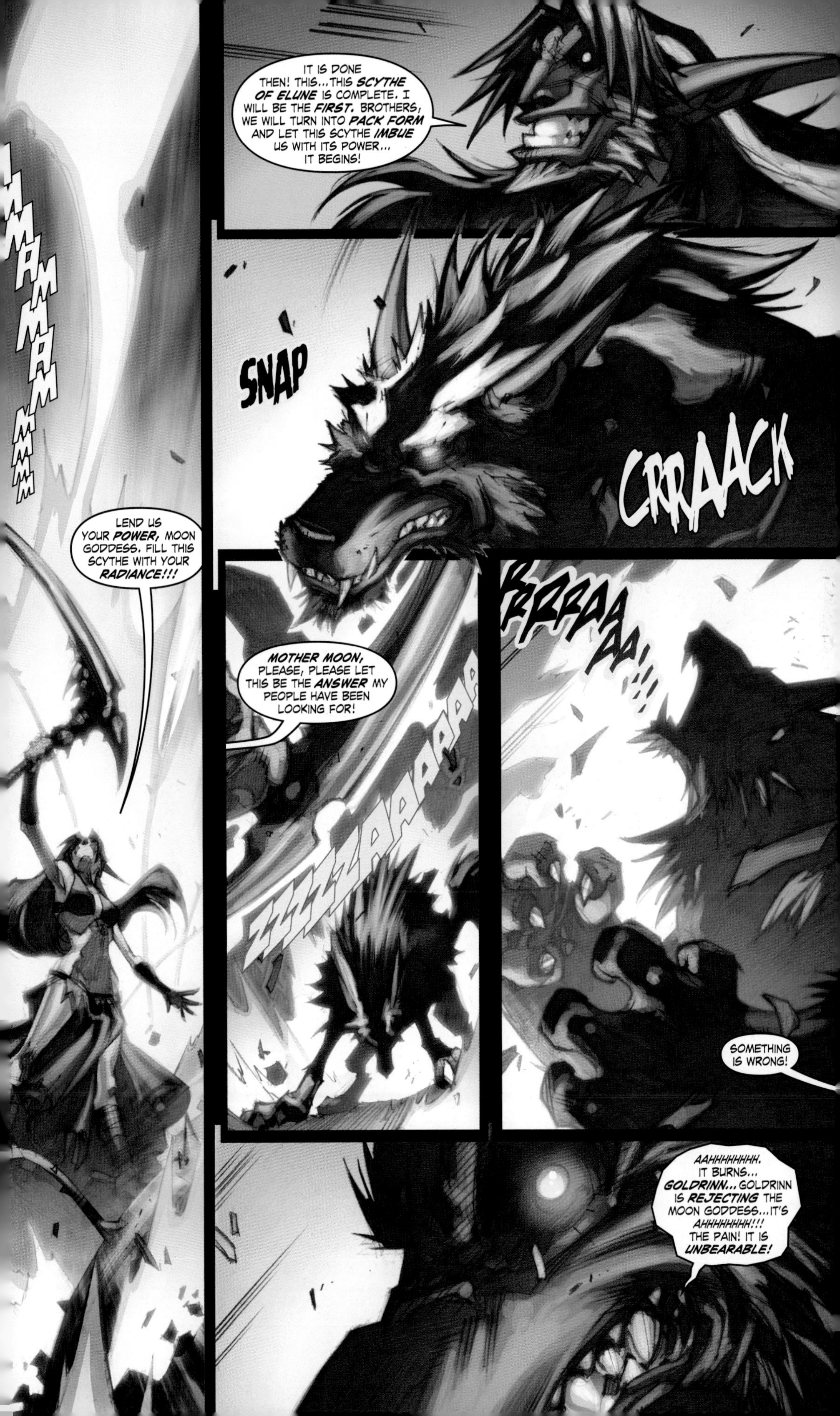
IT IS DONE THEN! THIS...THIS SCYTHE OF ELUNE IS COMPLETE. I WILL BE THE FIRST. BROTHERS, WE WILL TURN INTO PACK FORM AND LET THIS SCYTHE IMBUE US WITH ITS POWER... IT BEGINS!
SNAP
CRRAACK
LEND US YOUR POWER, MOON GODDESS. FILL THIS SCYTHE WITH YOUR RADIANCE!!!
MOTHER MOON, PLEASE, PLEASE LET THIS BE THE ANSWER MY PEOPLE HAVE BEEN LOOKING FOR!
SOMETHING IS WRONG!
AAHHHHHHHHH. IT BURNS... GOLDRINN... GOLDRINN IS REJECTING THE MOON GODDESS...IT'S AHHHHHHHH!!! THE PAIN! IT IS UNBEARABLE!

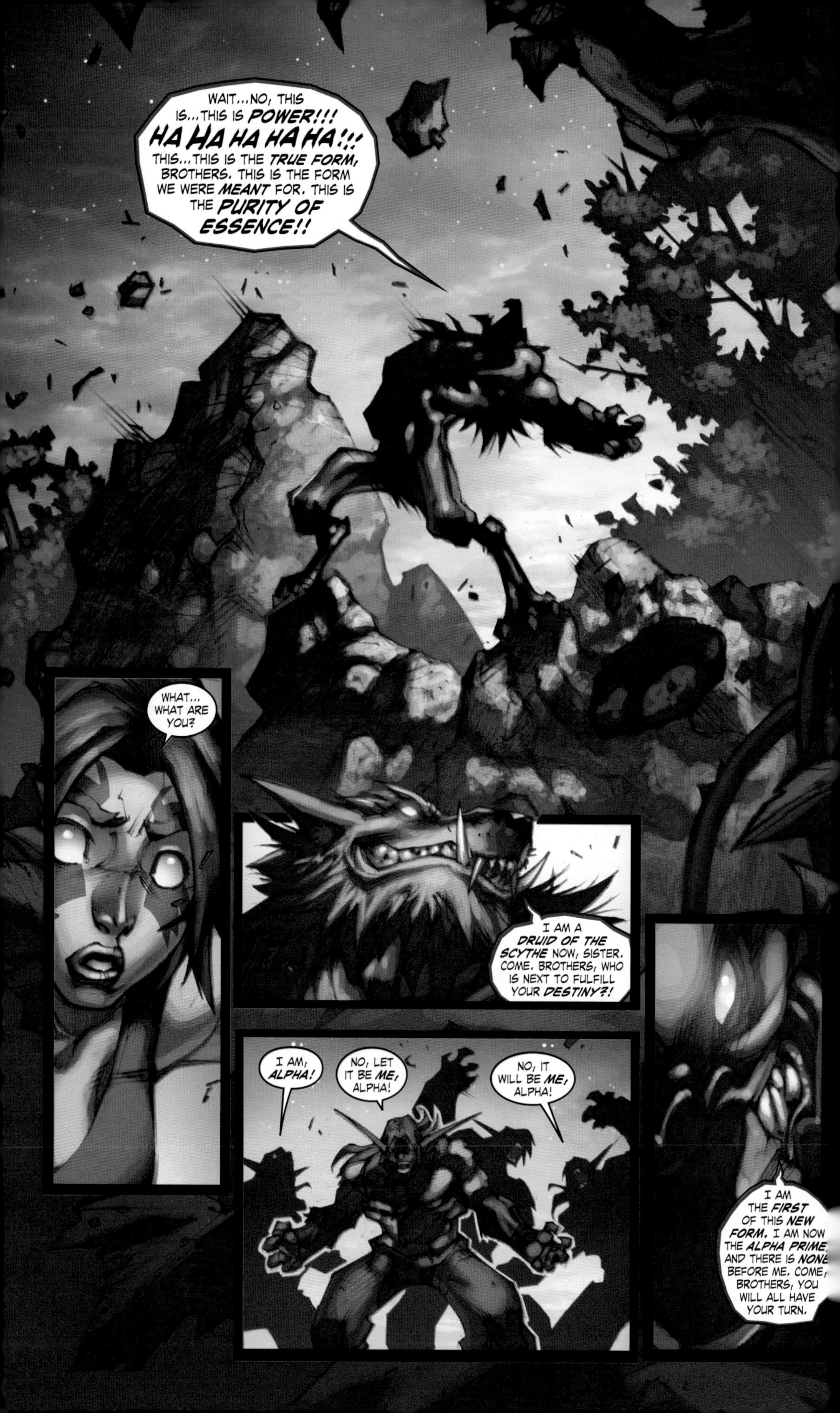
WAIT...NO, THIS IS...THIS IS POWER!!! HA HA HA HA HA!!! THIS...THIS IS THE TRUE FORM, BROTHERS. THIS IS THE FORM WE WERE MEANT FOR. THIS IS THE PURITY OF ESSENCE!!
WHAT... WHAT ARE YOU?
I AM A DRUID OF THE SCYTHE NOW, SISTER. COME. BROTHERS, WHO IS NEXT TO FULFILL YOUR DESTINY?!
I AM, ALPHA!
NO, LET IT BE ME, ALPHA!
NO, IT WILL BE ME, ALPHA!
I AM THE FIRST OF THIS NEW FORM. I AM NOW THE ALPHA PRIME AND THERE IS NONE BEFORE ME. COME, BROTHERS, YOU WILL ALL HAVE YOUR TURN.

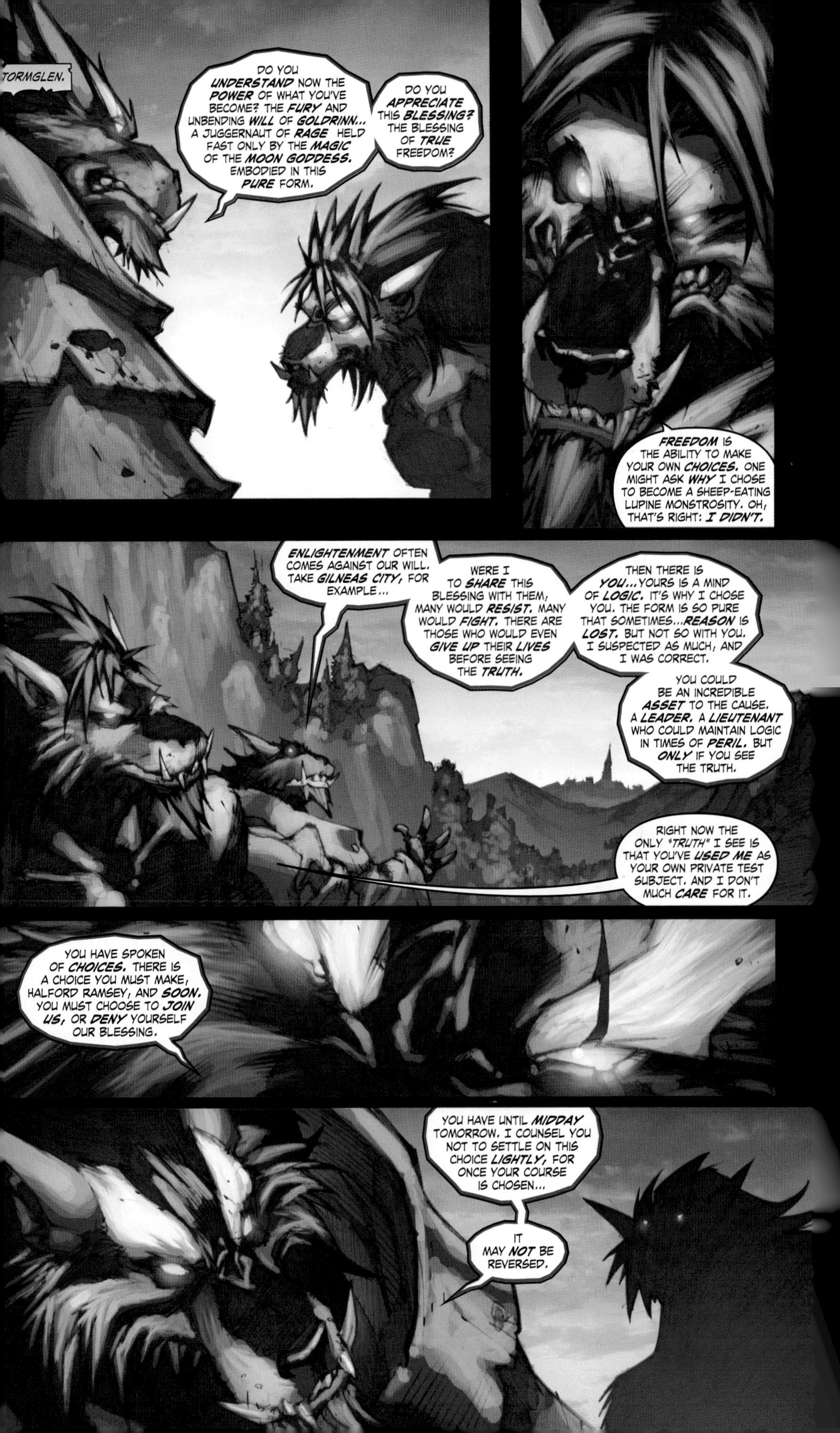
TORMGLEN.
DO YOU UNDERSTAND NOW THE POWER OF WHAT YOU'VE BECOME? THE FURY AND UNBENDING WILL OF GOLDRINN... A JUGGERNAUT OF RAGE HELD FAST ONLY BY THE MAGIC OF THE MOON GODDESS. EMBODIED IN THIS PURE FORM.
DO YOU APPRECIATE THIS BLESSING? THE BLESSING OF TRUE FREEDOM?
FREEDOM IS THE ABILITY TO MAKE YOUR OWN CHOICES. ONE MIGHT ASK WHY I CHOSE TO BECOME A SHEEP-EATING LUPINE MONSTROSITY. OH, THAT'S RIGHT: I DIDN'T.
ENLIGHTENMENT OFTEN COMES AGAINST OUR WILL. TAKE GILNEAS CITY, FOR EXAMPLE...
WERE I TO SHARE THIS BLESSING WITH THEM, MANY WOULD RESIST. MANY WOULD FIGHT. THERE ARE THOSE WHO WOULD EVEN GIVE UP THEIR LIVES BEFORE SEEING THE TRUTH.
THEN THERE IS YOU...YOURS IS A MIND OF LOGIC. IT'S WHY I CHOSE YOU. THE FORM IS SO PURE THAT SOMETIMES...REASON IS LOST. BUT NOT SO WITH YOU. I SUSPECTED AS MUCH, AND I WAS CORRECT.
YOU COULD BE AN INCREDIBLE ASSET TO THE CAUSE. A LEADER. A LIEUTENANT WHO COULD MAINTAIN LOGIC IN TIMES OF PERIL. BUT ONLY IF YOU SEE THE TRUTH.
RIGHT NOW THE ONLY "TRUTH" I SEE IS THAT YOU'VE USED ME AS YOUR OWN PRIVATE TEST SUBJECT. AND I DON'T MUCH CARE FOR IT.
YOU HAVE SPOKEN OF CHOICES. THERE IS A CHOICE YOU MUST MAKE, HALFORD RAMSEY, AND SOON. YOU MUST CHOOSE TO JOIN US, OR DENY YOURSELF OUR BLESSING.
YOU HAVE UNTIL MIDDAY TOMORROW. I COUNSEL YOU NOT TO SETTLE ON THIS CHOICE LIGHTLY, FOR ONCE YOUR COURSE IS CHOSEN...
IT MAY NOT BE REVERSED.

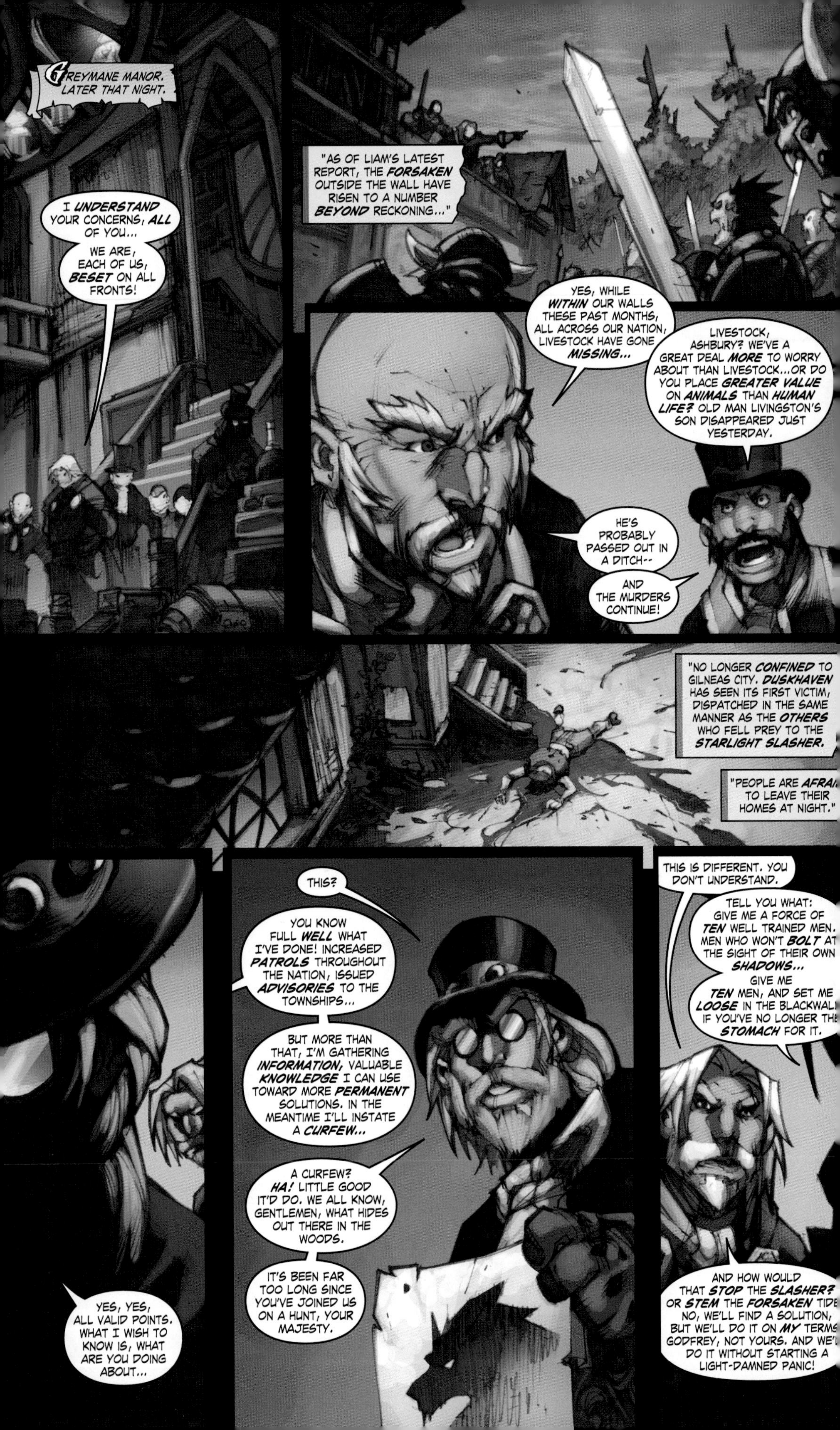
GREYMANE MANOR. LATER THAT NIGHT.
I UNDERSTAND YOUR CONCERNS, ALL OF YOU...
WE ARE, EACH OF US, BESET ON ALL FRONTS!
"AS OF LIAM'S LATEST REPORT, THE FORSAKEN OUTSIDE THE WALL HAVE RISEN TO A NUMBER BEYOND RECKONING..."
YES, WHILE WITHIN OUR WALLS THESE PAST MONTHS, ALL ACROSS OUR NATION, LIVESTOCK HAVE GONE MISSING...
LIVESTOCK, ASHBURY? WE'VE A GREAT DEAL MORE TO WORRY ABOUT THAN LIVESTOCK...OR DO YOU PLACE GREATER VALUE ON ANIMALS THAN HUMAN LIFE? OLD MAN LIVINGSTON'S SON DISAPPEARED JUST YESTERDAY.
HE'S PROBABLY PASSED OUT IN A DITCH--
AND THE MURDERS CONTINUE!
"NO LONGER CONFINED TO GILNEAS CITY. DUSKHAVEN HAS SEEN ITS FIRST VICTIM, DISPATCHED IN THE SAME MANNER AS THE OTHERS WHO FELL PREY TO THE STARLIGHT SLASHER.
"PEOPLE ARE AFRAI TO LEAVE THEIR HOMES AT NIGHT."
YES, YES, ALL VALID POINTS. WHAT I WISH TO KNOW IS, WHAT ARE YOU DOING ABOUT...
THIS?
YOU KNOW FULL WELL WHAT I'VE DONE! INCREASED PATROLS THROUGHOUT THE NATION, ISSUED ADVISORIES TO THE TOWNSHIPS...
BUT MORE THAN THAT, I'M GATHERING INFORMATION, VALUABLE KNOWLEDGE I CAN USE TOWARD MORE PERMANENT SOLUTIONS. IN THE MEANTIME I'LL INSTATE A CURFEW...
A CURFEW? HA! LITTLE GOOD IT'D DO. WE ALL KNOW, GENTLEMEN, WHAT HIDES OUT THERE IN THE WOODS.
IT'S BEEN FAR TOO LONG SINCE YOU'VE JOINED US ON A HUNT, YOUR MAJESTY.
THIS IS DIFFERENT. YOU DON'T UNDERSTAND.
TELL YOU WHAT: GIVE ME A FORCE OF TEN WELL TRAINED MEN. MEN WHO WON'T BOLT AT THE SIGHT OF THEIR OWN SHADOWS...
GIVE ME TEN MEN, AND SET ME LOOSE IN THE BLACKWAL IF YOU'VE NO LONGER TH STOMACH FOR IT.
AND HOW WOULD THAT STOP THE SLASHER? OR STEM THE FORSAKEN TIDE NO, WE'LL FIND A SOLUTION, BUT WE'LL DO IT ON MY TERMS GODFREY, NOT YOURS. AND WE'L DO IT WITHOUT STARTING A LIGHT-DAMNED PANIC!

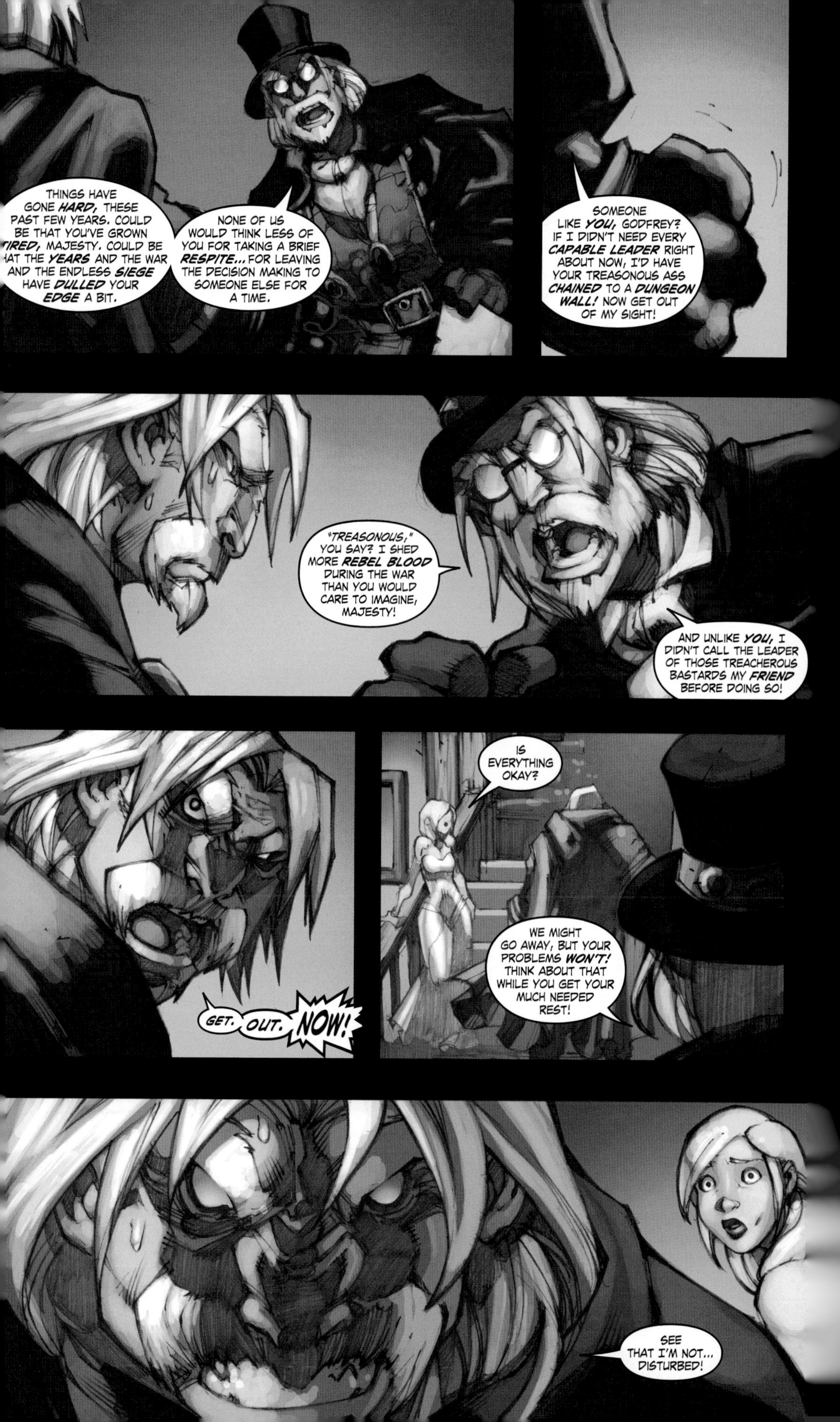
THINGS HAVE GONE HARD, THESE PAST FEW YEARS. COULD BE THAT YOU'VE GROWN TIRED, MAJESTY. COULD BE THAT THE YEARS AND THE WAR AND THE ENDLESS SIEGE HAVE DULLED YOUR EDGE A BIT.
NONE OF US WOULD THINK LESS OF YOU FOR TAKING A BRIEF RESPITE... FOR LEAVING THE DECISION MAKING TO SOMEONE ELSE FOR A TIME.
SOMEONE LIKE YOU, GODFREY? IF I DIDN'T NEED EVERY CAPABLE LEADER RIGHT ABOUT NOW, I'D HAVE YOUR TREASONOUS ASS CHAINED TO A DUNGEON WALL! NOW GET OUT OF MY SIGHT!
"TREASONOUS," YOU SAY? I SHED MORE REBEL BLOOD DURING THE WAR THAN YOU WOULD CARE TO IMAGINE, MAJESTY!
AND UNLIKE YOU, I DIDN'T CALL THE LEADER OF THOSE TREACHEROUS BASTARDS MY FRIEND BEFORE DOING SO!
GET. OUT. NOW!
IS EVERYTHING OKAY?
WE MIGHT GO AWAY, BUT YOUR PROBLEMS WON'T! THINK ABOUT THAT WHILE YOU GET YOUR MUCH NEEDED REST!
SEE THAT I'M NOT... DISTURBED!

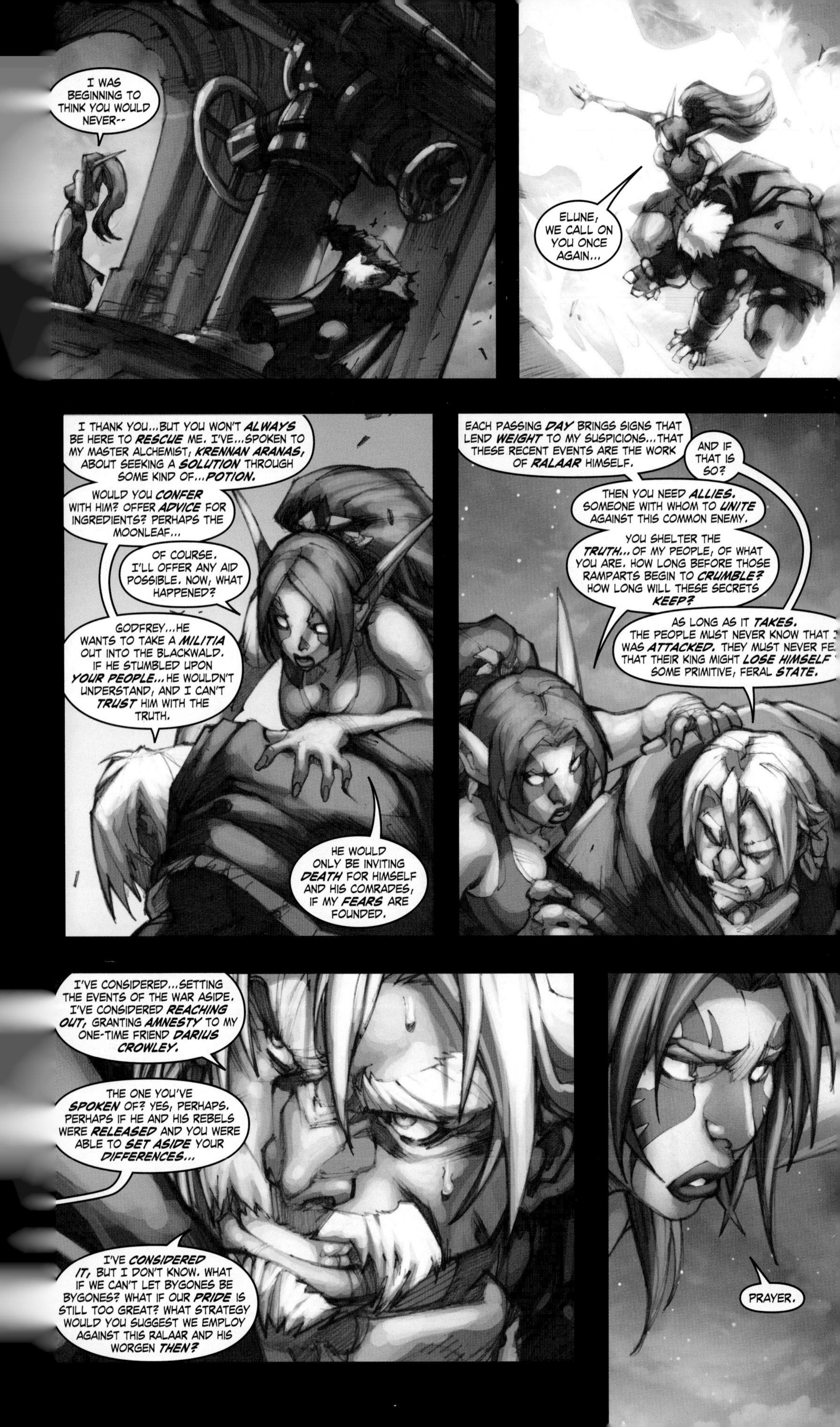
I WAS BEGINNING TO THINK YOU WOULD NEVER--
ELUNE, WE CALL ON YOU ONCE AGAIN...
I THANK YOU...BUT YOU WON'T ALWAYS BE HERE TO RESCUE ME. I'VE...SPOKEN TO MY MASTER ALCHEMIST, KRENNAN ARANAS, ABOUT SEEKING A SOLUTION THROUGH SOME KIND OF...POTION.
WOULD YOU CONFER WITH HIM? OFFER ADVICE FOR INGREDIENTS? PERHAPS THE MOONLEAF...
OF COURSE. I'LL OFFER ANY AID POSSIBLE. NOW, WHAT HAPPENED?
GODFREY...HE WANTS TO TAKE A MILITIA OUT INTO THE BLACKWALD. IF HE STUMBLED UPON YOUR PEOPLE...HE WOULDN'T UNDERSTAND, AND I CAN'T TRUST HIM WITH THE TRUTH.
HE WOULD ONLY BE INVITING DEATH FOR HIMSELF AND HIS COMRADES, IF MY FEARS ARE FOUNDED.
EACH PASSING DAY BRINGS SIGNS THAT LEND WEIGHT TO MY SUSPICIONS...THAT THESE RECENT EVENTS ARE THE WORK OF RALAAR HIMSELF.
AND IF THAT IS SO?
THEN YOU NEED ALLIES. SOMEONE WITH WHOM TO UNITE AGAINST THIS COMMON ENEMY.
YOU SHELTER THE TRUTH... OF MY PEOPLE, OF WHAT YOU ARE. HOW LONG BEFORE THOSE RAMPARTS BEGIN TO CRUMBLE? HOW LONG WILL THESE SECRETS KEEP?
AS LONG AS IT TAKES. THE PEOPLE MUST NEVER KNOW THAT WAS ATTACKED. THEY MUST NEVER FE THAT THEIR KING MIGHT LOSE HIMSELF SOME PRIMITIVE, FERAL STATE.
I'VE CONSIDERED...SETTING THE EVENTS OF THE WAR ASIDE. I'VE CONSIDERED REACHING OUT, GRANTING AMNESTY TO MY ONE-TIME FRIEND DARIUS CROWLEY.
THE ONE YOU'VE SPOKEN OF? YES, PERHAPS. PERHAPS IF HE AND HIS REBELS WERE RELEASED AND YOU WERE ABLE TO SET ASIDE YOUR DIFFERENCES...
I'VE CONSIDERED IT, BUT I DON'T KNOW. WHAT IF WE CAN'T LET BYGONES BE BYGONES? WHAT IF OUR PRIDE IS STILL TOO GREAT? WHAT STRATEGY WOULD YOU SUGGEST WE EMPLOY AGAINST THIS RALAAR AND HIS WORGEN THEN?
PRAYER.

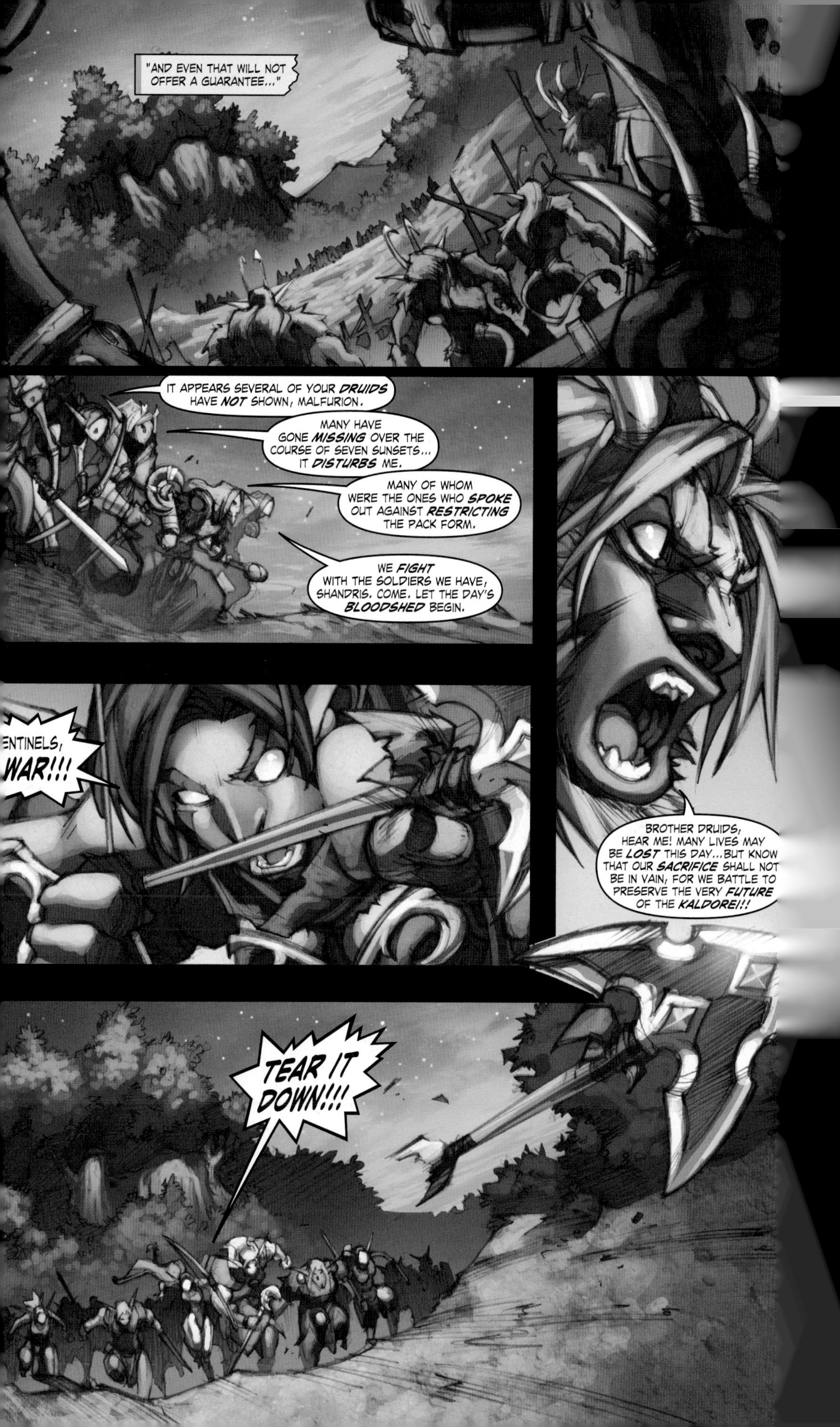

"AND EVEN THAT WILL NOT OFFER A GUARANTEE..."
IT APPEARS SEVERAL OF YOUR DRUIDS HAVE NOT SHOWN, MALFURION.
MANY HAVE GONE MISSING OVER THE COURSE OF SEVEN SUNSETS... IT DISTURBS ME.
MANY OF WHOM WERE THE ONES WHO SPOKE OUT AGAINST RESTRICTING THE PACK FORM.
WE FIGHT WITH THE SOLDIERS WE HAVE, SHANDRIS. COME. LET THE DAY'S BLOODSHED BEGIN.
BROTHER DRUIDS, HEAR ME! MANY LIVES MAY BE LOST THIS DAY...BUT KNOW THAT OUR SACRIFICE SHALL NOT BE IN VAIN, FOR WE BATTLE TO PRESERVE THE VERY FUTURE OF THE KALDORE!!!
ENTINELS, WAR!!!
TEAR IT DOWN!!!

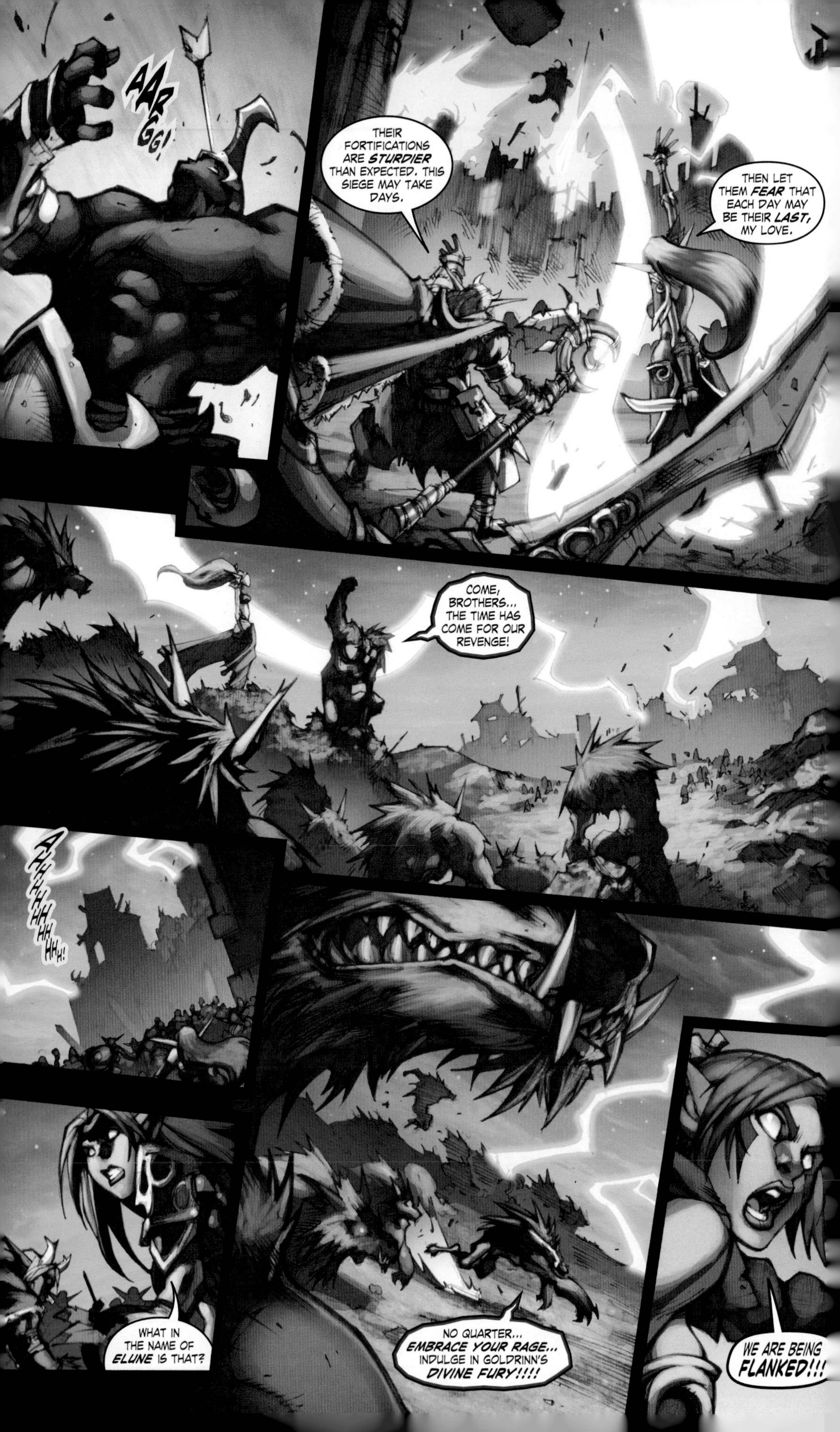
AARGG!
THEIR FORTIFICATIONS ARE STURDIER THAN EXPECTED. THIS SIEGE MAY TAKE DAYS.
THEN LET THEM FEAR THAT EACH DAY MAY BE THEIR LAST, MY LOVE.
COME, BROTHERS... THE TIME HAS COME FOR OUR REVENGE!
AHHHHHHHHH!
WHAT IN THE NAME OF ELUNE IS THAT?
NO QUARTER... EMBRACE YOUR RAGE... INDULGE IN GOLDRINN'S DIVINE FURY!!!!
WE ARE BEING FLANKED!!!

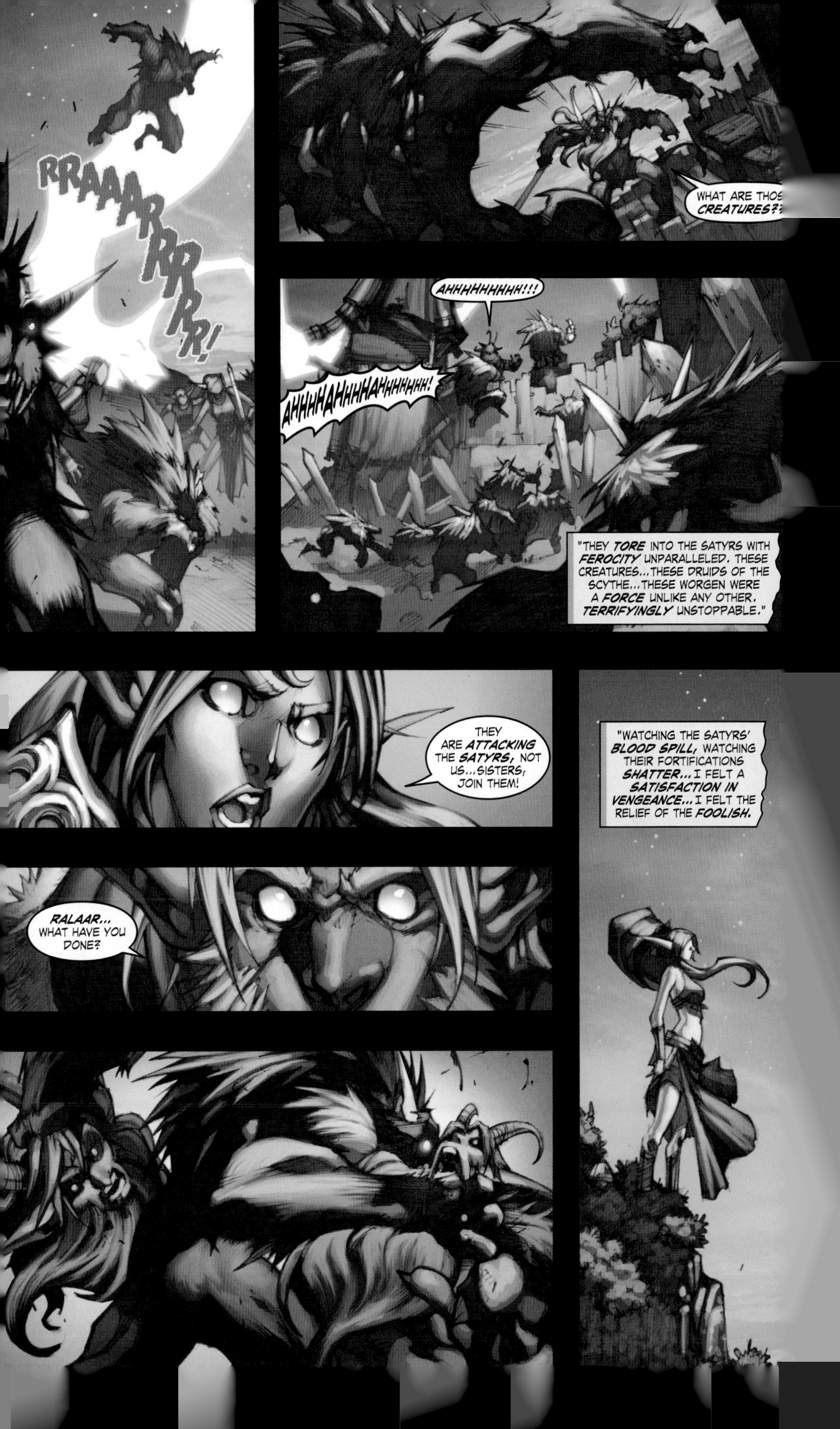
RRAAAARRRRRR!
WHAT ARE THOS
CREATURES??
AHHHHHHHHH!!!
AHHHHAHHHHAHHHHHHH!
"THEY TORE INTO THE SATYRS WITH FEROCITY UNPARALLELED. THESE CREATURES...THESE DRUIDS OF THE SCYTHE...THESE WORGEN WERE A FORCE UNLIKE ANY OTHER. TERRIFYINGLY UNSTOPPABLE."
THEY ARE ATTACKING THE SATYRS, NOT US...SISTERS, JOIN THEM!
RALAAR... WHAT HAVE YOU DONE?
"WATCHING THE SATYRS' BLOOD SPILL, WATCHING THEIR FORTIFICATIONS SHATTER...I FELT A SATISFACTION IN VENGEANCE...I FELT THE RELIEF OF THE FOOLISH.

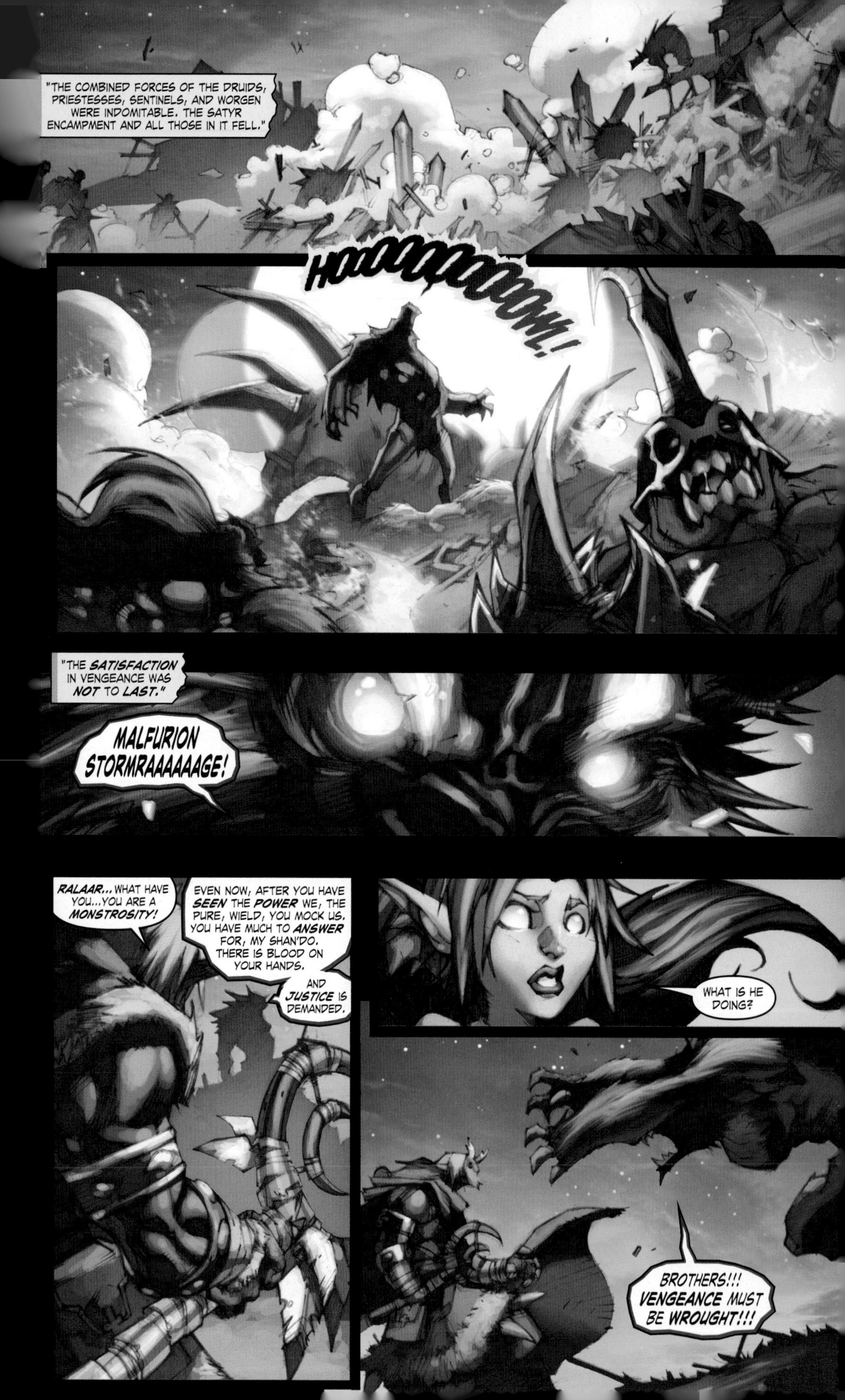
"THE COMBINED FORCES OF THE DRUIDS, PRIESTESSES, SENTINELS, AND WORGEN WERE INDOMITABLE. THE SATYR ENCAMPMENT AND ALL THOSE IN IT FELL."
HOOOOOOOOOOWL!
"THE SATISFACTION IN VENGEANCE WAS NOT TO LAST."
MALFURION STORMRAAAAAAGE!
RALAAR... WHAT HAVE YOU...YOU ARE A MONSTROSITY!
EVEN NOW, AFTER YOU HAVE SEEN THE POWER WE, THE PURE, WIELD, YOU MOCK US. YOU HAVE MUCH TO ANSWER FOR, MY SHAN'DO. THERE IS BLOOD ON YOUR HANDS.
AND JUSTICE IS DEMANDED.
WHAT IS HE DOING?
BROTHERS!!! VENGEANCE MUST BE WROUGHT!!!

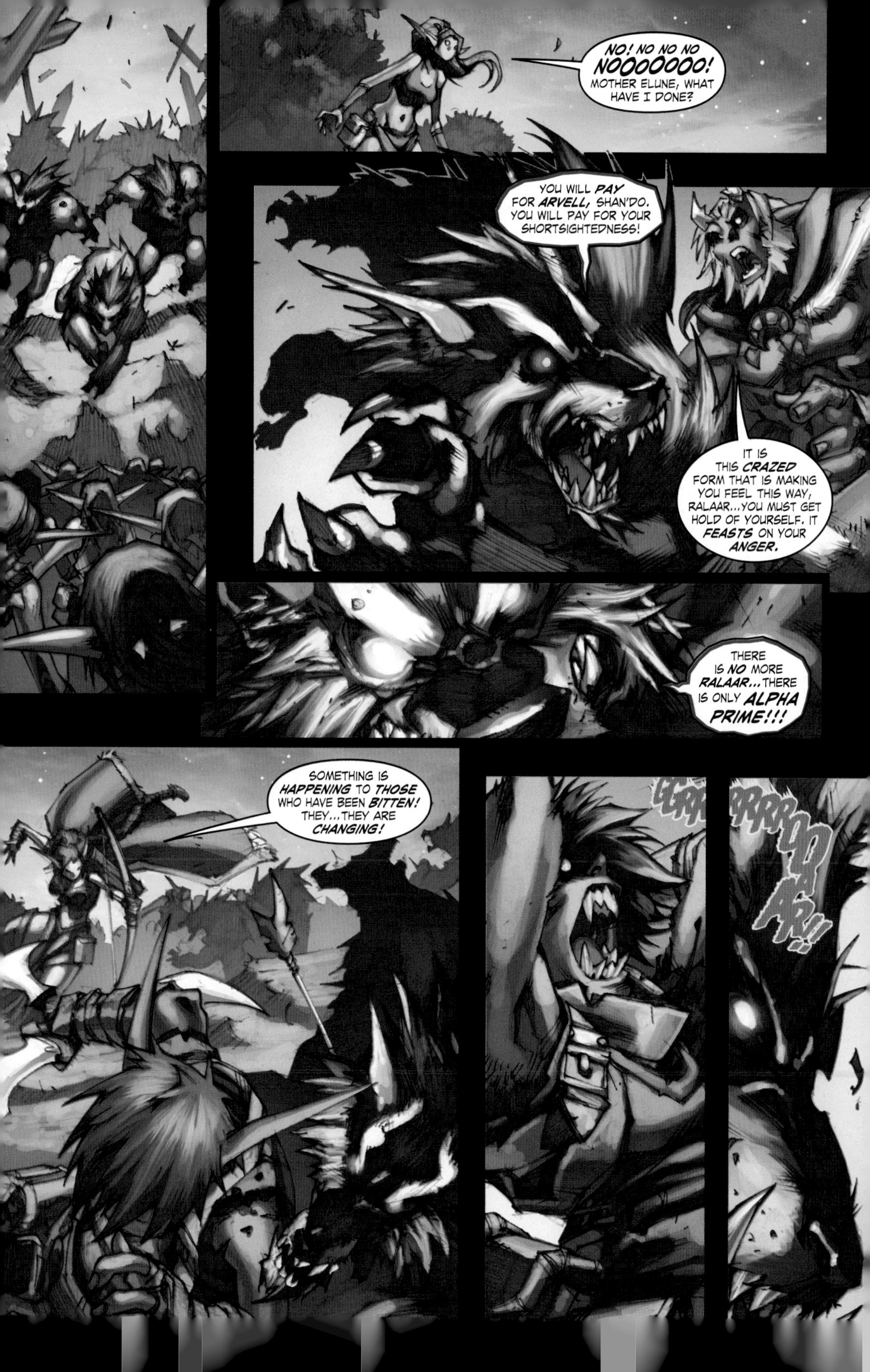
NO! NO NO NO NOOOOOOO! MOTHER ELUNE, WHAT HAVE I DONE?
YOU WILL PAY FOR ARVELL, SHAN'DO. YOU WILL PAY FOR YOUR SHORTSIGHTEDNESS!
IT IS THIS CRAZED FORM THAT IS MAKING YOU FEEL THIS WAY, RALAAR...YOU MUST GET HOLD OF YOURSELF. IT FEASTS ON YOUR ANGER.
THERE IS NO MORE RALAAR...THERE IS ONLY ALPHA PRIME!!!
SOMETHING IS HAPPENING TO THOSE WHO HAVE BEEN BITTEN! THEY...THEY ARE CHANGING!
GGRRRRRRRROOOAAR!!

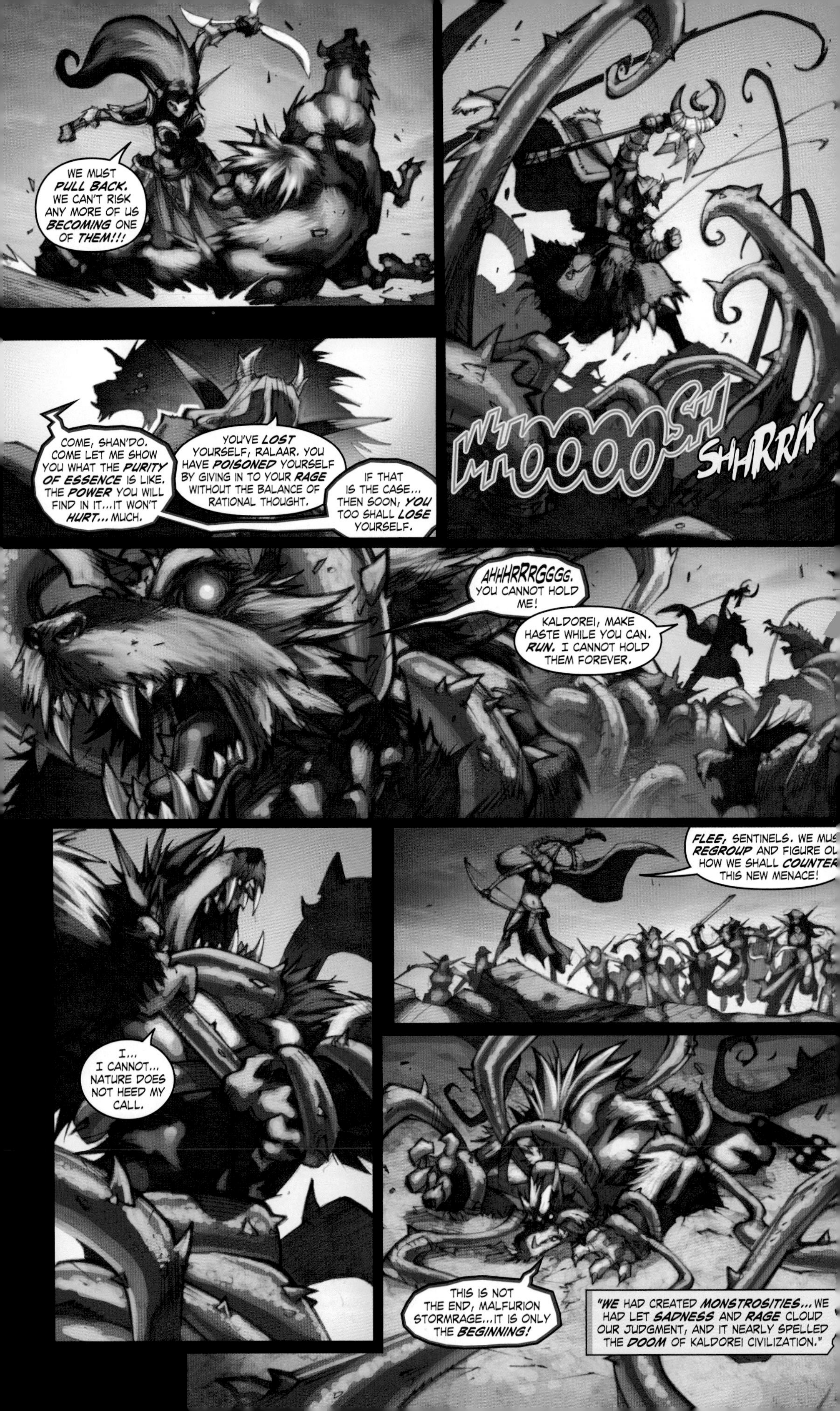
WE MUST PULL BACK. WE CAN'T RISK ANY MORE OF US BECOMING ONE OF THEM!!!
COME, SHAN'DO. COME LET ME SHOW YOU WHAT THE PURITY OF ESSENCE IS LIKE. THE POWER YOU WILL FIND IN IT... IT WON'T HURT... MUCH.
YOU'VE LOST YOURSELF, RALAAR. YOU HAVE POISONED YOURSELF BY GIVING IN TO YOUR RAGE WITHOUT THE BALANCE OF RATIONAL THOUGHT.
IF THAT IS THE CASE... THEN SOON, YOU TOO SHALL LOSE YOURSELF.
WHOOOOOSH
SHHRRK
AHHHRRRGGGG. YOU CANNOT HOLD ME!
KALDOREI, MAKE HASTE WHILE YOU CAN. RUN. I CANNOT HOLD THEM FOREVER.
I... I CANNOT... NATURE DOES NOT HEED MY CALL.
FLEE, SENTINELS. WE MUS REGROUP AND FIGURE OU HOW WE SHALL COUNTER THIS NEW MENACE!
THIS IS NOT THE END, MALFURION STORMRAGE... IT IS ONLY THE BEGINNING!
"WE HAD CREATED MONSTROSITIES... WE HAD LET SADNESS AND RAGE CLOUD OUR JUDGMENT, AND IT NEARLY SPELLED THE DOOM OF KALDOREI CIVILIZATION."

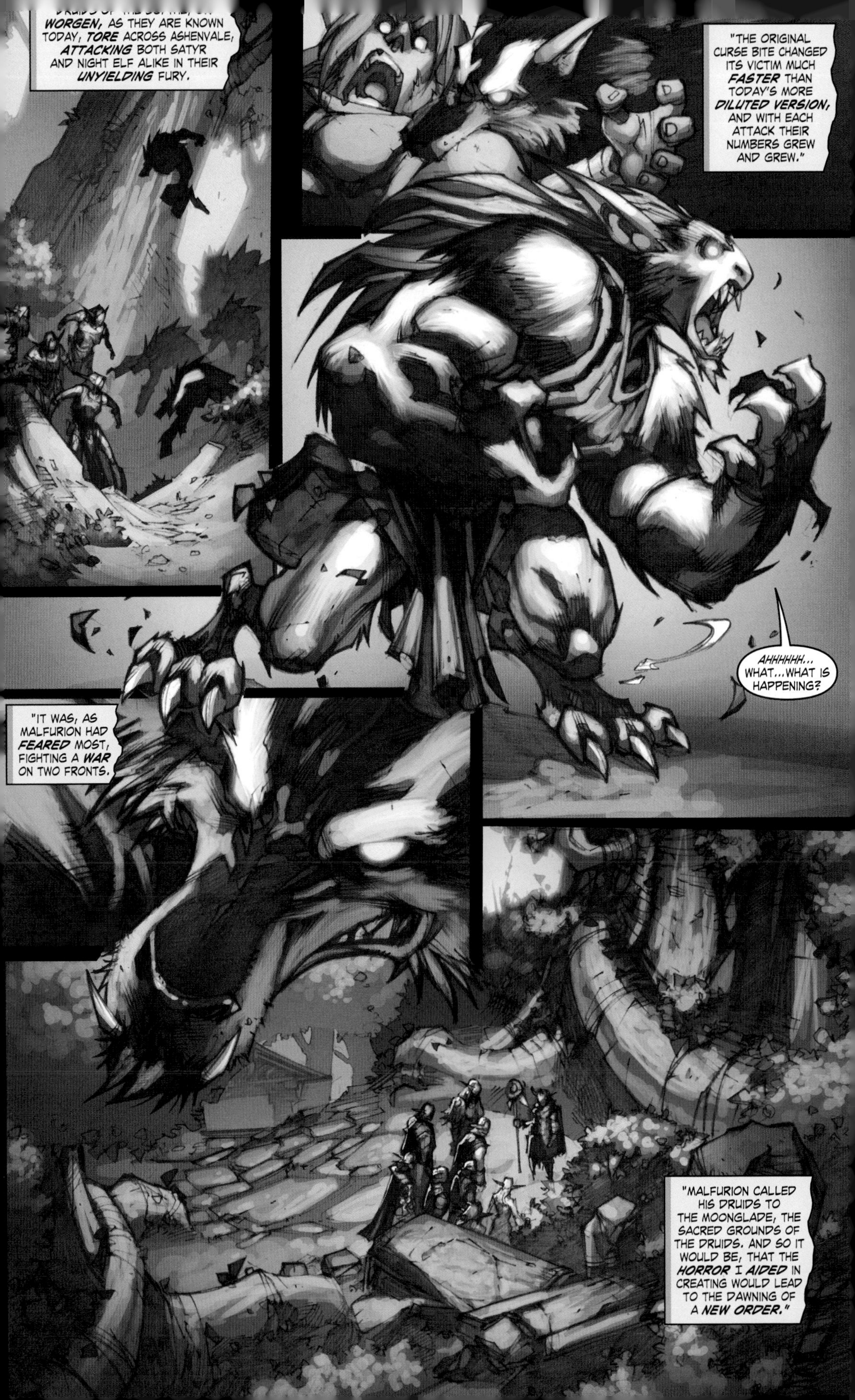
WORGEN, AS THEY ARE KNOWN TODAY, TORE ACROSS ASHENVALE, ATTACKING BOTH SATYR AND NIGHT ELF ALIKE IN THEIR UNYIELDING FURY.
"THE ORIGINAL CURSE BITE CHANGED ITS VICTIM MUCH FASTER THAN TODAY'S MORE DILUTED VERSION, AND WITH EACH ATTACK THEIR NUMBERS GREW AND GREW."
AHHHHHH... WHAT...WHAT IS HAPPENING?
"IT WAS, AS MALFURION HAD FEARED MOST, FIGHTING A WAR ON TWO FRONTS.
"MALFURION CALLED HIS DRUIDS TO THE MOONGLADE, THE SACRED GROUNDS OF THE DRUIDS. AND SO IT WOULD BE, THAT THE HORROR I AIDED IN CREATING WOULD LEAD TO THE DAWNING OF A NEW ORDER."

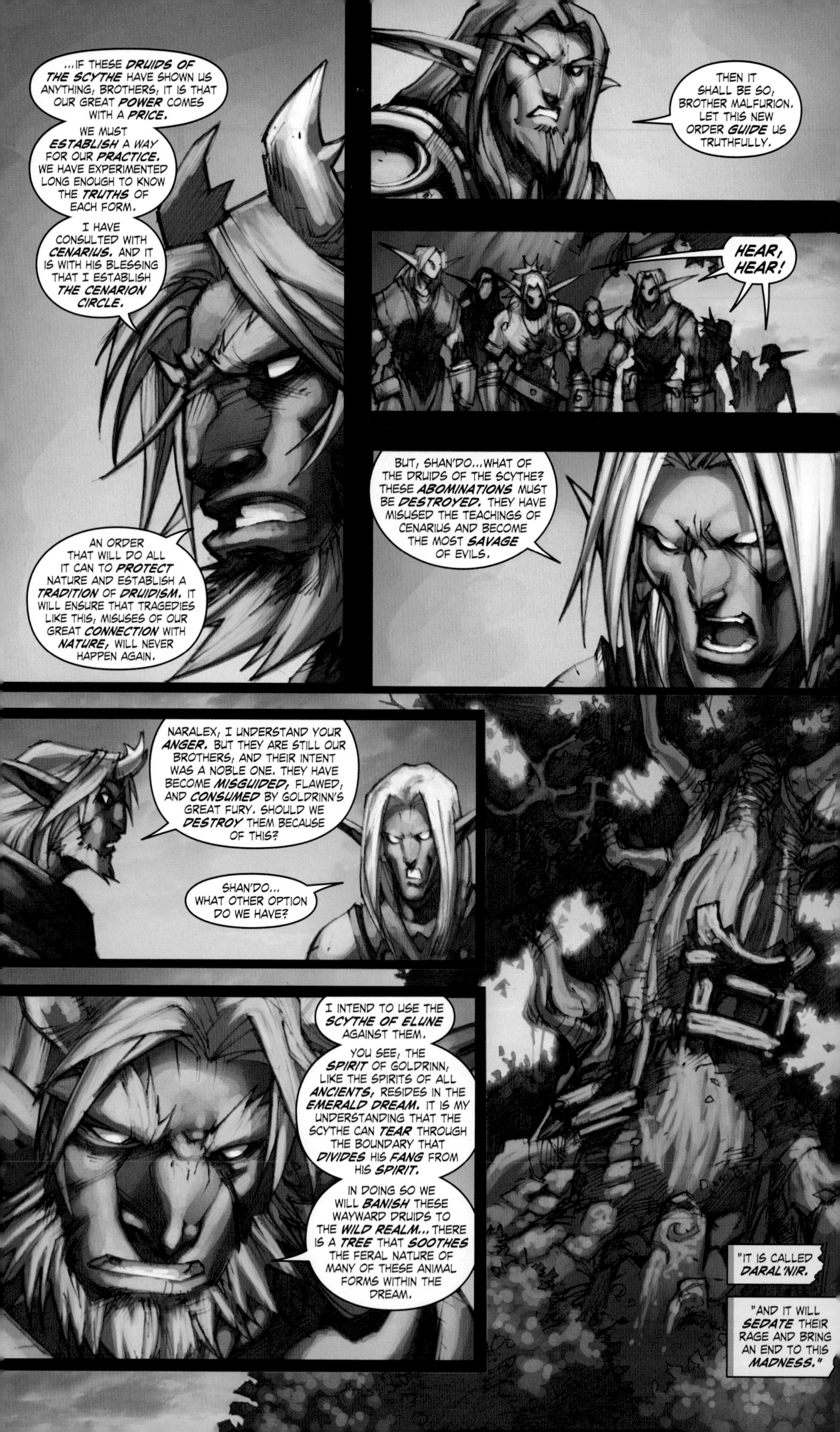

...IF THESE DRUIDS OF THE SCYTHE HAVE SHOWN US ANYTHING, BROTHERS, IT IS THAT OUR GREAT POWER COMES WITH A PRICE.
WE MUST ESTABLISH A WAY FOR OUR PRACTICE. WE HAVE EXPERIMENTED LONG ENOUGH TO KNOW THE TRUTHS OF EACH FORM.
I HAVE CONSULTED WITH CENARIUS. AND IT IS WITH HIS BLESSING THAT I ESTABLISH THE CENARION CIRCLE.
AN ORDER THAT WILL DO ALL IT CAN TO PROTECT NATURE AND ESTABLISH A TRADITION OF DRUIDISM. IT WILL ENSURE THAT TRAGEDIES LIKE THIS, MISUSES OF OUR GREAT CONNECTION WITH NATURE, WILL NEVER HAPPEN AGAIN.
THEN IT SHALL BE SO, BROTHER MALFURION. LET THIS NEW ORDER GUIDE US TRUTHFULLY.
HEAR, HEAR!
BUT, SHAN'DO...WHAT OF THE DRUIDS OF THE SCYTHE? THESE ABOMINATIONS MUST BE DESTROYED. THEY HAVE MISUSED THE TEACHINGS OF CENARIUS AND BECOME THE MOST SAVAGE OF EVILS.
NARALEX, I UNDERSTAND YOUR ANGER. BUT THEY ARE STILL OUR BROTHERS, AND THEIR INTENT WAS A NOBLE ONE. THEY HAVE BECOME MISGUIDED, FLAWED, AND CONSUMED BY GOLDRINN'S GREAT FURY. SHOULD WE DESTROY THEM BECAUSE OF THIS?
SHAN'DO... WHAT OTHER OPTION DO WE HAVE?
I INTEND TO USE THE SCYTHE OF ELUNE AGAINST THEM.
YOU SEE, THE SPIRIT OF GOLDRINN, LIKE THE SPIRITS OF ALL ANCIENTS, RESIDES IN THE EMERALD DREAM. IT IS MY UNDERSTANDING THAT THE SCYTHE CAN TEAR THROUGH THE BOUNDARY THAT DIVIDES HIS FANG FROM HIS SPIRIT.
IN DOING SO WE WILL BANISH THESE WAYWARD DRUIDS TO THE WILD REALM... THERE IS A TREE THAT SOOTHES THE FERAL NATURE OF MANY OF THESE ANIMAL FORMS WITHIN THE DREAM.
"IT IS CALLED DARAL'NIR.
"AND IT WILL SEDATE THEIR RAGE AND BRING AN END TO THIS MADNESS."

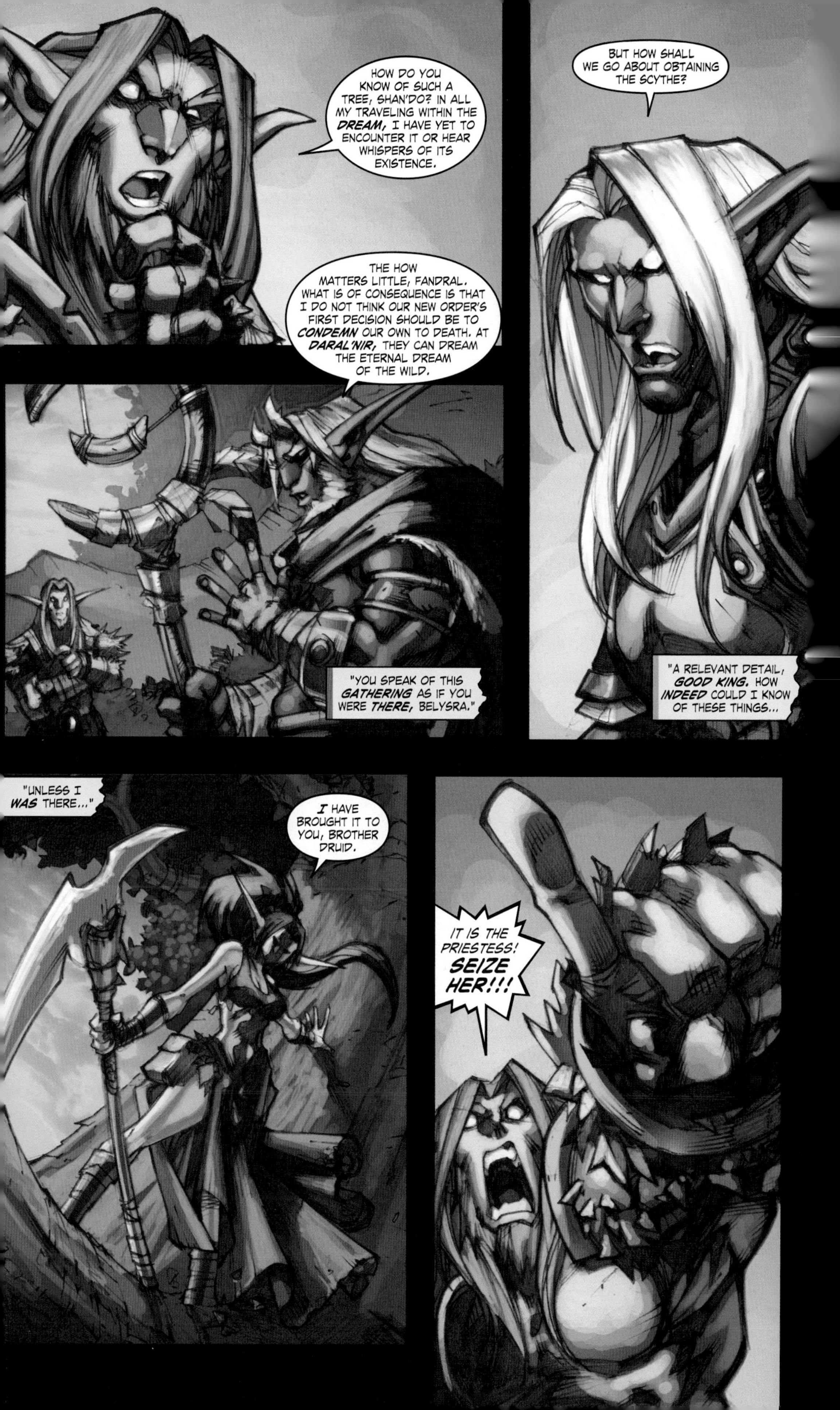
HOW DO YOU KNOW OF SUCH A TREE, SHAN'DO? IN ALL MY TRAVELING WITHIN THE DREAM, I HAVE YET TO ENCOUNTER IT OR HEAR WHISPERS OF ITS EXISTENCE.
THE HOW MATTERS LITTLE, FANDRAL. WHAT IS OF CONSEQUENCE IS THAT I DO NOT THINK OUR NEW ORDER'S FIRST DECISION SHOULD BE TO CONDEMN OUR OWN TO DEATH. AT DARAL'NIR, THEY CAN DREAM THE ETERNAL DREAM OF THE WILD.
"YOU SPEAK OF THIS GATHERING AS IF YOU WERE THERE, BELYSRA."
BUT HOW SHALL WE GO ABOUT OBTAINING THE SCYTHE?
"A RELEVANT DETAIL, GOOD KING. HOW INDEED COULD I KNOW OF THESE THINGS...
"UNLESS I WAS THERE..."
I HAVE BROUGHT IT TO YOU, BROTHER DRUID.
IT IS THE PRIESTESS! SEIZE HER!!!

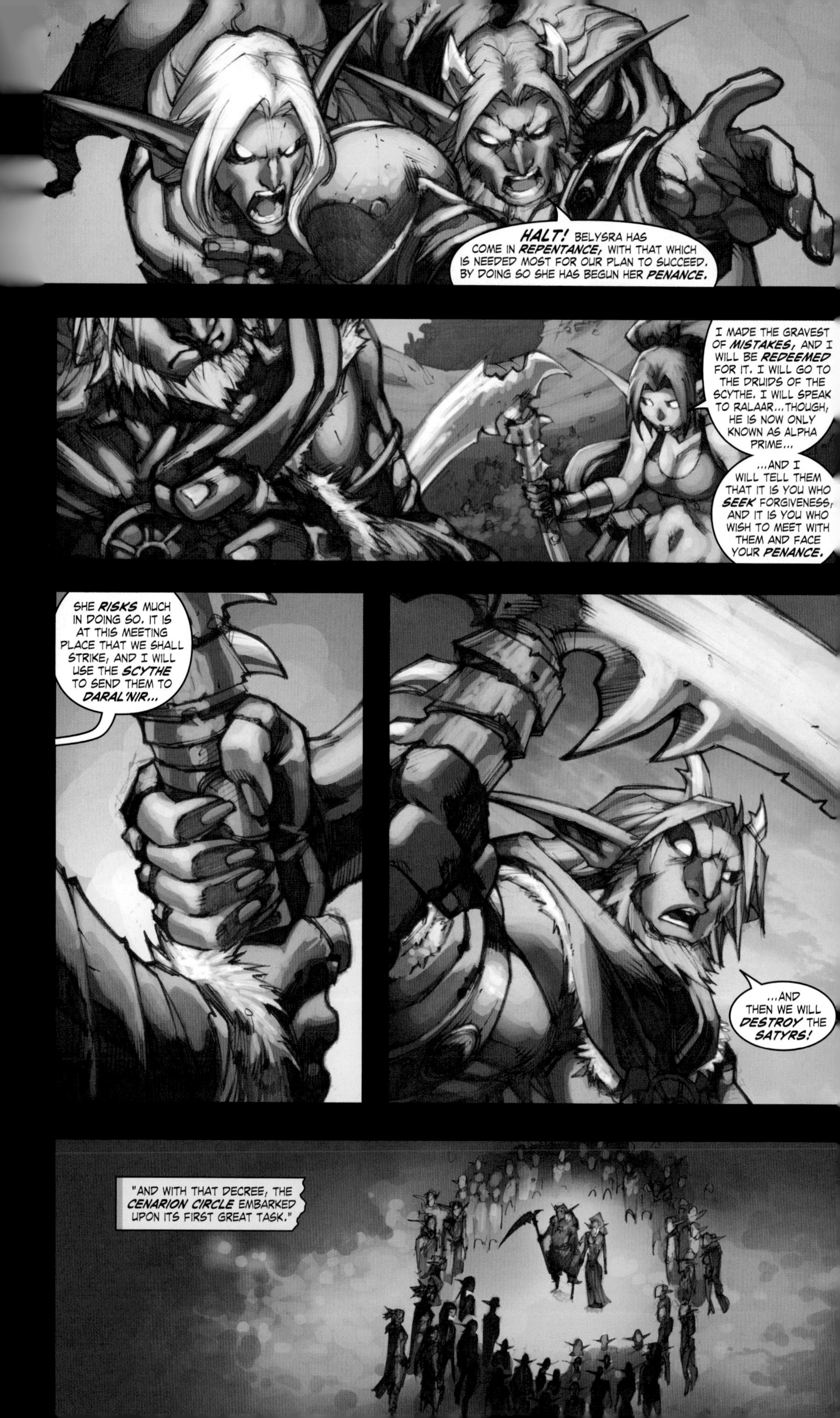
HALT! BELYSRA HAS COME IN REPENTANCE, WITH THAT WHICH IS NEEDED MOST FOR OUR PLAN TO SUCCEED. BY DOING SO SHE HAS BEGUN HER PENANCE.
I MADE THE GRAVEST OF MISTAKES, AND I WILL BE REDEEMED FOR IT. I WILL GO TO THE DRUIDS OF THE SCYTHE. I WILL SPEAK TO RALAAR...THOUGH, HE IS NOW ONLY KNOWN AS ALPHA PRIME...
...AND I WILL TELL THEM THAT IT IS YOU WHO SEEK FORGIVENESS, AND IT IS YOU WHO WISH TO MEET WITH THEM AND FACE YOUR PENANCE.
SHE RISKS MUCH IN DOING SO. IT IS AT THIS MEETING PLACE THAT WE SHALL STRIKE, AND I WILL USE THE SCYTHE TO SEND THEM TO DARAL'NIR...
...AND THEN WE WILL DESTROY THE SATYRS!
"AND WITH THAT DECREE, THE CENARION CIRCLE EMBARKED UPON ITS FIRST GREAT TASK."

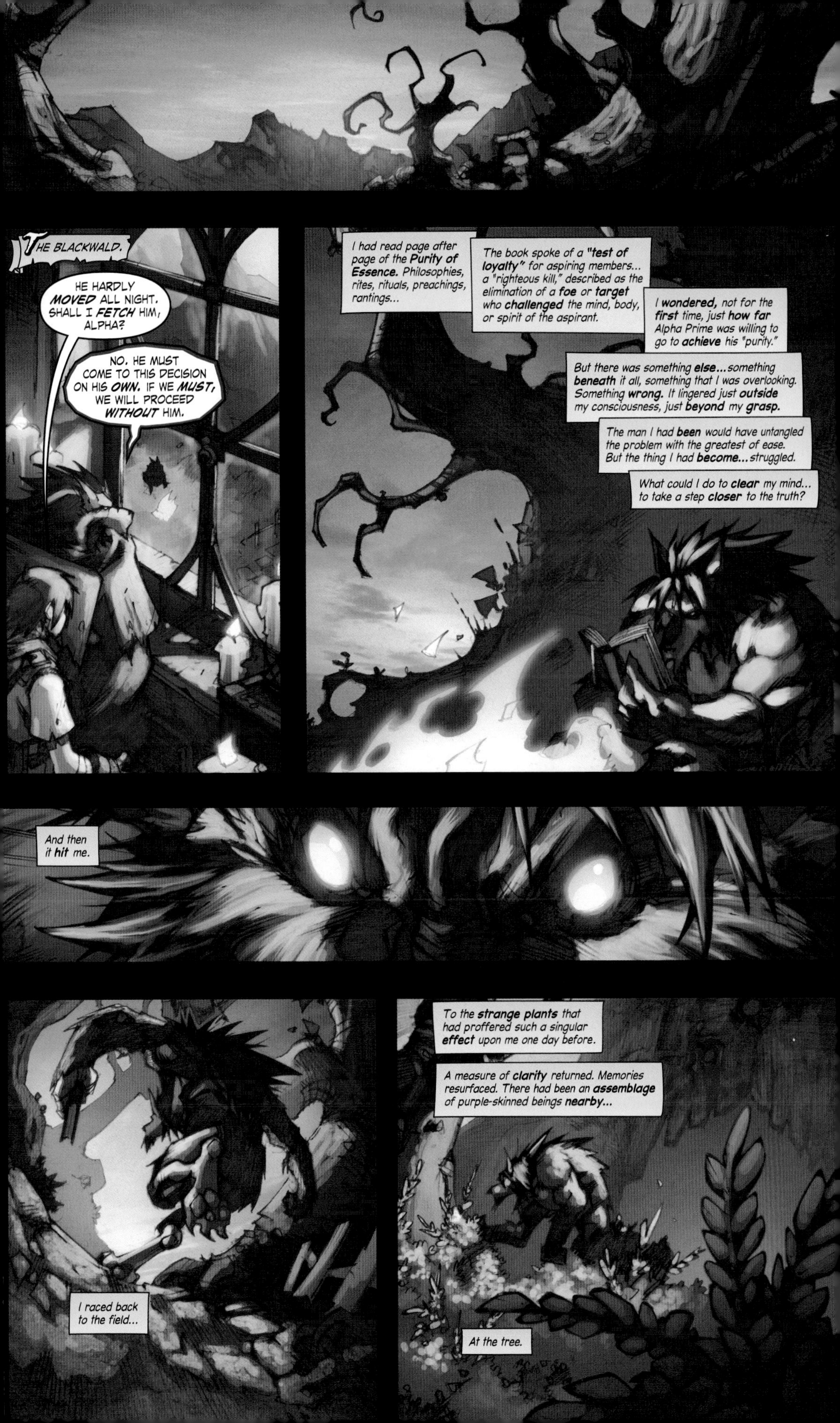
THE BLACKWALD.
HE HARDLY MOVED ALL NIGHT. SHALL I FETCH HIM, ALPHA?
NO. HE MUST COME TO THIS DECISION ON HIS OWN. IF WE MUST, WE WILL PROCEED WITHOUT HIM.
I had read page after page of the Purity of Essence. Philosophies, rites, rituals, preachings, rantings...
The book spoke of a "test of loyalty" for aspiring members... a "righteous kill," described as the elimination of a foe or target who challenged the mind, body, or spirit of the aspirant.
I wondered, not for the first time, just how far Alpha Prime was willing to go to achieve his "purity."
But there was something else... something beneath it all, something that I was overlooking. Something wrong. It lingered just outside my consciousness, just beyond my grasp.
The man I had been would have untangled the problem with the greatest of ease. But the thing I had become... struggled.
What could I do to clear my mind... to take a step closer to the truth?
And then it hit me.
I raced back to the field...
To the strange plants that had proffered such a singular effect upon me one day before.
A measure of clarity returned. Memories resurfaced. There had been an assemblage of purple-skinned beings nearby...
At the tree.

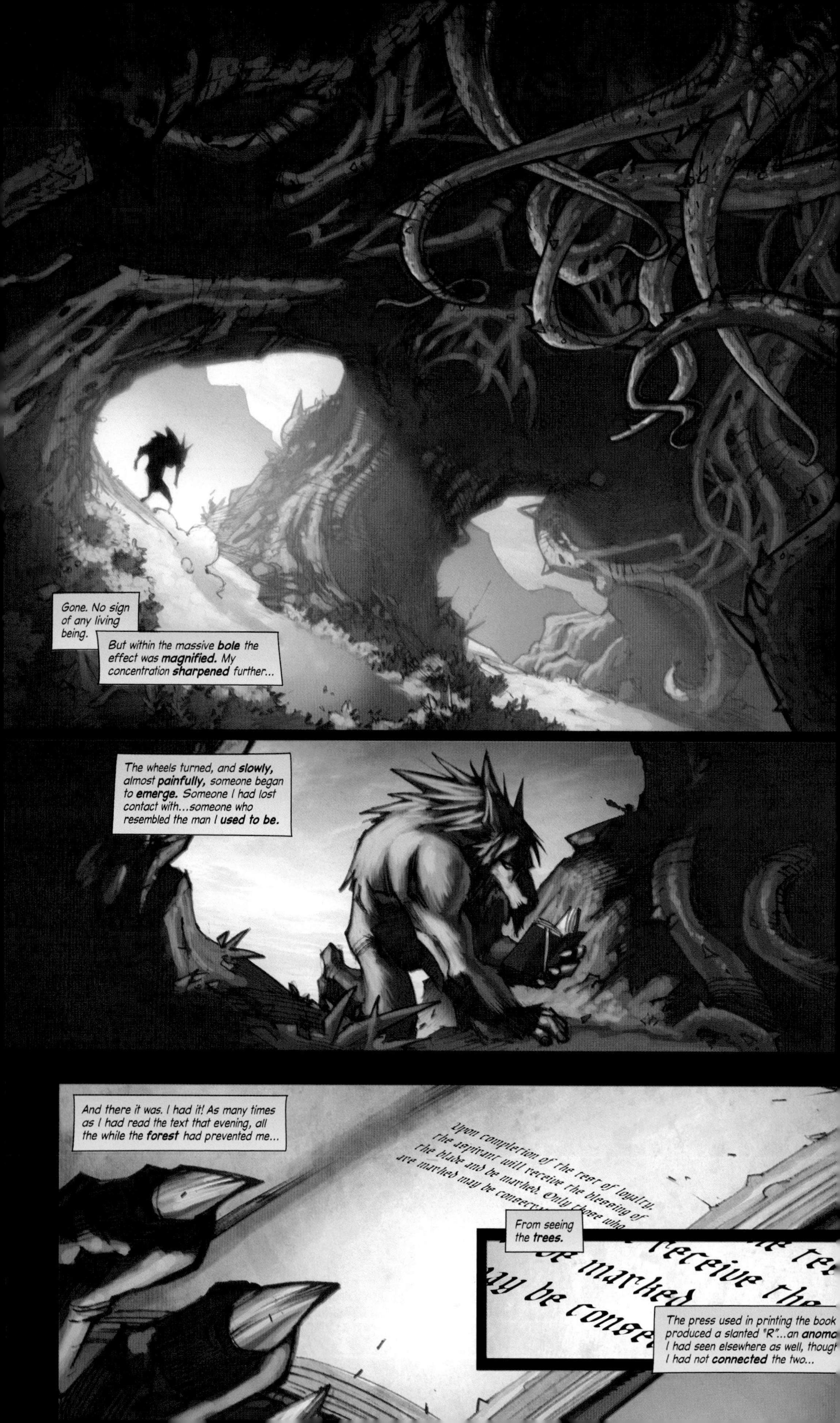

Gone. No sign of any living being.
But within the massive **bole** the effect was **magnified.** My concentration **sharpened** further...
The wheels turned, and **slowly,** almost **painfully,** someone began to **emerge.** Someone I had lost contact with...someone who resembled the man I **used to be.**
And there it was. I had it! As many times as I had read the text that evening, all the while the **forest** had prevented me...
Upon completion of the test of loyalty,
the aspirant will receive the blessing of
the blade and be marked. Only those who
are marked may be
From seeing the **trees.**
The press used in printing the book produced a slanted "R"...an **anoma**
I had seen elsewhere as well, thoug
I had not **connected** the two...

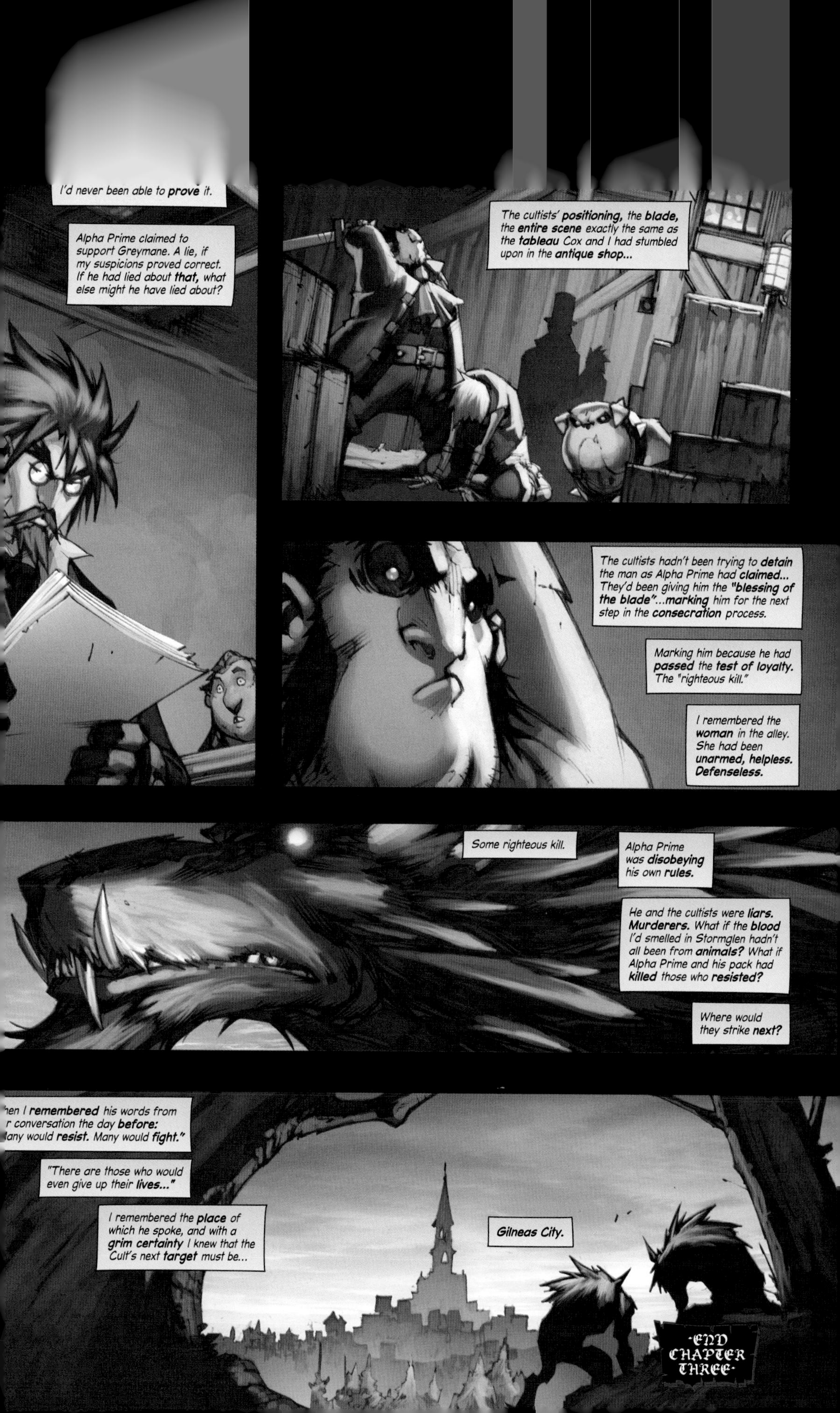
I'd never been able to prove it.
Alpha Prime claimed to support Greymane. A lie, if my suspicions proved correct. If he had lied about that, what else might he have lied about?
The cultists' positioning, the blade, the entire scene exactly the same as the tableau Cox and I had stumbled upon in the antique shop...
The cultists hadn't been trying to detain the man as Alpha Prime had claimed... They'd been giving him the "blessing of the blade"...marking him for the next step in the consecration process.
Marking him because he had passed the test of loyalty. The "righteous kill."
I remembered the woman in the alley. She had been unarmed, helpless. Defenseless.
Some righteous kill.
Alpha Prime was disobeying his own rules.
He and the cultists were liars. Murderers. What if the blood I'd smelled in Stormglen hadn't all been from animals? What if Alpha Prime and his pack had killed those who resisted?
Where would they strike next?
hen I remembered his words from r conversation the day before: lany would resist. Many would fight."
"There are those who would even give up their lives..."
I remembered the place of which he spoke, and with a grim certainty I knew that the Cult's next target must be...
Gilneas City.
END CHAPTER THREE

CHAPTER 4 Cover by Glenn Rane

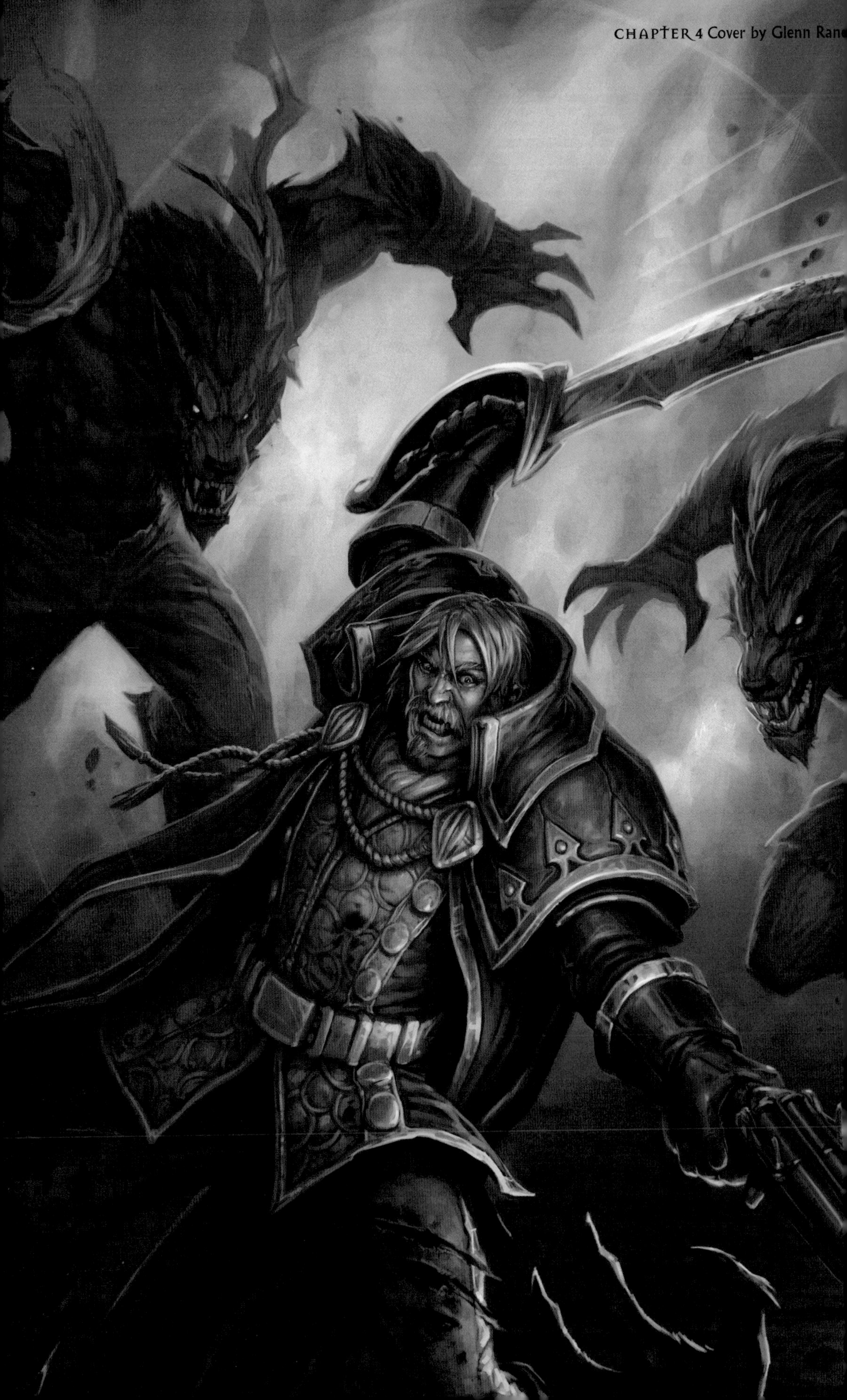

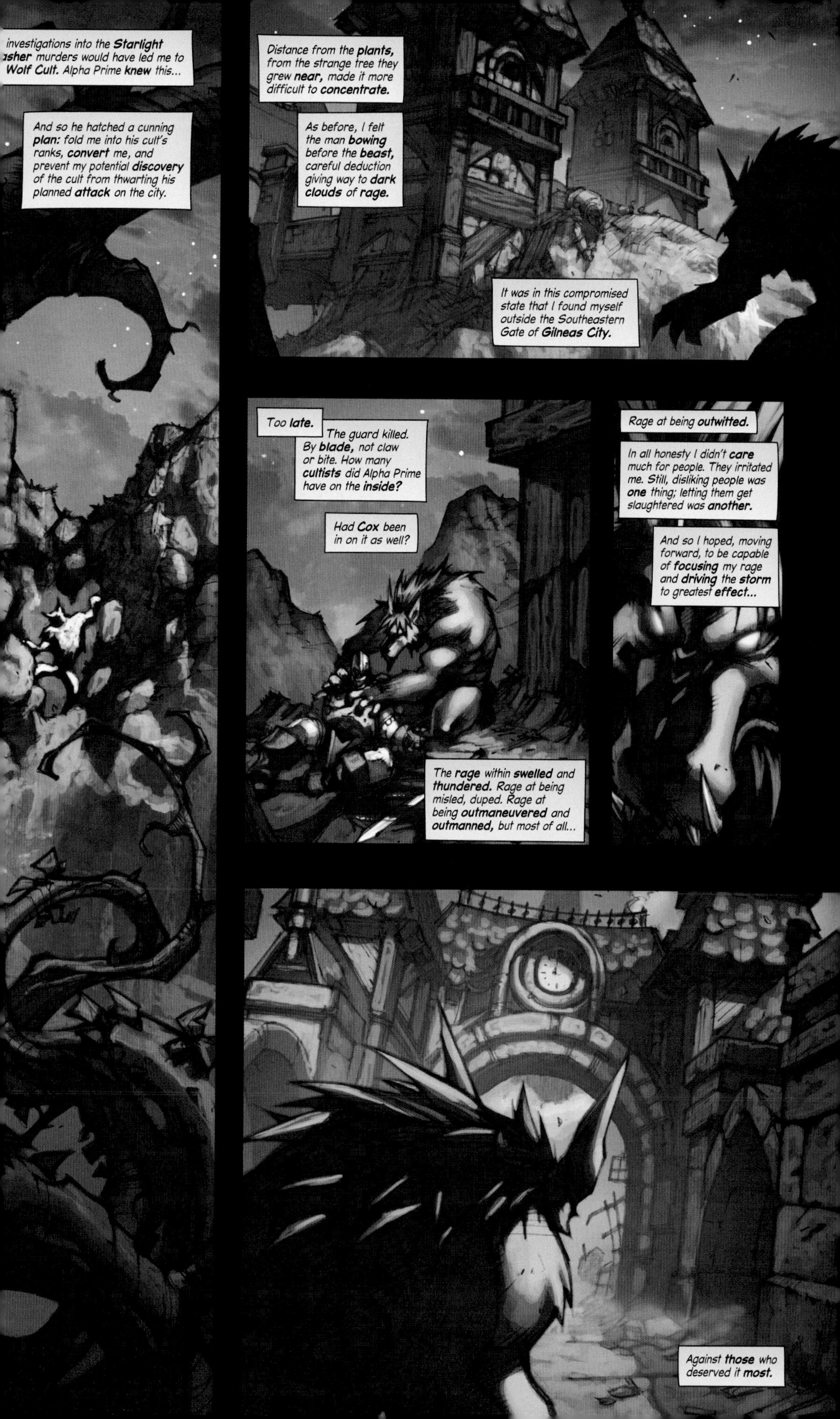

investigations into the Starlight
ısher murders would have led me to
Wolf Cult. Alpha Prime knew this...
And so he hatched a cunning plan: fold me into his cult's ranks, convert me, and prevent my potential discovery of the cult from thwarting his planned attack on the city.
Distance from the plants, from the strange tree they grew near, made it more difficult to concentrate.
As before, I felt the man bowing before the beast, careful deduction giving way to dark clouds of rage.
It was in this compromised state that I found myself outside the Southeastern Gate of Gilneas City.
Too late.
The guard killed. By blade, not claw or bite. How many cultists did Alpha Prime have on the inside?
Had Cox been in on it as well?
The rage within swelled and thundered. Rage at being misled, duped. Rage at being outmaneuvered and outmanned, but most of all...
Rage at being outwitted.
In all honesty I didn't care much for people. They irritated me. Still, disliking people was one thing; letting them get slaughtered was another.
And so I hoped, moving forward, to be capable of focusing my rage and driving the storm to greatest effect...
Against those who deserved it most.

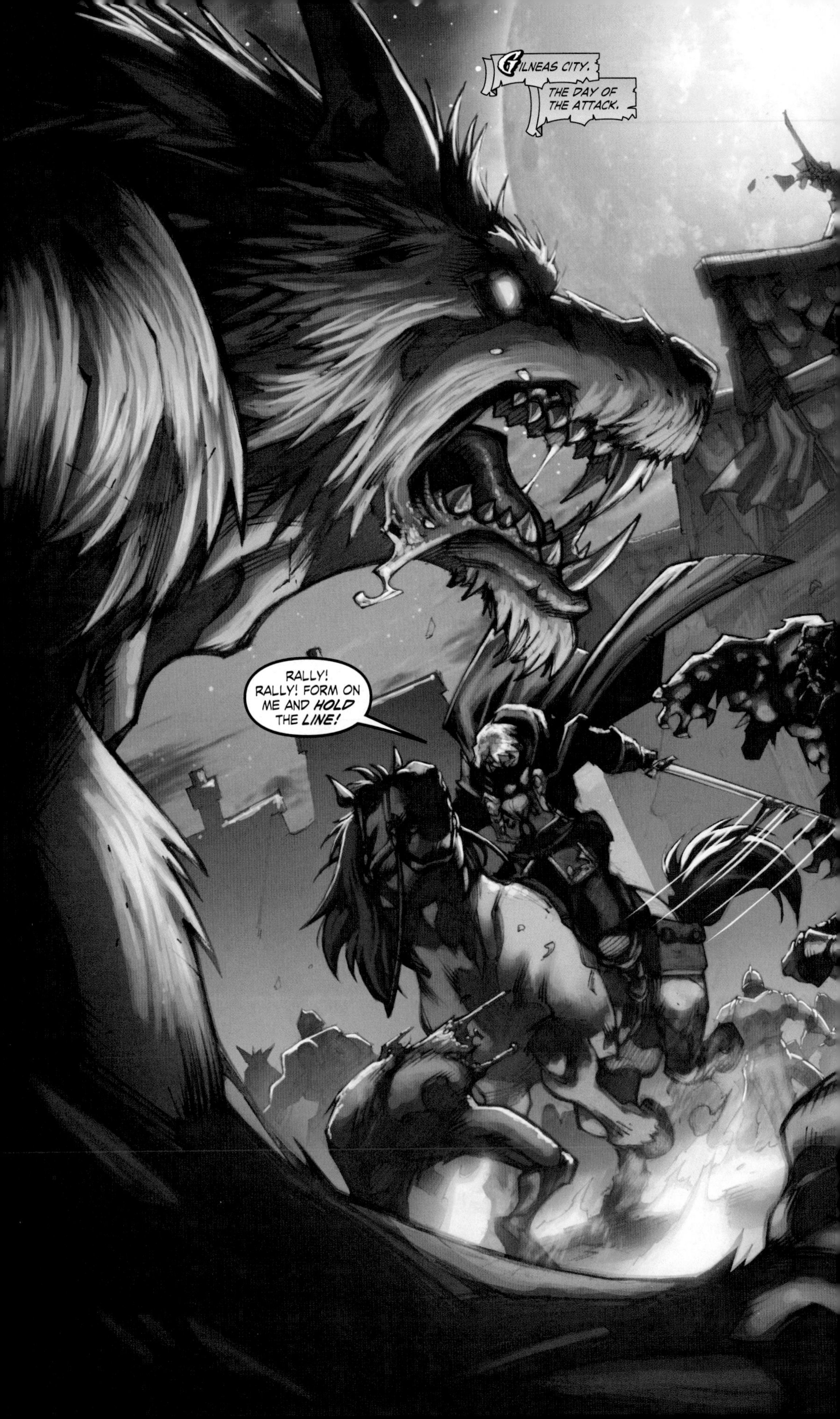
GILNEAS CITY.
THE DAY OF THE ATTACK.
RALLY! RALLY! FORM ON ME AND HOLD THE LINE!

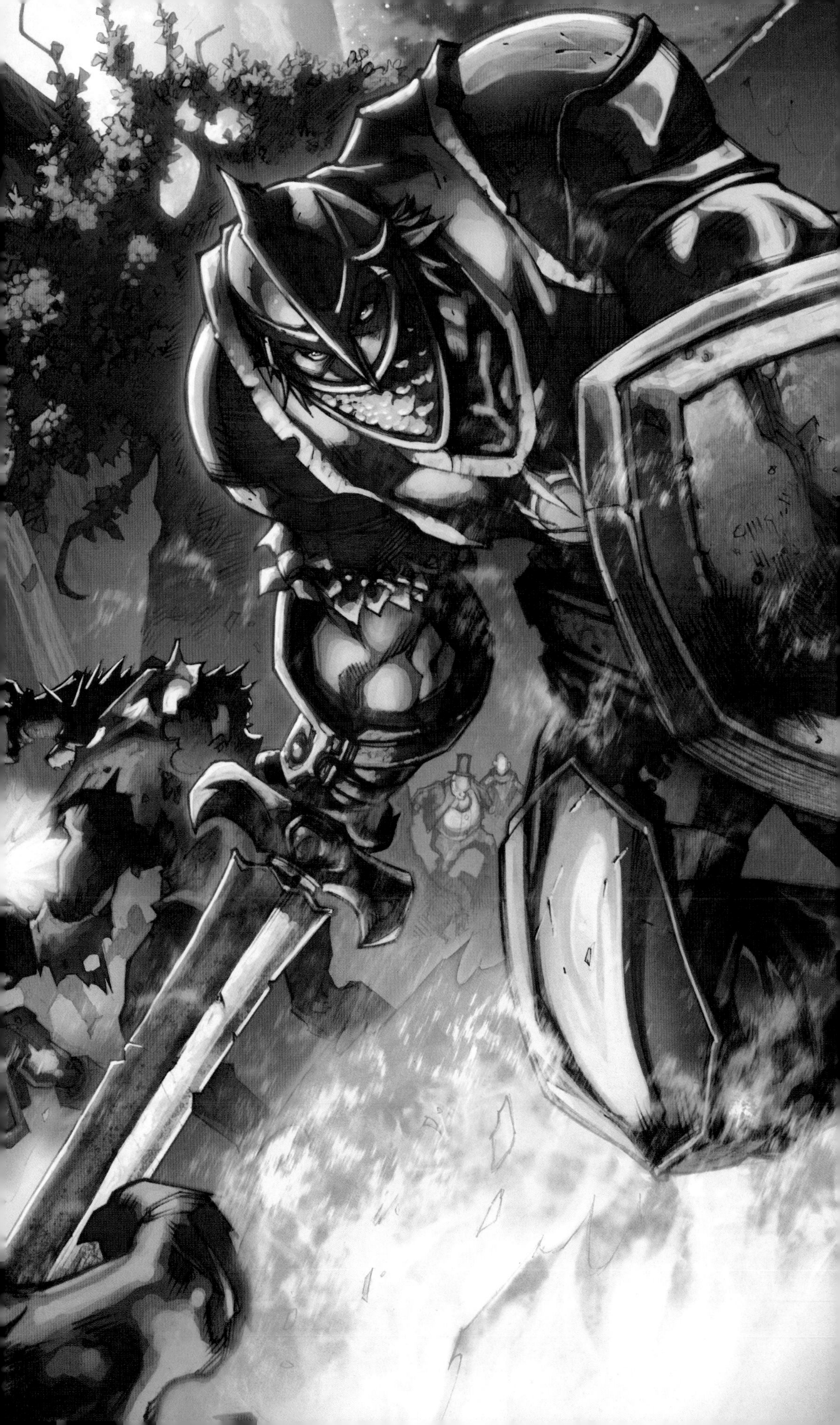

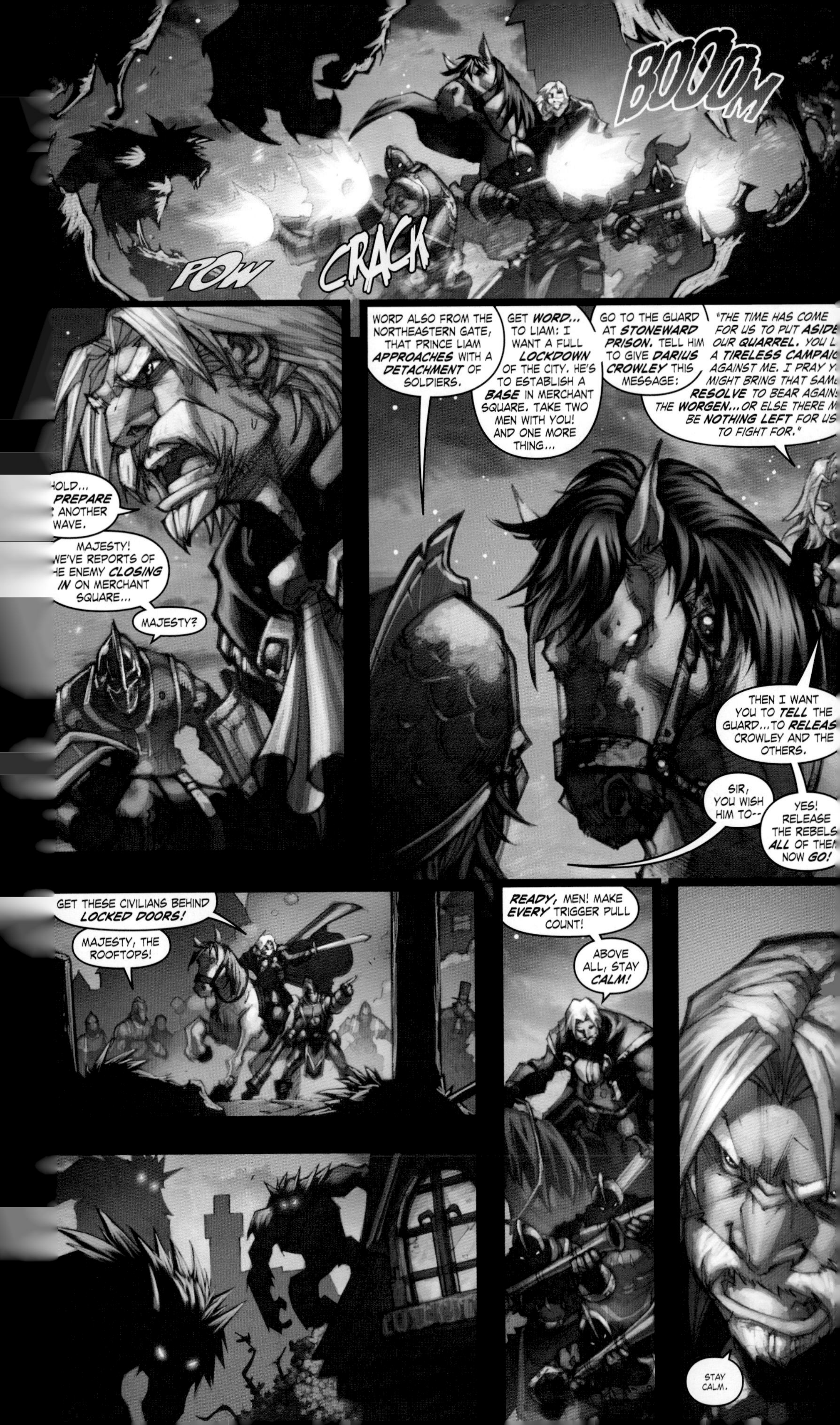
BOOOM
POW
CRACK
HOLD... PREPARE ANOTHER WAVE.
MAJESTY! WE'VE REPORTS OF THE ENEMY CLOSING IN ON MERCHANT SQUARE...
MAJESTY?
WORD ALSO FROM THE NORTHEASTERN GATE, THAT PRINCE LIAM APPROACHES WITH A DETACHMENT OF SOLDIERS.
GET WORD... TO LIAM: I WANT A FULL LOCKDOWN OF THE CITY. HE'S TO ESTABLISH A BASE IN MERCHANT SQUARE. TAKE TWO MEN WITH YOU! AND ONE MORE THING...
GO TO THE GUARD AT STONEWARD PRISON. TELL HIM TO GIVE DARIUS CROWLEY THIS MESSAGE:
THEN I WANT YOU TO TELL THE GUARD...TO RELEAS CROWLEY AND THE OTHERS.
SIR, YOU WISH HIM TO--
YES! RELEASE THE REBELS ALL OF THE NOW GO!
GET THESE CIVILIANS BEHIND LOCKED DOORS!
MAJESTY, THE ROOFTOPS!
READY, MEN! MAKE EVERY TRIGGER PULL COUNT!
ABOVE ALL, STAY CALM!
STAY CALM.

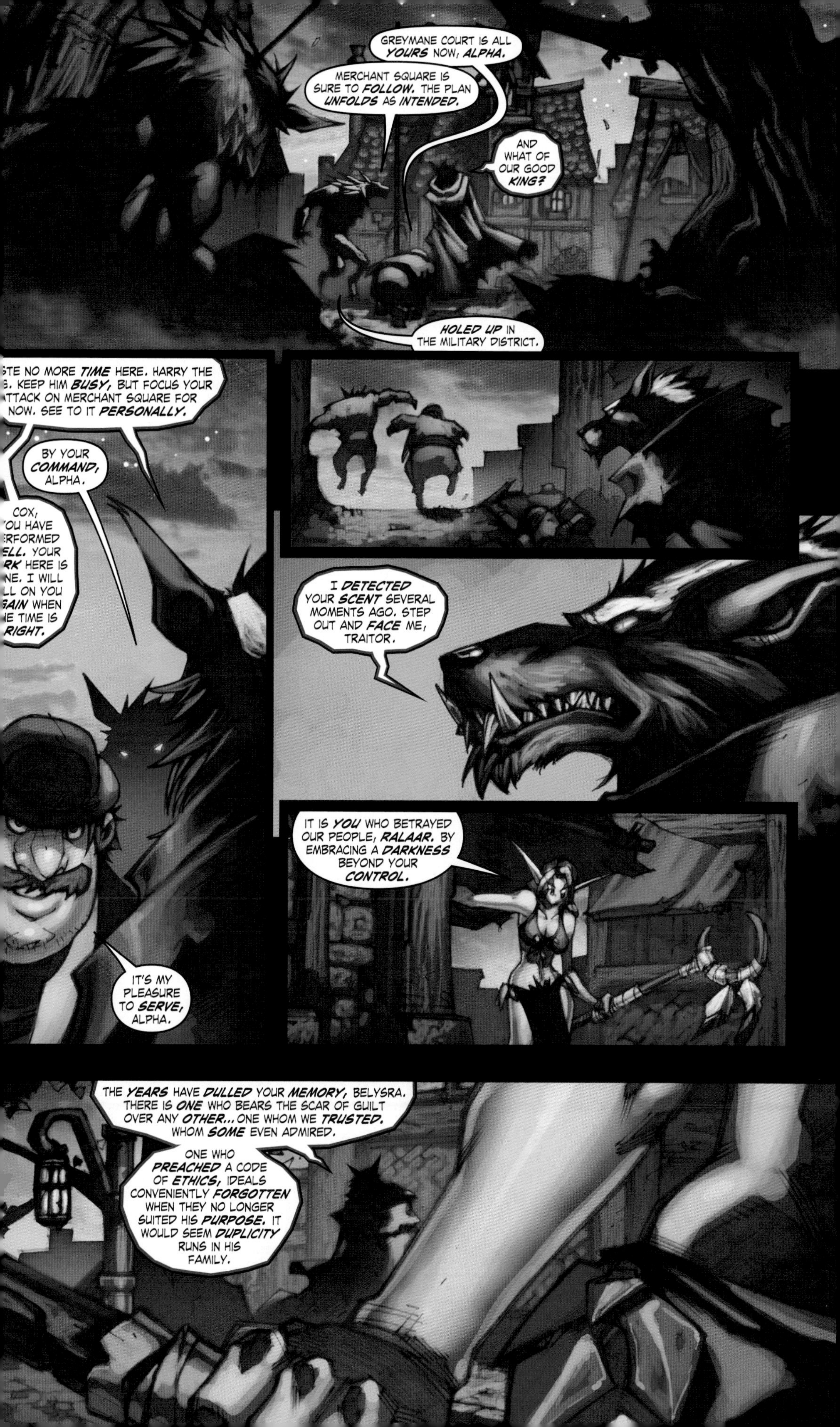
GREYMANE COURT IS ALL YOURS NOW, ALPHA.
MERCHANT SQUARE IS SURE TO FOLLOW. THE PLAN UNFOLDS AS INTENDED.
AND WHAT OF OUR GOOD KING?
HOLED UP IN THE MILITARY DISTRICT.
STE NO MORE TIME HERE. HARRY THE G. KEEP HIM BUSY, BUT FOCUS YOUR TTACK ON MERCHANT SQUARE FOR NOW. SEE TO IT PERSONALLY.
BY YOUR COMMAND, ALPHA.
COX, OU HAVE RFORMED ELL. YOUR RK HERE IS NE. I WILL LL ON YOU GAIN WHEN E TIME IS RIGHT.
IT'S MY PLEASURE TO SERVE, ALPHA.
I DETECTED YOUR SCENT SEVERAL MOMENTS AGO. STEP OUT AND FACE ME, TRAITOR.
IT IS YOU WHO BETRAYED OUR PEOPLE, RALAAR. BY EMBRACING A DARKNESS BEYOND YOUR CONTROL.
THE YEARS HAVE DULLED YOUR MEMORY, BELYSRA. THERE IS ONE WHO BEARS THE SCAR OF GUILT OVER ANY OTHER... ONE WHOM WE TRUSTED. WHOM SOME EVEN ADMIRED.
ONE WHO PREACHED A CODE OF ETHICS, IDEALS CONVENIENTLY FORGOTTEN WHEN THEY NO LONGER SUITED HIS PURPOSE. IT WOULD SEEM DUPLICITY RUNS IN HIS FAMILY.

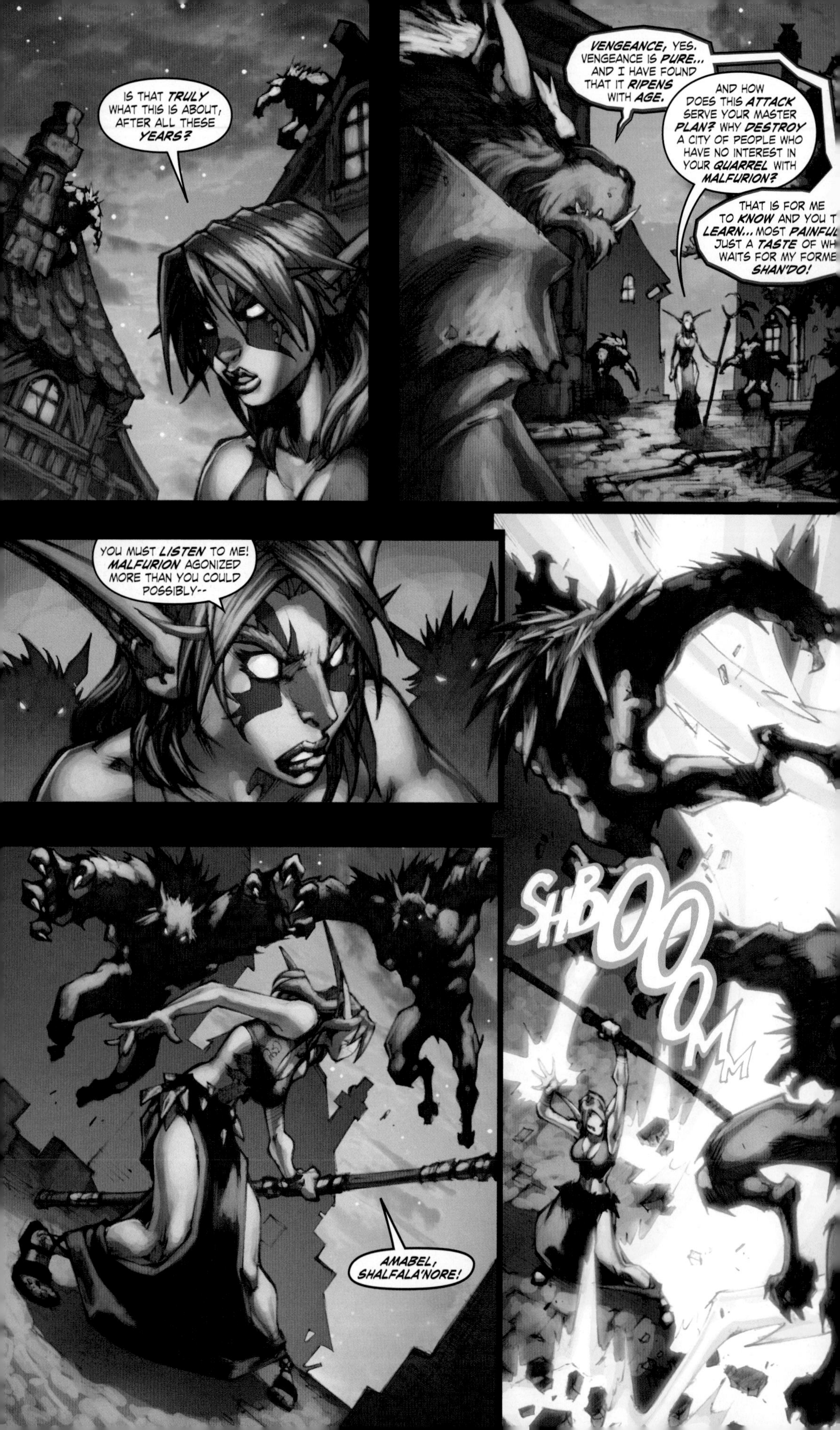
IS THAT TRULY WHAT THIS IS ABOUT, AFTER ALL THESE YEARS?
VENGEANCE, YES. VENGEANCE IS PURE... AND I HAVE FOUND THAT IT RIPENS WITH AGE.
AND HOW DOES THIS ATTACK SERVE YOUR MASTER PLAN? WHY DESTROY A CITY OF PEOPLE WHO HAVE NO INTEREST IN YOUR QUARREL WITH MALFURION?
THAT IS FOR ME TO KNOW AND YOU T LEARN... MOST PAINFUL JUST A TASTE OF WH WAITS FOR MY FORME SHAN'DO!
YOU MUST LISTEN TO ME! MALFURION AGONIZED MORE THAN YOU COULD POSSIBLY--
AMABEL, SHALFALA'NORE!
SHBOOOOMM

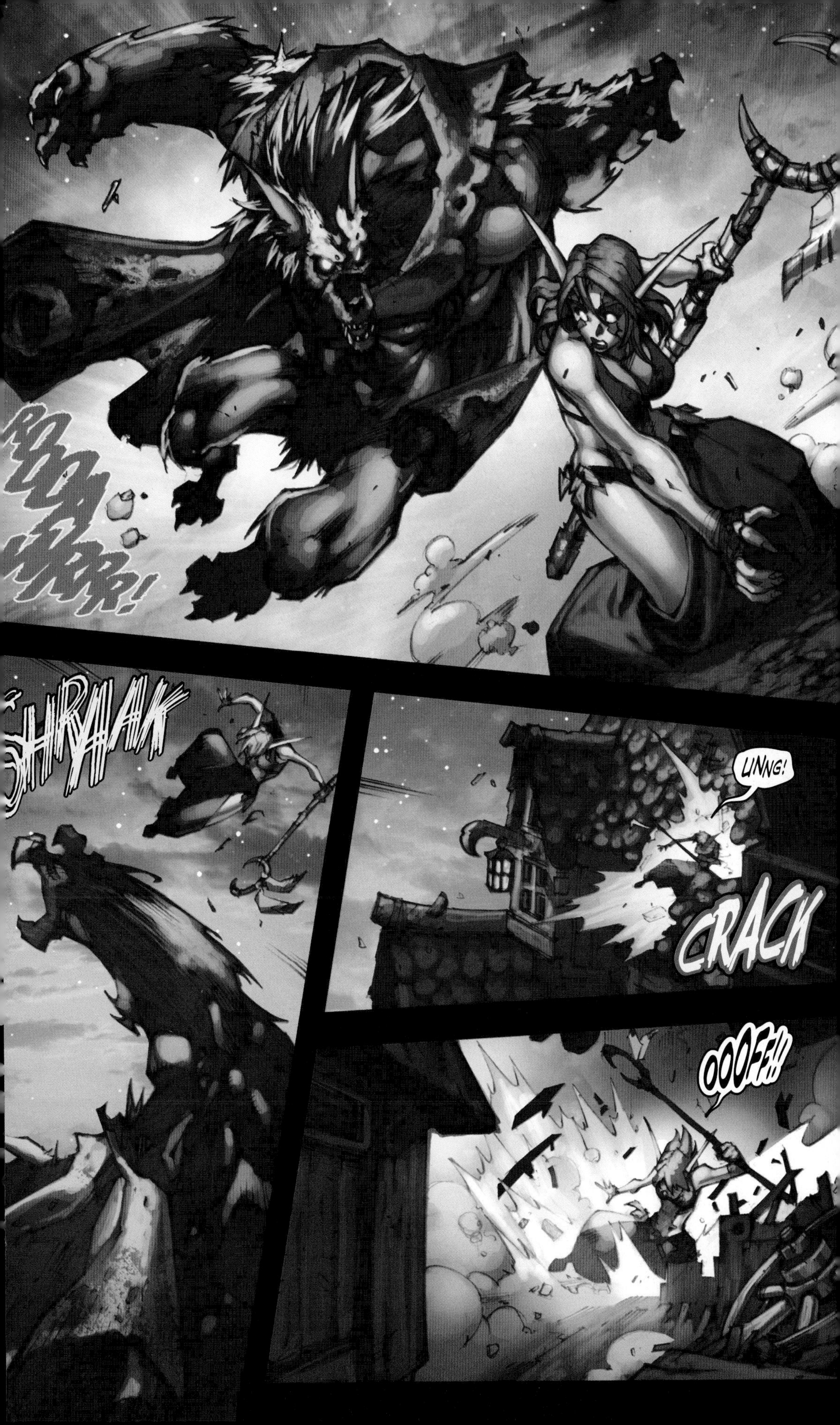
UNNG!
CRACK
OOOFF!!

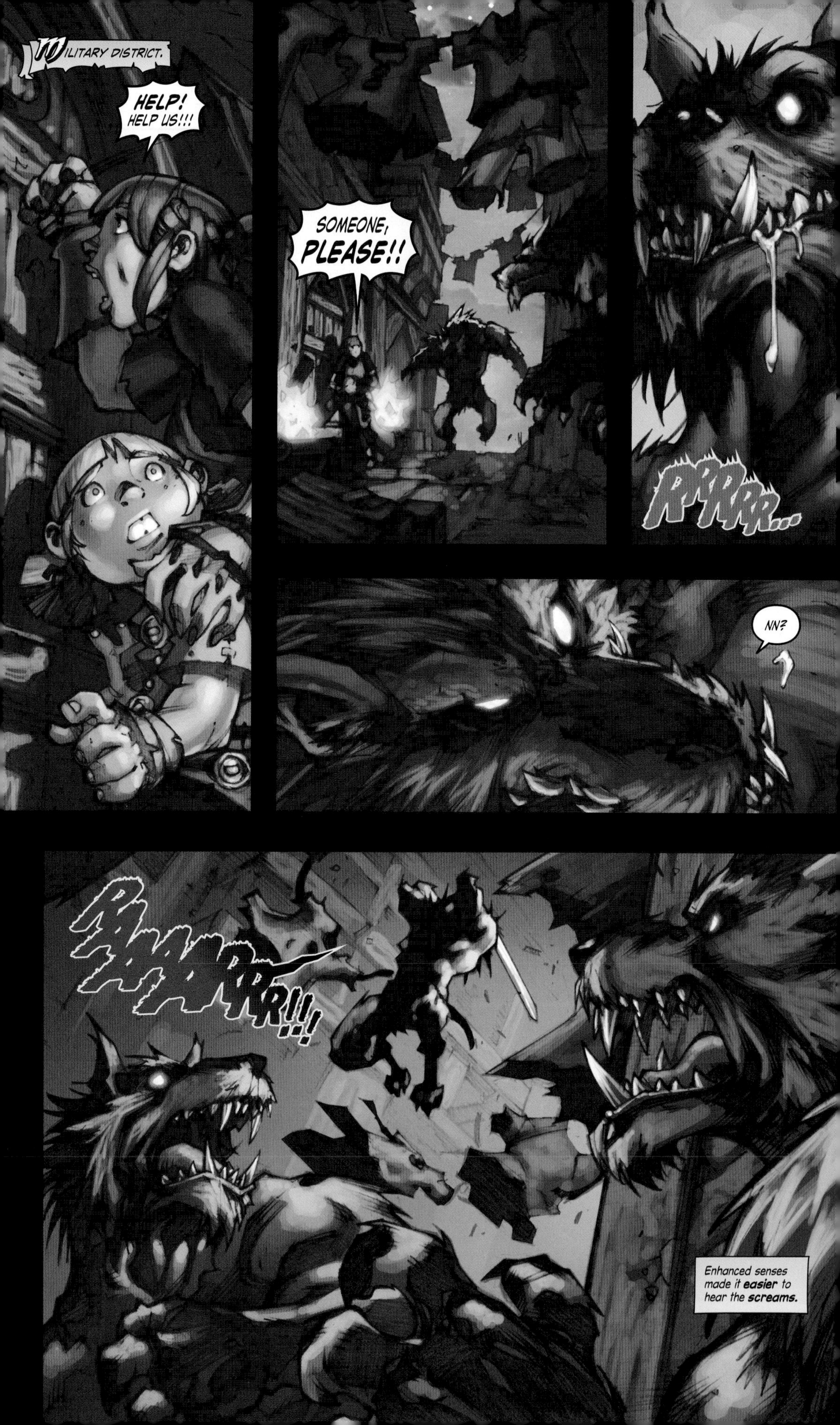
Military district.
HELP! HELP US!!!
SOMEONE, PLEASE!!
RRRRR...
NN?
RAAARRRAARRRR!!!
Enhanced senses made it **easier** to hear the **screams.**

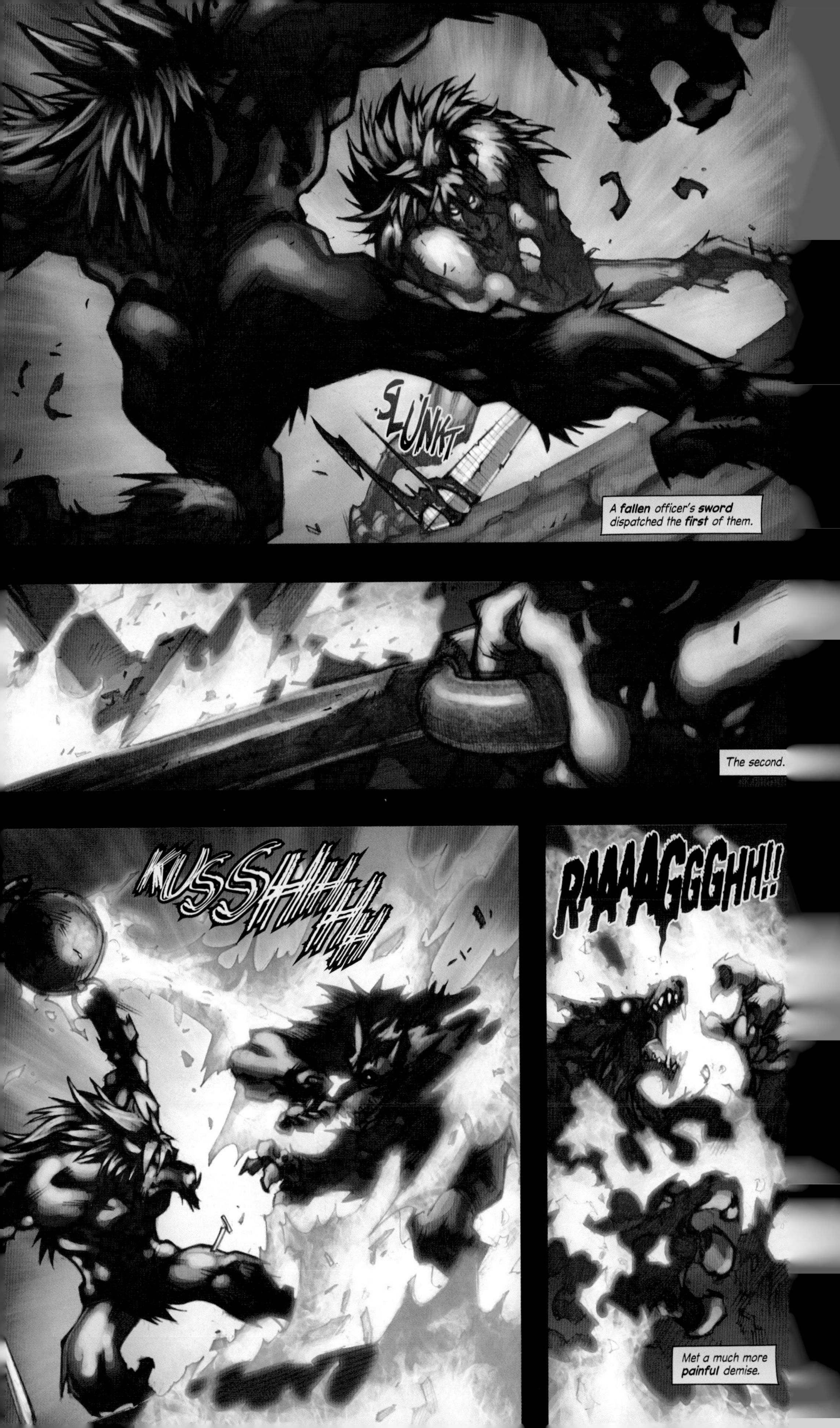
SLUNKT
A fallen officer's sword dispatched the first of them.
The second.
KUSSHHHH
RAAAAGGGHH!!
Met a much more painful demise.

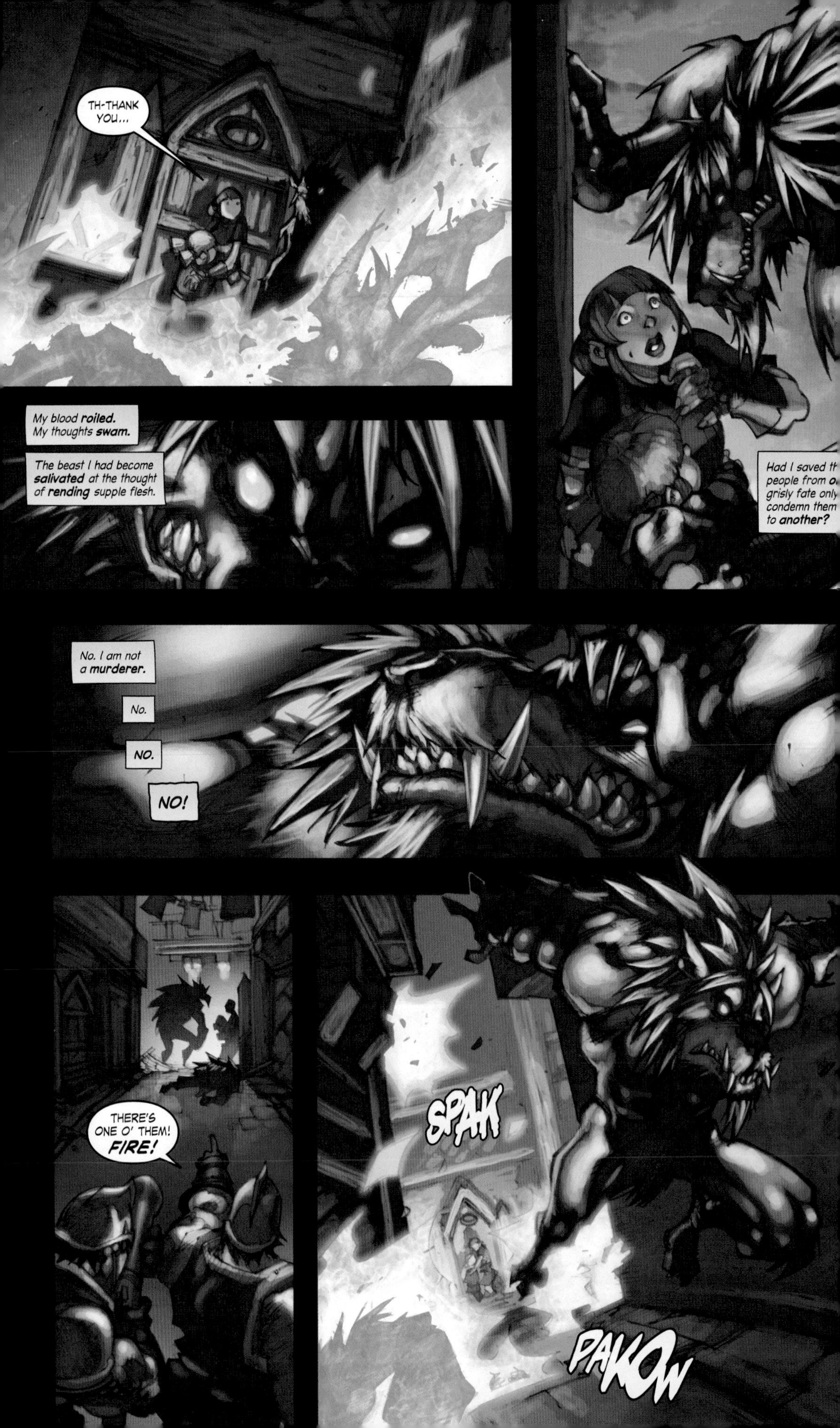

TH-THANK YOU...
My blood roiled. My thoughts swam.
The beast I had become salivated at the thought of rending supple flesh.
Had I saved th people from o grisly fate only condemn them to another?
No. I am not a murderer.
No.
NO.
NO!
THERE'S ONE O' THEM! FIRE!
SPAK
PAKOW

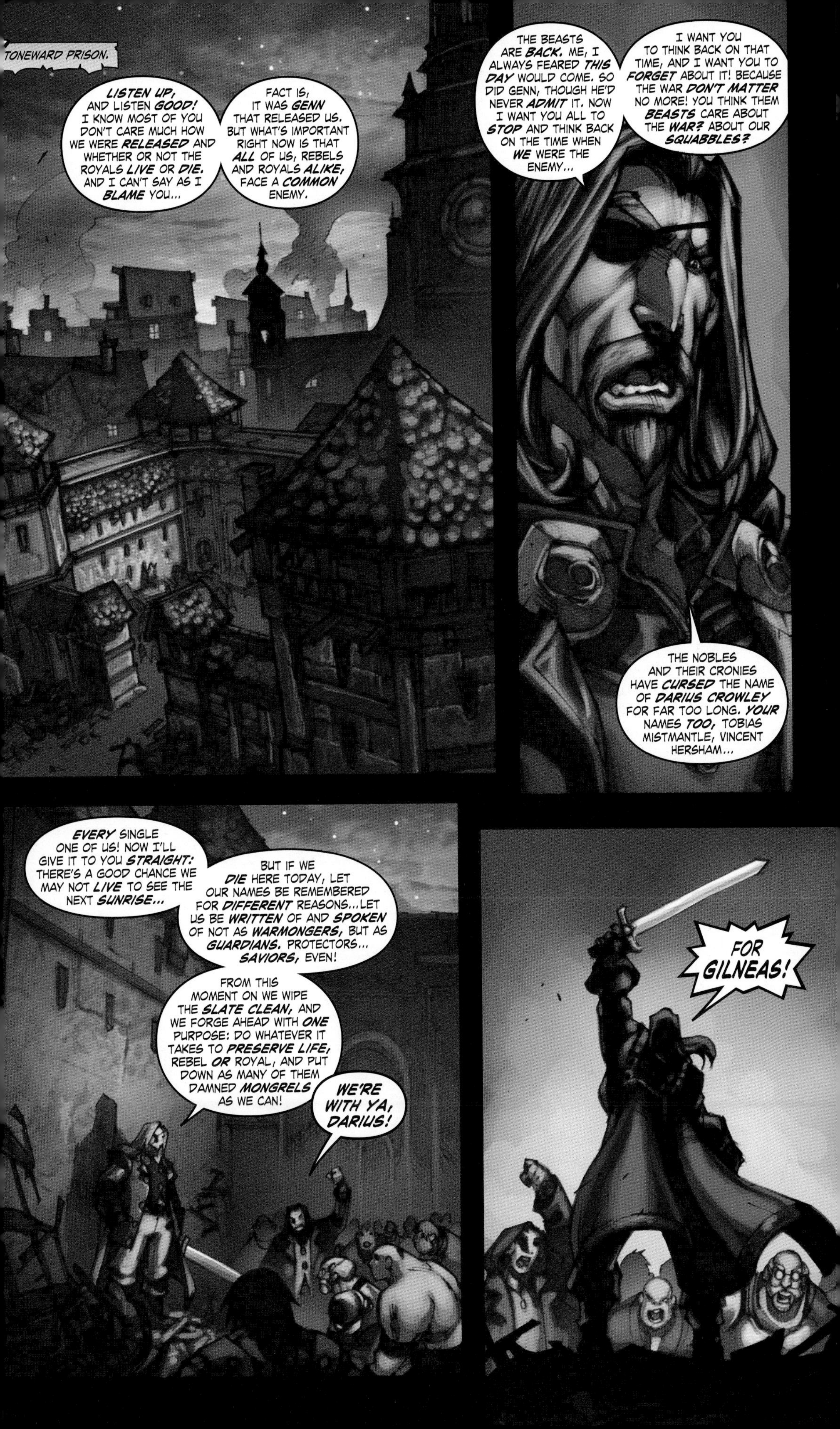
TONEWARD PRISON.
LISTEN UP, AND LISTEN GOOD! I KNOW MOST OF YOU DON'T CARE MUCH HOW WE WERE RELEASED AND WHETHER OR NOT THE ROYALS LIVE OR DIE. AND I CAN'T SAY AS I BLAME YOU...
FACT IS, IT WAS GENN THAT RELEASED US. BUT WHAT'S IMPORTANT RIGHT NOW IS THAT ALL OF US, REBELS AND ROYALS ALIKE, FACE A COMMON ENEMY.
THE BEASTS ARE BACK. ME, I ALWAYS FEARED THIS DAY WOULD COME. SO DID GENN, THOUGH HE'D NEVER ADMIT IT. NOW I WANT YOU ALL TO STOP AND THINK BACK ON THE TIME WHEN WE WERE THE ENEMY...
I WANT YOU TO THINK BACK ON THAT TIME, AND I WANT YOU TO FORGET ABOUT IT! BECAUSE THE WAR DON'T MATTER NO MORE! YOU THINK THEM BEASTS CARE ABOUT THE WAR? ABOUT OUR SQUABBLES?
THE NOBLES AND THEIR CRONIES HAVE CURSED THE NAME OF DARIUS CROWLEY FOR FAR TOO LONG. YOUR NAMES TOO, TOBIAS MISTMANTLE, VINCENT HERSHAM...
EVERY SINGLE ONE OF US! NOW I'LL GIVE IT TO YOU STRAIGHT: THERE'S A GOOD CHANCE WE MAY NOT LIVE TO SEE THE NEXT SUNRISE...
BUT IF WE DIE HERE TODAY, LET OUR NAMES BE REMEMBERED FOR DIFFERENT REASONS...LET US BE WRITTEN OF AND SPOKEN OF NOT AS WARMONGERS, BUT AS GUARDIANS. PROTECTORS... SAVIORS, EVEN!
FROM THIS MOMENT ON WE WIPE THE SLATE CLEAN, AND WE FORGE AHEAD WITH ONE PURPOSE: DO WHATEVER IT TAKES TO PRESERVE LIFE, REBEL OR ROYAL, AND PUT DOWN AS MANY OF THEM DAMNED MONGRELS AS WE CAN!
WE'RE WITH YA, DARIUS!
FOR GILNEAS!

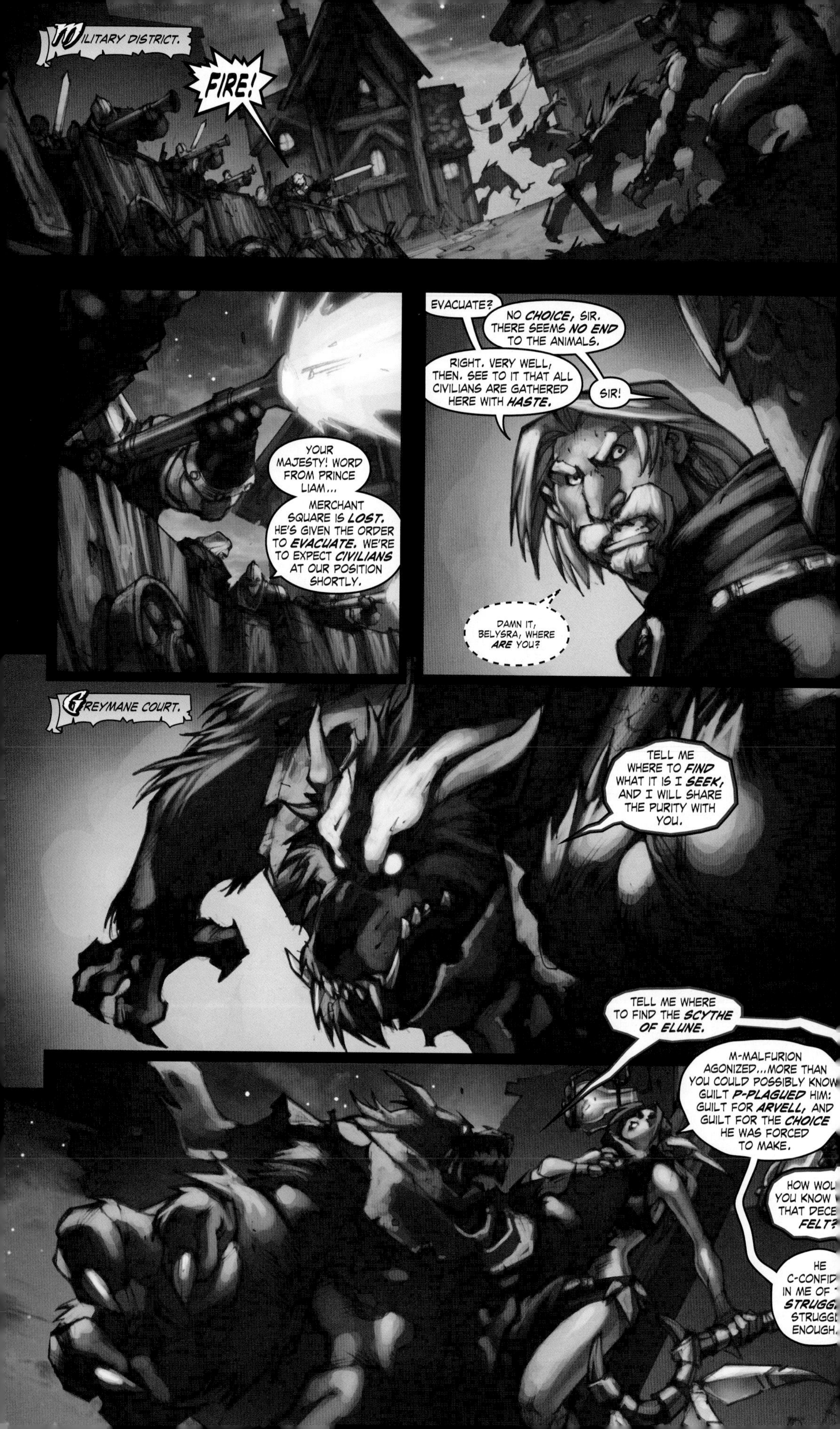
MILITARY DISTRICT.
FIRE!
YOUR MAJESTY! WORD FROM PRINCE LIAM...
MERCHANT SQUARE IS LOST. HE'S GIVEN THE ORDER TO EVACUATE. WE'RE TO EXPECT CIVILIANS AT OUR POSITION SHORTLY.
EVACUATE?
NO CHOICE, SIR. THERE SEEMS NO END TO THE ANIMALS.
RIGHT. VERY WELL, THEN. SEE TO IT THAT ALL CIVILIANS ARE GATHERED HERE WITH HASTE.
SIR!
DAMN IT, BELYSRA, WHERE ARE YOU?
GREYMANE COURT.
TELL ME WHERE TO FIND WHAT IT IS I SEEK, AND I WILL SHARE THE PURITY WITH YOU.
TELL ME WHERE TO FIND THE SCYTHE OF ELUNE.
M-MALFURION AGONIZED...MORE THAN YOU COULD POSSIBLY KNOW. GUILT P-PLAGUED HIM: GUILT FOR ARVELL, AND GUILT FOR THE CHOICE HE WAS FORCED TO MAKE.
HOW WOL YOU KNOW THAT DECE FELT?
HE C-CONFID IN ME OF STRUGG STRUGG ENOUGH.

"TO WARRANT AN *AUDIENCE*... WITH THE DEMIGOD *CENARIUS* HIMSELF..."

SHAN'DO...I SEEK YOUR COUNSEL ONCE MORE. THE PATH I AM SET TO TREAD IS NOT ONE I WISH TO EMBARK UPON WITHOUT YOUR...ASSENT.

THERE COMES A TIME, THERO'SHAN, TO LET GO OF THE NEED FOR MY APPROVAL. YOU MUST EMBRACE WHAT YOU HAVE BECOME, MALFURION STORMRAGE. SOMEONE LOOKED TO AS A LEADER.

A TRUE ARCHDRUID. THOSE OF YOUR ORDER WILL TRUST YOU TO CHOOSE THE RIGHT PATH AND AVOID THAT WHICH WILL LEAD THEM ASTRAY.

KNOW THAT THE MANTLE OF LEADERSHIP IS ONE OF GREAT BURDEN. YOU MUST TAKE OWNERSHIP OF YOUR DECISIONS, FOR GOOD OR ILL. SEEK COUNSEL, YES, BUT NOT PERMISSION.

THIS MAY BE TRUE... BUT, LONG AGO RALAAR POSSESSED GREATEST OF POTENTIAL, YET ALSO WITHIN HIM I DETECTED A SMOLDERING FIRE. I THOUGHT THAT...HE REMINDED ME OF...

I THOUGHT THAT THERE WOULD COME A TIME WHEN WOULD LEARN TO EXTINGUISH HIS RAGE... PERHAPS THIS IS TRULY MY FAILURE MORE THAN IT IS HIS.

WE ARE NOT IN AGREEMENT ON THIS. RALAAR'S DECISIONS WERE HIS OWN. THE CHOICES WE MAKE ARE INEVITABLY WHAT DEFINE US. RALAAR MADE HIS CHOICE. NOT YOU.

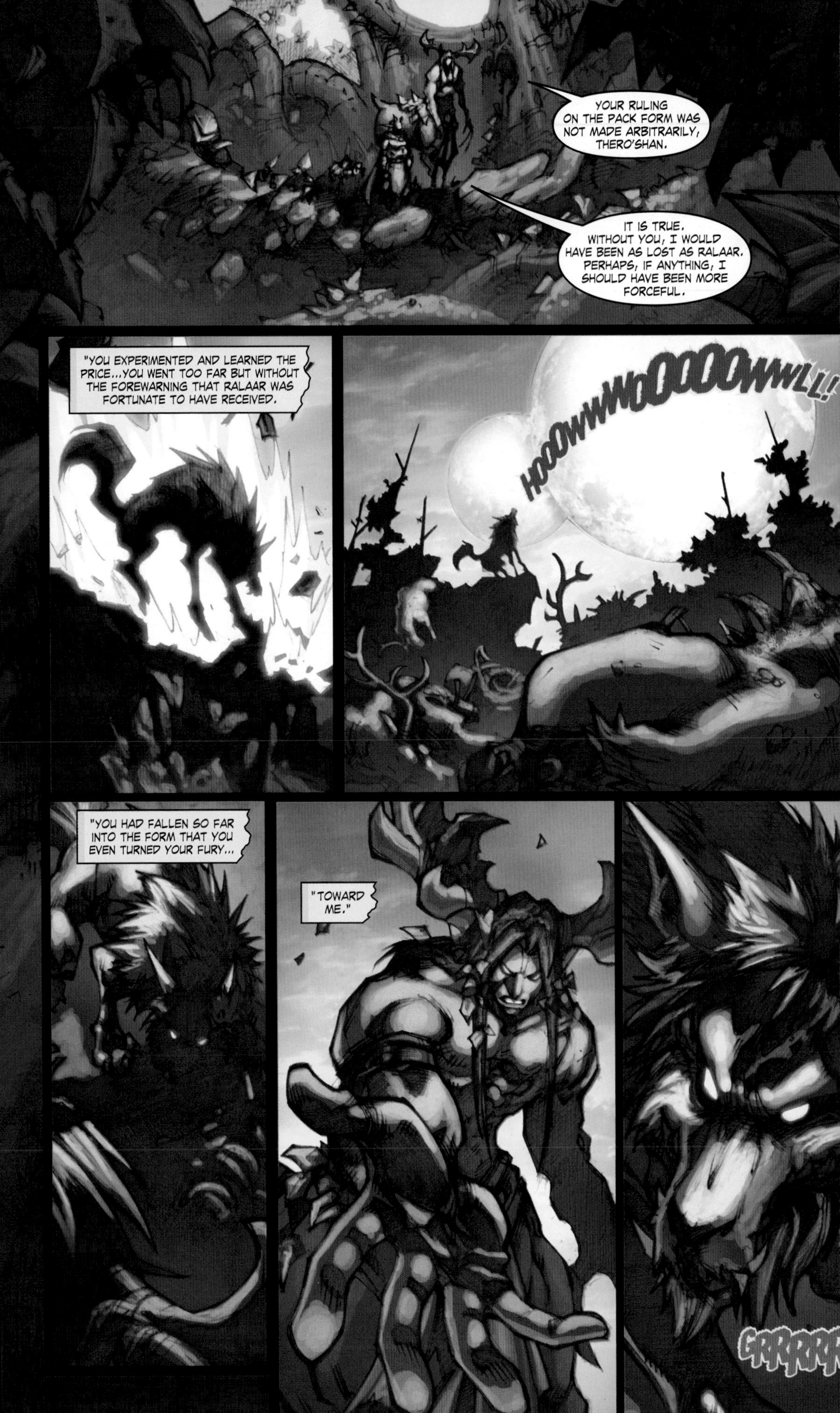
YOUR RULING ON THE PACK FORM WAS NOT MADE ARBITRARILY, THERO'SHAN.
IT IS TRUE. WITHOUT YOU, I WOULD HAVE BEEN AS LOST AS RALAAR. PERHAPS, IF ANYTHING, I SHOULD HAVE BEEN MORE FORCEFUL.
"YOU EXPERIMENTED AND LEARNED THE PRICE...YOU WENT TOO FAR BUT WITHOUT THE FOREWARNING THAT RALAAR WAS FORTUNATE TO HAVE RECEIVED.
HOOOWWWOOOOOWWLL!
"YOU HAD FALLEN SO FAR INTO THE FORM THAT YOU EVEN TURNED YOUR FURY...
"TOWARD ME."
GRRRRR

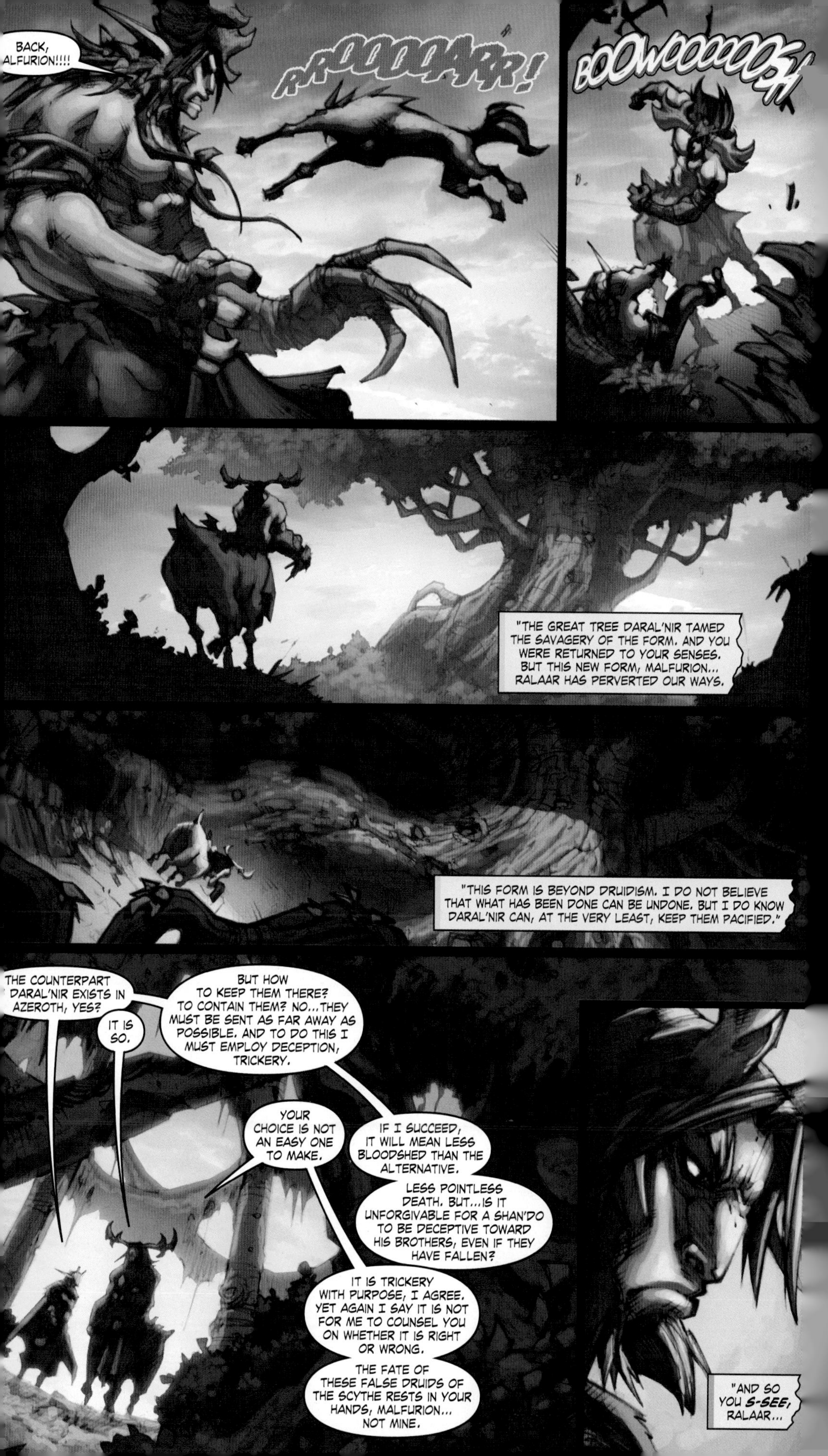
BACK, ALFURION!!!!
RRROOOOARRR!
BOOWOOOOOOSH
"THE GREAT TREE DARAL'NIR TAMED THE SAVAGERY OF THE FORM, AND YOU WERE RETURNED TO YOUR SENSES. BUT THIS NEW FORM, MALFURION... RALAAR HAS PERVERTED OUR WAYS.
"THIS FORM IS BEYOND DRUIDISM. I DO NOT BELIEVE THAT WHAT HAS BEEN DONE CAN BE UNDONE. BUT I DO KNOW DARAL'NIR CAN, AT THE VERY LEAST, KEEP THEM PACIFIED."
THE COUNTERPART DARAL'NIR EXISTS IN AZEROTH, YES?
IT IS SO.
BUT HOW TO KEEP THEM THERE? TO CONTAIN THEM? NO...THEY MUST BE SENT AS FAR AWAY AS POSSIBLE. AND TO DO THIS I MUST EMPLOY DECEPTION, TRICKERY.
IF I SUCCEED, IT WILL MEAN LESS BLOODSHED THAN THE ALTERNATIVE.
LESS POINTLESS DEATH. BUT...IS IT UNFORGIVABLE FOR A SHAN'DO TO BE DECEPTIVE TOWARD HIS BROTHERS, EVEN IF THEY HAVE FALLEN?
YOUR CHOICE IS NOT AN EASY ONE TO MAKE.
IT IS TRICKERY WITH PURPOSE, I AGREE. YET AGAIN I SAY IT IS NOT FOR ME TO COUNSEL YOU ON WHETHER IT IS RIGHT OR WRONG.
THE FATE OF THESE FALSE DRUIDS OF THE SCYTHE RESTS IN YOUR HANDS, MALFURION... NOT MINE.
"AND SO YOU ***S-SEE,*** RALAAR...

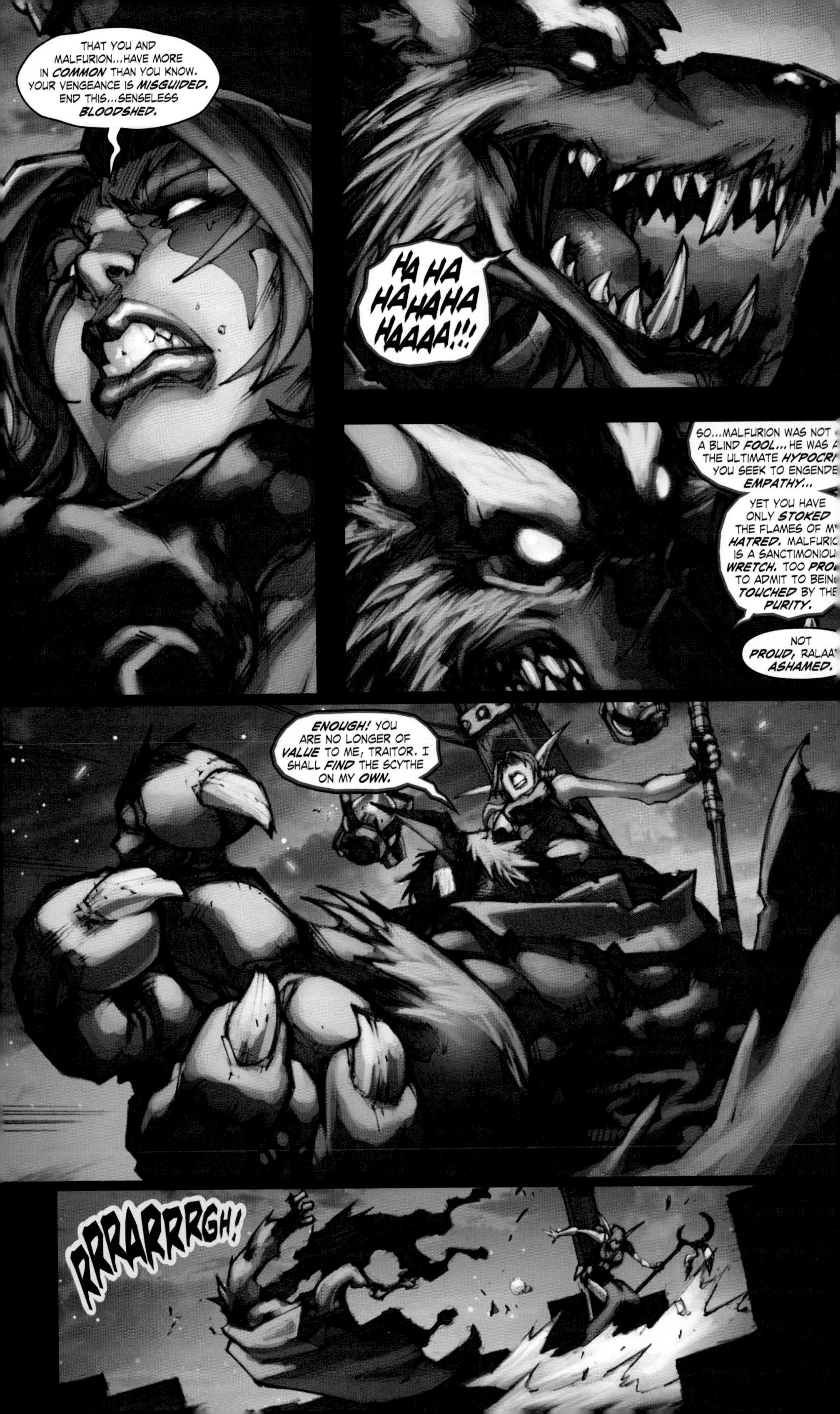
THAT YOU AND MALFURION...HAVE MORE IN COMMON THAN YOU KNOW. YOUR VENGEANCE IS MISGUIDED. END THIS...SENSELESS BLOODSHED.
HA HA HAHAHA HAAAA!!!
SO...MALFURION WAS NOT A BLIND FOOL...HE WAS A THE ULTIMATE HYPOCRI YOU SEEK TO ENGENDE EMPATHY...
YET YOU HAVE ONLY STOKED THE FLAMES OF MY HATRED. MALFURIC IS A SANCTIMONIOU WRETCH. TOO PRO TO ADMIT TO BEIN TOUCHED BY THE PURITY.
NOT PROUD, RALAA ASHAMED.
ENOUGH! YOU ARE NO LONGER OF VALUE TO ME, TRAITOR. I SHALL FIND THE SCYTHE ON MY OWN.
RRRARRRGH!

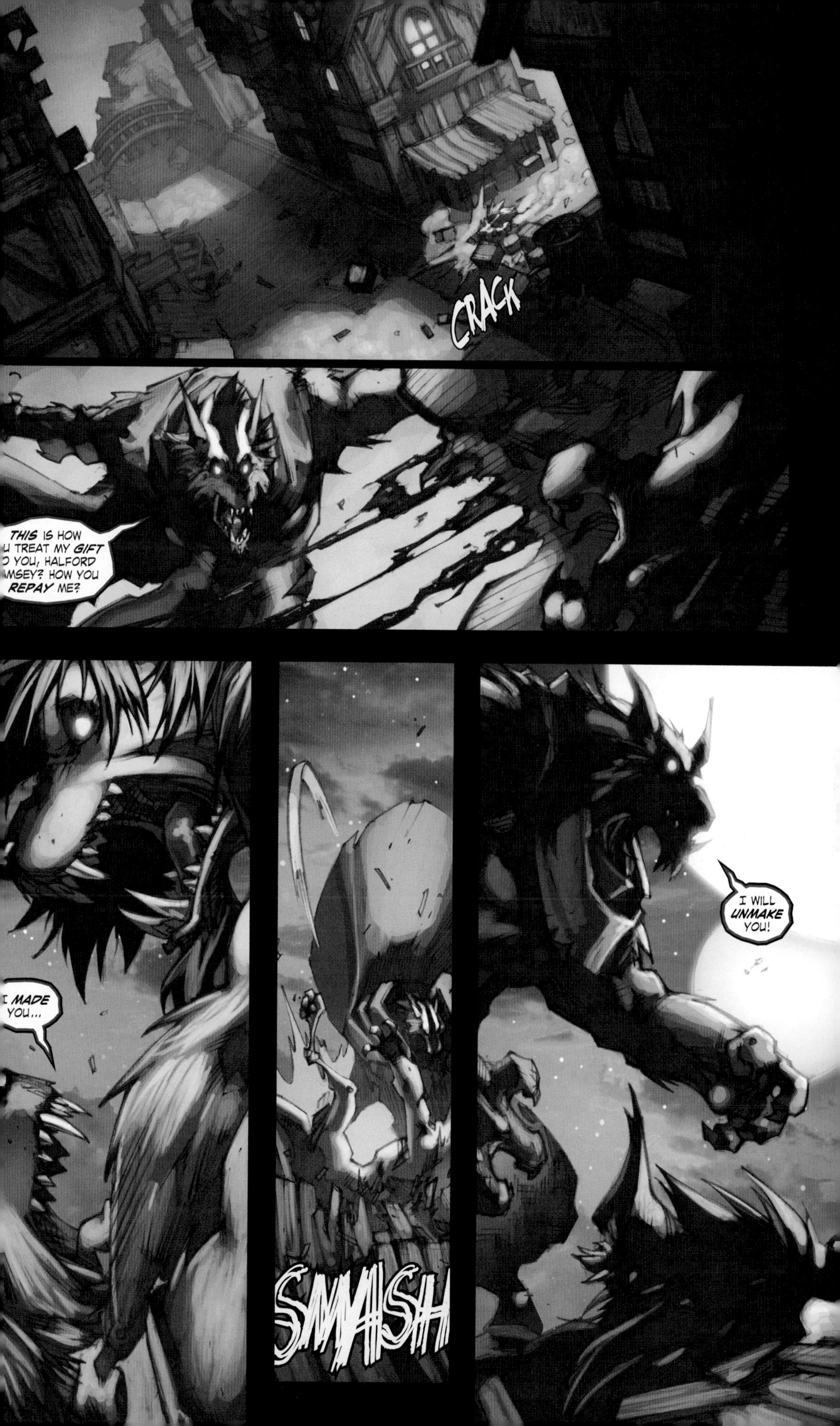
CRACK
THIS IS HOW U TREAT MY GIFT O YOU, HALFORD MSEY? HOW YOU REPAY ME?
I MADE YOU...
SMASH
I WILL UNMAKE YOU!

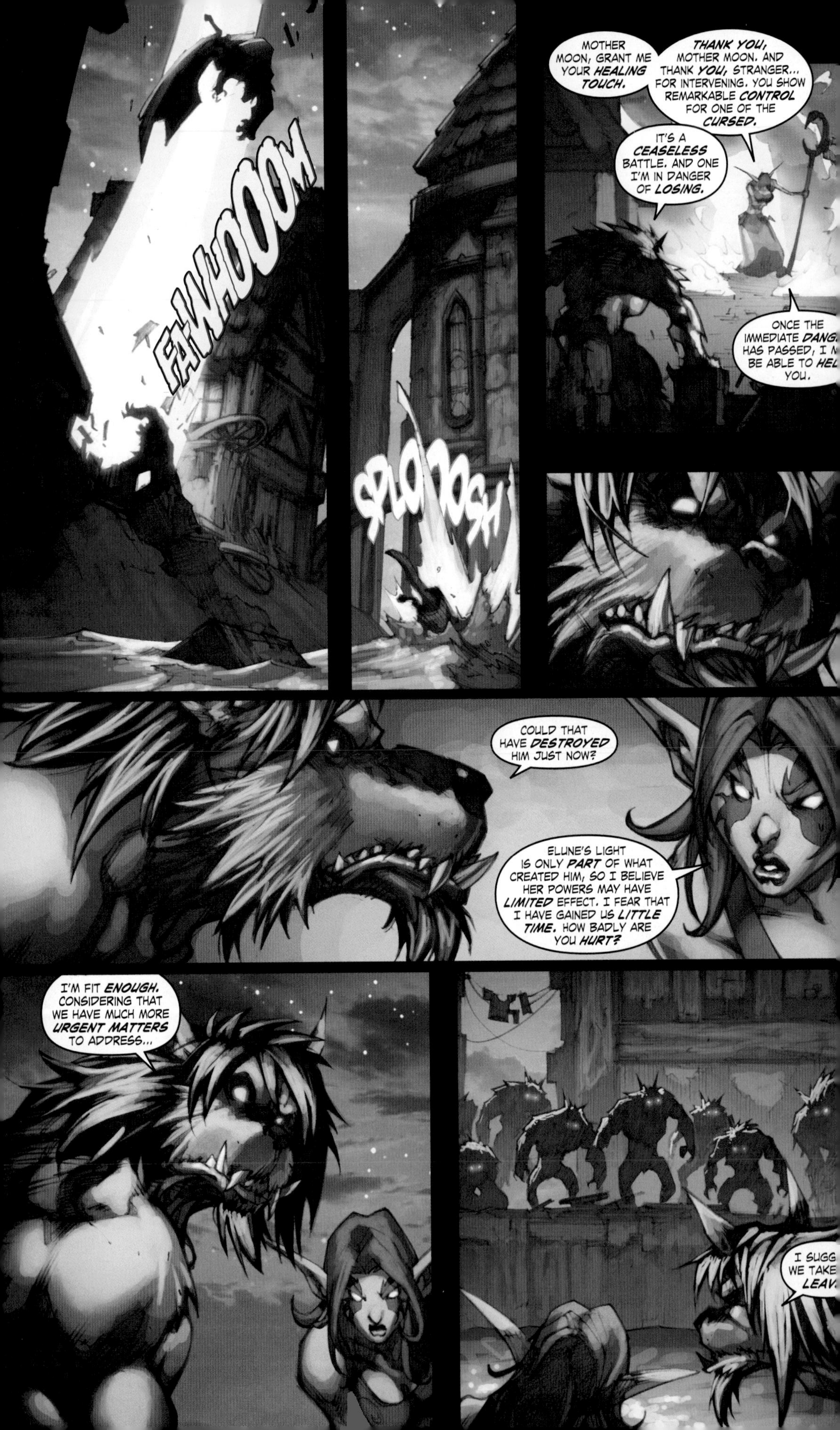

FA-WHOOOM
SPLOOOSH
MOTHER MOON, GRANT ME YOUR HEALING TOUCH.
THANK YOU, MOTHER MOON. AND THANK YOU, STRANGER... FOR INTERVENING. YOU SHOW REMARKABLE CONTROL FOR ONE OF THE CURSED.
IT'S A CEASELESS BATTLE. AND ONE I'M IN DANGER OF LOSING.
ONCE THE IMMEDIATE DANG HAS PASSED, I M BE ABLE TO HEL YOU.
COULD THAT HAVE DESTROYED HIM JUST NOW?
ELUNE'S LIGHT IS ONLY PART OF WHAT CREATED HIM, SO I BELIEVE HER POWERS MAY HAVE LIMITED EFFECT. I FEAR THAT I HAVE GAINED US LITTLE TIME. HOW BADLY ARE YOU HURT?
I'M FIT ENOUGH. CONSIDERING THAT WE HAVE MUCH MORE URGENT MATTERS TO ADDRESS...
I SUGG WE TAKE LEAV

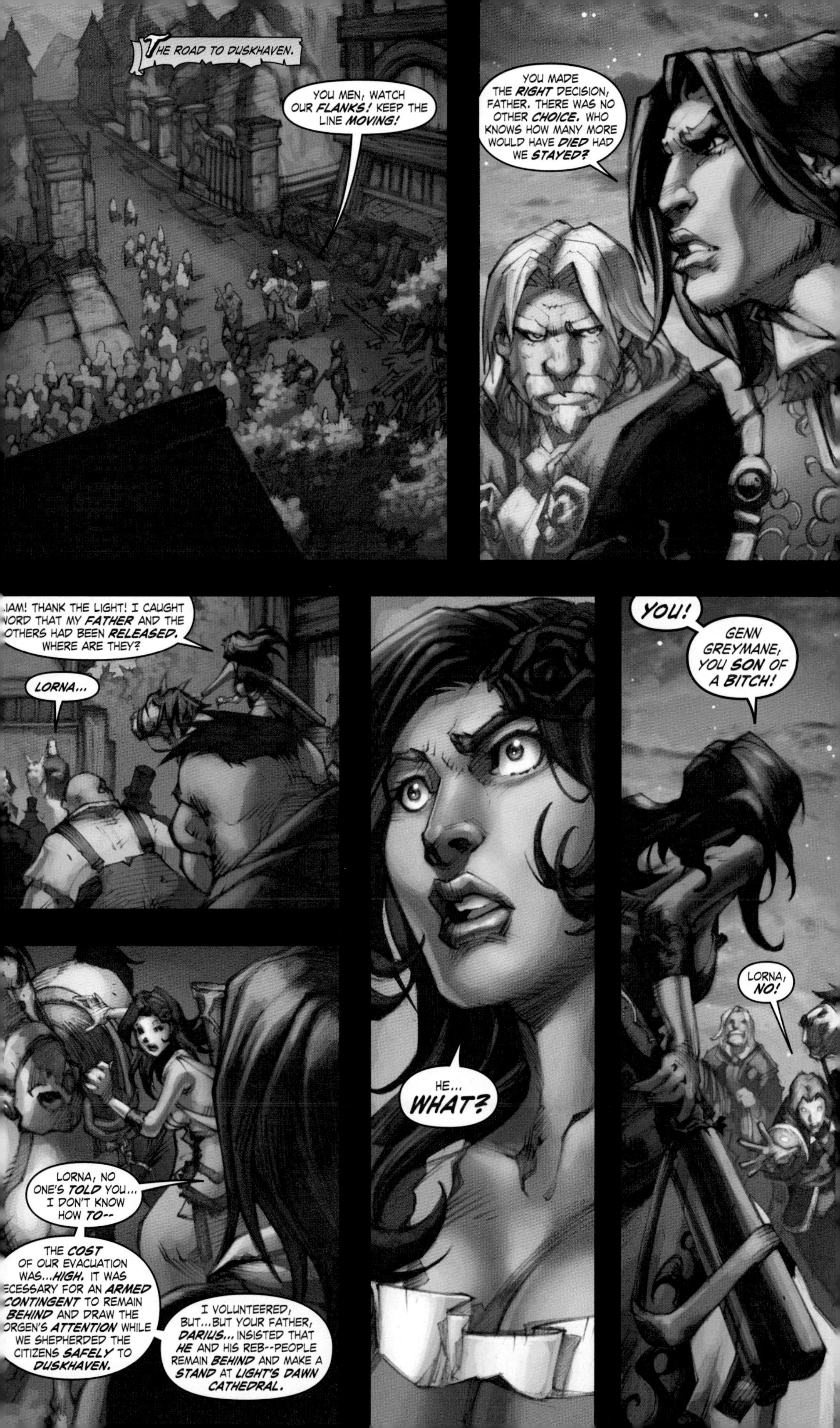
THE ROAD TO DUSKHAVEN.
YOU MEN, WATCH OUR FLANKS! KEEP THE LINE MOVING!
YOU MADE THE RIGHT DECISION, FATHER. THERE WAS NO OTHER CHOICE. WHO KNOWS HOW MANY MORE WOULD HAVE DIED HAD WE STAYED?
IAM! THANK THE LIGHT! I CAUGHT WORD THAT MY FATHER AND THE OTHERS HAD BEEN RELEASED. WHERE ARE THEY?
LORNA...
LORNA, NO ONE'S TOLD YOU... I DON'T KNOW HOW TO--
THE COST OF OUR EVACUATION WAS...HIGH. IT WAS ECESSARY FOR AN ARMED CONTINGENT TO REMAIN BEHIND AND DRAW THE ORGEN'S ATTENTION WHILE WE SHEPHERDED THE CITIZENS SAFELY TO DUSKHAVEN.
I VOLUNTEERED, BUT...BUT YOUR FATHER, DARIUS... INSISTED THAT HE AND HIS REB--PEOPLE REMAIN BEHIND AND MAKE A STAND AT LIGHT'S DAWN CATHEDRAL.
HE... WHAT?
YOU!
GENN GREYMANE, YOU SON OF A BITCH!
LORNA, NO!

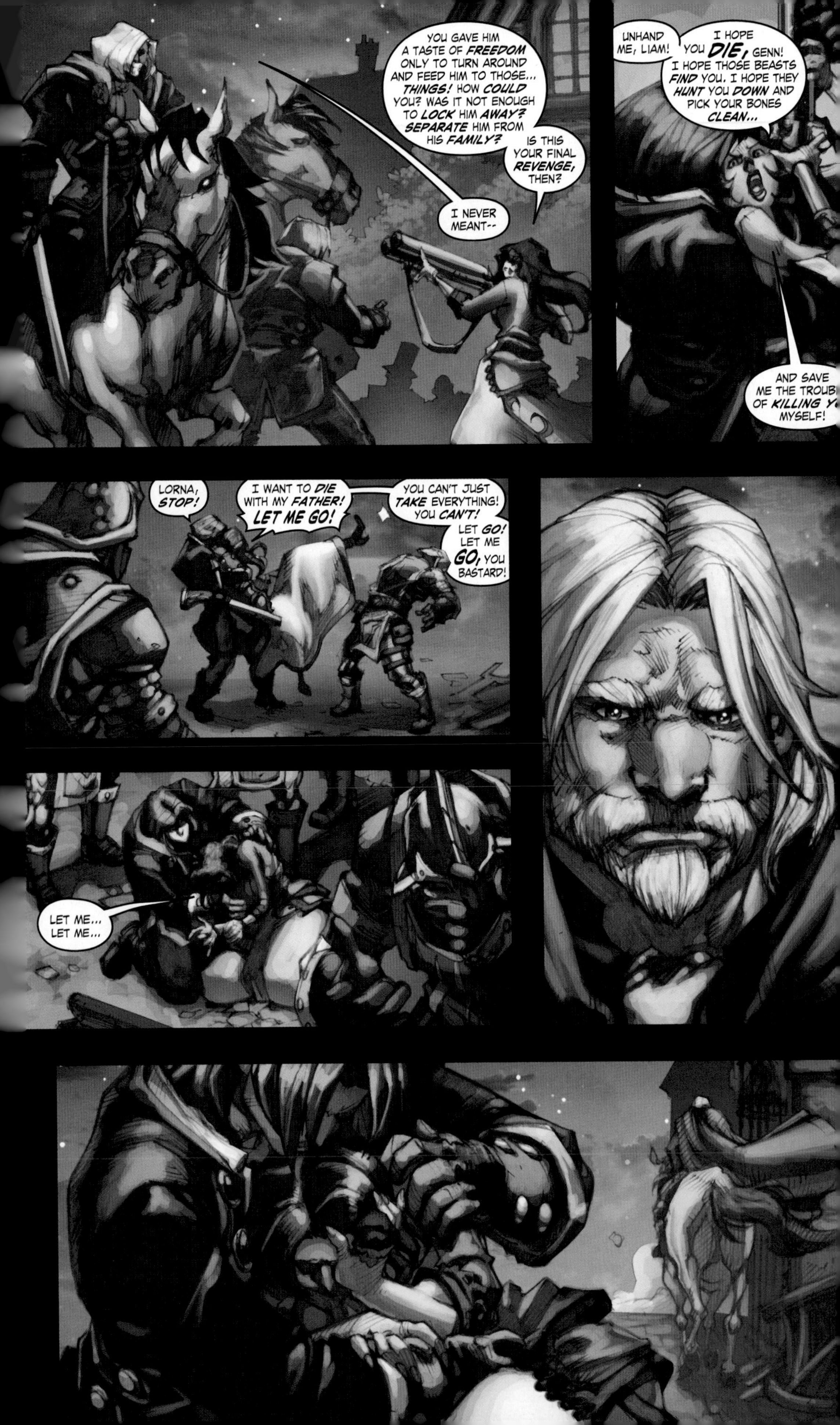
YOU GAVE HIM A TASTE OF FREEDOM ONLY TO TURN AROUND AND FEED HIM TO THOSE... THINGS! HOW COULD YOU? WAS IT NOT ENOUGH TO LOCK HIM AWAY? SEPARATE HIM FROM HIS FAMILY?
I NEVER MEANT--
IS THIS YOUR FINAL REVENGE, THEN?
UNHAND ME, LIAM!
I HOPE YOU DIE, GENN! I HOPE THOSE BEASTS FIND YOU. I HOPE THEY HUNT YOU DOWN AND PICK YOUR BONES CLEAN...
AND SAVE ME THE TROUB
OF KILLING Y
MYSELF!
LORNA, STOP!
I WANT TO DIE WITH MY FATHER! LET ME GO!
YOU CAN'T JUST TAKE EVERYTHING! YOU CAN'T!
LET GO! LET ME GO, YOU BASTARD!
LET ME... LET ME...

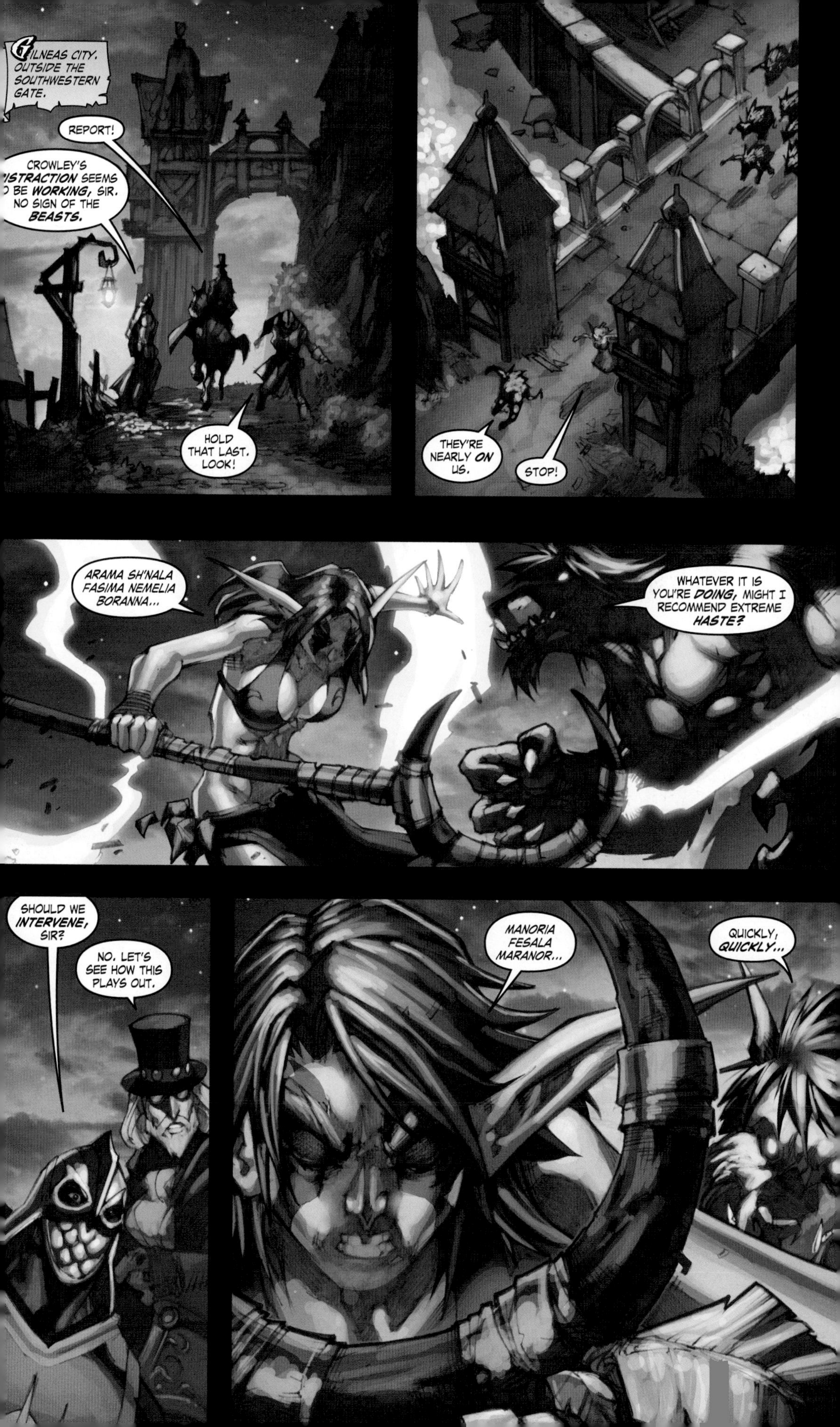
GILNEAS CITY. OUTSIDE THE SOUTHWESTERN GATE.
REPORT!
CROWLEY'S ISTRACTION SEEMS O BE WORKING, SIR. NO SIGN OF THE BEASTS.
HOLD THAT LAST. LOOK!
THEY'RE NEARLY ON US.
STOP!
ARAMA SH'NALA FASIMA NEMELIA BORANNA...
WHATEVER IT IS YOU'RE DOING, MIGHT I RECOMMEND EXTREME HASTE?
SHOULD WE INTERVENE, SIR?
NO. LET'S SEE HOW THIS PLAYS OUT.
MANORIA FESALA MARANOR...
QUICKLY, QUICKLY...

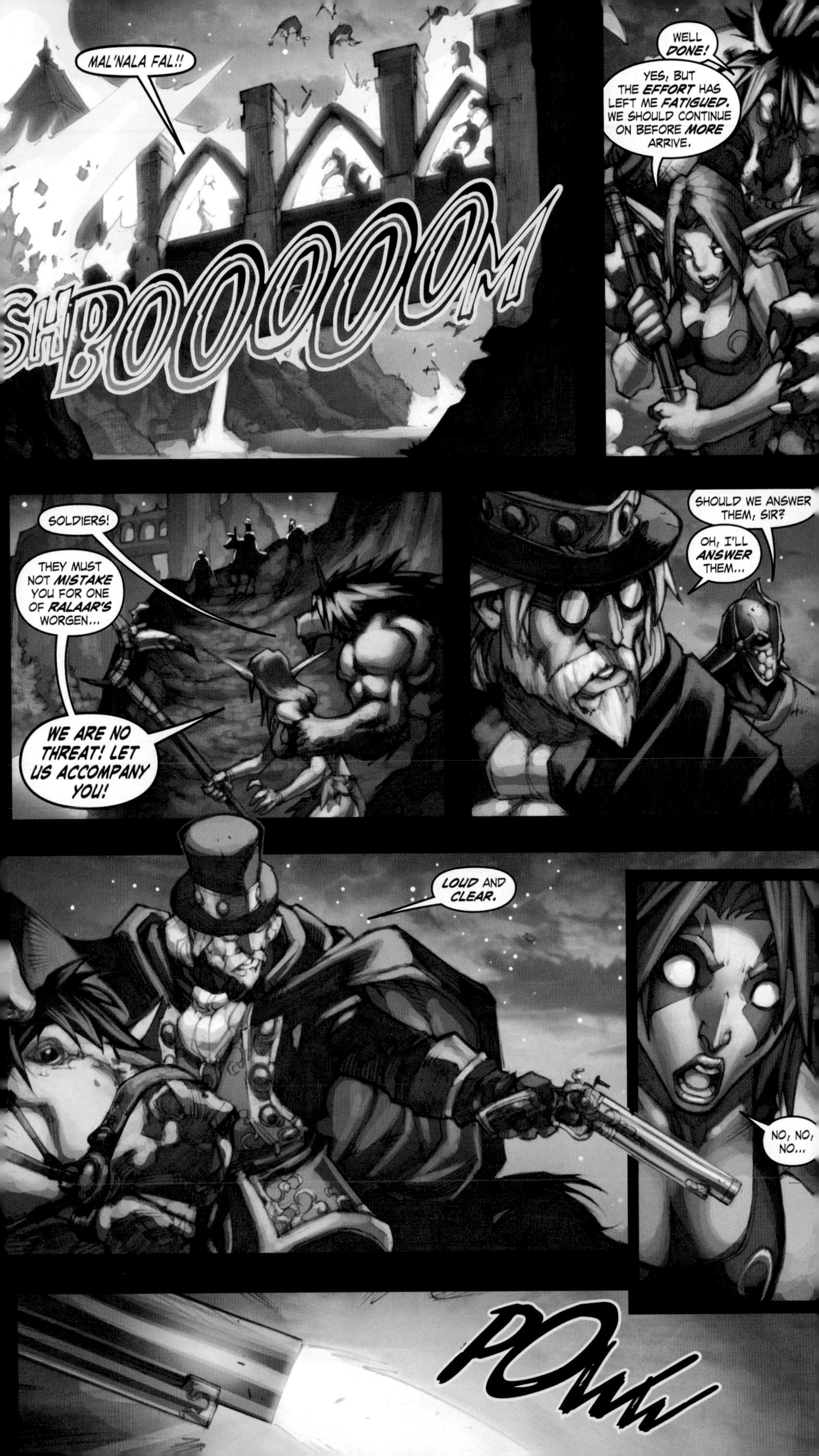
MAL'NALA FAL!!
SHBOOOOOOM
WELL DONE!
YES, BUT THE EFFORT HAS LEFT ME FATIGUED. WE SHOULD CONTINUE ON BEFORE MORE ARRIVE.
SOLDIERS!
THEY MUST NOT MISTAKE YOU FOR ONE OF RALAAR'S WORGEN...
WE ARE NO THREAT! LET US ACCOMPANY YOU!
SHOULD WE ANSWER THEM, SIR?
OH, I'LL ANSWER THEM...
LOUD AND CLEAR.
NO, NO, NO...
POW

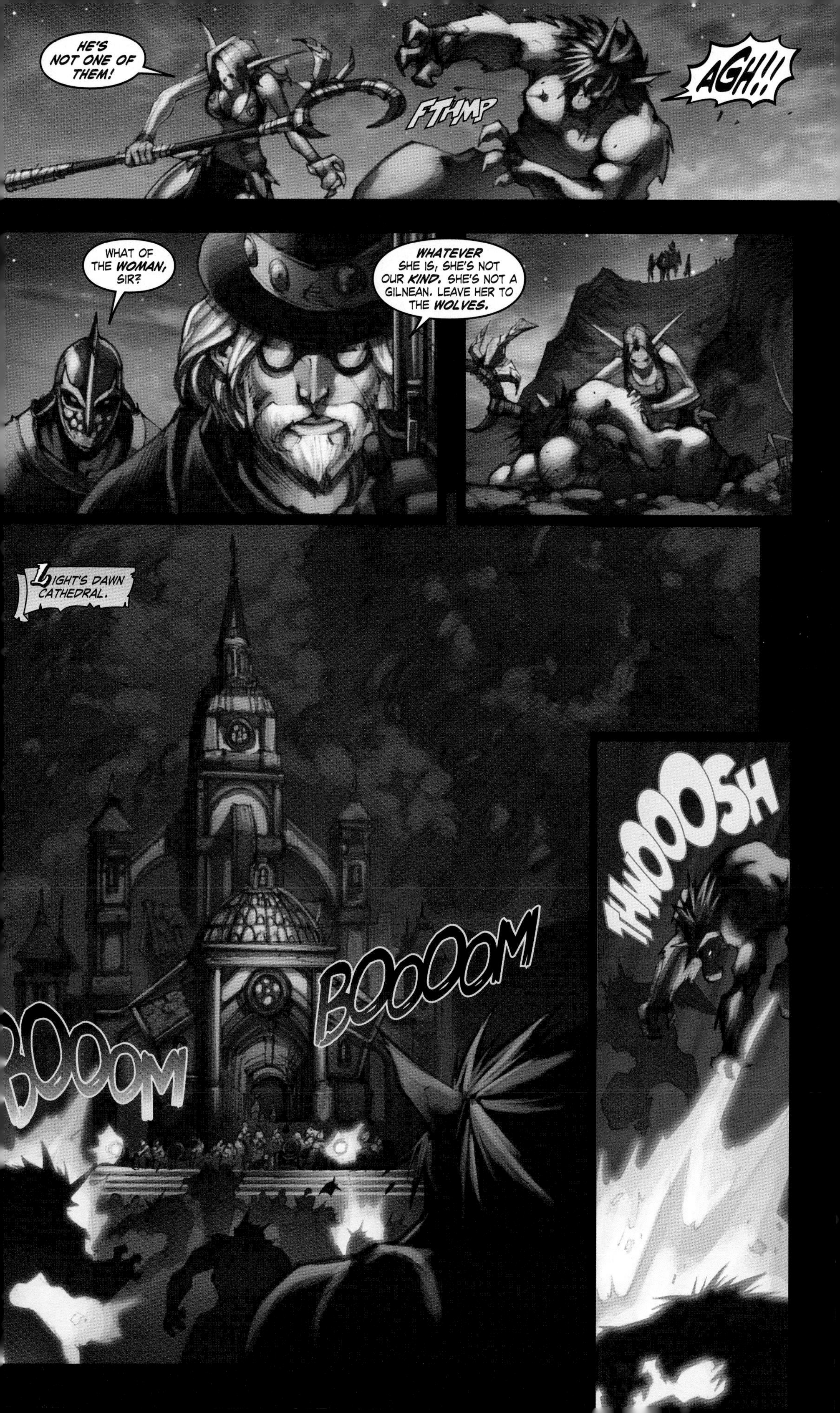
HE'S NOT ONE OF THEM!
FTHMP
AGH!!
WHAT OF THE WOMAN, SIR?
WHATEVER SHE IS, SHE'S NOT OUR KIND. SHE'S NOT A GILNEAN. LEAVE HER TO THE WOLVES.
LIGHT'S DAWN CATHEDRAL.
BOOOOM
BOOOOM
THWOOOOSH

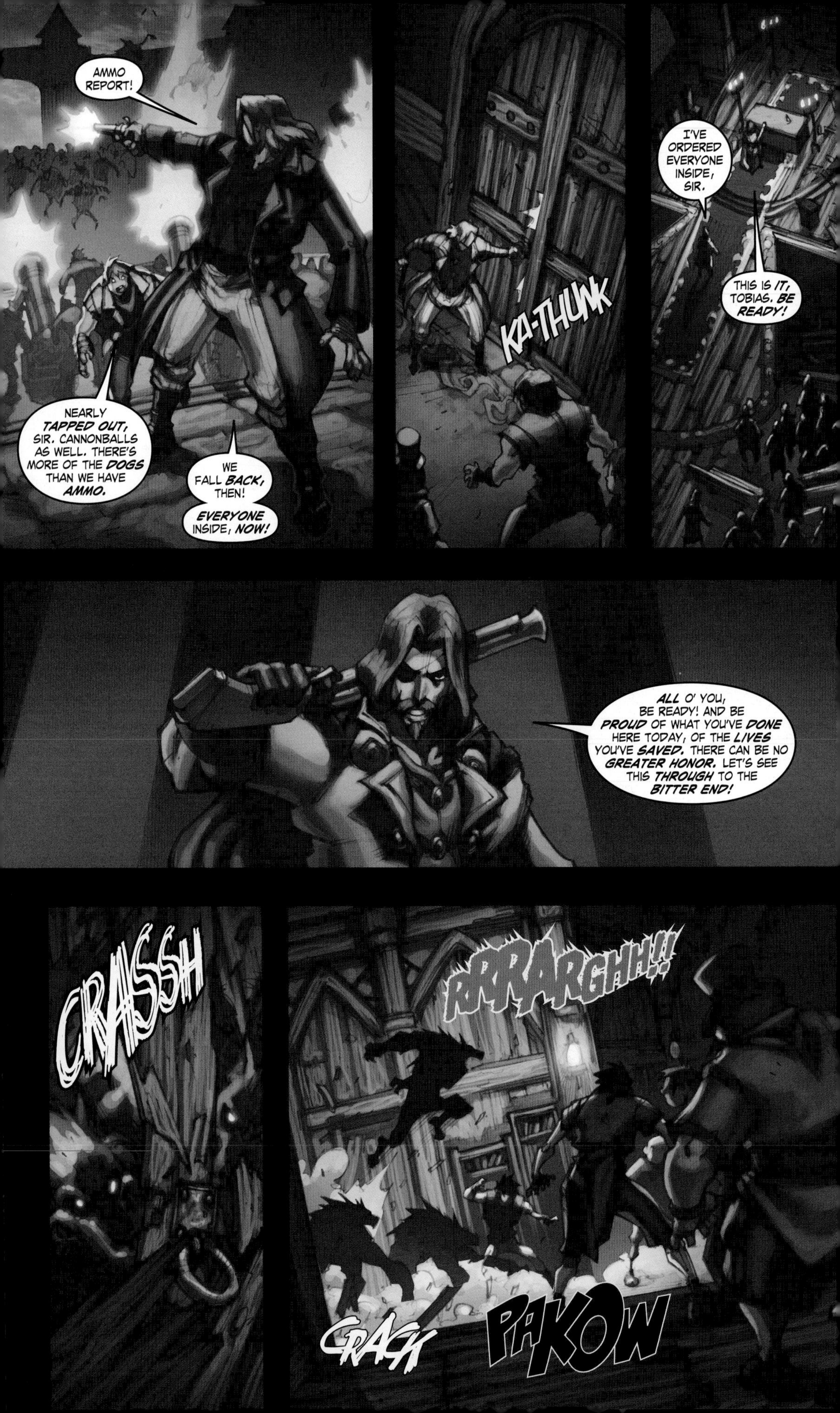
AMMO REPORT!
NEARLY *TAPPED OUT*, SIR. CANNONBALLS AS WELL. THERE'S MORE OF THE *DOGS* THAN WE HAVE *AMMO.*
WE FALL *BACK*, THEN!
EVERYONE INSIDE; *NOW!*
KA-THUNK
I'VE ORDERED EVERYONE INSIDE, SIR.
THIS IS *IT*, TOBIAS. *BE READY!*
ALL O' YOU, BE READY! AND BE *PROUD* OF WHAT YOU'VE *DONE* HERE TODAY, OF THE *LIVES* YOU'VE *SAVED.* THERE CAN BE NO *GREATER HONOR.* LET'S SEE THIS *THROUGH* TO THE *BITTER END!*
CRASSH
RRRRARGHH!!
CRACK
PAKOW

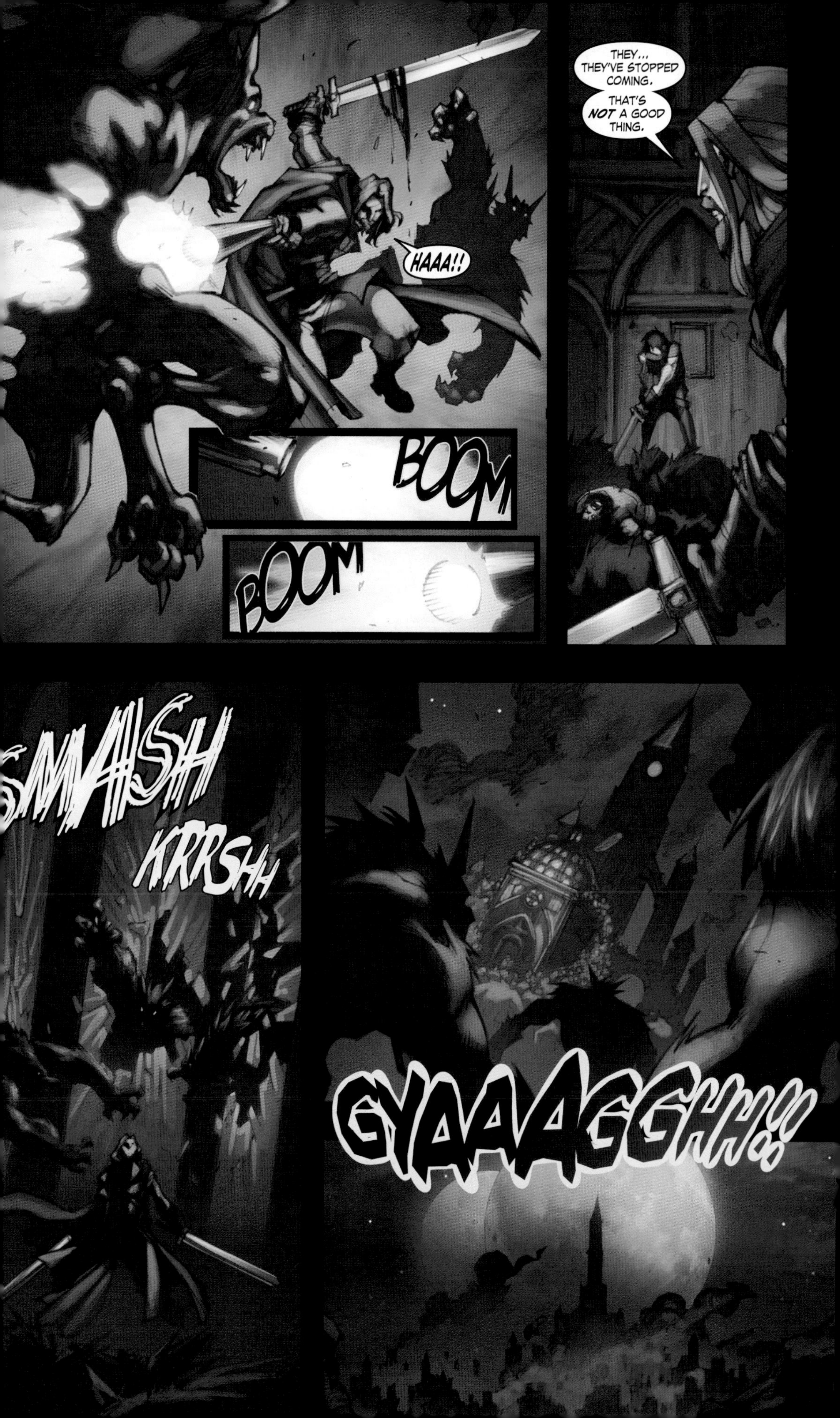
HAAA!!
BOOM
BOOM
THEY... THEY'VE STOPPED COMING.
THAT'S NOT A GOOD THING.
SMASH
KRRSHH
GYAAAGGHH!!

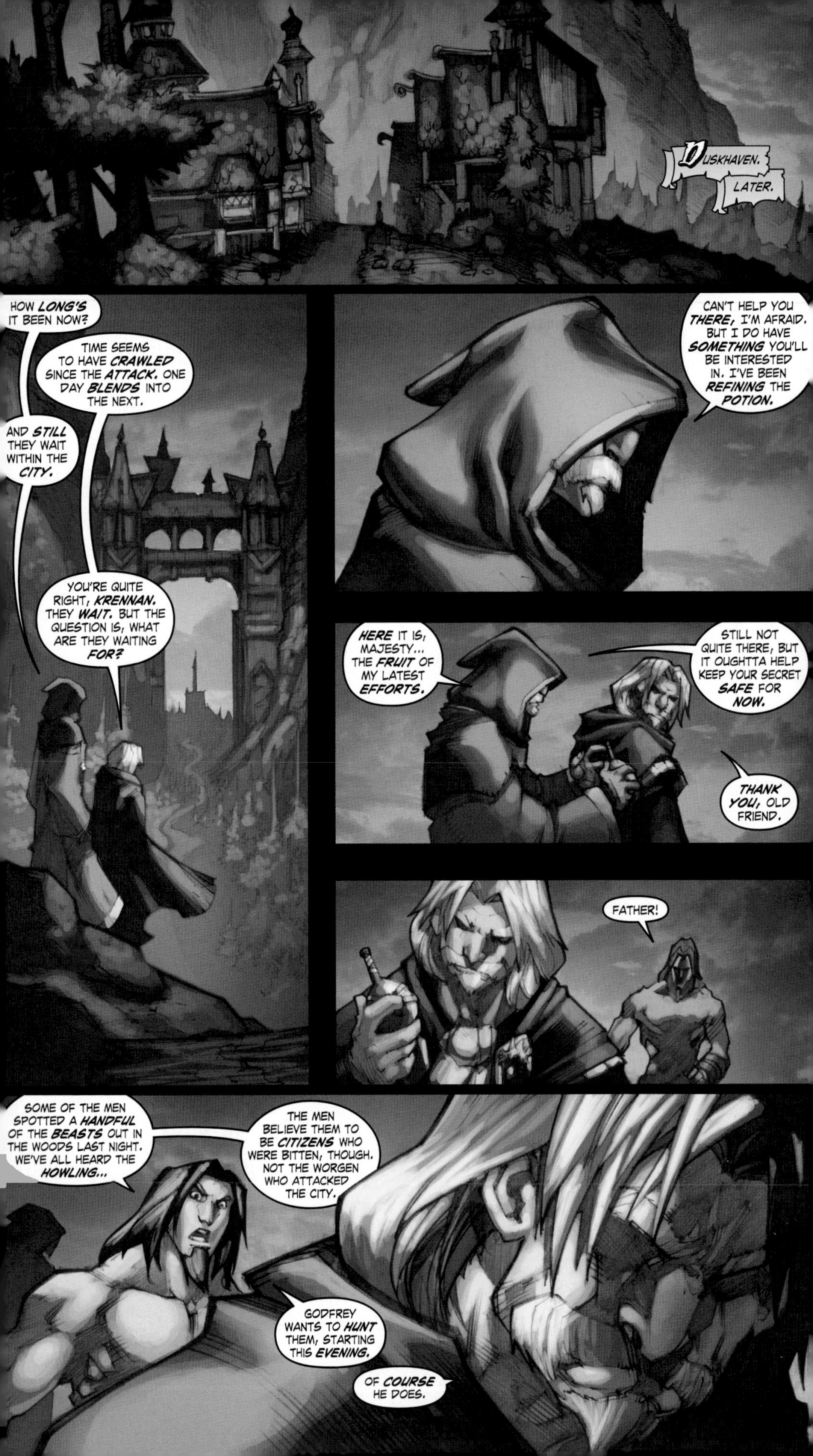
DUSKHAVEN.
LATER.
HOW LONG'S IT BEEN NOW?
TIME SEEMS TO HAVE CRAWLED SINCE THE ATTACK. ONE DAY BLENDS INTO THE NEXT.
AND STILL THEY WAIT WITHIN THE CITY.
YOU'RE QUITE RIGHT, KRENNAN. THEY WAIT. BUT THE QUESTION IS, WHAT ARE THEY WAITING FOR?
CAN'T HELP YOU THERE, I'M AFRAID. BUT I DO HAVE SOMETHING YOU'LL BE INTERESTED IN. I'VE BEEN REFINING THE POTION.
HERE IT IS, MAJESTY... THE FRUIT OF MY LATEST EFFORTS.
STILL NOT QUITE THERE, BUT IT OUGHTTA HELP KEEP YOUR SECRET SAFE FOR NOW.
THANK YOU, OLD FRIEND.
FATHER!
SOME OF THE MEN SPOTTED A HANDFUL OF THE BEASTS OUT IN THE WOODS LAST NIGHT. WE'VE ALL HEARD THE HOWLING...
THE MEN BELIEVE THEM TO BE CITIZENS WHO WERE BITTEN, THOUGH. NOT THE WORGEN WHO ATTACKED THE CITY.
GODFREY WANTS TO HUNT THEM, STARTING THIS EVENING.
OF COURSE HE DOES.

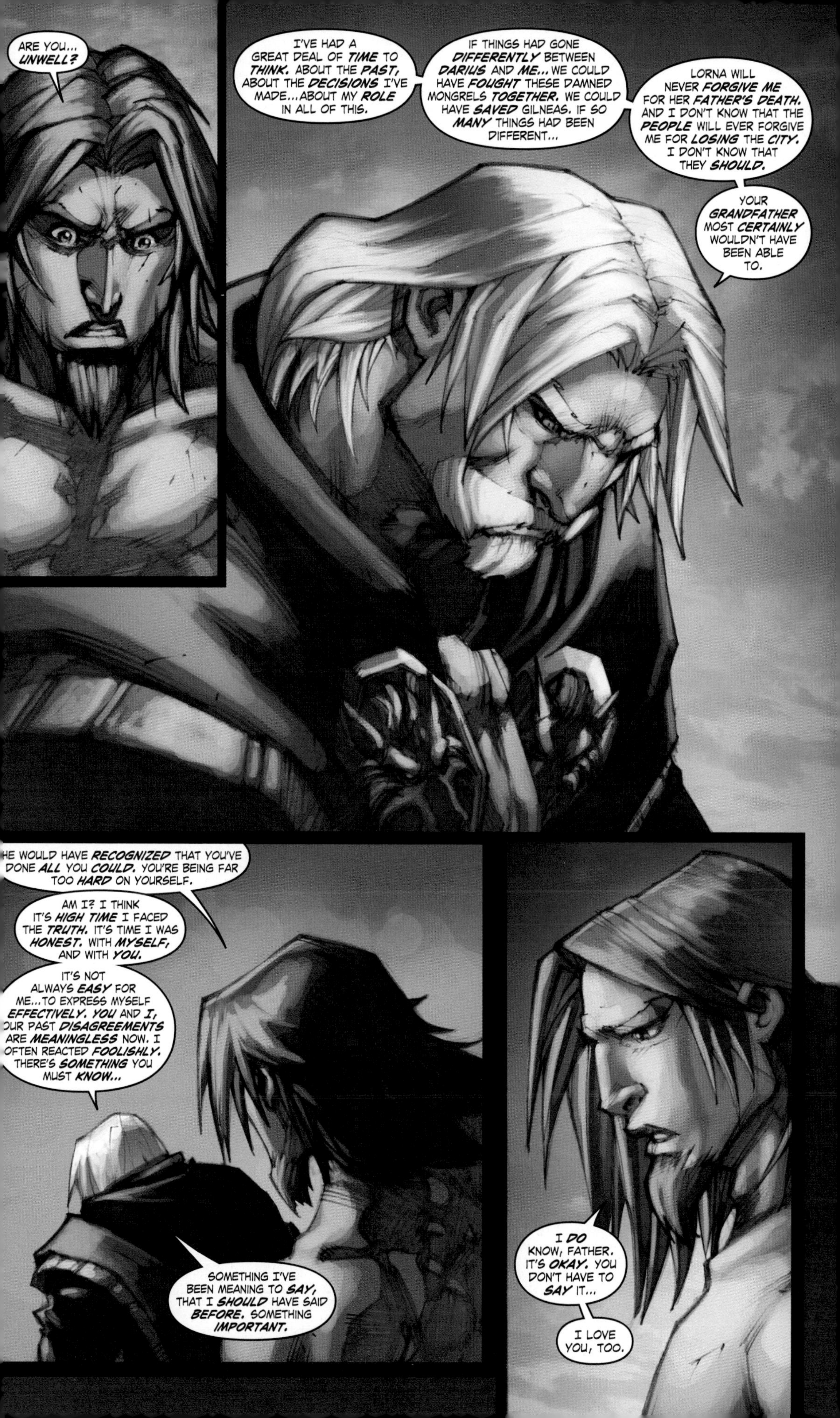
ARE YOU... UNWELL?
I'VE HAD A GREAT DEAL OF TIME TO THINK. ABOUT THE PAST, ABOUT THE DECISIONS I'VE MADE...ABOUT MY ROLE IN ALL OF THIS.
IF THINGS HAD GONE DIFFERENTLY BETWEEN DARIUS AND ME... WE COULD HAVE FOUGHT THESE DAMNED MONGRELS TOGETHER. WE COULD HAVE SAVED GILNEAS. IF SO MANY THINGS HAD BEEN DIFFERENT...
LORNA WILL NEVER FORGIVE ME FOR HER FATHER'S DEATH. AND I DON'T KNOW THAT THE PEOPLE WILL EVER FORGIVE ME FOR LOSING THE CITY. I DON'T KNOW THAT THEY SHOULD.
YOUR GRANDFATHER MOST CERTAINLY WOULDN'T HAVE BEEN ABLE TO.
HE WOULD HAVE RECOGNIZED THAT YOU'VE DONE ALL YOU COULD. YOU'RE BEING FAR TOO HARD ON YOURSELF.
AM I? I THINK IT'S HIGH TIME I FACED THE TRUTH. IT'S TIME I WAS HONEST. WITH MYSELF, AND WITH YOU.
IT'S NOT ALWAYS EASY FOR ME...TO EXPRESS MYSELF EFFECTIVELY. YOU AND I, OUR PAST DISAGREEMENTS ARE MEANINGLESS NOW. I OFTEN REACTED FOOLISHLY. THERE'S SOMETHING YOU MUST KNOW...
SOMETHING I'VE BEEN MEANING TO SAY, THAT I SHOULD HAVE SAID BEFORE. SOMETHING IMPORTANT.
I DO KNOW, FATHER. IT'S OKAY. YOU DON'T HAVE TO SAY IT...
I LOVE YOU, TOO.

YOU'RE A GREAT *LEADER*. YOU'VE ALWAYS DONE WHAT YOU *BELIEVED* WAS *BEST* FOR YOUR PEOPLE. BUT IN THE RECENT PAST I FEEL AS THOUGH YOU'VE *LOST FAITH* IN YOURSELF.

IF YOU CAN JUST *FIND* A WAY TO *BELIEVE* IN YOURSELF ONCE AGAIN...YOUR *PEOPLE* WILL BELIEVE IN *YOU*. AND THEY WILL *FORGIVE* YOU. FOR *ANYTHING*.

ANYTHING...

AND WOULD *YOU* FORGIVE ME?

IN MY MIND, THERE'S *NOTHING* TO *FORGIVE*.

I SHOULD GET BACK TO THE *OTHERS*.

LIAM! TELL GODFREY...TELL HIM THE WORGEN ARE *NOT* TO BE KILLED. I WANT HIM TO SET *TRAPS* ONLY. I WANT TO *CATCH* AS MANY OF THEM *ALIVE* AS POSSIBLE.

HE WON'T WANT TO HE IT, BUT I'L TELL HIM

SAY THAT THERE'S A *GOOD REASON*. TELL HIM THAT THEY MAY PROVE...

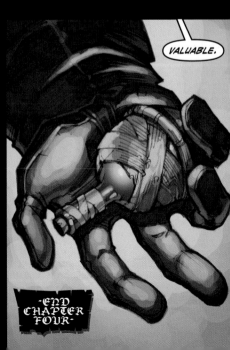

VALUABLE.

-END CHAPTER FOUR-

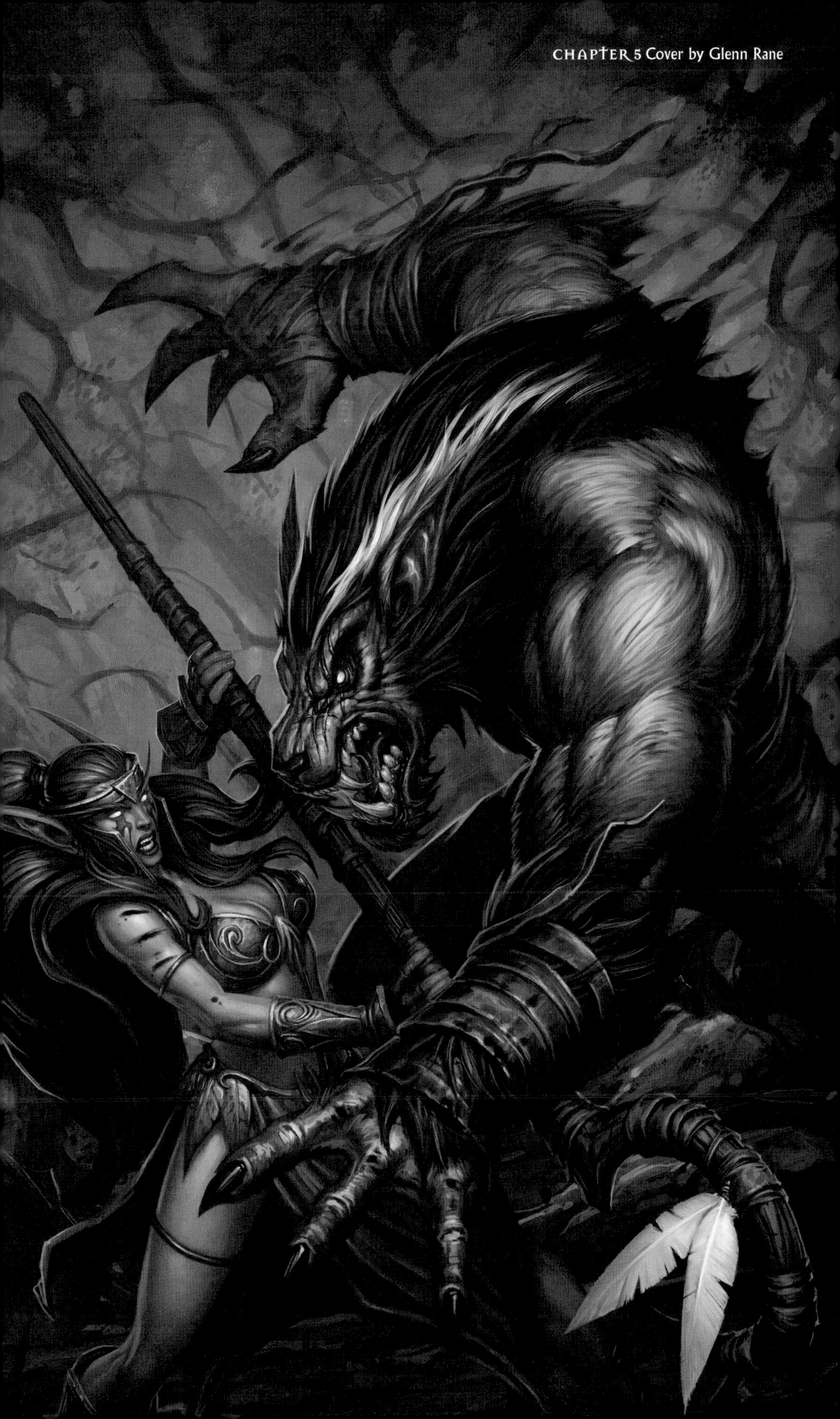

CHAPTER 5 Cover by Glenn Rane

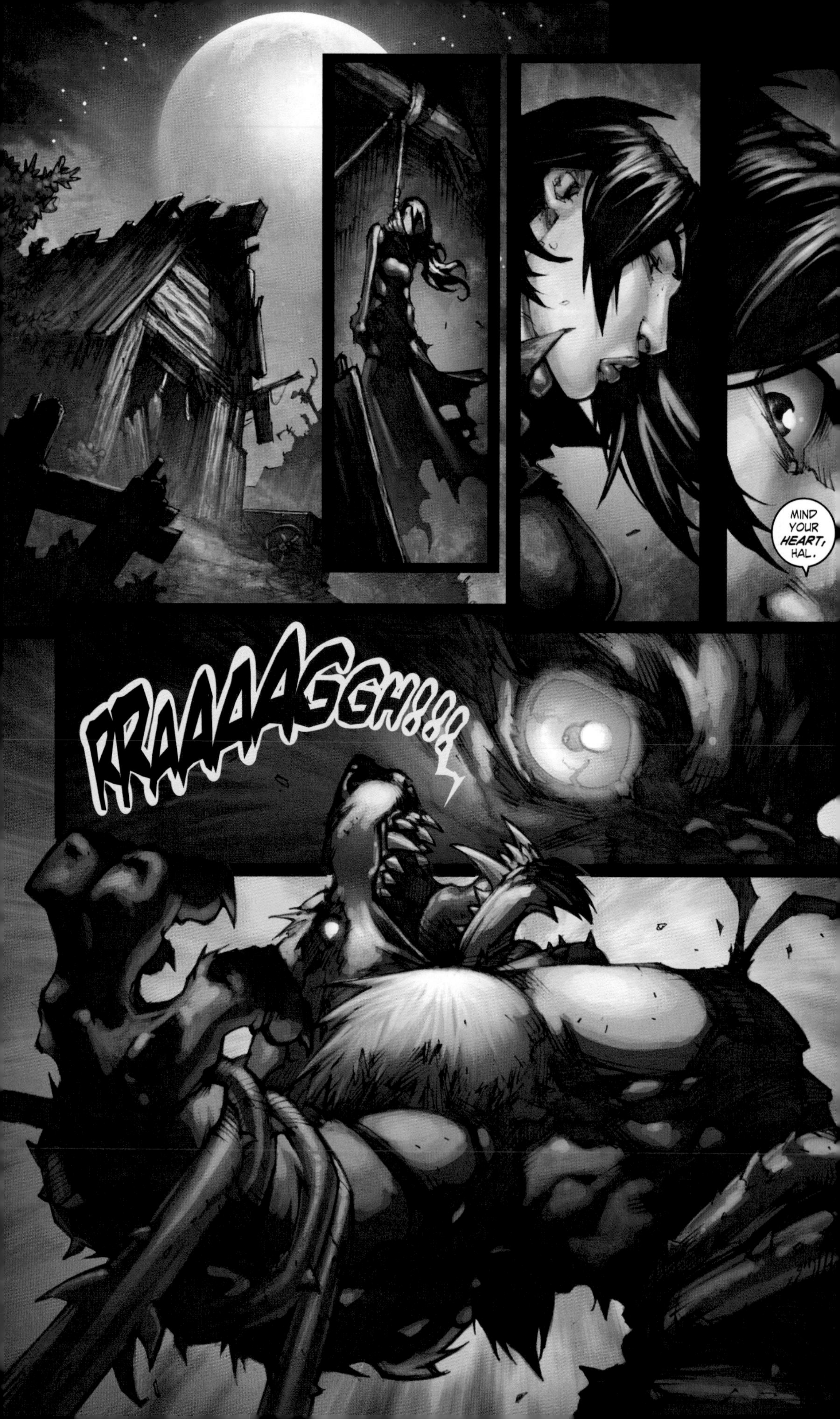
MIND YOUR HEART, HAL.
RRAAAAGGH!!!

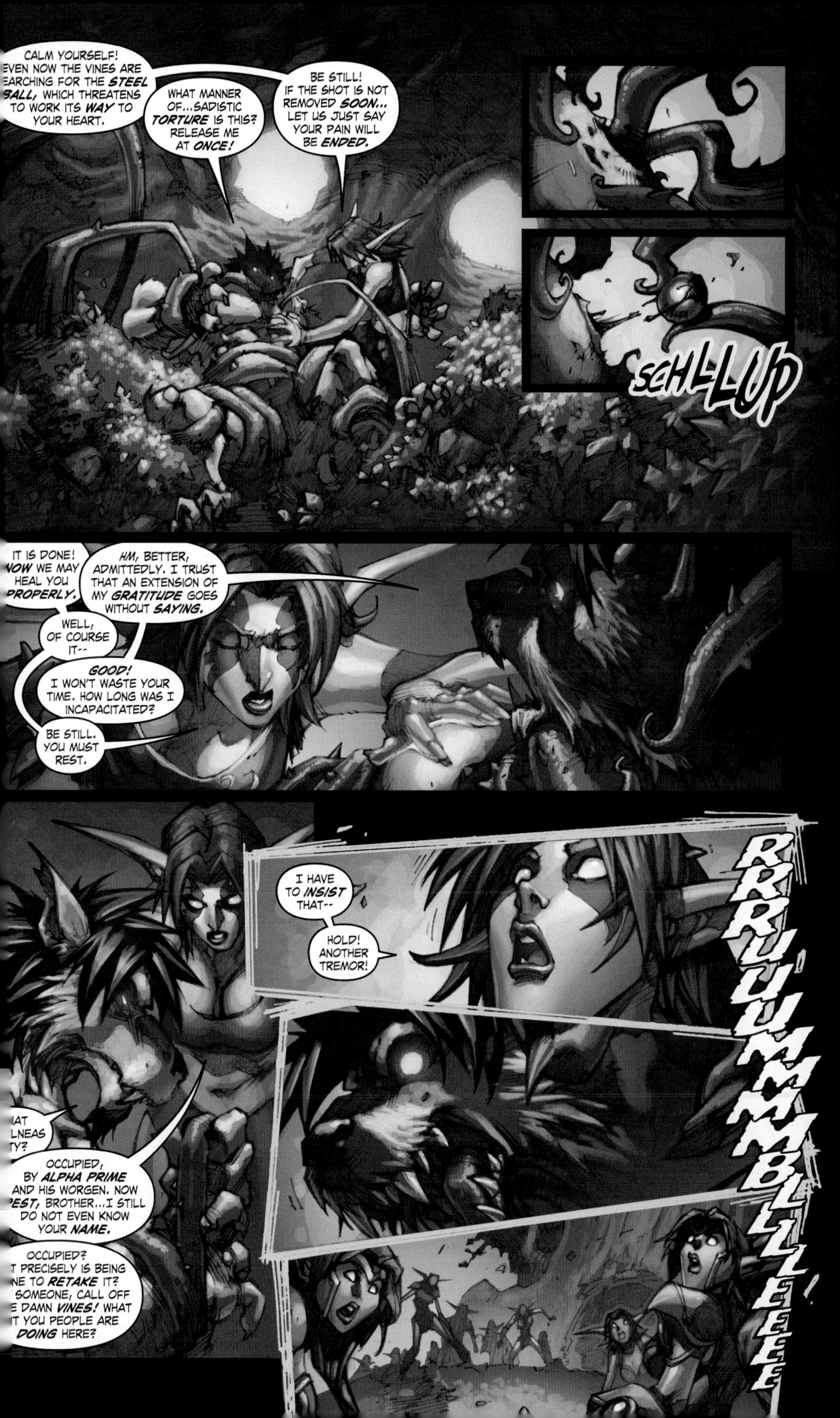
CALM YOURSELF! EVEN NOW THE VINES ARE EARCHING FOR THE STEEL BALL, WHICH THREATENS TO WORK ITS WAY TO YOUR HEART.
WHAT MANNER OF...SADISTIC TORTURE IS THIS? RELEASE ME AT ONCE!
BE STILL! IF THE SHOT IS NOT REMOVED SOON... LET US JUST SAY YOUR PAIN WILL BE ENDED.
SCHLLUP
IT IS DONE! NOW WE MAY HEAL YOU PROPERLY.
HM, BETTER, ADMITTEDLY. I TRUST THAT AN EXTENSION OF MY GRATITUDE GOES WITHOUT SAYING.
WELL, OF COURSE IT--
GOOD! I WON'T WASTE YOUR TIME. HOW LONG WAS I INCAPACITATED?
BE STILL. YOU MUST REST.
OCCUPIED, BY ALPHA PRIME AND HIS WORGEN. NOW EST, BROTHER...I STILL DO NOT EVEN KNOW YOUR NAME.
OCCUPIED? T PRECISELY IS BEING NE TO RETAKE IT? SOMEONE, CALL OFF E DAMN VINES! WHAT T YOU PEOPLE ARE DOING HERE?
I HAVE TO INSIST THAT--
HOLD! ANOTHER TREMOR!
RRRUUUMMMBLLEEEE!

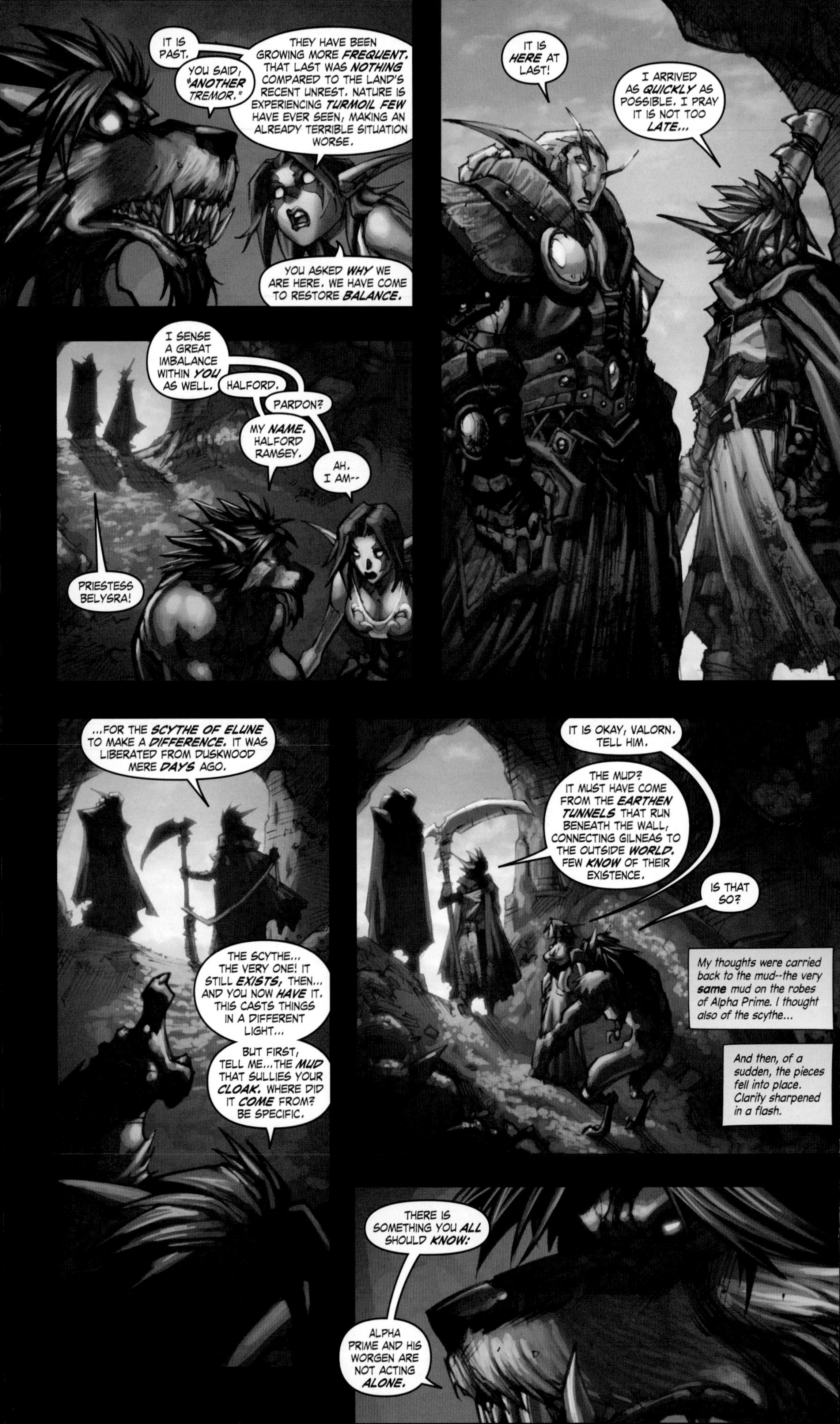
IT IS PAST.
YOU SAID, "ANOTHER TREMOR."
THEY HAVE BEEN GROWING MORE FREQUENT. THAT LAST WAS NOTHING COMPARED TO THE LAND'S RECENT UNREST. NATURE IS EXPERIENCING TURMOIL FEW HAVE EVER SEEN, MAKING AN ALREADY TERRIBLE SITUATION WORSE.
YOU ASKED WHY WE ARE HERE. WE HAVE COME TO RESTORE BALANCE.
IT IS HERE AT LAST!
I ARRIVED AS QUICKLY AS POSSIBLE. I PRAY IT IS NOT TOO LATE...
I SENSE A GREAT IMBALANCE WITHIN YOU AS WELL.
HALFORD.
PARDON?
MY NAME. HALFORD RAMSEY.
AH. I AM--
PRIESTESS BELYSRA!
...FOR THE SCYTHE OF ELUNE TO MAKE A DIFFERENCE. IT WAS LIBERATED FROM DUSKWOOD MERE DAYS AGO.
THE SCYTHE... THE VERY ONE! IT STILL EXISTS, THEN... AND YOU NOW HAVE IT. THIS CASTS THINGS IN A DIFFERENT LIGHT...
BUT FIRST, TELL ME...THE MUD THAT SULLIES YOUR CLOAK. WHERE DID IT COME FROM? BE SPECIFIC.
IT IS OKAY, VALORN. TELL HIM.
THE MUD? IT MUST HAVE COME FROM THE EARTHEN TUNNELS THAT RUN BENEATH THE WALL, CONNECTING GILNEAS TO THE OUTSIDE WORLD. FEW KNOW OF THEIR EXISTENCE.
IS THAT SO?
My thoughts were carried back to the mud--the very same mud on the robes of Alpha Prime. I thought also of the scythe...
And then, of a sudden, the pieces fell into place. Clarity sharpened in a flash.
THERE IS SOMETHING YOU ALL SHOULD KNOW:
ALPHA PRIME AND HIS WORGEN ARE NOT ACTING ALONE.

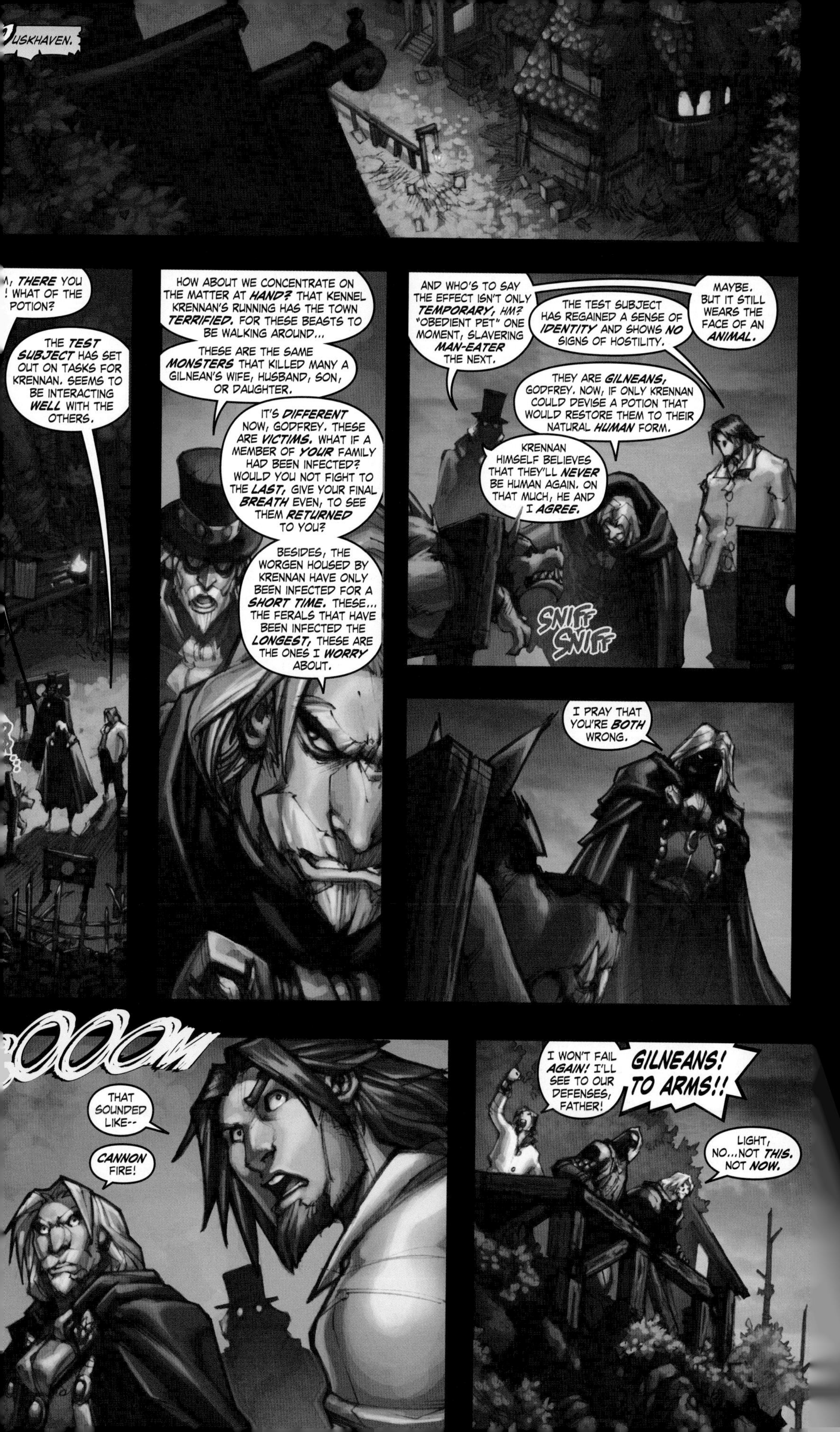

USKHAVEN.
M, THERE YOU ! WHAT OF THE POTION?
THE TEST SUBJECT HAS SET OUT ON TASKS FOR KRENNAN. SEEMS TO BE INTERACTING WELL WITH THE OTHERS.
HOW ABOUT WE CONCENTRATE ON THE MATTER AT HAND? THAT KENNEL KRENNAN'S RUNNING HAS THE TOWN TERRIFIED. FOR THESE BEASTS TO BE WALKING AROUND...
THESE ARE THE SAME MONSTERS THAT KILLED MANY A GILNEAN'S WIFE, HUSBAND, SON, OR DAUGHTER.
IT'S DIFFERENT NOW, GODFREY. THESE ARE VICTIMS. WHAT IF A MEMBER OF YOUR FAMILY HAD BEEN INFECTED? WOULD YOU NOT FIGHT TO THE LAST, GIVE YOUR FINAL BREATH EVEN, TO SEE THEM RETURNED TO YOU?
BESIDES, THE WORGEN HOUSED BY KRENNAN HAVE ONLY BEEN INFECTED FOR A SHORT TIME. THESE... THE FERALS THAT HAVE BEEN INFECTED THE LONGEST, THESE ARE THE ONES I WORRY ABOUT.
AND WHO'S TO SAY THE EFFECT ISN'T ONLY TEMPORARY, HM? "OBEDIENT PET" ONE MOMENT, SLAVERING MAN-EATER THE NEXT.
THE TEST SUBJECT HAS REGAINED A SENSE OF IDENTITY AND SHOWS NO SIGNS OF HOSTILITY.
MAYBE. BUT IT STILL WEARS THE FACE OF AN ANIMAL.
THEY ARE GILNEANS, GODFREY. NOW, IF ONLY KRENNAN COULD DEVISE A POTION THAT WOULD RESTORE THEM TO THEIR NATURAL HUMAN FORM.
KRENNAN HIMSELF BELIEVES THAT THEY'LL NEVER BE HUMAN AGAIN. ON THAT MUCH, HE AND I AGREE.
SNIFF SNIFF
I PRAY THAT YOU'RE BOTH WRONG.
OOOOM
THAT SOUNDED LIKE--
CANNON FIRE!
I WON'T FAIL AGAIN! I'LL SEE TO OUR DEFENSES, FATHER!
GILNEANS! TO ARMS!!
LIGHT, NO...NOT THIS. NOT NOW.

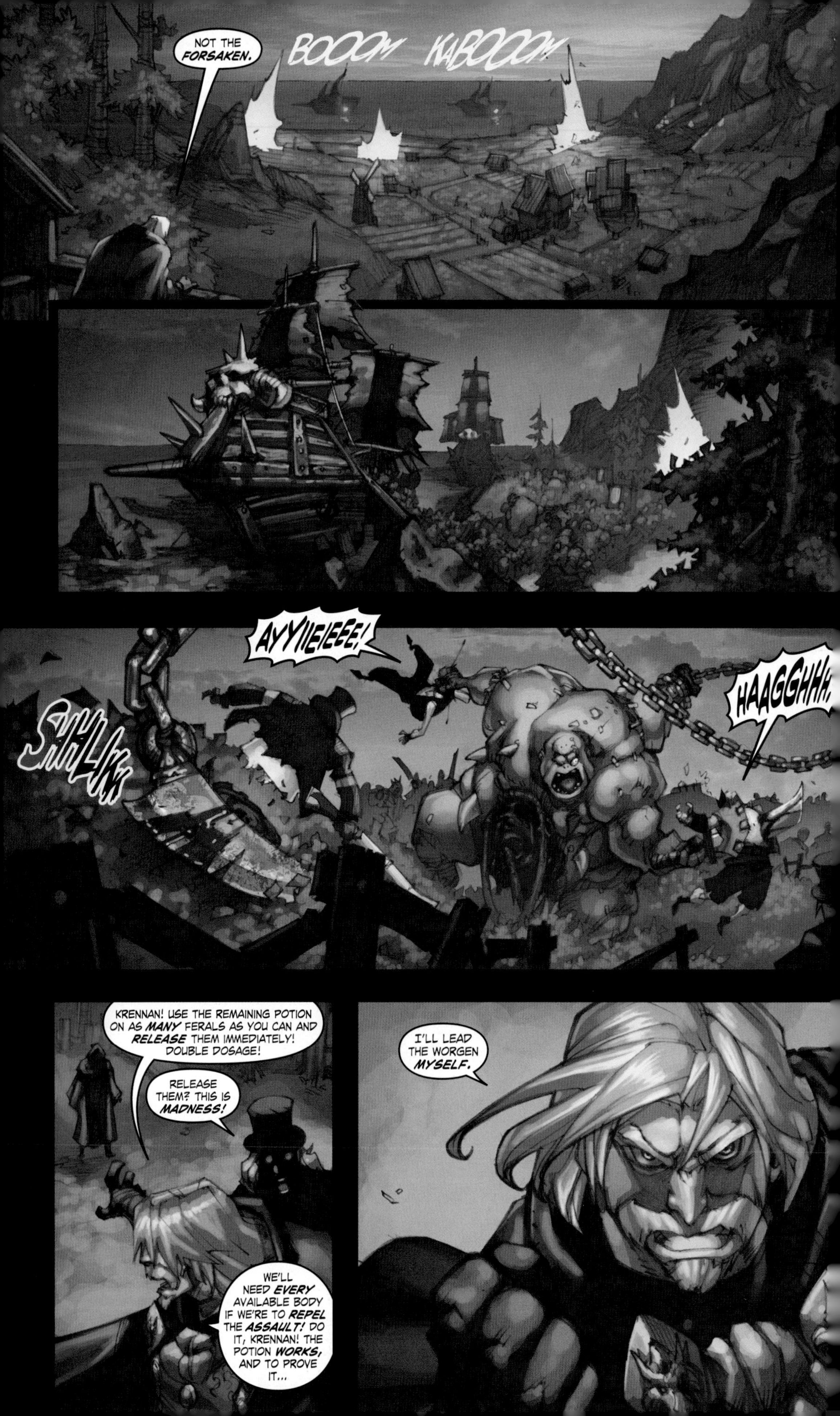

NOT THE *FORSAKEN.*
BOOOM KABOOOM
AYYIIEIEEE!
SHHLIKK
HAAGGHHH
KRENNAN! USE THE REMAINING POTION ON AS *MANY* FERALS AS YOU CAN AND *RELEASE* THEM IMMEDIATELY! DOUBLE DOSAGE!
RELEASE THEM? THIS IS *MADNESS!*
WE'LL NEED *EVERY* AVAILABLE BODY IF WE'RE TO *REPEL* THE *ASSAULT!* DO IT, KRENNAN! THE POTION *WORKS,* AND TO PROVE IT...
I'LL LEAD THE WORGEN *MYSELF.*

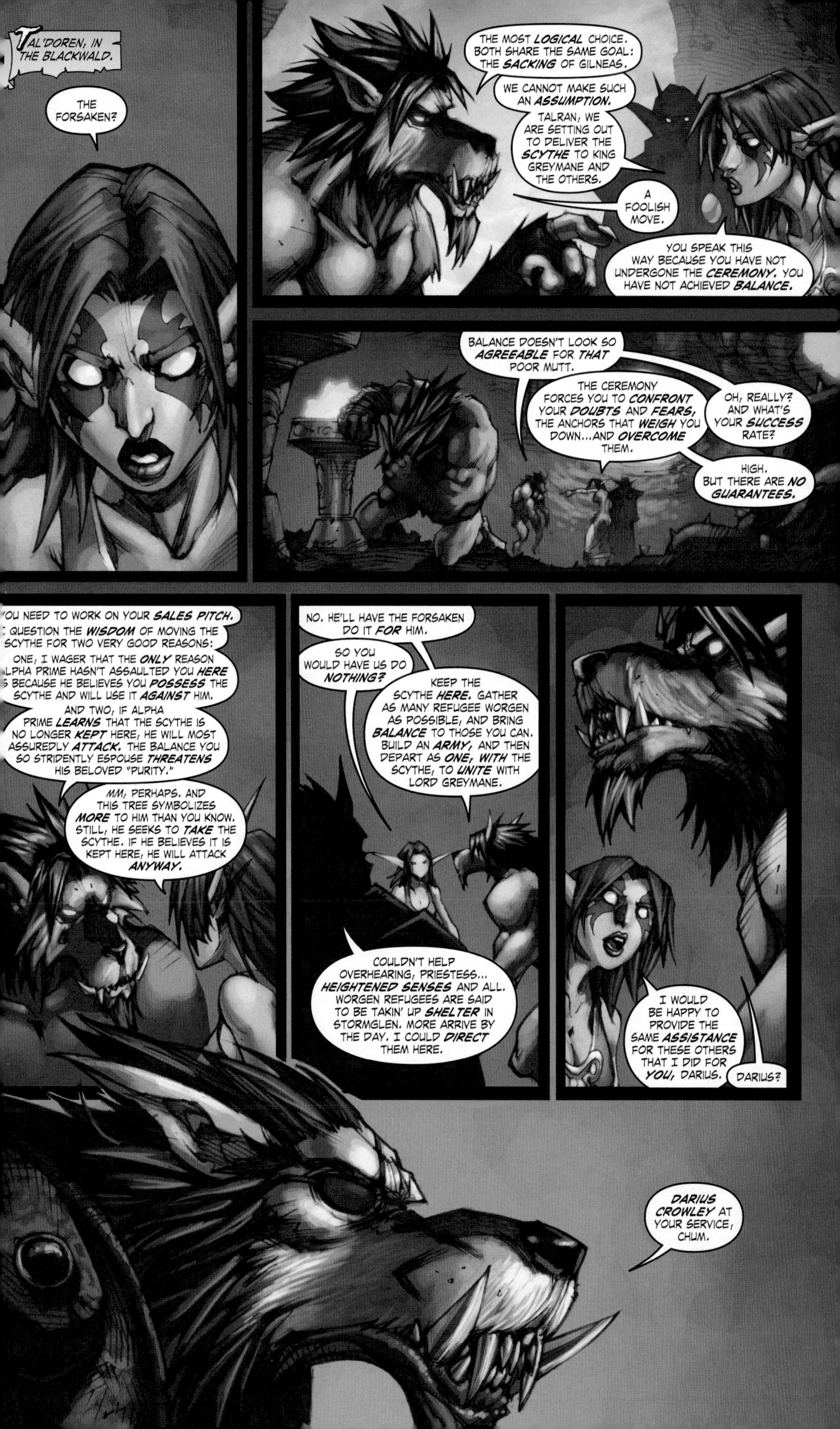
TAL'DOREN, IN THE BLACKWALD.
THE FORSAKEN?
THE MOST LOGICAL CHOICE. BOTH SHARE THE SAME GOAL: THE SACKING OF GILNEAS.
WE CANNOT MAKE SUCH AN ASSUMPTION.
TALRAN, WE ARE SETTING OUT TO DELIVER THE SCYTHE TO KING GREYMANE AND THE OTHERS.
A FOOLISH MOVE.
YOU SPEAK THIS WAY BECAUSE YOU HAVE NOT UNDERGONE THE CEREMONY. YOU HAVE NOT ACHIEVED BALANCE.
BALANCE DOESN'T LOOK SO AGREEABLE FOR THAT POOR MUTT.
THE CEREMONY FORCES YOU TO CONFRONT YOUR DOUBTS AND FEARS, THE ANCHORS THAT WEIGH YOU DOWN...AND OVERCOME THEM.
OH, REALLY? AND WHAT'S YOUR SUCCESS RATE?
HIGH. BUT THERE ARE NO GUARANTEES.
YOU NEED TO WORK ON YOUR SALES PITCH. I QUESTION THE WISDOM OF MOVING THE SCYTHE FOR TWO VERY GOOD REASONS:
ONE, I WAGER THAT THE ONLY REASON ALPHA PRIME HASN'T ASSAULTED YOU HERE IS BECAUSE HE BELIEVES YOU POSSESS THE SCYTHE AND WILL USE IT AGAINST HIM.
AND TWO, IF ALPHA PRIME LEARNS THAT THE SCYTHE IS NO LONGER KEPT HERE, HE WILL MOST ASSUREDLY ATTACK. THE BALANCE YOU SO STRIDENTLY ESPOUSE THREATENS HIS BELOVED "PURITY."
MM, PERHAPS. AND THIS TREE SYMBOLIZES MORE TO HIM THAN YOU KNOW. STILL, HE SEEKS TO TAKE THE SCYTHE. IF HE BELIEVES IT IS KEPT HERE, HE WILL ATTACK ANYWAY.
NO. HE'LL HAVE THE FORSAKEN DO IT FOR HIM.
SO YOU WOULD HAVE US DO NOTHING?
KEEP THE SCYTHE HERE. GATHER AS MANY REFUGEE WORGEN AS POSSIBLE, AND BRING BALANCE TO THOSE YOU CAN. BUILD AN ARMY, AND THEN DEPART AS ONE, WITH THE SCYTHE, TO UNITE WITH LORD GREYMANE.
COULDN'T HELP OVERHEARING, PRIESTESS... HEIGHTENED SENSES AND ALL. WORGEN REFUGEES ARE SAID TO BE TAKIN' UP SHELTER IN STORMGLEN. MORE ARRIVE BY THE DAY. I COULD DIRECT THEM HERE.
I WOULD BE HAPPY TO PROVIDE THE SAME ASSISTANCE FOR THESE OTHERS THAT I DID FOR YOU, DARIUS.
DARIUS?
DARIUS CROWLEY AT YOUR SERVICE, CHUM.

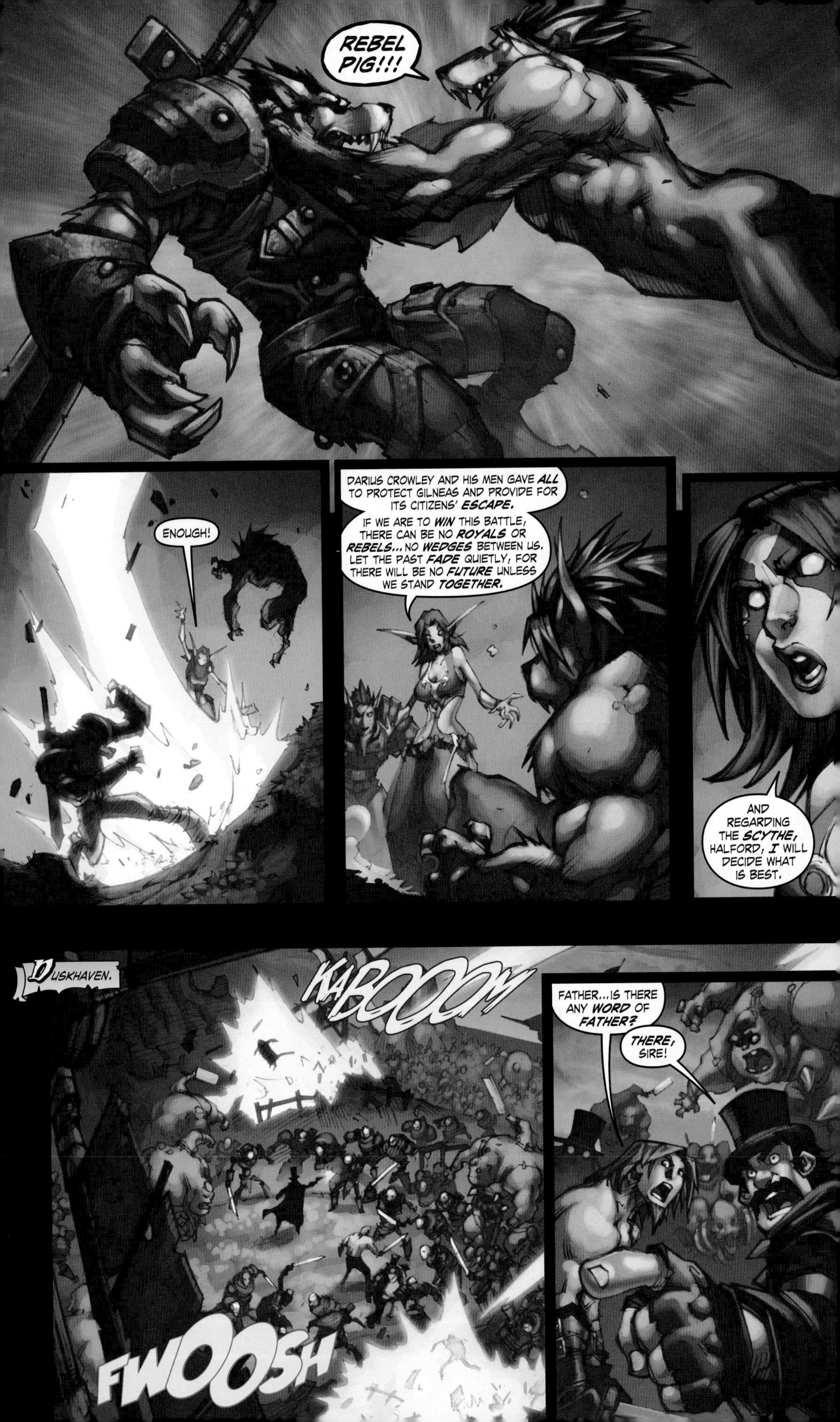
REBEL PIG!!!
ENOUGH!
DARIUS CROWLEY AND HIS MEN GAVE ALL TO PROTECT GILNEAS AND PROVIDE FOR ITS CITIZENS' ESCAPE.
IF WE ARE TO WIN THIS BATTLE, THERE CAN BE NO ROYALS OR REBELS... NO WEDGES BETWEEN US. LET THE PAST FADE QUIETLY, FOR THERE WILL BE NO FUTURE UNLESS WE STAND TOGETHER.
AND REGARDING THE SCYTHE, HALFORD, I WILL DECIDE WHAT IS BEST.
DUSKHAVEN.
KABOOOM
FATHER... IS THERE ANY WORD OF FATHER?
THERE, SIRE!
FWOOSH

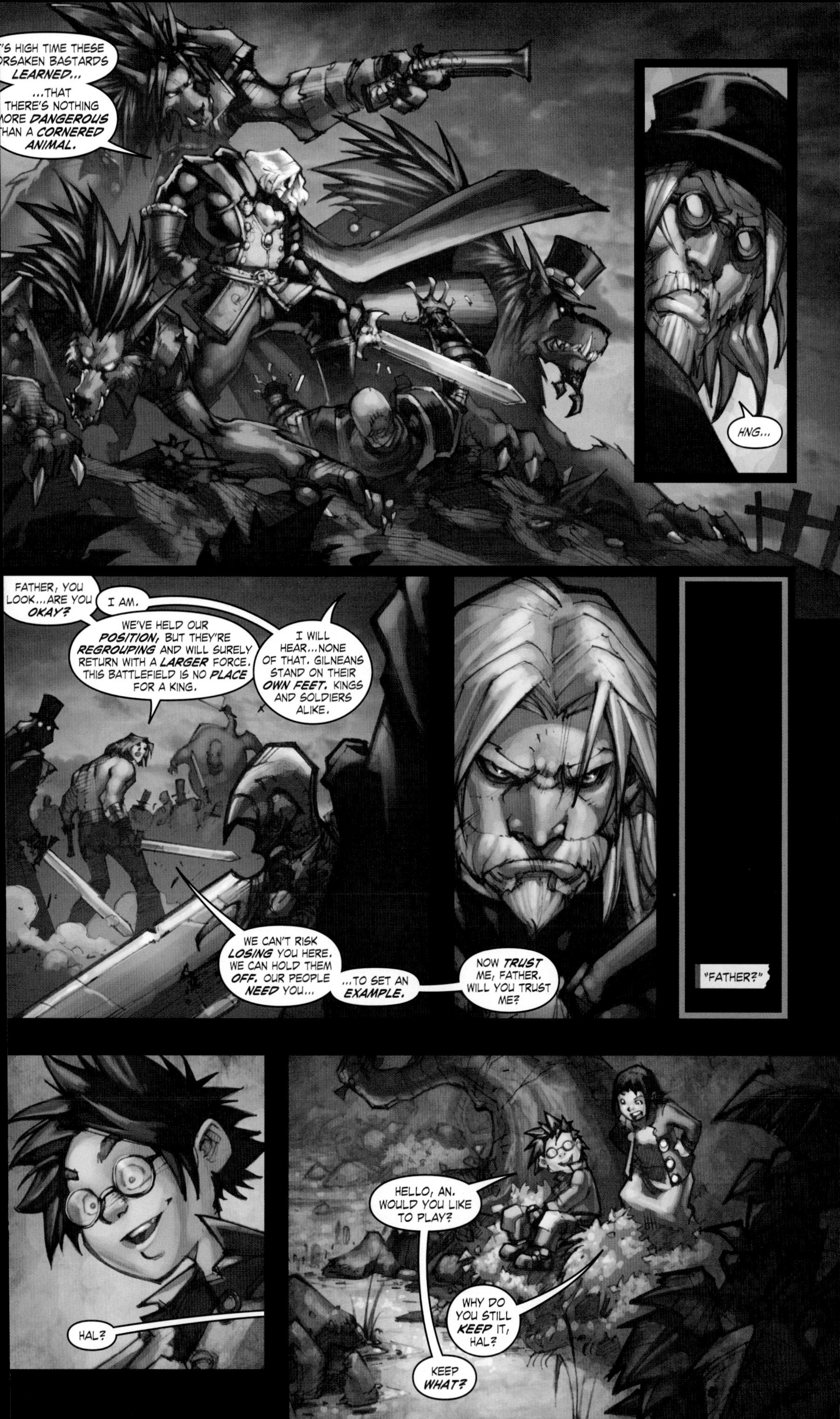

'S HIGH TIME THESE
ORSAKEN BASTARDS
LEARNED...
...THAT THERE'S NOTHING MORE DANGEROUS THAN A CORNERED ANIMAL.
HNG...
FATHER, YOU LOOK...ARE YOU OKAY?
I AM.
WE'VE HELD OUR POSITION, BUT THEY'RE REGROUPING AND WILL SURELY RETURN WITH A LARGER FORCE. THIS BATTLEFIELD IS NO PLACE FOR A KING.
I WILL HEAR...NONE OF THAT. GILNEANS STAND ON THEIR OWN FEET. KINGS AND SOLDIERS ALIKE.
WE CAN'T RISK LOSING YOU HERE. WE CAN HOLD THEM OFF. OUR PEOPLE NEED YOU...
...TO SET AN EXAMPLE.
NOW TRUST ME, FATHER. WILL YOU TRUST ME?
"FATHER?"
HAL?
HELLO, AN. WOULD YOU LIKE TO PLAY?
WHY DO YOU STILL KEEP IT, HAL?
KEEP WHAT?

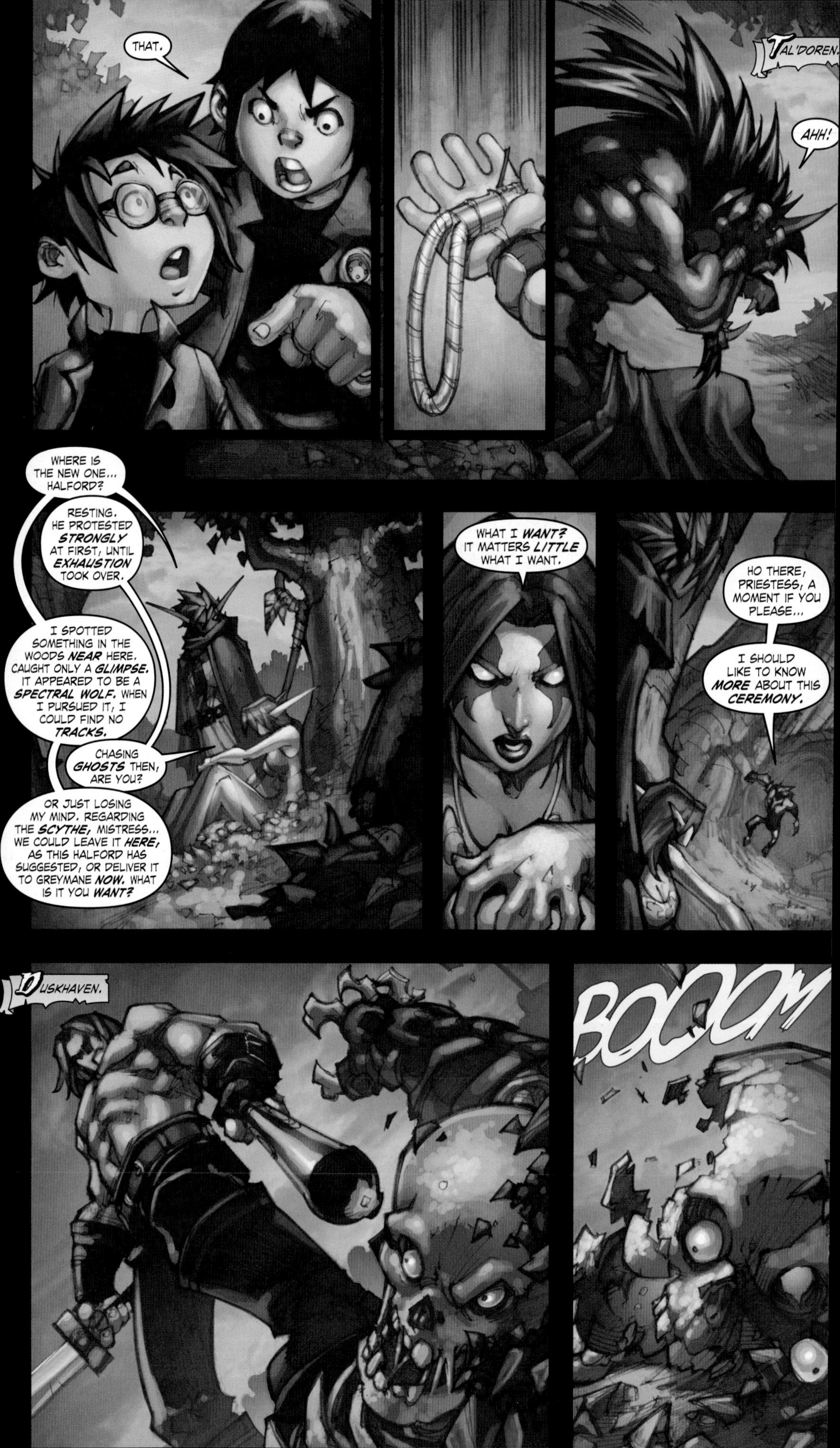
THAT.
TAL'DOREN.
AHH!
WHERE IS THE NEW ONE... HALFORD?
RESTING. HE PROTESTED STRONGLY AT FIRST, UNTIL EXHAUSTION TOOK OVER.
I SPOTTED SOMETHING IN THE WOODS NEAR HERE. CAUGHT ONLY A GLIMPSE. IT APPEARED TO BE A SPECTRAL WOLF. WHEN I PURSUED IT, I COULD FIND NO TRACKS.
CHASING GHOSTS THEN, ARE YOU?
OR JUST LOSING MY MIND. REGARDING THE SCYTHE, MISTRESS... WE COULD LEAVE IT HERE, AS THIS HALFORD HAS SUGGESTED, OR DELIVER IT TO GREYMANE NOW. WHAT IS IT YOU WANT?
WHAT I WANT? IT MATTERS LITTLE WHAT I WANT.
HO THERE, PRIESTESS, A MOMENT IF YOU PLEASE...
I SHOULD LIKE TO KNOW MORE ABOUT THIS CEREMONY.
DUSKHAVEN.
BOOOM

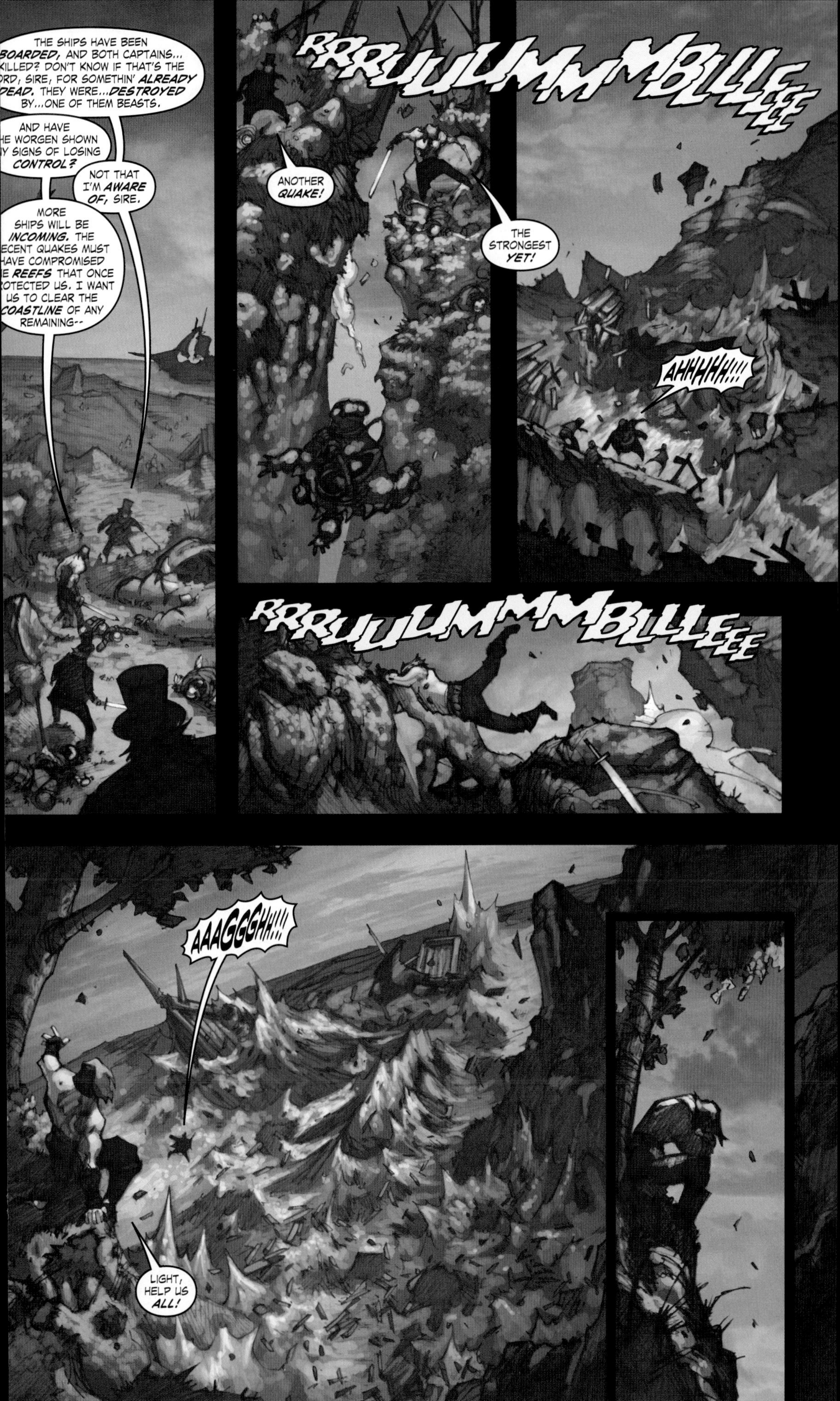

THE SHIPS HAVE BEEN BOARDED, AND BOTH CAPTAINS... KILLED? DON'T KNOW IF THAT'S THE ORD, SIRE, FOR SOMETHIN' ALREADY DEAD. THEY WERE...DESTROYED BY...ONE OF THEM BEASTS.
AND HAVE HE WORGEN SHOWN Y SIGNS OF LOSING CONTROL?
NOT THAT I'M AWARE OF, SIRE.
MORE SHIPS WILL BE INCOMING. THE ECENT QUAKES MUST HAVE COMPROMISED E REEFS THAT ONCE ROTECTED US. I WANT US TO CLEAR THE COASTLINE OF ANY REMAINING--
RRRUUUUMMMMBLLLEEE
ANOTHER QUAKE!
THE STRONGEST YET!
AHHHHH!!!
RRRUUUUMMMMBLLLEEE
AAAGGGHH!!!
LIGHT, HELP US ALL!

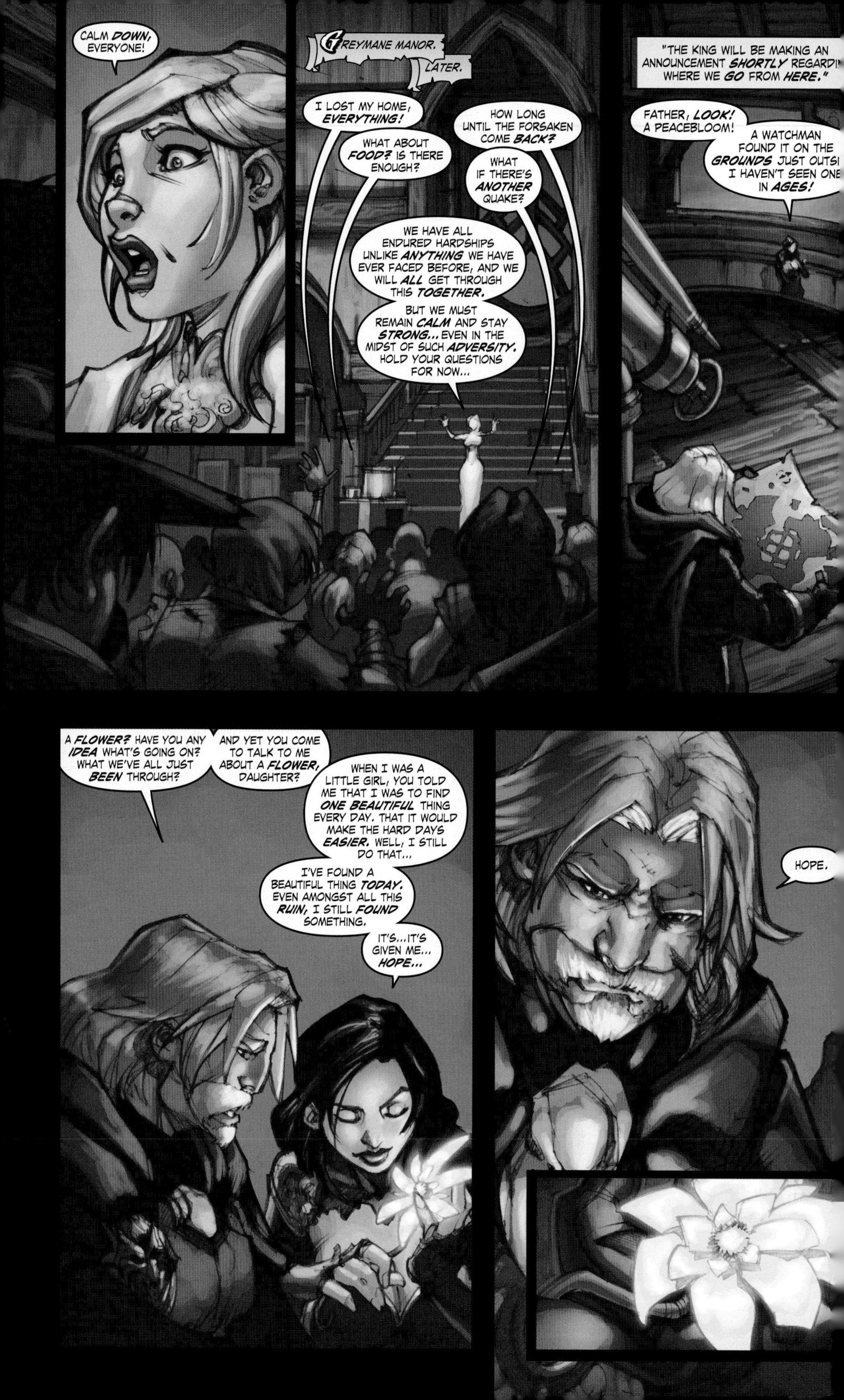
CALM DOWN, EVERYONE!
GREYMANE MANOR.
LATER.
I LOST MY HOME, EVERYTHING!
WHAT ABOUT FOOD? IS THERE ENOUGH?
HOW LONG UNTIL THE FORSAKEN COME BACK?
WHAT IF THERE'S ANOTHER QUAKE?
WE HAVE ALL ENDURED HARDSHIPS UNLIKE ANYTHING WE HAVE EVER FACED BEFORE, AND WE WILL ALL GET THROUGH THIS TOGETHER.
BUT WE MUST REMAIN CALM AND STAY STRONG... EVEN IN THE MIDST OF SUCH ADVERSITY. HOLD YOUR QUESTIONS FOR NOW...
"THE KING WILL BE MAKING AN ANNOUNCEMENT SHORTLY REGARDI WHERE WE GO FROM HERE."
FATHER, LOOK! A PEACEBLOOM!
A WATCHMAN FOUND IT ON THE GROUNDS JUST OUTSI I HAVEN'T SEEN ONE IN AGES!
A FLOWER? HAVE YOU ANY IDEA WHAT'S GOING ON? WHAT WE'VE ALL JUST BEEN THROUGH?
AND YET YOU COME TO TALK TO ME ABOUT A FLOWER, DAUGHTER?
WHEN I WAS A LITTLE GIRL, YOU TOLD ME THAT I WAS TO FIND ONE BEAUTIFUL THING EVERY DAY. THAT IT WOULD MAKE THE HARD DAYS EASIER. WELL, I STILL DO THAT...
I'VE FOUND A BEAUTIFUL THING TODAY. EVEN AMONGST ALL THIS RUIN, I STILL FOUND SOMETHING.
IT'S...IT'S GIVEN ME... HOPE...
HOPE.

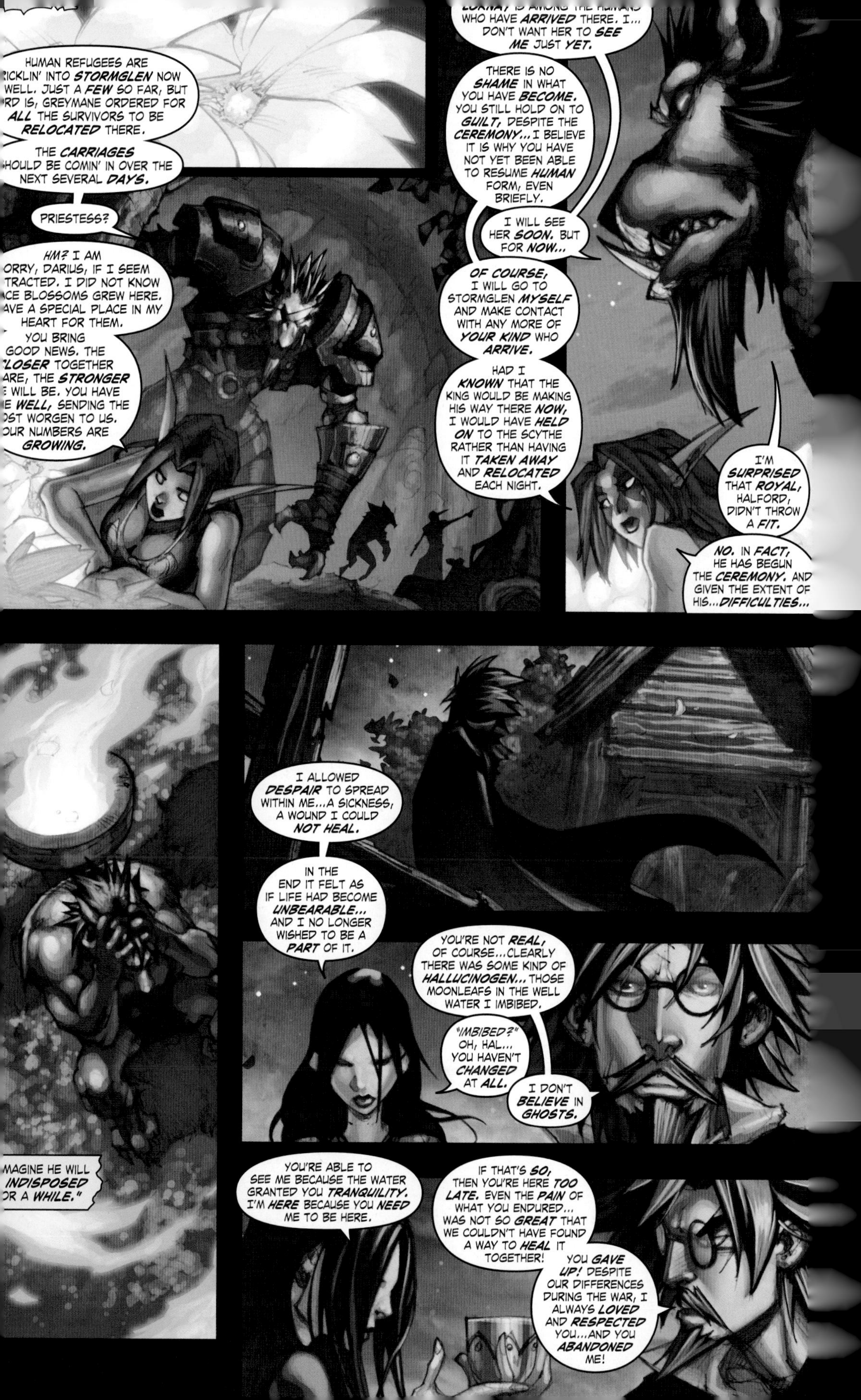

HUMAN REFUGEES ARE RICKLIN' INTO STORMGLEN NOW WELL. JUST A FEW SO FAR, BUT RD IS, GREYMANE ORDERED FOR ALL THE SURVIVORS TO BE RELOCATED THERE.
THE CARRIAGES HOULD BE COMIN' IN OVER THE NEXT SEVERAL DAYS.
PRIESTESS?
HM? I AM ORRY, DARIUS, IF I SEEM TRACTED. I DID NOT KNOW ACE BLOSSOMS GREW HERE. AVE A SPECIAL PLACE IN MY HEART FOR THEM.
YOU BRING GOOD NEWS. THE LOSER TOGETHER ARE, THE STRONGER E WILL BE. YOU HAVE E WELL, SENDING THE OST WORGEN TO US. OUR NUMBERS ARE GROWING.
WHO HAVE ARRIVED THERE. I... DON'T WANT HER TO SEE ME JUST YET.
THERE IS NO SHAME IN WHAT YOU HAVE BECOME. YOU STILL HOLD ON TO GUILT, DESPITE THE CEREMONY... I BELIEVE IT IS WHY YOU HAVE NOT YET BEEN ABLE TO RESUME HUMAN FORM, EVEN BRIEFLY.
I WILL SEE HER SOON. BUT FOR NOW...
OF COURSE; I WILL GO TO STORMGLEN MYSELF AND MAKE CONTACT WITH ANY MORE OF YOUR KIND WHO ARRIVE.
HAD I KNOWN THAT THE KING WOULD BE MAKING HIS WAY THERE NOW, I WOULD HAVE HELD ON TO THE SCYTHE RATHER THAN HAVING IT TAKEN AWAY AND RELOCATED EACH NIGHT.
I'M SURPRISED THAT ROYAL, HALFORD, DIDN'T THROW A FIT.
NO. IN FACT, HE HAS BEGUN THE CEREMONY. AND GIVEN THE EXTENT OF HIS...DIFFICULTIES...
MAGINE HE WILL INDISPOSED OR A WHILE."
I ALLOWED DESPAIR TO SPREAD WITHIN ME...A SICKNESS, A WOUND I COULD NOT HEAL.
IN THE END IT FELT AS IF LIFE HAD BECOME UNBEARABLE... AND I NO LONGER WISHED TO BE A PART OF IT.
YOU'RE NOT REAL, OF COURSE...CLEARLY THERE WAS SOME KIND OF HALLUCINOGEN... THOSE MOONLEAFS IN THE WELL WATER I IMBIBED.
"IMBIBED?" OH, HAL... YOU HAVEN'T CHANGED AT ALL.
I DON'T BELIEVE IN GHOSTS.
YOU'RE ABLE TO SEE ME BECAUSE THE WATER GRANTED YOU TRANQUILITY. I'M HERE BECAUSE YOU NEED ME TO BE HERE.
IF THAT'S SO, THEN YOU'RE HERE TOO LATE. EVEN THE PAIN OF WHAT YOU ENDURED... WAS NOT SO GREAT THAT WE COULDN'T HAVE FOUND A WAY TO HEAL IT TOGETHER!
YOU GAVE UP! DESPITE OUR DIFFERENCES DURING THE WAR, I ALWAYS LOVED AND RESPECTED YOU...AND YOU ABANDONED ME!

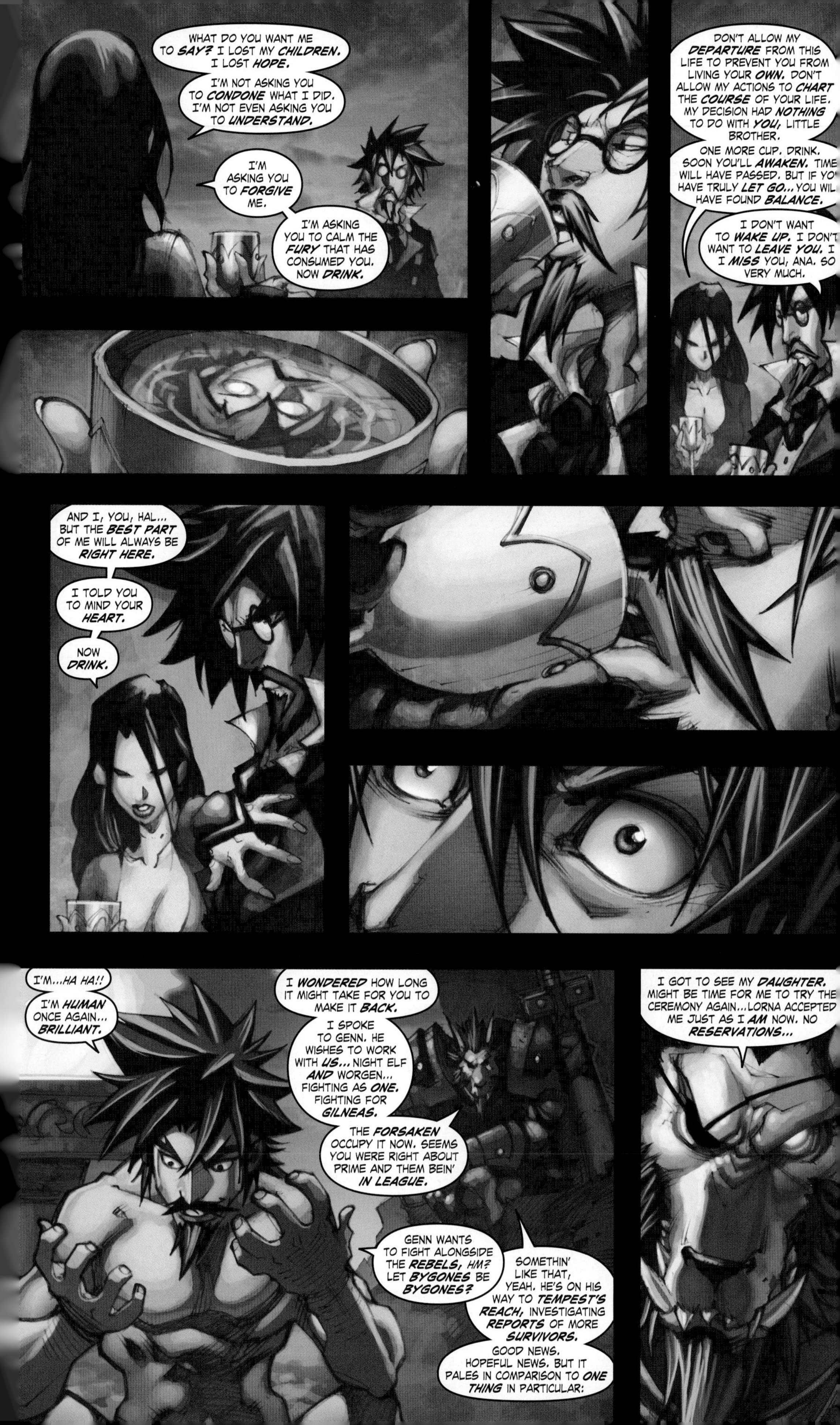
WHAT DO YOU WANT ME TO SAY? I LOST MY CHILDREN. I LOST HOPE.
I'M NOT ASKING YOU TO CONDONE WHAT I DID. I'M NOT EVEN ASKING YOU TO UNDERSTAND.
I'M ASKING YOU TO FORGIVE ME.
I'M ASKING YOU TO CALM THE FURY THAT HAS CONSUMED YOU. NOW DRINK.
DON'T ALLOW MY DEPARTURE FROM THIS LIFE TO PREVENT YOU FROM LIVING YOUR OWN. DON'T ALLOW MY ACTIONS TO CHART THE COURSE OF YOUR LIFE. MY DECISION HAD NOTHING TO DO WITH YOU, LITTLE BROTHER.
ONE MORE CUP. DRINK. SOON YOU'LL AWAKEN. TIME WILL HAVE PASSED. BUT IF YO HAVE TRULY LET GO...YOU WIL HAVE FOUND BALANCE.
I DON'T WANT TO WAKE UP. I DON'T WANT TO LEAVE YOU. I I MISS YOU, ANA. SO VERY MUCH.
AND I, YOU, HAL... BUT THE BEST PART OF ME WILL ALWAYS BE RIGHT HERE.
I TOLD YOU TO MIND YOUR HEART.
NOW DRINK.
I'M...HA HA!!
I'M HUMAN ONCE AGAIN... BRILLIANT.
I WONDERED HOW LONG IT MIGHT TAKE FOR YOU TO MAKE IT BACK.
I SPOKE TO GENN. HE WISHES TO WORK WITH US... NIGHT ELF AND WORGEN... FIGHTING AS ONE. FIGHTING FOR GILNEAS.
THE FORSAKEN OCCUPY IT NOW. SEEMS YOU WERE RIGHT ABOUT PRIME AND THEM BEIN' IN LEAGUE.
GENN WANTS TO FIGHT ALONGSIDE THE REBELS, HM? LET BYGONES BE BYGONES?
SOMETHIN' LIKE THAT, YEAH. HE'S ON HIS WAY TO TEMPEST'S REACH, INVESTIGATING REPORTS OF MORE SURVIVORS.
GOOD NEWS. HOPEFUL NEWS. BUT IT PALES IN COMPARISON TO ONE THING IN PARTICULAR:
I GOT TO SEE MY DAUGHTER. MIGHT BE TIME FOR ME TO TRY THE CEREMONY AGAIN...LORNA ACCEPTED ME JUST AS I AM NOW. NO RESERVATIONS...

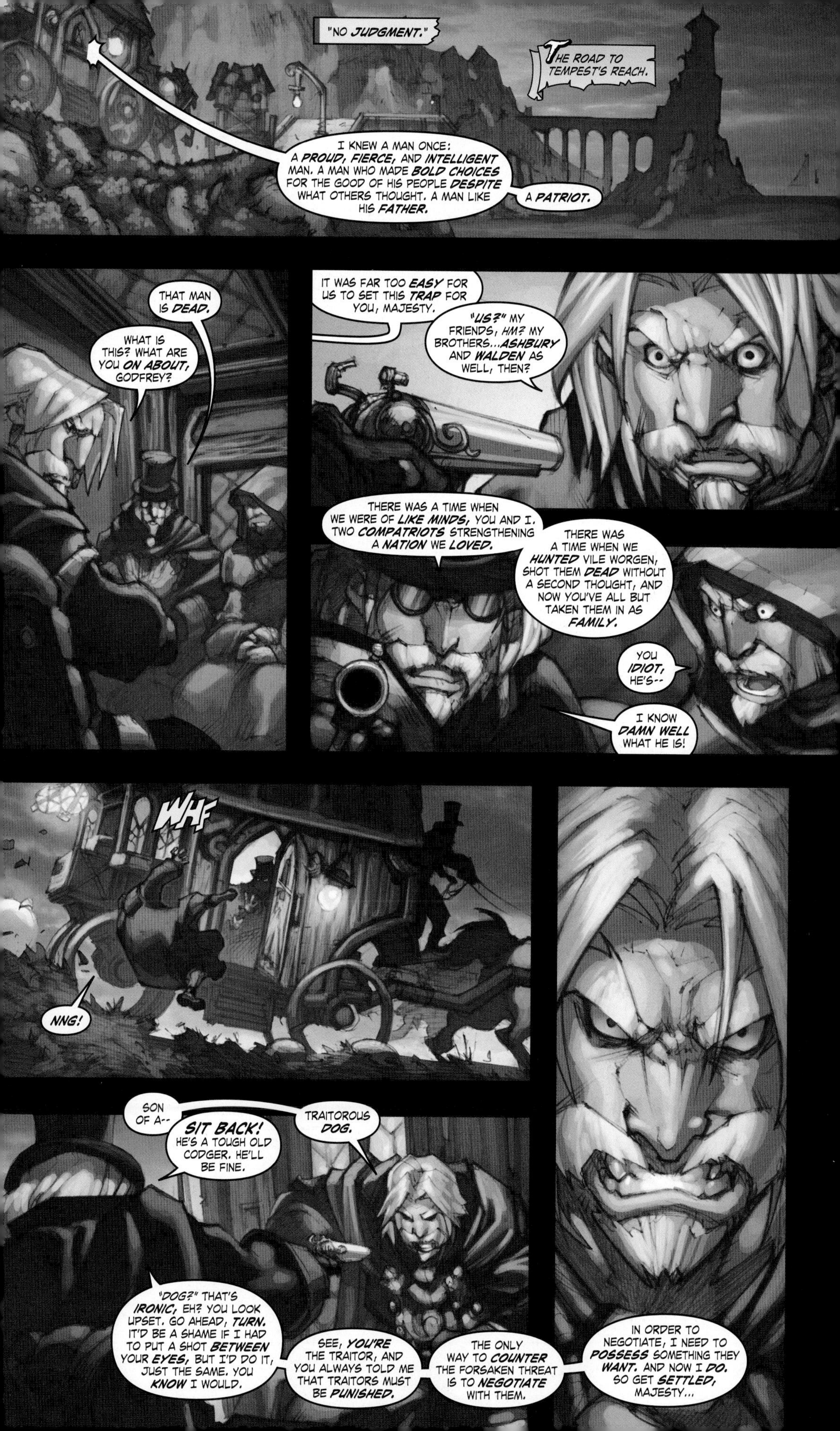

"NO JUDGMENT."
THE ROAD TO TEMPEST'S REACH.
I KNEW A MAN ONCE: A PROUD, FIERCE, AND INTELLIGENT MAN. A MAN WHO MADE BOLD CHOICES FOR THE GOOD OF HIS PEOPLE DESPITE WHAT OTHERS THOUGHT. A MAN LIKE HIS FATHER.
A PATRIOT.
THAT MAN IS DEAD.
WHAT IS THIS? WHAT ARE YOU ON ABOUT, GODFREY?
IT WAS FAR TOO EASY FOR US TO SET THIS TRAP FOR YOU, MAJESTY.
"US?" MY FRIENDS, HM? MY BROTHERS...ASHBURY AND WALDEN AS WELL, THEN?
THERE WAS A TIME WHEN WE WERE OF LIKE MINDS, YOU AND I. TWO COMPATRIOTS STRENGTHENING A NATION WE LOVED.
THERE WAS A TIME WHEN WE HUNTED VILE WORGEN, SHOT THEM DEAD WITHOUT A SECOND THOUGHT, AND NOW YOU'VE ALL BUT TAKEN THEM IN AS FAMILY.
YOU IDIOT, HE'S--
I KNOW DAMN WELL WHAT HE IS!
WHF
NNG!
SON OF A--
TRAITOROUS DOG.
SIT BACK! HE'S A TOUGH OLD CODGER. HE'LL BE FINE.
"DOG?" THAT'S IRONIC, EH? YOU LOOK UPSET. GO AHEAD, TURN. IT'D BE A SHAME IF I HAD TO PUT A SHOT BETWEEN YOUR EYES, BUT I'D DO IT, JUST THE SAME. YOU KNOW I WOULD.
SEE, YOU'RE THE TRAITOR, AND YOU ALWAYS TOLD ME THAT TRAITORS MUST BE PUNISHED.
THE ONLY WAY TO COUNTER THE FORSAKEN THREAT IS TO NEGOTIATE WITH THEM.
IN ORDER TO NEGOTIATE, I NEED TO POSSESS SOMETHING THEY WANT. AND NOW I DO. SO GET SETTLED, MAJESTY...

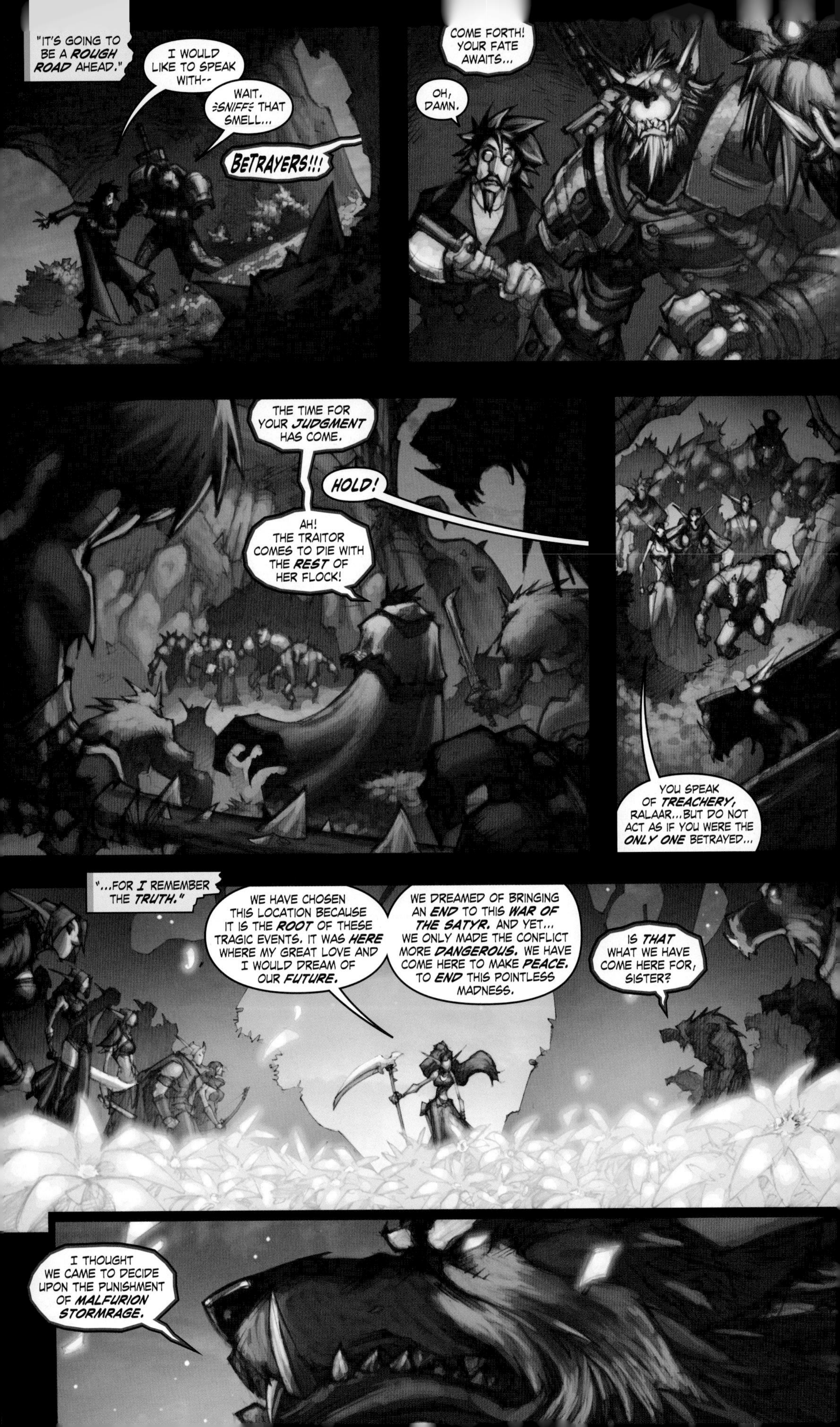
"IT'S GOING TO BE A ROUGH ROAD AHEAD."
I WOULD LIKE TO SPEAK WITH--
WAIT. SNIFF THAT SMELL...
BETRAYERS!!!
COME FORTH! YOUR FATE AWAITS...
OH, DAMN.
THE TIME FOR YOUR JUDGMENT HAS COME.
HOLD!
AH! THE TRAITOR COMES TO DIE WITH THE REST OF HER FLOCK!
YOU SPEAK OF TREACHERY, RALAAR...BUT DO NOT ACT AS IF YOU WERE THE ONLY ONE BETRAYED...
"...FOR I REMEMBER THE TRUTH."
WE HAVE CHOSEN THIS LOCATION BECAUSE IT IS THE ROOT OF THESE TRAGIC EVENTS. IT WAS HERE WHERE MY GREAT LOVE AND I WOULD DREAM OF OUR FUTURE.
WE DREAMED OF BRINGING AN END TO THIS WAR OF THE SATYR. AND YET... WE ONLY MADE THE CONFLICT MORE DANGEROUS. WE HAVE COME HERE TO MAKE PEACE. TO END THIS POINTLESS MADNESS.
IS THAT WHAT WE HAVE COME HERE FOR, SISTER?
I THOUGHT WE CAME TO DECIDE UPON THE PUNISHMENT OF MALFURION STORMRAGE.

IT *PAINS* ME TO SEE YOU LIKE THIS, MY *THERO'SHAN.* YOU HAVE LOST SIGHT OF THE *TRUTH* OF YOUR CALLING. *BALANCE.* NO DRUID WAS EVER MEANT TO LIVE IN A FORM *PERMANENTLY.*

LET US *RESOLVE* THIS MATTER AND BRING *PEACE,* RALAAR. WE NEED NOT CONTINUE OUR *WAR.*

THERE IS NO MORE RALAAR... AND THERE WILL BE *NO* PEACE THIS DAY...

DRUIDS OF THE SCYTHE, *NOW* IS THE TIME FOR OUR *VENGEANCE!!!* *STRIKE!!!!*

BETRAYAL WAS THEIR PLAN *ALL ALONG!!!!*

THE TIME IS RIGHT FOR *OURS,* THEN!

BELYSRA... *NOW!!!!*

ELUNE, *GUIDE* MY HAND!!

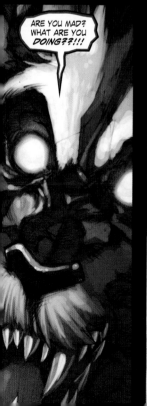

ARE YOU MAD? WHAT ARE YOU *DOING??!!!*

TWUUMP

TRAITOR!!!

THEY HAVE THE SCYTHE!

THE *FANG* OF THE *FATHER!!!*

IT COMES TO AN END *NOW,* RALAAR. YOU HAVE MURDERED *HUNDREDS.* YOU HAVE TURNED MANY INTO MONSTERS JUST LIKE *YOU.* YOUR FURY KNOWS NO *BOUNDS.*

AND FOR *THAT,* YOU WILL BE BANISHED.

BROTHER DRUIDS, *NOW!*

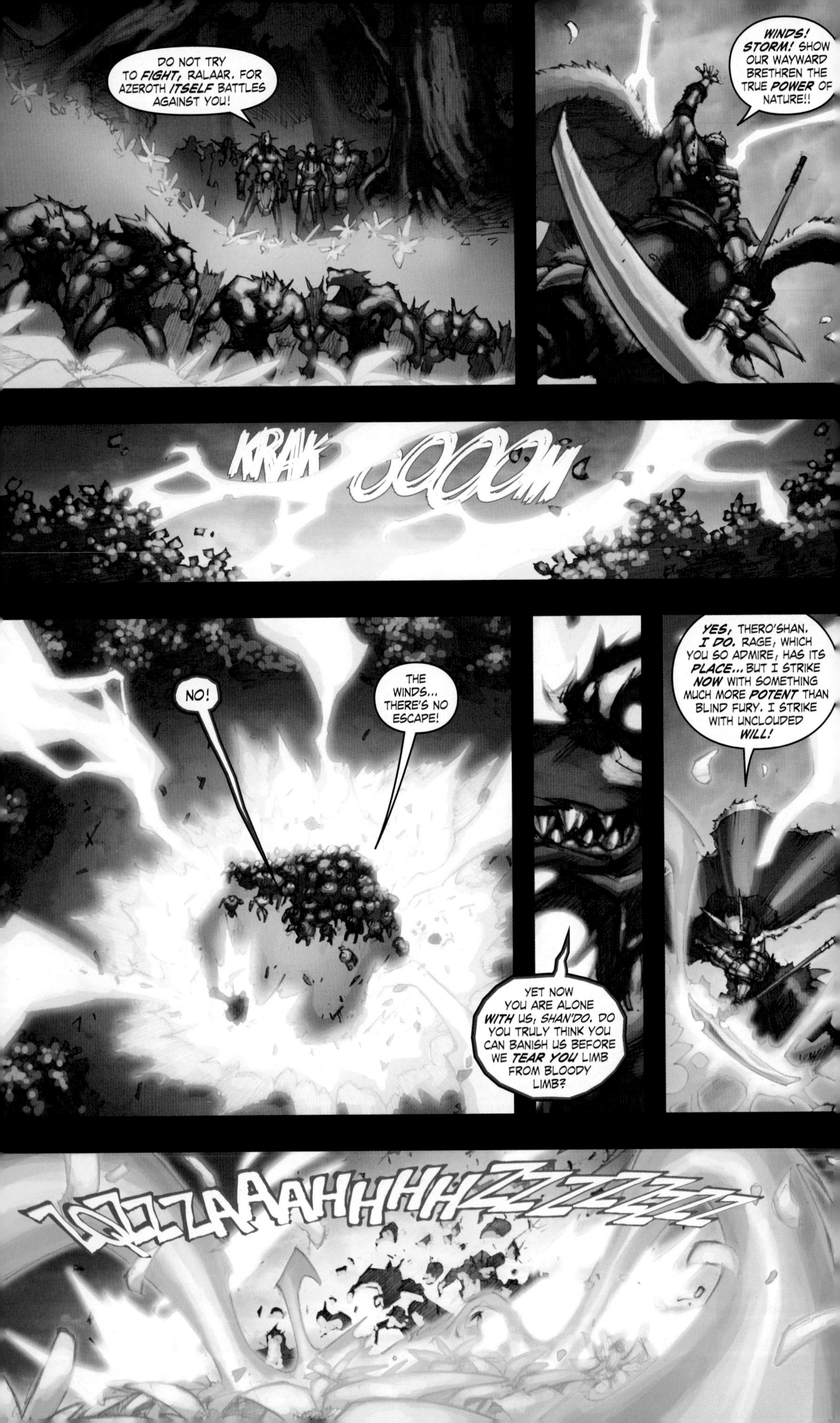

DO NOT TRY TO *FIGHT*, RALAAR. FOR AZEROTH *ITSELF* BATTLES AGAINST YOU!
WINDS! STORM! SHOW OUR WAYWARD BRETHREN THE TRUE *POWER* OF NATURE!!
KRAK OOOOOM
NO!
THE WINDS... THERE'S NO ESCAPE!
YET NOW YOU ARE ALONE *WITH* US, *SHAN'DO*. DO YOU TRULY THINK YOU CAN BANISH US BEFORE WE *TEAR YOU* LIMB FROM BLOODY LIMB?
YES, THERO'SHAN. *I DO.* RAGE, WHICH YOU SO ADMIRE, HAS ITS *PLACE...* BUT I STRIKE *NOW* WITH SOMETHING MUCH MORE *POTENT* THAN BLIND FURY. I STRIKE WITH UNCLOUDED *WILL!*

NOOOOOoooo...
AND SO IT *ENDS.* REST SOUNDLY. SLEEP IN THE *CALM* OF THE *EMERALD DREAM,* AND...
DREAM THE *DREAMS* OF THE *WILD.*
BE AT *PEACE. FOREVER.*

"BE AT PEACE?"
AT *PEACE?!*
WE ARE MEANT TO *RUN!*
TO *HUNT!*

THE *EXILE* OF THE DREAM WAS
A TORTURE YOU COULD NEVER POSSIBLY
COMPREHEND! YOU CANNOT TAME WHAT
IS MEANT TO BE *WILD!*

YOU LEFT US NO *CHOICE.*
IT IS NOT TOO *LATE* TO TURN FROM
THIS FOOLISH *QUEST,* RALAAR.

OH, I'LL NOT BE *ABANDONING* MY
QUEST. I LEARNED NOT *LONG AGO* THAT THE
FORSAKEN HAVE LAID CLAIM TO THE SCYTHE.
A *PITY* YOU MAY NO LONGER HIDE *BEHIND* IT.

YOU AR
ABSOLUTE
CORREC
RALAAR.

THE FORSAKEN DID
TAKE POSSESSION OF T
SCYTHE...FOR A *TIME.* BU
WAS SECURED BY ONE OF
VERY *CITIZENS* YOU *CURS
TALRAN, IF YOU PLEASE

IMBUED WITH THE *POWERS* OF
MY BROTHER DRUIDS, THE SCYTHE WILL NOW
STILL THE CHAOS YOU HAVE SOWN...I WILL SEND
YOU BACK TO THE *"TORTURE"* YOU ESCAPED.

NO!
NOT AGAI
NEVER!

BACK TO
THE DREAM,
RALAAR!

ATTAAAC

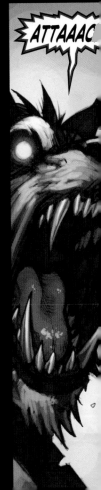

THUNKT

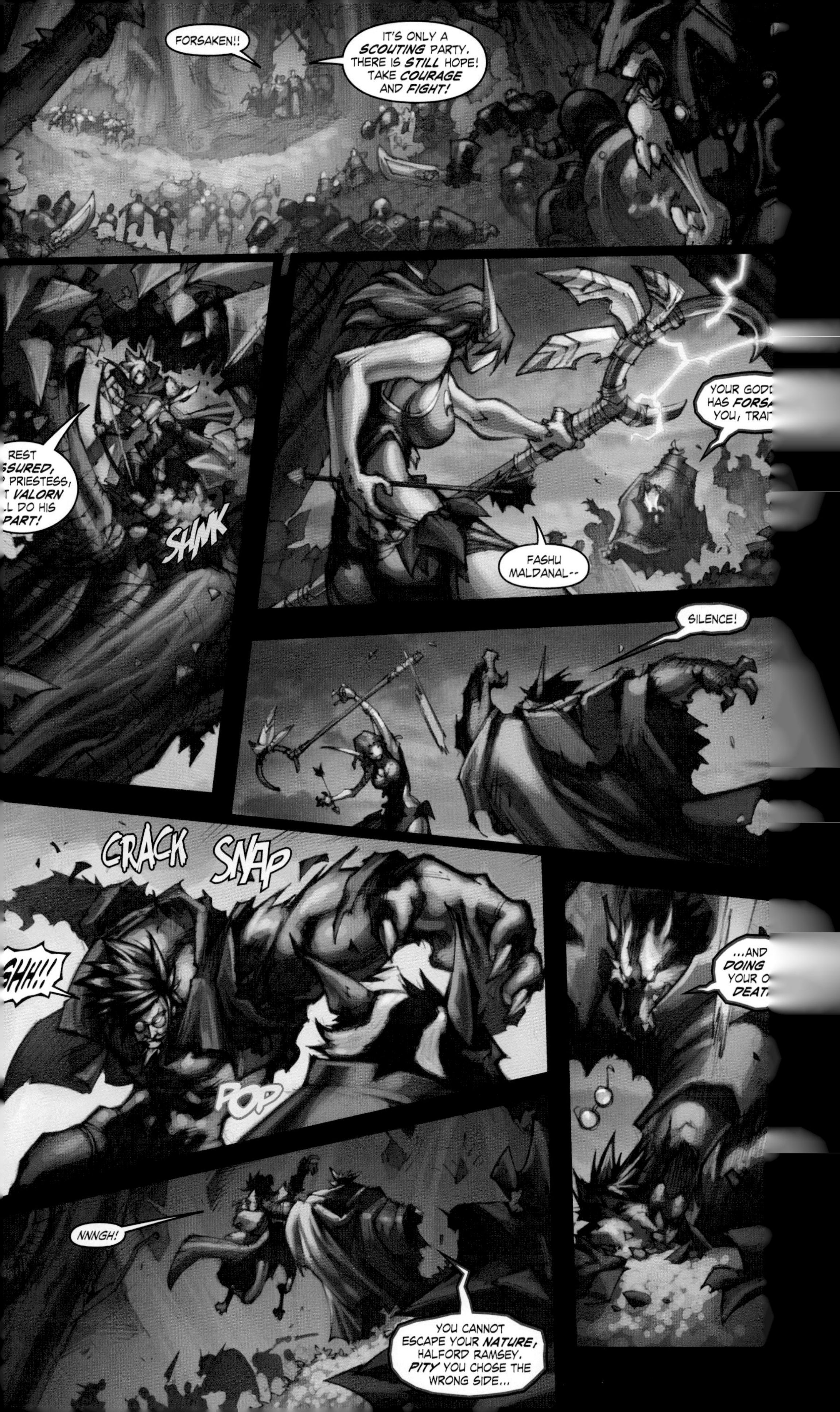
FORSAKEN!!
IT'S ONLY A SCOUTING PARTY. THERE IS STILL HOPE! TAKE COURAGE AND FIGHT!
REST SSURED, PRIESTESS, T VALORN L DO HIS PART!
SHNK
YOUR GODD HAS FORSA YOU, TRAI
FASHU MALDANAL--
SILENCE!
CRACK
SNAP
GHH!!
POP
...AND DOING YOUR O DEAT
NNNGH!
YOU CANNOT ESCAPE YOUR NATURE, HALFORD RAMSEY. PITY YOU CHOSE THE WRONG SIDE...

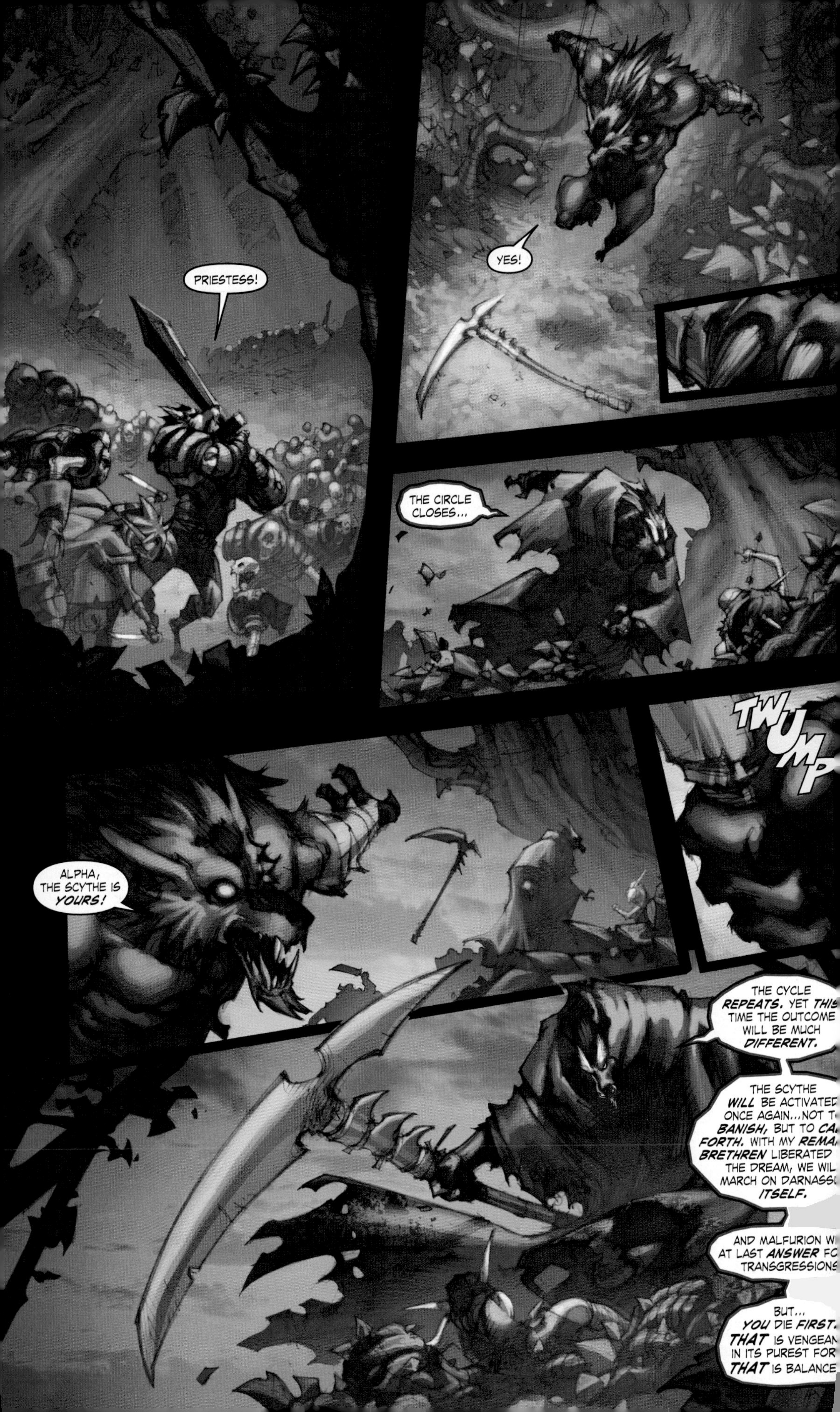
PRIESTESS!
YES!
THE CIRCLE CLOSES...
TWUMP
ALPHA, THE SCYTHE IS YOURS!
THE CYCLE REPEATS. YET THIS TIME THE OUTCOME WILL BE MUCH DIFFERENT.
THE SCYTHE WILL BE ACTIVATED ONCE AGAIN...NOT T BANISH, BUT TO CA FORTH. WITH MY REMA BRETHREN LIBERATED THE DREAM, WE WIL MARCH ON DARNASS ITSELF.
AND MALFURION W AT LAST ANSWER FO TRANSGRESSIONS
BUT... YOU DIE FIRST. THAT IS VENGEAN IN ITS PUREST FOR THAT IS BALANCE

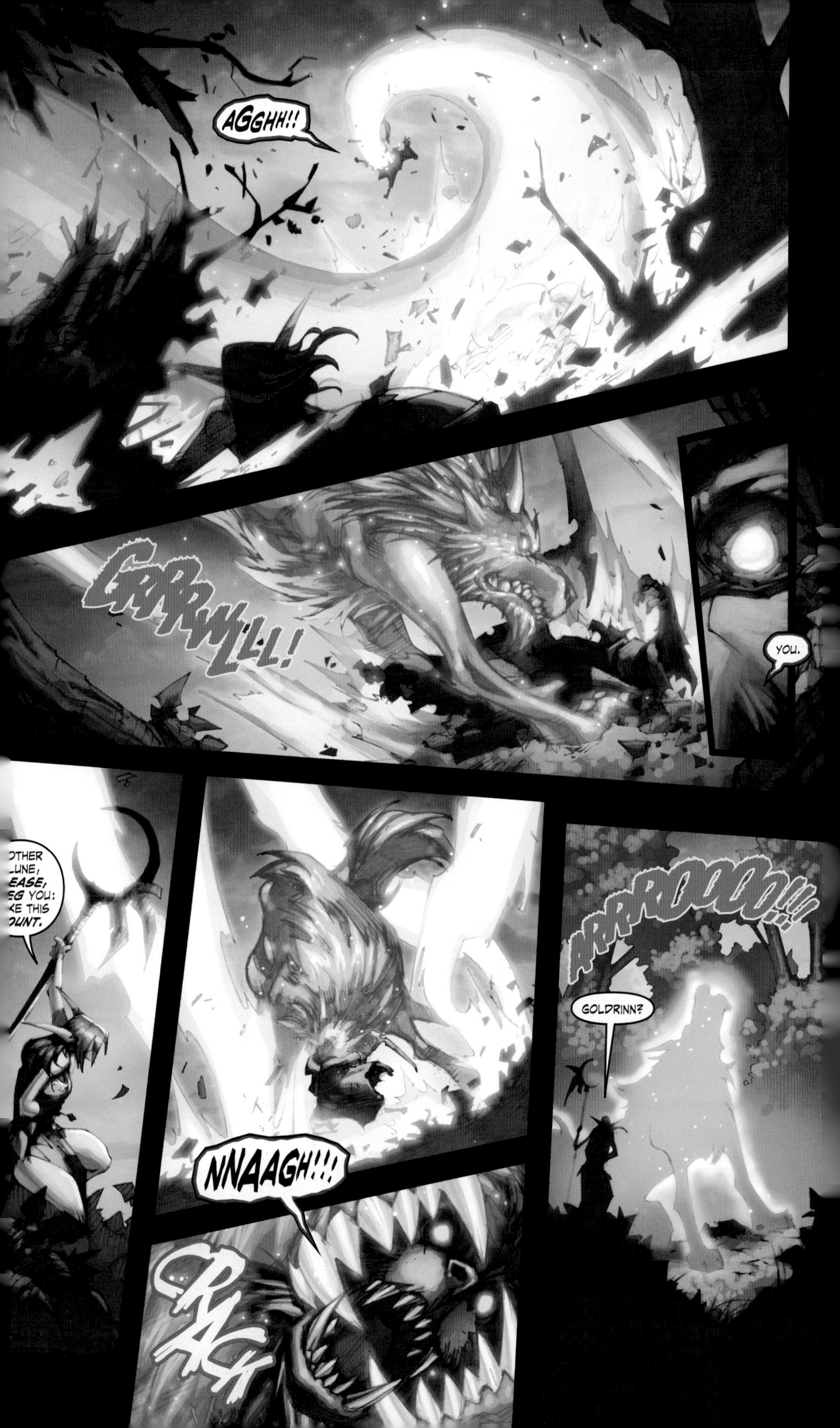
AGGHH!!
GRRRWLLL!
YOU.
OTHER
LUNE,
EASE,
EG YOU:
KE THIS
OUNT.
NNAAGH!!!
CRACK
ARRRROOOO!!!
GOLDRINN?

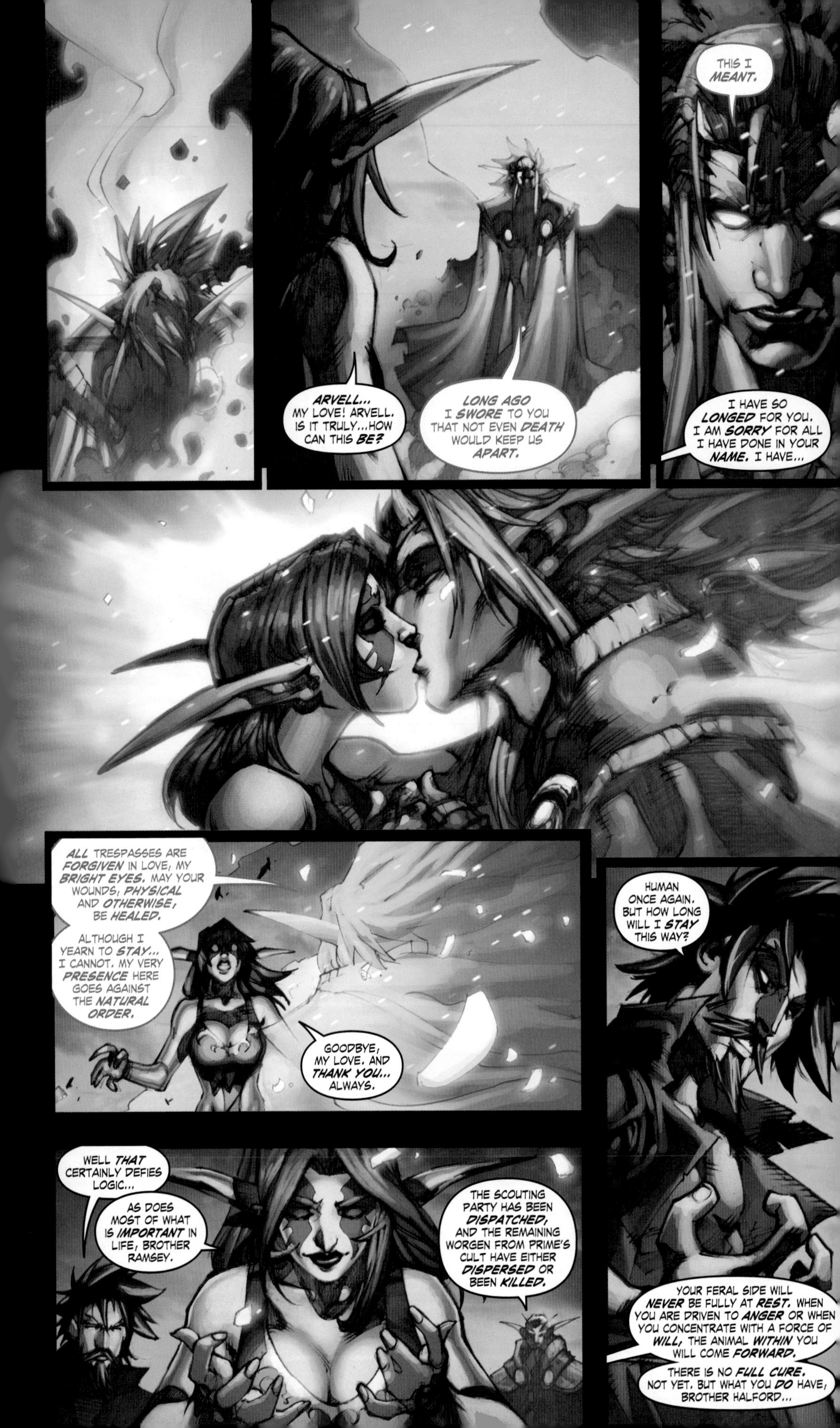
ARVELL... MY LOVE! ARVELL. IS IT TRULY...HOW CAN THIS BE?
LONG AGO I SWORE TO YOU THAT NOT EVEN DEATH WOULD KEEP US APART.
THIS I MEANT.
I HAVE SO LONGED FOR YOU. I AM SORRY FOR ALL I HAVE DONE IN YOUR NAME. I HAVE...
ALL TRESPASSES ARE FORGIVEN IN LOVE, MY BRIGHT EYES. MAY YOUR WOUNDS, PHYSICAL AND OTHERWISE, BE HEALED.
ALTHOUGH I YEARN TO STAY... I CANNOT. MY VERY PRESENCE HERE GOES AGAINST THE NATURAL ORDER.
GOODBYE, MY LOVE. AND THANK YOU... ALWAYS.
HUMAN ONCE AGAIN. BUT HOW LONG WILL I STAY THIS WAY?
WELL THAT CERTAINLY DEFIES LOGIC...
AS DOES MOST OF WHAT IS IMPORTANT IN LIFE, BROTHER RAMSEY.
THE SCOUTING PARTY HAS BEEN DISPATCHED, AND THE REMAINING WORGEN FROM PRIME'S CULT HAVE EITHER DISPERSED OR BEEN KILLED.
YOUR FERAL SIDE WILL NEVER BE FULLY AT REST. WHEN YOU ARE DRIVEN TO ANGER OR WHEN YOU CONCENTRATE WITH A FORCE OF WILL, THE ANIMAL WITHIN YOU WILL COME FORWARD.
THERE IS NO FULL CURE. NOT YET. BUT WHAT YOU DO HAVE, BROTHER HALFORD...

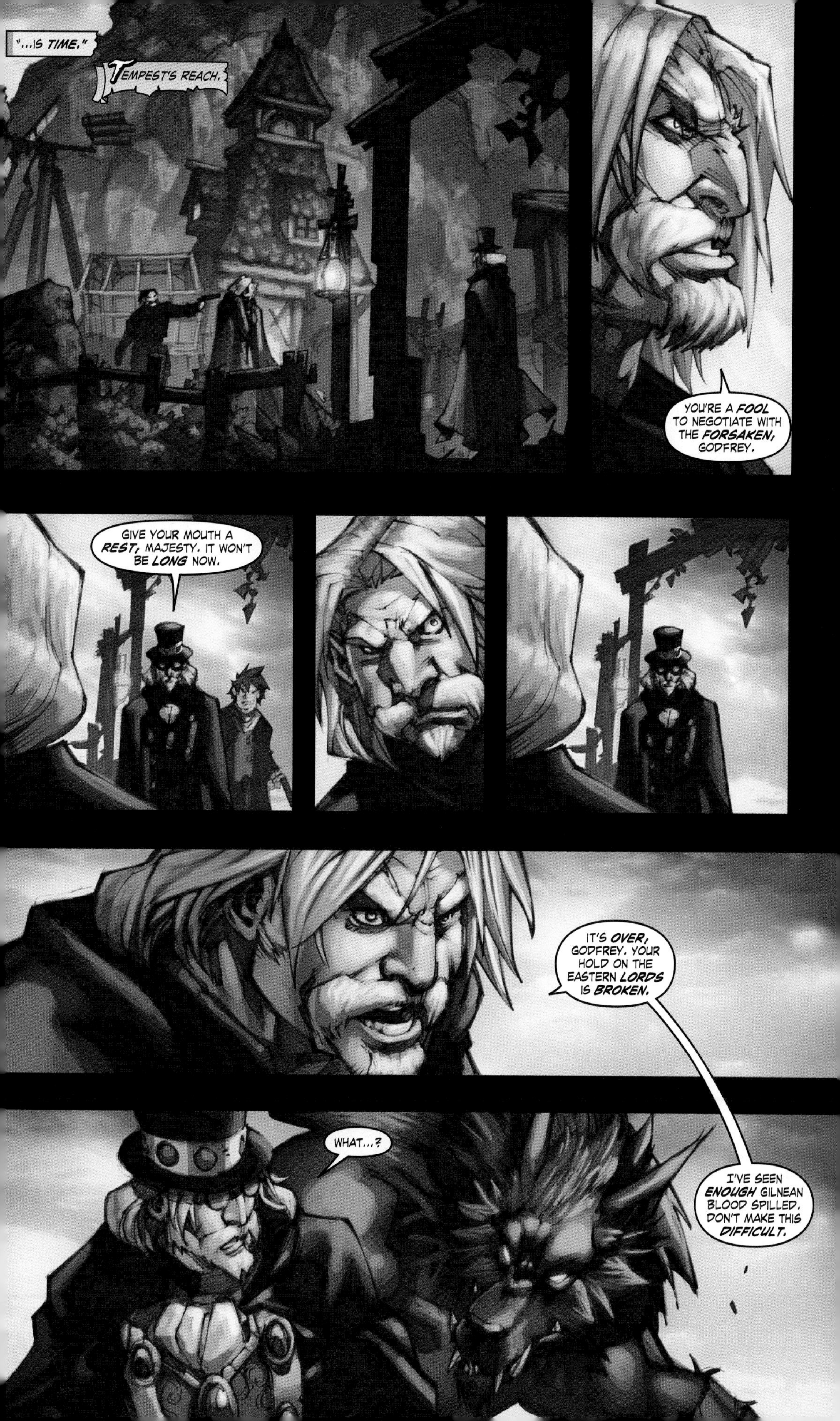
"...IS TIME."
TEMPEST'S REACH.
YOU'RE A FOOL TO NEGOTIATE WITH THE FORSAKEN, GODFREY.
GIVE YOUR MOUTH A REST, MAJESTY. IT WON'T BE LONG NOW.
IT'S OVER, GODFREY. YOUR HOLD ON THE EASTERN LORDS IS BROKEN.
WHAT...?
I'VE SEEN ENOUGH GILNEAN BLOOD SPILLED. DON'T MAKE THIS DIFFICULT.

NO... I'D SOONER *DIE* THAN HAVE ONE OF *YOUR KIND* FOR A *KING!*

GODFREY, *NO!!*

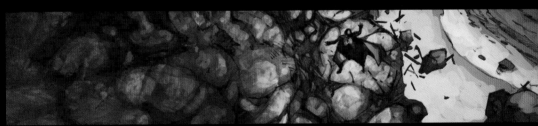

THEY'RE READY TO *HEAR* YOU, FATHER.

OUTSIDE GILNEAS CITY. DAYS LATER.

FIRST, THERE'S SOMETHING I WISH TO *SHARE* WITH YOU...SOMETHING *IMPORTANT.*

OUR NATION'S *GREAT WALL* HAS ISOLATED *MORE* THAN A KINGDOM. IT'S ISOLATED THE *LIES* OF ITS *KING* AS WELL. THE TIME HAS *COME* NOW...

...FOR THE *WALLS* TO COME *DOWN.*

YOU REMEMBER ARUGAL?

YES, OF COURSE, THAT *IMBECILE* OF *ARCHMAGE!* H— RECKLESSLY CAST *SPELL* THAT *PULL—* THE WORGEN IN— OUR WORLD.

WHAT YOU HAVE *NOT* KNOWN, WHAT NEVER *TOLD* YOU THAT ARUGAL...

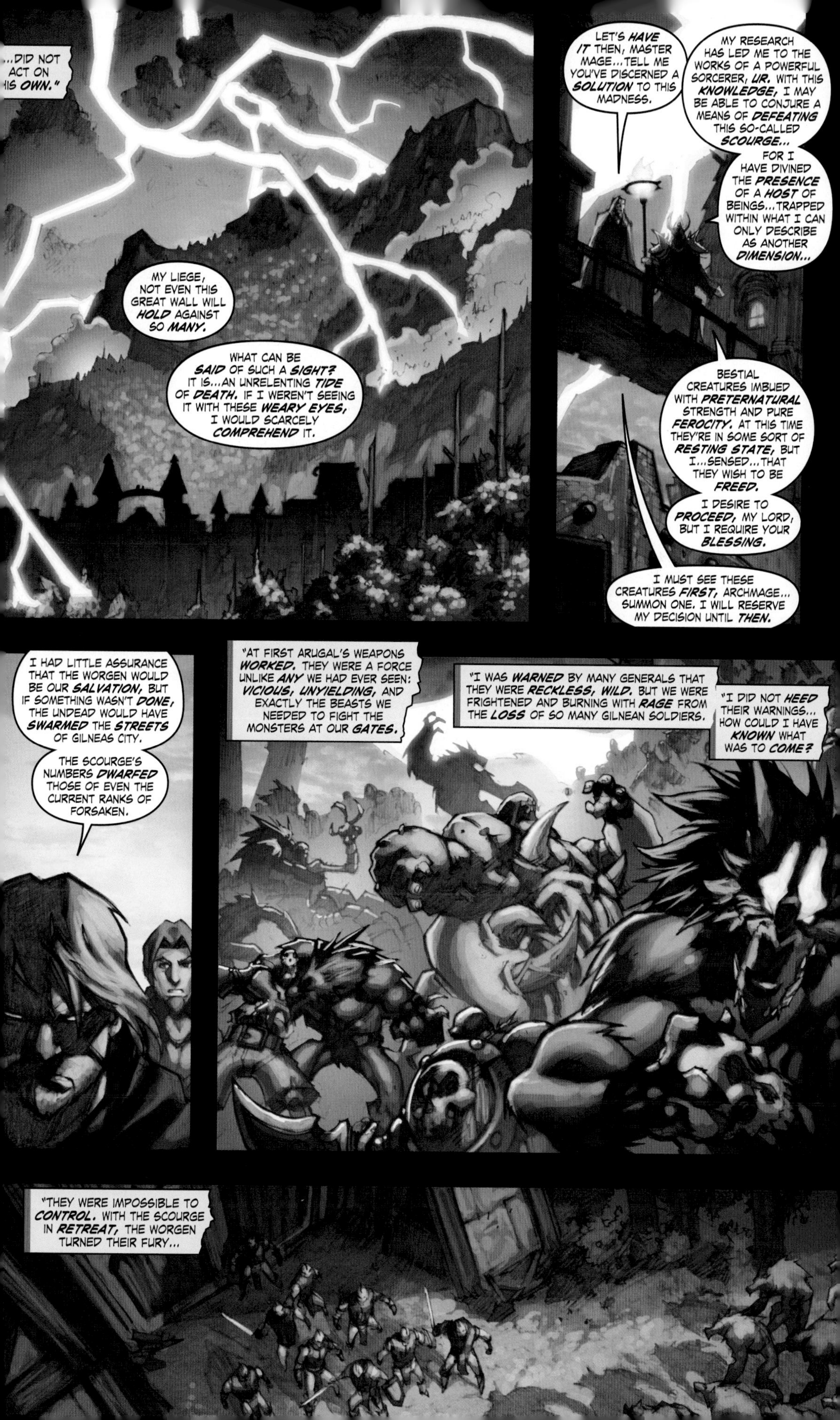

...DID NOT ACT ON HIS OWN."
MY LIEGE, NOT EVEN THIS GREAT WALL WILL HOLD AGAINST SO MANY.
WHAT CAN BE SAID OF SUCH A SIGHT? IT IS...AN UNRELENTING TIDE OF DEATH. IF I WEREN'T SEEING IT WITH THESE WEARY EYES, I WOULD SCARCELY COMPREHEND IT.
LET'S HAVE IT THEN, MASTER MAGE...TELL ME YOU'VE DISCERNED A SOLUTION TO THIS MADNESS.
MY RESEARCH HAS LED ME TO THE WORKS OF A POWERFUL SORCERER, UR. WITH THIS KNOWLEDGE, I MAY BE ABLE TO CONJURE A MEANS OF DEFEATING THIS SO-CALLED SCOURGE...
FOR I HAVE DIVINED THE PRESENCE OF A HOST OF BEINGS...TRAPPED WITHIN WHAT I CAN ONLY DESCRIBE AS ANOTHER DIMENSION...
BESTIAL CREATURES IMBUED WITH PRETERNATURAL STRENGTH AND PURE FEROCITY. AT THIS TIME THEY'RE IN SOME SORT OF RESTING STATE; BUT I...SENSED...THAT THEY WISH TO BE FREED.
I DESIRE TO PROCEED, MY LORD, BUT I REQUIRE YOUR BLESSING.
I MUST SEE THESE CREATURES FIRST, ARCHMAGE... SUMMON ONE. I WILL RESERVE MY DECISION UNTIL THEN.
I HAD LITTLE ASSURANCE THAT THE WORGEN WOULD BE OUR SALVATION, BUT IF SOMETHING WASN'T DONE, THE UNDEAD WOULD HAVE SWARMED THE STREETS OF GILNEAS CITY.
THE SCOURGE'S NUMBERS DWARFED THOSE OF EVEN THE CURRENT RANKS OF FORSAKEN.
"AT FIRST ARUGAL'S WEAPONS WORKED. THEY WERE A FORCE UNLIKE ANY WE HAD EVER SEEN: VICIOUS, UNYIELDING, AND EXACTLY THE BEASTS WE NEEDED TO FIGHT THE MONSTERS AT OUR GATES.
"I WAS WARNED BY MANY GENERALS THAT THEY WERE RECKLESS, WILD. BUT WE WERE FRIGHTENED AND BURNING WITH RAGE FROM THE LOSS OF SO MANY GILNEAN SOLDIERS.
"I DID NOT HEED THEIR WARNINGS... HOW COULD I HAVE KNOWN WHAT WAS TO COME?
"THEY WERE IMPOSSIBLE TO CONTROL. WITH THE SCOURGE IN RETREAT, THE WORGEN TURNED THEIR FURY...

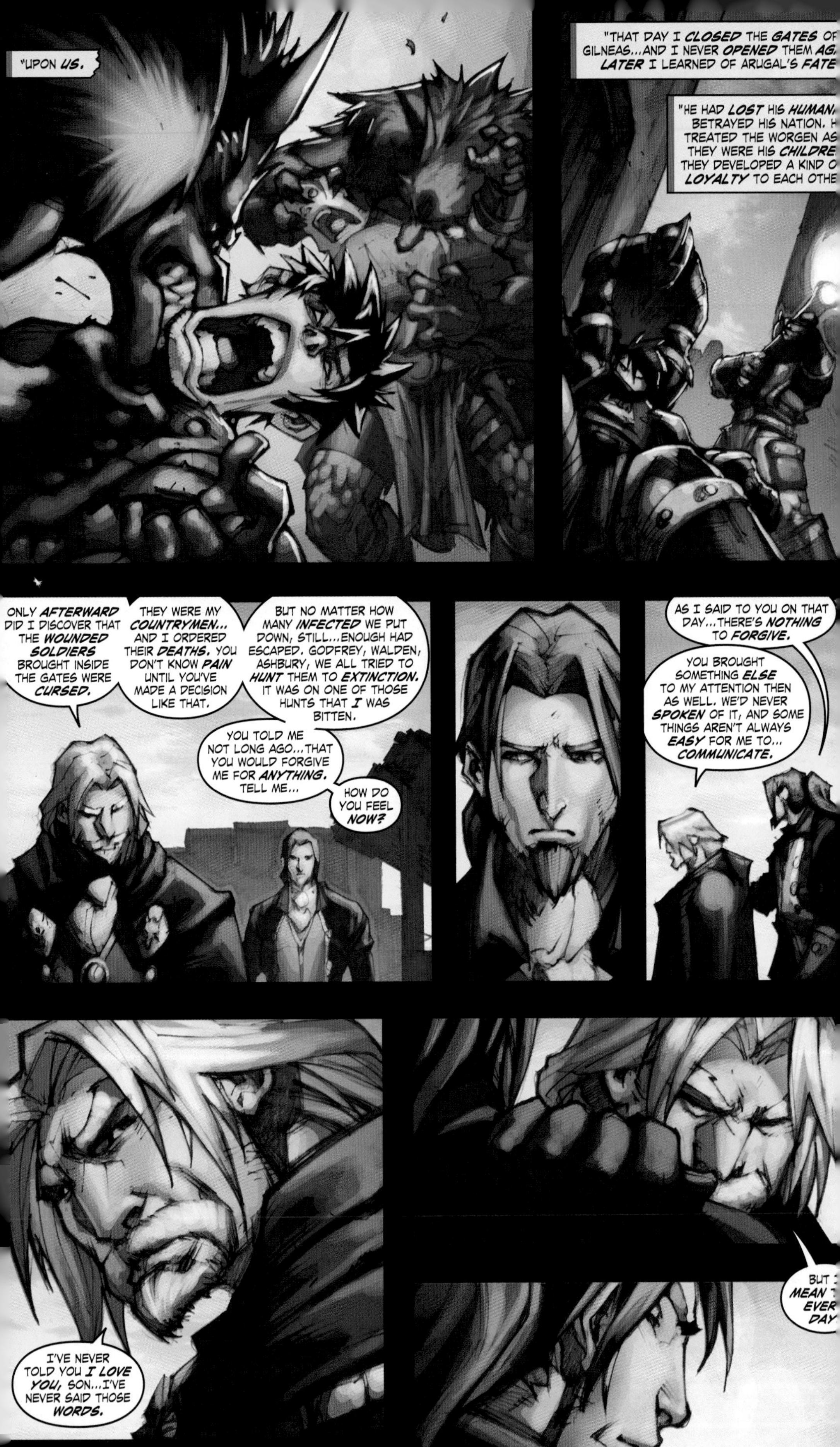

"UPON US.
"THAT DAY I CLOSED THE GATES OF GILNEAS...AND I NEVER OPENED THEM AG LATER I LEARNED OF ARUGAL'S FATE
"HE HAD LOST HIS HUMAN BETRAYED HIS NATION. H TREATED THE WORGEN AS THEY WERE HIS CHILDRE THEY DEVELOPED A KIND O LOYALTY TO EACH OTHE
ONLY AFTERWARD DID I DISCOVER THAT THE WOUNDED SOLDIERS BROUGHT INSIDE THE GATES WERE CURSED.
THEY WERE MY COUNTRYMEN... AND I ORDERED THEIR DEATHS. YOU DON'T KNOW PAIN UNTIL YOU'VE MADE A DECISION LIKE THAT.
BUT NO MATTER HOW MANY INFECTED WE PUT DOWN, STILL...ENOUGH HAD ESCAPED. GODFREY, WALDEN, ASHBURY, WE ALL TRIED TO HUNT THEM TO EXTINCTION. IT WAS ON ONE OF THOSE HUNTS THAT I WAS BITTEN.
YOU TOLD ME NOT LONG AGO...THAT YOU WOULD FORGIVE ME FOR ANYTHING. TELL ME...
HOW DO YOU FEEL NOW?
AS I SAID TO YOU ON THAT DAY...THERE'S NOTHING TO FORGIVE.
YOU BROUGHT SOMETHING ELSE TO MY ATTENTION THEN AS WELL. WE'D NEVER SPOKEN OF IT, AND SOME THINGS AREN'T ALWAYS EASY FOR ME TO... COMMUNICATE.
I'VE NEVER TOLD YOU I LOVE YOU, SON...I'VE NEVER SAID THOSE WORDS.
BUT MEAN EVER DAY

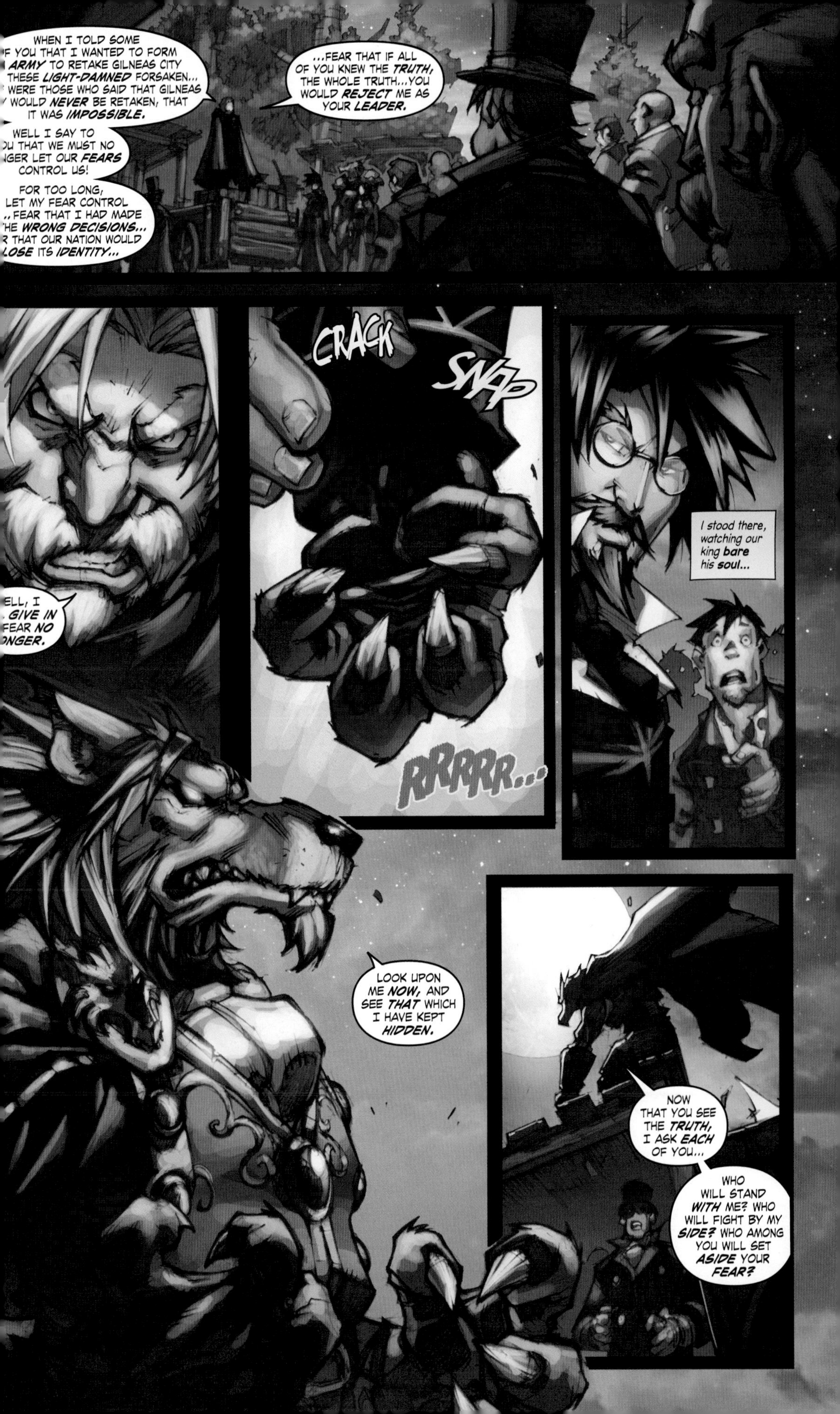
WHEN I TOLD SOME F YOU THAT I WANTED TO FORM ARMY TO RETAKE GILNEAS CITY THESE LIGHT-DAMNED FORSAKEN... WERE THOSE WHO SAID THAT GILNEAS WOULD NEVER BE RETAKEN; THAT IT WAS IMPOSSIBLE.
WELL I SAY TO U THAT WE MUST NO GER LET OUR FEARS CONTROL US!
FOR TOO LONG, LET MY FEAR CONTROL .. FEAR THAT I HAD MADE HE WRONG DECISIONS... R THAT OUR NATION WOULD LOSE ITS IDENTITY...
...FEAR THAT IF ALL OF YOU KNEW THE TRUTH, THE WHOLE TRUTH...YOU WOULD REJECT ME AS YOUR LEADER.
ELL, I GIVE IN FEAR NO NGER.
CRACK
SNAP
RRRRR...
I stood there, watching our king bare his soul...
LOOK UPON ME NOW, AND SEE THAT WHICH I HAVE KEPT HIDDEN.
NOW THAT YOU SEE THE TRUTH, I ASK EACH OF YOU...
WHO WILL STAND WITH ME? WHO WILL FIGHT BY MY SIDE? WHO AMONG YOU WILL SET ASIDE YOUR FEAR?

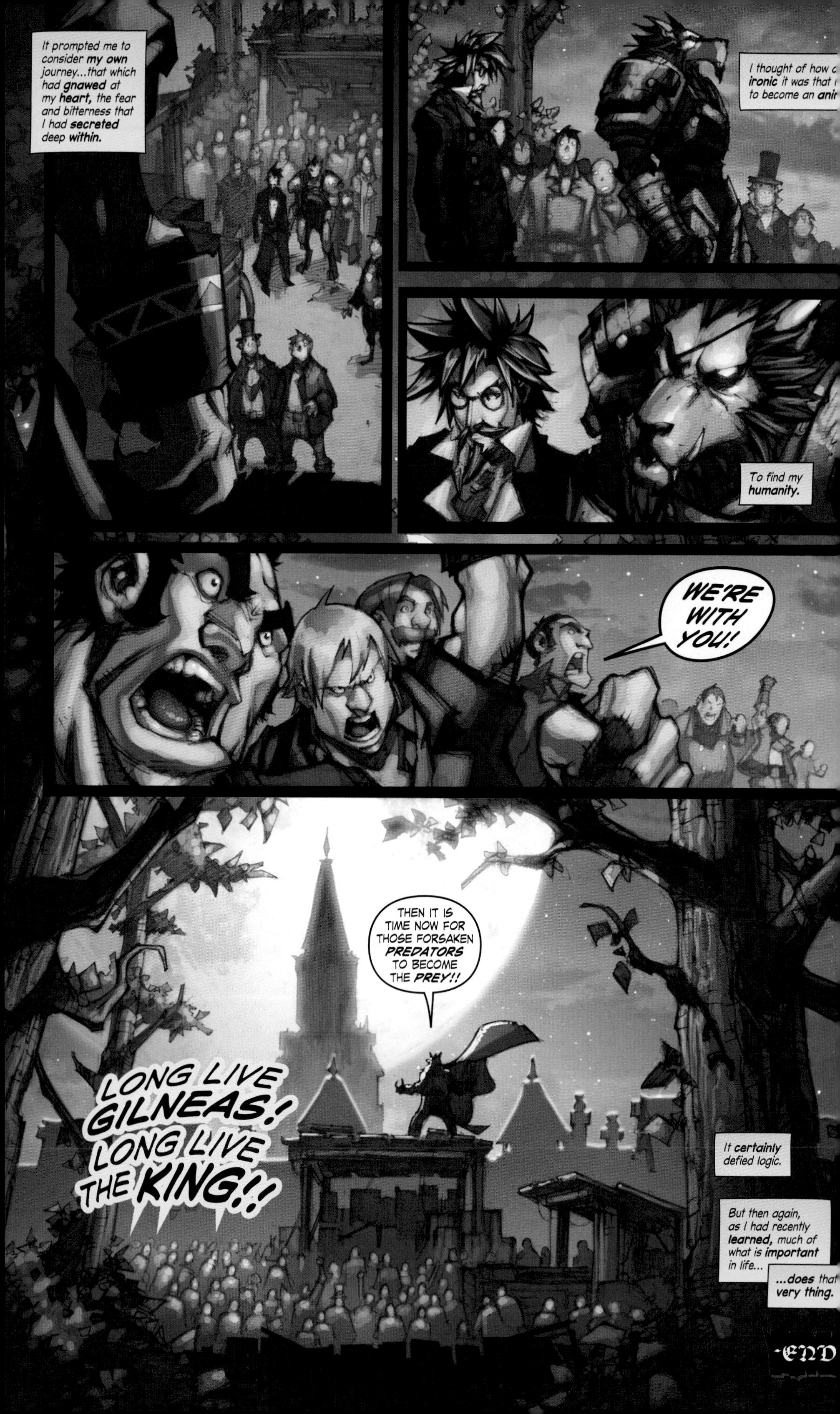
It prompted me to consider my own journey...that which had gnawed at my heart, the fear and bitterness that I had secreted deep within.
To find my humanity.
WE'RE WITH YOU!
THEN IT IS TIME NOW FOR THOSE FORSAKEN PREDATORS TO BECOME THE PREY!!
LONG LIVE GILNEAS! LONG LIVE THE KING!!
It certainly defied logic.
But then again, as I had recently learned, much of what is important in life...
...does that very thing.
-END

EPILOGUE

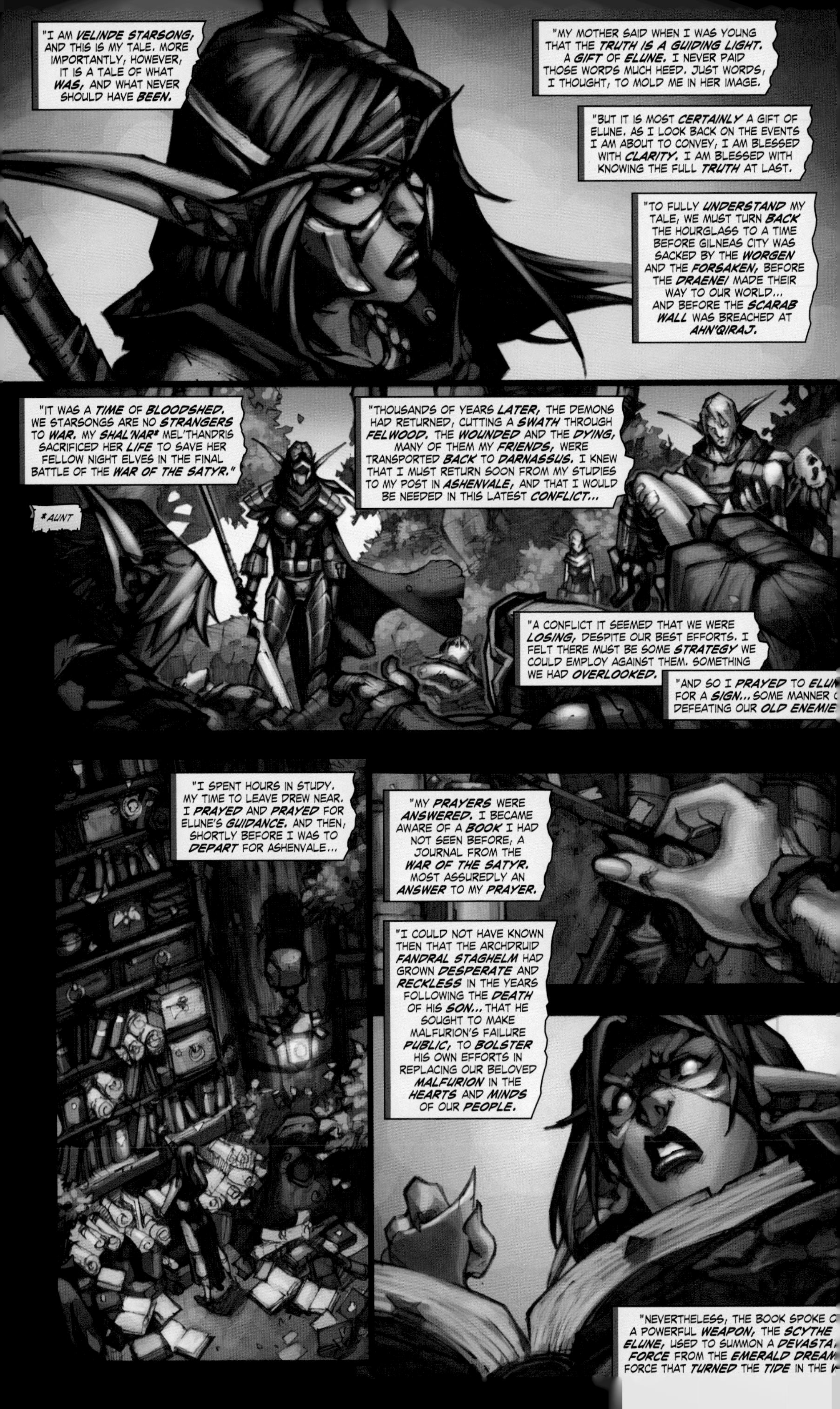
"I AM VELINDE STARSONG, AND THIS IS MY TALE. MORE IMPORTANTLY, HOWEVER, IT IS A TALE OF WHAT WAS, AND WHAT NEVER SHOULD HAVE BEEN.
"MY MOTHER SAID WHEN I WAS YOUNG THAT THE TRUTH IS A GUIDING LIGHT. A GIFT OF ELUNE. I NEVER PAID THOSE WORDS MUCH HEED. JUST WORDS, I THOUGHT, TO MOLD ME IN HER IMAGE.
"BUT IT IS MOST CERTAINLY A GIFT OF ELUNE. AS I LOOK BACK ON THE EVENTS I AM ABOUT TO CONVEY, I AM BLESSED WITH CLARITY. I AM BLESSED WITH KNOWING THE FULL TRUTH AT LAST.
"TO FULLY UNDERSTAND MY TALE, WE MUST TURN BACK THE HOURGLASS TO A TIME BEFORE GILNEAS CITY WAS SACKED BY THE WORGEN AND THE FORSAKEN, BEFORE THE DRAENEI MADE THEIR WAY TO OUR WORLD... AND BEFORE THE SCARAB WALL WAS BREACHED AT AHN'QIRAJ.
"IT WAS A TIME OF BLOODSHED. WE STARSONGS ARE NO STRANGERS TO WAR. MY SHAL'NAR* MEL'THANDRIS SACRIFICED HER LIFE TO SAVE HER FELLOW NIGHT ELVES IN THE FINAL BATTLE OF THE WAR OF THE SATYR."
*AUNT
"THOUSANDS OF YEARS LATER, THE DEMONS HAD RETURNED, CUTTING A SWATH THROUGH FELWOOD. THE WOUNDED AND THE DYING, MANY OF THEM MY FRIENDS, WERE TRANSPORTED BACK TO DARNASSUS. I KNEW THAT I MUST RETURN SOON FROM MY STUDIES TO MY POST IN ASHENVALE, AND THAT I WOULD BE NEEDED IN THIS LATEST CONFLICT...
"A CONFLICT IT SEEMED THAT WE WERE LOSING, DESPITE OUR BEST EFFORTS. I FELT THERE MUST BE SOME STRATEGY WE COULD EMPLOY AGAINST THEM. SOMETHING WE HAD OVERLOOKED.
"AND SO I PRAYED TO ELUN FOR A SIGN... SOME MANNER DEFEATING OUR OLD ENEMIE
"I SPENT HOURS IN STUDY. MY TIME TO LEAVE DREW NEAR. I PRAYED AND PRAYED FOR ELUNE'S GUIDANCE. AND THEN, SHORTLY BEFORE I WAS TO DEPART FOR ASHENVALE...
"MY PRAYERS WERE ANSWERED. I BECAME AWARE OF A BOOK I HAD NOT SEEN BEFORE, A JOURNAL FROM THE WAR OF THE SATYR. MOST ASSUREDLY AN ANSWER TO MY PRAYER.
"I COULD NOT HAVE KNOWN THEN THAT THE ARCHDRUID FANDRAL STAGHELM HAD GROWN DESPERATE AND RECKLESS IN THE YEARS FOLLOWING THE DEATH OF HIS SON... THAT HE SOUGHT TO MAKE MALFURION'S FAILURE PUBLIC, TO BOLSTER HIS OWN EFFORTS IN REPLACING OUR BELOVED MALFURION IN THE HEARTS AND MINDS OF OUR PEOPLE.
"NEVERTHELESS, THE BOOK SPOKE O A POWERFUL WEAPON, THE SCYTHE ELUNE, USED TO SUMMON A DEVASTA FORCE FROM THE EMERALD DREAM FORCE THAT TURNED THE TIDE IN THE

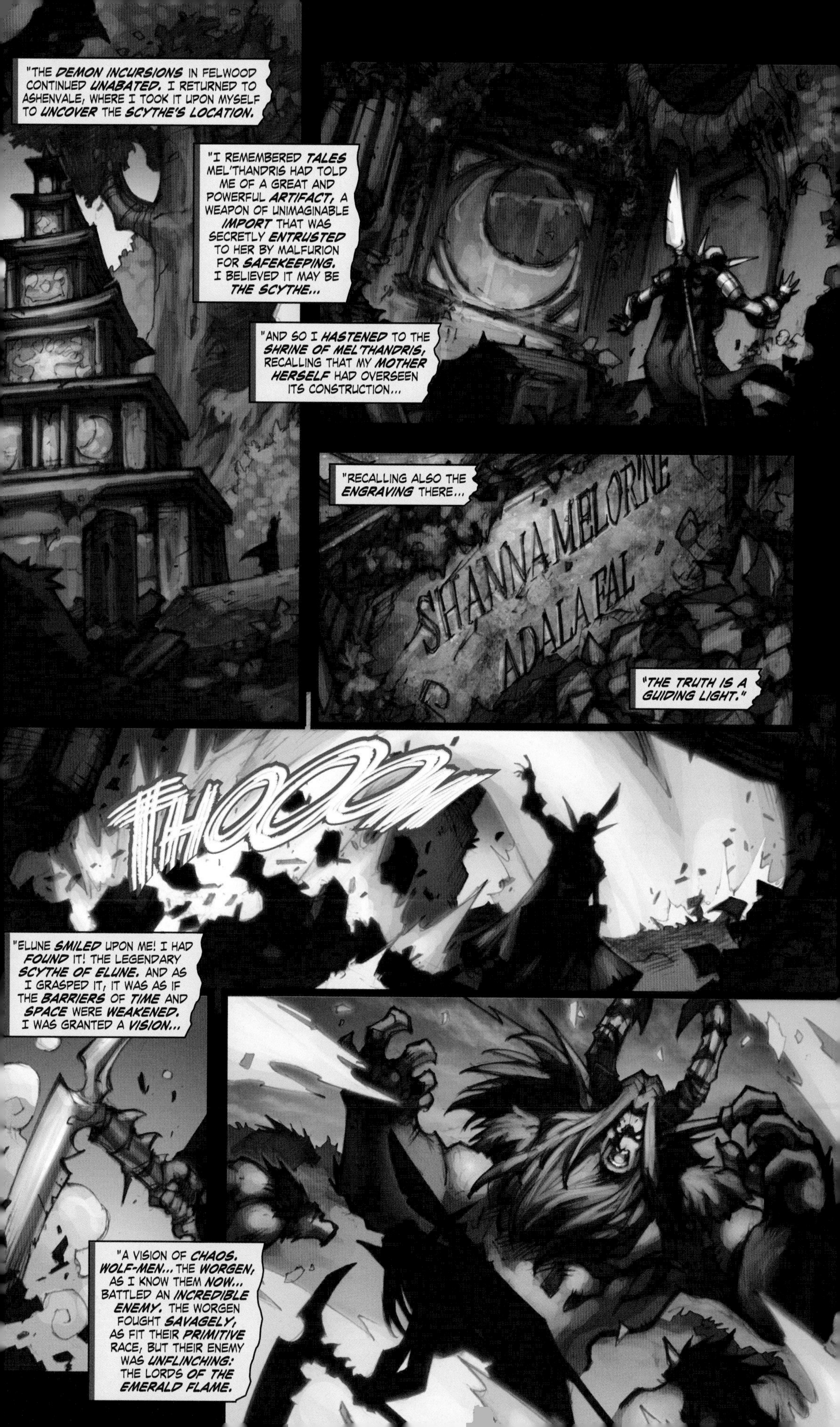
"THE DEMON INCURSIONS IN FELWOOD CONTINUED UNABATED. I RETURNED TO ASHENVALE, WHERE I TOOK IT UPON MYSELF TO UNCOVER THE SCYTHE'S LOCATION.
"I REMEMBERED TALES MEL'THANDRIS HAD TOLD ME OF A GREAT AND POWERFUL ARTIFACT, A WEAPON OF UNIMAGINABLE IMPORT THAT WAS SECRETLY ENTRUSTED TO HER BY MALFURION FOR SAFEKEEPING. I BELIEVED IT MAY BE THE SCYTHE...
"AND SO I HASTENED TO THE SHRINE OF MEL'THANDRIS, RECALLING THAT MY MOTHER HERSELF HAD OVERSEEN ITS CONSTRUCTION...
"RECALLING ALSO THE ENGRAVING THERE...
SHANNA MELOR'NE
ADALA FAL
"THE TRUTH IS A GUIDING LIGHT."
THOOOM
"ELUNE SMILED UPON ME! I HAD FOUND IT! THE LEGENDARY SCYTHE OF ELUNE. AND AS I GRASPED IT, IT WAS AS IF THE BARRIERS OF TIME AND SPACE WERE WEAKENED. I WAS GRANTED A VISION...
"A VISION OF CHAOS. WOLF-MEN... THE WORGEN, AS I KNOW THEM NOW... BATTLED AN INCREDIBLE ENEMY. THE WORGEN FOUGHT SAVAGELY, AS FIT THEIR PRIMITIVE RACE, BUT THEIR ENEMY WAS UNFLINCHING: THE LORDS OF THE EMERALD FLAME.

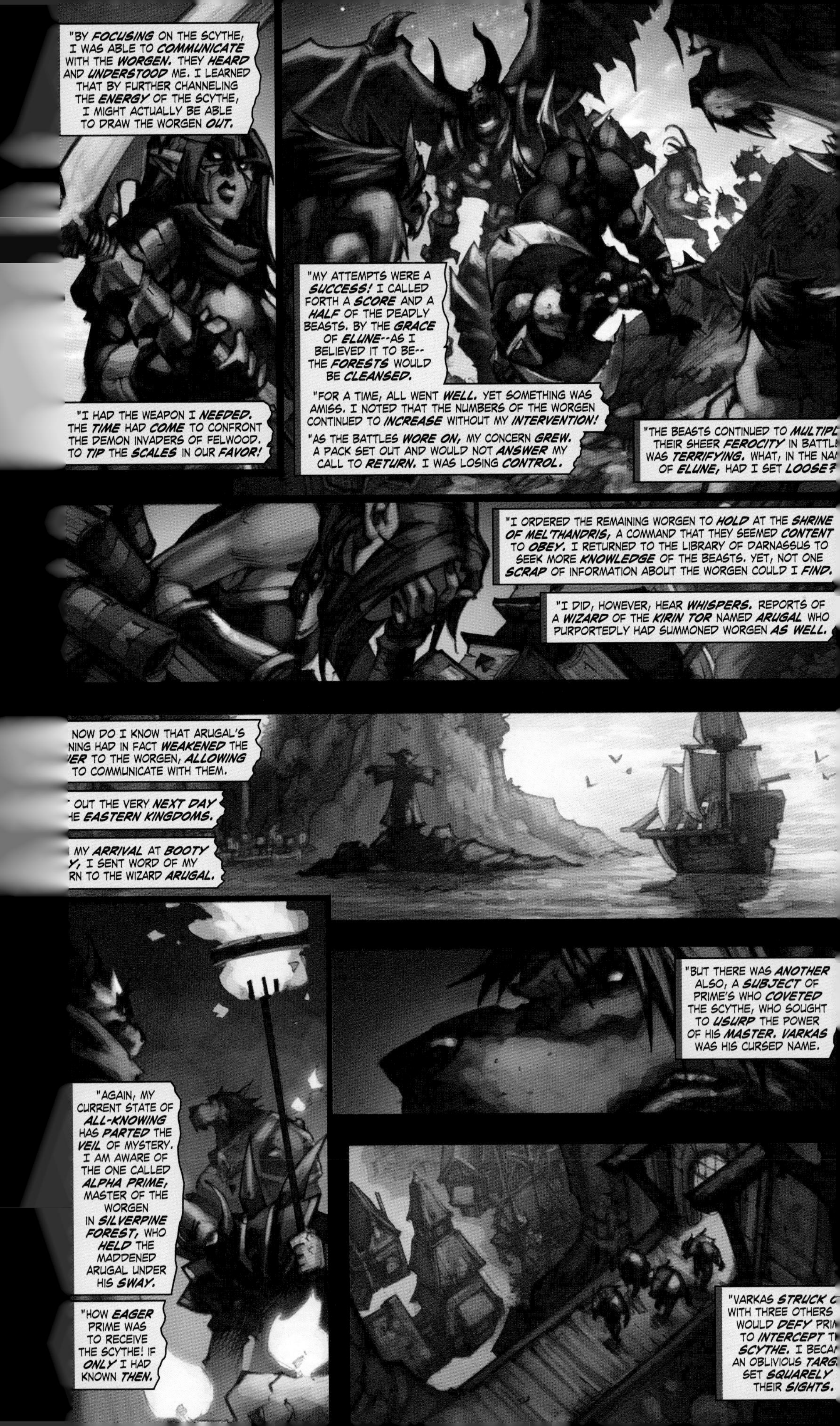
"BY FOCUSING ON THE SCYTHE, I WAS ABLE TO COMMUNICATE WITH THE WORGEN. THEY HEARD AND UNDERSTOOD ME. I LEARNED THAT BY FURTHER CHANNELING THE ENERGY OF THE SCYTHE, I MIGHT ACTUALLY BE ABLE TO DRAW THE WORGEN OUT.
"I HAD THE WEAPON I NEEDED. THE TIME HAD COME TO CONFRONT THE DEMON INVADERS OF FELWOOD. TO TIP THE SCALES IN OUR FAVOR!
"MY ATTEMPTS WERE A SUCCESS! I CALLED FORTH A SCORE AND A HALF OF THE DEADLY BEASTS. BY THE GRACE OF ELUNE--AS I BELIEVED IT TO BE--THE FORESTS WOULD BE CLEANSED.
"FOR A TIME, ALL WENT WELL. YET SOMETHING WAS AMISS. I NOTED THAT THE NUMBERS OF THE WORGEN CONTINUED TO INCREASE WITHOUT MY INTERVENTION!
"AS THE BATTLES WORE ON, MY CONCERN GREW. A PACK SET OUT AND WOULD NOT ANSWER MY CALL TO RETURN. I WAS LOSING CONTROL.
"THE BEASTS CONTINUED TO MULTIPL THEIR SHEER FEROCITY IN BATTL WAS TERRIFYING. WHAT, IN THE NA OF ELUNE, HAD I SET LOOSE?
"I ORDERED THE REMAINING WORGEN TO HOLD AT THE SHRINE OF MEL'THANDRIS, A COMMAND THAT THEY SEEMED CONTENT TO OBEY. I RETURNED TO THE LIBRARY OF DARNASSUS TO SEEK MORE KNOWLEDGE OF THE BEASTS. YET, NOT ONE SCRAP OF INFORMATION ABOUT THE WORGEN COULD I FIND.
"I DID, HOWEVER, HEAR WHISPERS. REPORTS OF A WIZARD OF THE KIRIN TOR NAMED ARUGAL WHO PURPORTEDLY HAD SUMMONED WORGEN AS WELL.
NOW DO I KNOW THAT ARUGAL'S NING HAD IN FACT WEAKENED THE ER TO THE WORGEN, ALLOWING TO COMMUNICATE WITH THEM.
T OUT THE VERY NEXT DAY HE EASTERN KINGDOMS.
MY ARRIVAL AT BOOTY Y, I SENT WORD OF MY RN TO THE WIZARD ARUGAL.
"AGAIN, MY CURRENT STATE OF ALL-KNOWING HAS PARTED THE VEIL OF MYSTERY. I AM AWARE OF THE ONE CALLED ALPHA PRIME, MASTER OF THE WORGEN IN SILVERPINE FOREST, WHO HELD THE MADDENED ARUGAL UNDER HIS SWAY.
"HOW EAGER PRIME WAS TO RECEIVE THE SCYTHE! IF ONLY I HAD KNOWN THEN.
"BUT THERE WAS ANOTHER ALSO, A SUBJECT OF PRIME'S WHO COVETED THE SCYTHE, WHO SOUGHT TO USURP THE POWER OF HIS MASTER. VARKAS WAS HIS CURSED NAME.
"VARKAS STRUCK WITH THREE OTHERS WOULD DEFY PRI TO INTERCEPT T SCYTHE. I BECA AN OBLIVIOUS TARG SET SQUARELY THEIR SIGHTS.

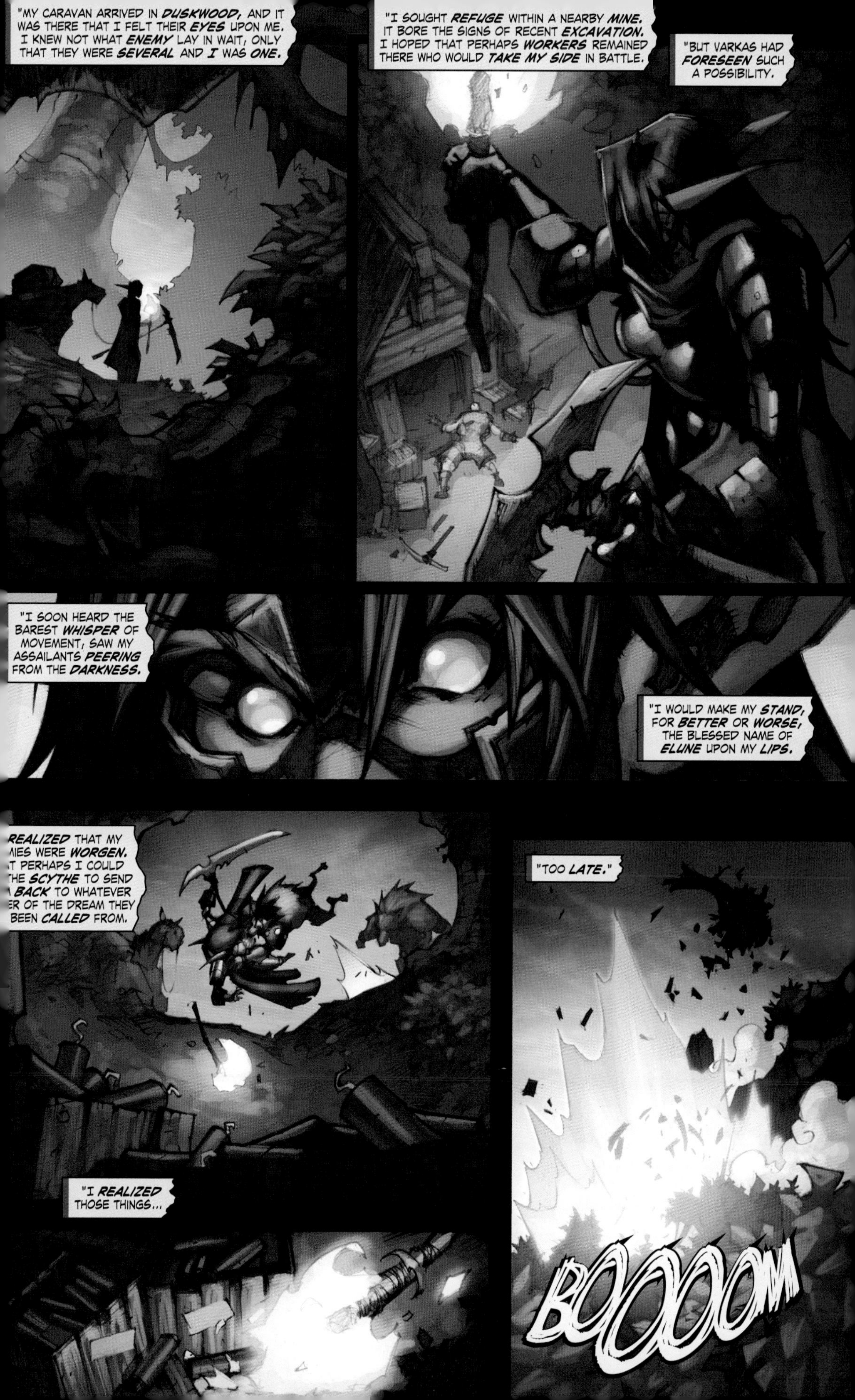
"MY CARAVAN ARRIVED IN DUSKWOOD, AND IT WAS THERE THAT I FELT THEIR EYES UPON ME. I KNEW NOT WHAT ENEMY LAY IN WAIT, ONLY THAT THEY WERE SEVERAL AND I WAS ONE.
"I SOUGHT REFUGE WITHIN A NEARBY MINE. IT BORE THE SIGNS OF RECENT EXCAVATION. I HOPED THAT PERHAPS WORKERS REMAINED THERE WHO WOULD TAKE MY SIDE IN BATTLE.
"BUT VARKAS HAD FORESEEN SUCH A POSSIBILITY.
"I SOON HEARD THE BAREST WHISPER OF MOVEMENT, SAW MY ASSAILANTS PEERING FROM THE DARKNESS.
"I WOULD MAKE MY STAND, FOR BETTER OR WORSE, THE BLESSED NAME OF ELUNE UPON MY LIPS.
REALIZED THAT MY MIES WERE WORGEN. T PERHAPS I COULD THE SCYTHE TO SEND BACK TO WHATEVER ER OF THE DREAM THEY BEEN CALLED FROM.
"I REALIZED THOSE THINGS...
"TOO LATE."
BOOOOOM

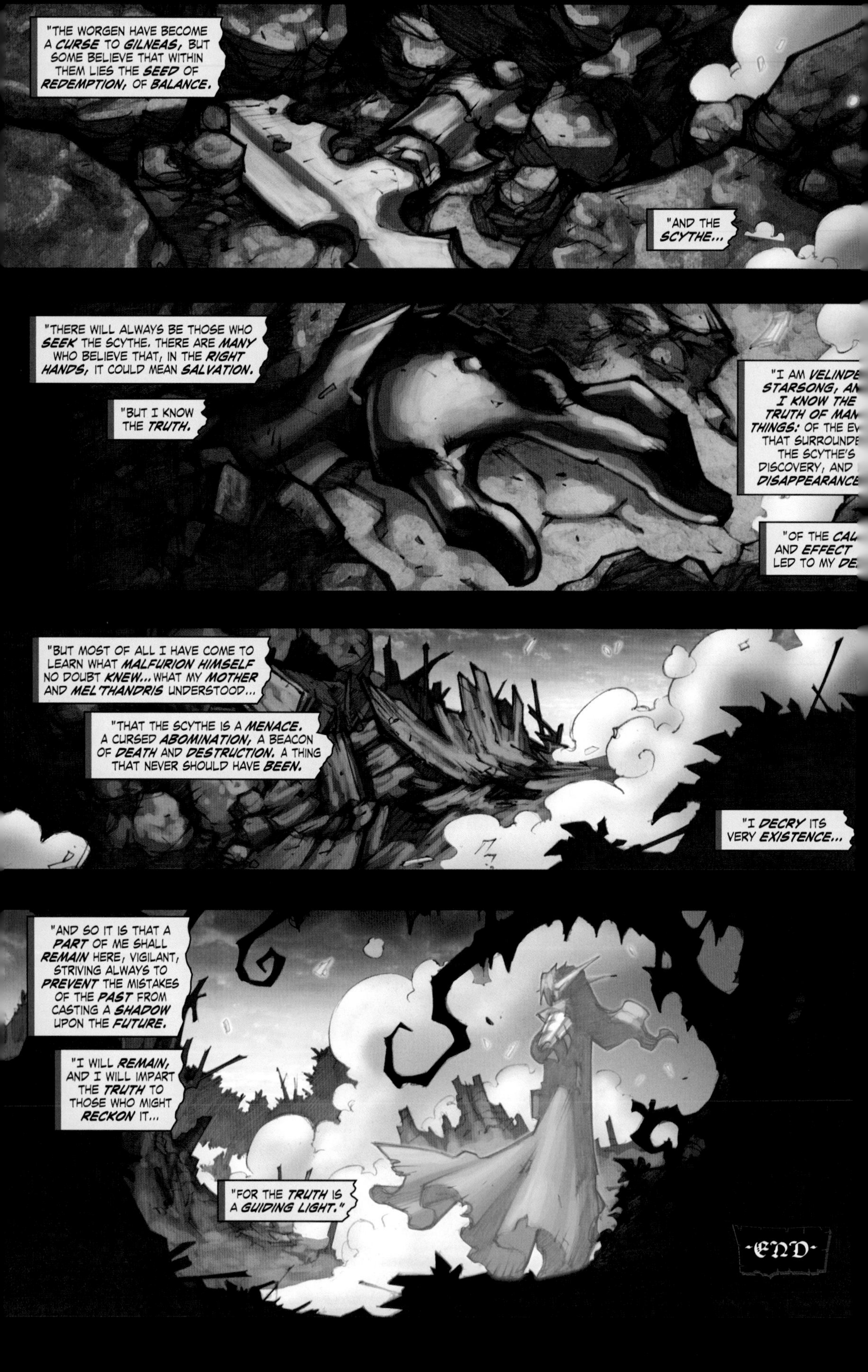
"THE WORGEN HAVE BECOME A CURSE TO GILNEAS, BUT SOME BELIEVE THAT WITHIN THEM LIES THE SEED OF REDEMPTION, OF BALANCE.
"AND THE SCYTHE...
"THERE WILL ALWAYS BE THOSE WHO SEEK THE SCYTHE. THERE ARE MANY WHO BELIEVE THAT, IN THE RIGHT HANDS, IT COULD MEAN SALVATION.
"BUT I KNOW THE TRUTH.
"I AM VELINDE STARSONG, AN I KNOW THE TRUTH OF MAN THINGS: OF THE EV THAT SURROUNDE THE SCYTHE'S DISCOVERY, AND DISAPPEARANCE
"OF THE CA AND EFFECT LED TO MY DE
"BUT MOST OF ALL I HAVE COME TO LEARN WHAT MALFURION HIMSELF NO DOUBT KNEW... WHAT MY MOTHER AND MEL'THANDRIS UNDERSTOOD...
"THAT THE SCYTHE IS A MENACE. A CURSED ABOMINATION, A BEACON OF DEATH AND DESTRUCTION. A THING THAT NEVER SHOULD HAVE BEEN.
"I DECRY ITS VERY EXISTENCE...
"AND SO IT IS THAT A PART OF ME SHALL REMAIN HERE, VIGILANT, STRIVING ALWAYS TO PREVENT THE MISTAKES OF THE PAST FROM CASTING A SHADOW UPON THE FUTURE.
"I WILL REMAIN, AND I WILL IMPART THE TRUTH TO THOSE WHO MIGHT RECKON IT...
"FOR THE TRUTH IS A GUIDING LIGHT."
END

WORLD OF WARCRAFT
Curse of the Worgen
FURTHER READING

 f you'd like to read more about the characters, situations, and settings featured in this comic book, the sources listed below offer additional pieces of the story of Azeroth.

 ore information about King Genn Greymane is revealed in *World of Warcraft: Wolfheart* and *Warcraft: Day of the Dragon* by Richard A. Knaak; *World of Warcraft: Tides of Darkness* by Aaron Rosenberg; *World of Warcraft: Beyond the Dark Portal* by Aaron Rosenberg and Christie Golden; and the short story "Lord of His Pack" by James Waugh (on http://us.battle.net/wow/en/game/lore/).

 alfurion Stormrage plays a key role in *World of Warcraft: Wolfheart* by Richard A. Knaak. Further insight regarding his past is offered in *World of Warcraft: Stormrage* and the *War of the Ancients Trilogy* (*Warcraft: The Well of Eternity*, *Warcraft: The Demon Soul*, and *Warcraft: The Sundering*) by Richard A. Knaak, as well as the short story "Seeds of Faith" by Valerie Watrous (on http://us.battle.net/wow/en/game/lore/).

 n the *War of the Ancients Trilogy* by Richard A. Knaak, Tyrande Whisperwind reluctantly establishes herself as the leader of the night elves. Other exciting events in Tyrande's life are portrayed in *World of Warcraft: Wolfheart* and *World of Warcraft: Stormrage* by Richard A. Knaak; issue #6 of the monthly *World of Warcraft* comic book by Walter Simonson, Ludo Lullabi, and Sandra Hope; and the short story "Seeds of Faith" by Valerie Watrous (on http://us.battle.net/wow/en/game/lore/).

 ou can learn more about Shandris Feathermoon in *World of Warcraft: Wolfheart*, *World of Warcraft: Stormrage*, and *Warcraft: The Demon Soul* and *Warcraft: The Sundering* (books two and three of the *War of the Ancients Trilogy*) by Richard A. Knaak, as well as "Seeds of Faith," a short story by Valerie Watrous (on http://us.battle.net/wow/en/game/lore/).

 ther details about the worgen curse and Gilneas, including characters such as Vincent Godfrey, Darius Crowley, and Baron Ashbury, are disclosed in the short story "Lord of His Pack" by James Waugh (on http://us.battle.net/wow/en/game/lore/).

 egends abound concerning the wolf Ancient, Goldrinn. You can learn more about him in *World of Warcraft: Stormrage* and *World of Warcraft: Wolfheart* by Richard A. Knaak, as well as issue #3 of the monthly *World of Warcraft* comic book by Walter Simonson, Ludo Lullabi, and Sandra Hope.

 he history of the great demigod Cenarius and his ties to the night elves are further explored in the *War of the Ancients Trilogy* and *World of Warcraft: Stormrage* by Richard A. Knaak.

 he fate of King Genn Greymane's family following the events of the *World of Warcraft: Curse of the Worgen* comic book is touched on in the short story "Lord of His Pack" by James Waugh (on http://us.battle.net/wow/en/game/lore/).

An amnesiac washes up on the shores of Kalimdor, starting the epic quest of the warrior Lo'Gosh, and his unlikely allies Broll Bearmantle and Valeera Sanguinar. Striking uneasy relationships with other races, as well as each other, they must fight both the Alliance and the Horde as they struggle to uncover the secrets of Lo'Gosh's past! Written by Walter Simonson (THE JUDAS COIN, Thor) and illustrated by Ludo Lullabi (Lanfeust Quest) and Sandra Hope (JUSTICE LEAGUE OF AMERICA), this is the latest saga set in the World of Warcraft!

WORLD OF WARCRAFT
SIMONSON • LULLABI • HOPE

WORLD OF WARCRAFT: BOOK 2

WORLD OF WARCRAFT
SIMONSON • BURAN • BOWDEN

Simonson • Buran Bowden

WORLD OF WARCRAFT: BOOK 3

WORLD OF WARCRAFT

Simonson • Buran Bowden

WORLD OF WARCRAFT: BOOK 4

WORLD OF WARCRAFT

Simonson • Buran Bowden

SEARCH THE GRAPHIC NOVELS SECTION OF
DCCOMICS.COM
FOR ART AND INFORMATION ON ALL OF OUR BOOKS!

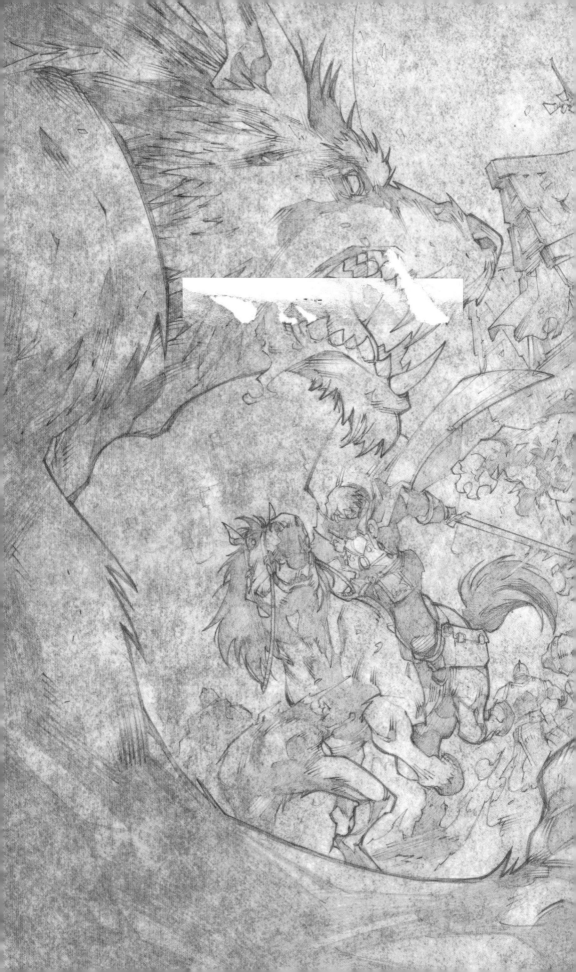